The Definitive Guide to NetBeans™ Platform 7

Heiko Böck

Apress®

The Definitive Guide to NetBeans™ Platform 7

Copyright © 2012 by Heiko Böck

ISBN-13 (pbk): 978-1-4302-4101-0

ISBN-13 (electronic): 978-1-4302-4102-7

President and Publisher: Paul Manning
Acquisitions Editor: Steve Anglin
Development Editor: Tom Welsh
Technical Reviewers: Jesse Glick and David Konecny
Editorial Board: Steve Anglin, Mark Beckner, Ewan Buckingham, Morgan Ertel, Jonathan Gennick, Jonathan Hassell, Robert Hutchinson, Michelle Lowman, James Markham, Matthew Moodie, Jeff Olson, Jeffrey Pepper, Douglas Pundick, Ben Renow-Clarke, Dominic Shakeshaft, Gwenan Spearing, Matt Wade, Tom Welsh
Coordinating Editor: Annie Beck
Copy Editor: Elizabeth Berry
Compositor: Bytheway Publishing Services
Indexer: BIM Indexing & Proofreading Services
Artist: SPI Global
Cover Designer: Anna Ishchenko

Distributed to the book trade worldwide by Springer Science+Business Media, LLC., 233 Spring Street, 6th Floor, New York, NY 10013. Phone 1-800-SPRINGER, fax (201) 348-4505, e-mail orders-ny@springer-sbm.com, or visit www.springeronline.com.

For information on translations, please e-mail rights@apress.com, or visit www.apress.com.

Apress and friends of ED books may be purchased in bulk for academic, corporate, or promotional use. eBook versions and licenses are also available for most titles. For more information, reference our Special Bulk Sales–eBook Licensing web page at www.apress.com/bulk-sales.

The source code for this book is available to readers at www.apress.com. You will need to answer questions pertaining to this book in order to successfully download the code.

Contents at a Glance

Contents

xvi

About the Author

 Heiko Böck has a Master of Science Degree in Computer Science and is a professional software development expert using Java. He has been working with the NetBeans Platform for years, and is a member of the NetBeans Dream Team. He is the author of the German books *NetBeans Platform 6* and *NetBeans Platform 7*, which have both been established as standard works on the subject. These days, he is writing his dissertation at Robert Bosch GmbH.

About the Translator

 Anne Böck studied English at the University of Tübingen and has, so to speak, dealt with the English language every day for years. She spent a semester studying in the U.S.A. at Indiana University. Additionally, she lived and worked in Canada for another six months. These days, she teaches English at a German school, and also works as a professional translator.

About the Technical Reviewers

Jesse Glick has worked on the NetBeans project since 1999, and saw it acquired by Sun Microsystems, made open source, and most recently incorporated into Oracle's tool portfolio. He has worked on basic components of the IDE such as the project system, the Ant and Maven integrations, and the Hudson integration.

Jesse has also contributed to the NetBeans Platform and its in-IDE tooling, co-authored an O'Reilly book on the subject, and spoken at several conferences on related topics.

David Konecny is a principal member of the technical staff at Oracle. He is technical leader of Java EE support in NetBeans IDE and has over the years worked on several different areas of the IDE. Prior to working for Sun and Oracle, he spent a decade in miscellaneous engineering roles. He is passionate about his work and anything he does in his life. Born in Czechoslovakia, he currently lives in New Zealand and works from home.

Acknowledgments

At this point I want to particularly thank my wife, Anne. With her tireless will she ensured that the successful German edition of *NetBeans Platform 7* is now available to the English-speaking software developer, too. In addition to her extraordinary performance (namely, in translating the book), I thank her for unconditionally backing up all my projects and for completing them together with me.

Furthermore, I want to thank Annie Beck, the coordinating editor, and all the staff of Apress, who have been involved in the realization of this book. Thanks to their smooth cooperation, it has been possible to implement this book quickly.

I also appreciate the steady reinforcement of numerous people, especially of my family, who always completely relied on me.

Introduction

With this work in your hands, you hold the most current and the most comprehensive guide to the Swing-based rich client platform, *NetBeans Platform 7*. The theme "richt client platform" is highly topical. In addition to the NetBeans Platform, Eclipse RCP is also a principal representative of this category. The development of these two platforms was mainly driven by the NetBeans and Eclipse integrated development environments (IDEs). Those two IDEs are based on their respective platforms and represent a rich client application themselves. The NetBeans Platform is completely based on the Java API with AWT and Swing and integrates the concepts of the Java Standard Edition (JSE), while the Eclipse RCP with SWT and JFace builds more and more on its own approaches and concepts.

Rich client platforms are flexible and used mainly for their constantly increasing requirements for applications and their architecture. One crucial aspect is their increased productivity and flexibility to be able to equip a product depending on its intended usage and to adapt it to a market. This is especially important for professional applications.

In my opinion, the NetBeans Platform is always worth using, even if an application is very small or quite huge, because of the comprehensive support actually provided by the NetBeans IDE. It is also already worth it because of the execution environment, and even more so because of the numerous APIs that provide practical solutions for frequently occurring problems and challenges with client application development. These solutions are very close to the practice and the application and increase productivity a lot.

However, this assumption is based on one basic condition: professional knowledge and use of the workings of the rich client platform. The application developer should at least know the main principles; only then can the real advantages of increased productivity and greater software quality be achieved in practice.

Many developers have assumed the platform was too complex, which is one of the main reasons the rich client platforms have not yet been established as quasi-standards for client application development. At first, developers may get the impression that there is a huge wall of APIs and concepts to master. However, once you begin to learn more, you find that there are immense synergies and simplifications possible, which make up for the challenges of the initial learning phase.

The NetBeans IDE simplifies both daily usage and developers' learning curve by providing comprehensive, helpful, and intuitive wizards. It is surely important that all NetBeans APIs and concepts build on the APIs and concepts of the Java Standard Edition (JSE). That fact simplifies everyday experiences with it and also facilitates the reuse of already existing components.

News of the NetBeans Platform

The NetBeans Platform 7 contains numerous innovations. One crucial innovation is the introduction of *Annotations*. Actions, for example, do not have to derive from a special class anymore. Thus, actions can be registered via annotations, and at the same time, actions can be added to a menu or to a toolbar, too. Before, you had to assign two separate configuration files for top components. Now, top components are registered via annotations and made public to the NetBeans Platform. Declarative information can now be directly and decentrally provided because of using annotations. Annotations are well documented and are checked by the editor or respectively by the compiler;, information is provided in a simpler manner and potential erratic entries in XML are avoided. Furthermore, the information is located exactly at the position it refers to, so no additional files have to be managed. This also simplifies refactoring and facilitates the NetBeans Platform's independence of the NetBeans IDE. Bear in mind that the necessary configuration files, or rather configuration entries, are created out of the annotations at compile time. This means using annotations is not mandatory; you can also manually create the necessary configuration as previously.

Whether or not you use annotations is a question of philosophy in the end, and also depends on the project's size and on your special needs. Of course, you can also look at the disadvantages of annotations. For example, the meta-information is scattered in the source files. A central file might be easier to adapt or to overlook.

The support of *OSGi* bundles is also a crucial innovation. Now OSGi bundles can be executed parallel to NetBeans modules within the NetBeans Platform 7. For this purpose, the OSGi framework, Felix or Equinox, is optionally integrated in the NetBeans Platform. It is also possible to convert the NetBeans Platform modules into OSGi bundles. This innovation allows the use of numerous existing OSGi bundles.

Out-of-the-box support of Maven can also be called an innovation. NetBeans Platform applications can now be completely developed via Maven. With the NetBeans Maven plugin and the availability of all NetBeans Platform modules in a public Maven repository, there is nothing that prevents using the NetBeans Platform outside the NetBeans IDE.

How This Book Is Structured

This book is aimed at Java developers who want to develop client applications based on the NetBeans Platform. No previous knowledge of rich client platforms is required. The main goal of this book is to provide the basic ideas and functionalities of the NetBeans Platform close to actual practice and to explain the very good support the NetBeans IDE provides for the development phase of your application as well as the interfaces and advantages of the NetBeans Platform. In this way I hope to motivate you to further use the NetBeans Platform—and to ask yourself why you have not been developing your applications on the basis of a rich client platform already, especially once you recognize the numerous advantages you could have benefited from in the past.

The separate chapters of the book are mostly independent of each other, in order to give you a way to get directly into individual chapters, and to provide you an optimal manual for developing rich client applications based on the NetBeans Platform. To keep the chapters clear and to facilitate direct access, the explanations within this book are supported by small examples without referring to an overall application. At the end of the book, I will show how to create a complete rich client application, from the draft phase over creating the basic structure to implementing the application logic. I will explain this in a tutorial-like format with the example of an MP3 manager. In this application you will integrate the Java Media Framework (JMF) as well as the Java DB database system, among others.

Part 1 deals with the basic features and concepts of the NetBeans Platform. At first, you will learn how a rich client is defined, which features a rich client platform generally contains, and which special advantages the Netbeans Platform provides. Additionally, because the module-based nature is crucial, I will cover both the NetBeans module system and the OSGi framework in the Part 1. The central topics of Lookup, actions, and data management complete the first part with one chapter each.

Part 2 is completely devoted to developing user interfaces. This part mainly deals with the Window System as well as the menu bar, toolbar, status bar, and progress bar. Due to the support of the Window System, you can implement and easily manage your own windows. Connected to the data management, which is explained in the first part, you will learn about the flexible node concept together with the

Explorer API in a separate chapter. This part also covers developing dialogs and wizards as well as using the powerful Visual Library API.

In Part 3 we will take a closer look at the standard modules of the NetBeans Platform which can be used directly without great effort. This includes the help system, the output window, the navigator, the properties window, the options dialog, and the palette module. I will explain how to use each of them in a separate chapter.

Part 4 is about using the very helpful APIs of the NetBeans Platform and the NetBeans IDE. Actually, you are not limited to the modules of the NetBeans Platform. One chapter explains how to use the Palette API and another how to use the Task List API. Additionally, we will take a closer look at the Quick Search and the Auto Update Services API by means of examples that are close to actual practice.

With Part 5 I put the NetBeans Platform in the context of databases and Java EE applications. First, you will use the Java DB as a client-side database solution within a NetBeans Platform application. Using Hibernate to facilitate accessing databases is covered in a following chapter. However, applying Hibernate does not need to be dependent on a special object-relational mapping (ORM) framework. In a later chapter, I will explain how to integrate the Java Persistence API (JPA) for this purpose. As an alternative to Java DB and Hibernate, I will also go deeper into the MySQL database solution in connection with EclipseLink. We will look at the topic of web services from both sides in this part: on the one hand, it is about using any available web services using SOAP. On the other hand, it is about connecting server-side Java EE applications using SOAP and REST-based web services. A final chapter will answer questions concerning authentication of users and specific adaptation of the application.

In Part 6 you will learn which possibilities the NetBeans Platform provides concerning internationalization and localization. Furthermore, this part covers the branding of the NetBeans Platform as well as packing the whole application as a deliverable unit. In another chapter you will learn about the update mechanism of the NetBeans Platform with which you can update your application in a simple and transparent manner after delivering.

Part 7 of this book is about the different development and test tools of the NetBeans Platform or, respectively, of the NetBeans IDE. First, it is about implementing NetBeans Platform applications using the Maven build system. In another chapter you learn about how to develop NetBeans Platform applications even within the Eclipse IDE using Maven. Additionally, one chapter will simplify changing from the Eclipse IDE to the NetBeans IDE to develop NetBeans Platform applications. In addition to the NetBeans and the Eclipse IDE, the IntelliJ IDEA can also be used to develop NetBeans Platform applications. The NetBeans IDE provides a powerful GUI builder for the efficient development of user interfaces. You will learn how to use it and how to debug and test your application in separate chapters.

Part 8 completes this guide with a fully functional example. In the course of this part, you develop an MP3 manager application step by step. The previously described concepts and technologies come together here and can be understood as in actual practice.

Downloading the Code

All examples and explanations in this book are based on Java 6 and NetBeans 7. You can download the Java Development Kit (JDK 6) at `http://java.oracle.com` and NetBeans 7 at `http://netbeans.org`.

Each of the source code examples in this book can be downloaded from the Source Code/Download area for this book on the Apress web site as a complete runnable NetBeans IDE project.

PART 1

Basics & Concepts: Basics of the NetBeans Platform

CHAPTER 1

Introduction

This chapter introduces you to rich client development. In the process, you will learn what a rich client is and how a rich client platform can help you. This chapter will also briefly touch on the main advantages and characteristics of the NetBeans Platform.

What Is a Rich Client?

In a client server architecture the term *rich client* is used for clients where the data processing occurs mainly on the client side. The client also provides the graphical user interface (GUI). Often rich clients are applications that are extendable via plugins and modules. In this way, rich clients are able to solve more than one problem.

Rich clients are typically developed on top of a framework. A framework offers a basic starting point on top of which the user can assemble logically related parts of the application, which are called modules. Ideally, unrelated solutions (such as those made available by different providers) can work together, so that all the modules appear to have been created as one whole.

Above and beyond all that, rich clients have the advantage that they are easy to distribute and update, such as via an automatic online update function within the client itself or through a mechanism that enables the rich client to start over the Internet (for example, via Java Web Start).

Here's an overview of the characteristics of a rich client:

- Flexible and modular application architecture

- Platform independence

- Adaptability to the end user

- Ability to work online as well as offline

- Simplified distribution to the end user

- Simplified updating of the client

What Is a Rich Client Platform?

A rich client platform is an application lifecycle environment, a basis for desktop applications. Most desktop applications have similar features, such as menus, toolbars, status bars, progress visualizations, data displays, customization settings, the saving and loading of user-specific data and configurations, splash screens, about boxes, internationalization, help systems, and so on. For these and other typical client application features, a rich client platform provides a framework with which the features can quickly and simply be put together.

The configurability and extensibility of an application take center stage in a framework of this kind. As a result, you can, for example, declaratively provide the menu entries of an application in a text file, then the menu will be loaded automatically by the framework. This means that the source code becomes considerably more focused and manageable, and developers are able to concentrate on the actual business needs of the application, while the menu is maximally configurable.

The most important aspect of a rich client platform is its architecture. Applications based on rich client platforms are written in the form of modules, within which logically coherent parts of an application are isolated. A module is described declaratively and automatically loaded by the platform. As a result, there is no explicit binding necessary between the source code and the application. In this way, a relatively loosely coupled relationship is established between independently functioning modules, by means of which the dynamic extensibility of the application and the ability to swap its constituent parts are enormously simplified. That way it is also very easy to assemble user- or domain-specific applications from individual modules.

A rich client platform also frees the developer from being concerned with tasks that have little to do with the application's business logic. At the end of the development cycle, you achieve a well-deserved and modern application architecture.

Advantages of a Rich Client Platform

Aside from the modularity offered by a rich client architecture,—which simultaneously implies a high degree of robustness and end user value—the extensive development support it provides should also be highlighted. These and other advantages of development based on rich client platforms are briefly described here.

Reduction of Development Time

A rich client platform provides a multitude of application programming interfaces (APIs) for desktop application development. For example, these APIs can be used by developers to manage windows and menus or support the display of customization options. Through the reusability of many predefined components, developers are able to concentrate very closely on the business logic of the application in question.

User Interface Consistency

Usability of an application is always of crucial concern, particularly when the application is intended to be used by professionals in a specific field. A rich client platform makes available a framework to display the user interface (UI), with an emphasis on consistency, accessibility, and usability.

Updating an Application

Using a rich client platform, it is possible to quickly and efficiently distribute new or updated modules to end users. As a result, not all the clients of an application need be informed by developers to switch to a new version. Updates can be distributed and installed in the form of modules, so distinct features can be developed and delivered by independently developer teams. The modular architecture of the application ensures that completed modules can be distributed without having to wait for other modules to be finalized.

Platform Independence

Rich client platforms are based on international standards and reusable components. As a result, Java applications based on rich client platforms can be automatically deployed to multiple systems, such as Windows or Linux, so long as an implementation of the Java Runtime Environment is available. Since the feature set and the applicability of applications keep changing, it is very important that they are developed in such a way that they are extendable and can be deployed to different target systems. All this is provided by a rich client platform, saving time and money. Applications based on rich client platforms do not require further libraries or components, other than the Java Runtime Environment.

Reusability and Reliability

Rich client platforms make a range of features and modules available, which can be used in the developer's own applications. If the module does not completely match the application's requirements, it is entirely possible to use it as a starting point, while extending it or changing it as needed. Since most platforms also make their source code available, it may also, in some cases, be worth considering changing or extending the platform itself. These factors imply a high degree of reliability and freedom.

Characteristics of the NetBeans Platform

In addition to the generic advantages of a rich client platform, the NetBeans Platform offers numerous frameworks and several additional features that can be particularly useful to your applications. The important ones, which constitute the main characteristics of the NetBeans Platform, are outlined here.

User Interface Framework

Windows, menus, toolbars, and other components are made available by the platform. As a result, you focus on specific actions, which condense your code, making it better and less error prone. The complete user interface offered by the NetBeans Platform is completely based on AWT/Swing and can be extended with your own components.

Data Editor

The powerful NetBeans editor within the NetBeans integrated development environment (IDE) can be used by your own application. The tools and functionality of the editor can quickly and easily be extended and adapted to the purposes of the application.

Customization Display

A display of user- and application-specific settings is needed in every application. The NetBeans Platform makes a framework available, making it extremely simple to integrate your own options dialogs, letting the user save and restore settings in a way that is pleasing to the eye.

Wizard Framework

The NetBeans Platform offers simple tools to create extendable and user-friendly wizards, guiding the user through complex steps in the application.

Data Systems

In terms of the NetBeans Platform, data can be local or available via FTP, CVS, a database, or an XML file. By means of abstraction, data access by one module is transparent to all other modules. Actual data access itself is therefore not a concern, since it is dealt with by the NetBeans Platform's APIs.

Framework for the Management and Representation of Data

Based on the abstraction of files and saved data (described in the previous paragraph), the NetBeans Platform provides a framework with which data can be assigned with specific actions or functions. It is also part of the framework to manage and represent the data and its action on the user interface.

Central Service Management

The NetBeans Plaform provides a central service management with the lookup concept. This enables you to provide and use certain services provided within an application independently of each other. This concept is important, because it enables a loose coupling of application parts to be realized. This is one of the important goals which the application of the NetBeans Platform pursues.

Internationalization

The NetBeans Platform provides classes and methods enabling the internationalization of JavaHelp and other resources. You can easily store text constants in properties files. The NetBeans Platform also loads text constants and icons applicable to the current country and language settings.

Help System

By means of the standard JavaHelp System, the NetBeans Platform offers a central system for the integration and display of help topics to the end user. In addition, individual modules can contribute their own topics to the application's help system. On top of all that, the NetBeans Platform lets you provide context-sensitive help as well.

Summary

In this chapter you learned the difference that a rich client can make. and the advantages a rich client brings to the table, including its modular architecture, which is made possible by a module system unique to rich client platforms. However, a rich client platform offers many other advantages and features, including support for a consistent user interface and the ability to update applications with new features at runtime. Finally, this chapter introduced the most important characteristics of the NetBeans Platform.

CHAPTER 2

Structure of the NetBeans Platform

To give you an overview of how a rich client application is structured and to show the relationship of the application you're creating to the NetBeans Platform, this chapter will discuss the architecture of the NetBeans Platform. It will also introduce the independent building blocks of the NetBeans Platform and the responsibilities that the NetBeans runtime container handles for you. Finally, this chapter will explain the structure of the NetBeans classloader system along with the role it plays in applications built on top of the NetBeans Platform.

NetBeans Platform Architecture

The size and complexity of modern applications is steadily increasing. At the same time, professional applications need to be flexible, above all, so that they can be quickly and easily extended. This makes it necessary to divide an application into distinct parts. As a result, each distinct part is a building block that makes up a modular architecture. The distinct parts must be independent, making available well-defined interfaces that are used by other parts of the same application, with features that other parts of the application can use and extend.

The division of an application into modules—that is, logically interdependent parts—enhances the design of an application enormously. In contrast to a monolithic application, in which every class can make use of code from any other class, the architecture is far more flexible and, more importantly, far simpler to maintain. Although it is possible in Java to protect a class from access from the outside world, but such class-level protection is too finely grained to be useful to most applications. It is exactly this central aspect of modern client applications that the NetBeans Platform tackles. Its concepts and structures support the development and conceptualization of flexible and modular applications.

The basic building block of the NetBeans Platform is modules. A module is a collection of functionally-related classes together with a description of the interfaces that the module exposes, as well as a description of the other modules that it needs in order to function. The complete NetBeans Platform, as well as the application built on top of it, are divided into modules. These are loaded by the core of the NetBeans Platform, which is known as the *NetBeans runtime container*. The NetBeans runtime container loads the application's modules dynamically and automatically, after which it is responsible for running the application as well.

The NetBeans IDE is a very good example of a modular rich client application. The functionality and characteristics of an IDE, such as its Java language support or the code editor, are created in the form of modules on top of the NetBeans Platform, as shown in Figure 2-1. This offers a great advantage because the application can be extended by additional modules and adapted to specific user needs, allowing particular modules that are not used to be deactivated or uninstalled.

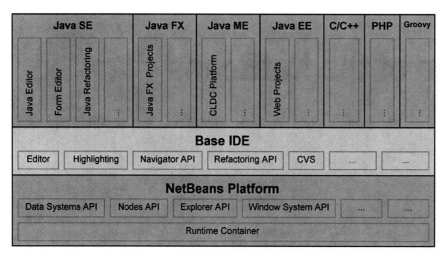

Figure 2-1. *Conceptual structure of the NetBeans IDE*

To enable your applications to attain this level of modularity, the NetBeans Platform on the one hand makes mechanisms and concepts available that enable modules to be extendable by other modules, and on the other hand enables them to communicate with each other without being dependent on each other. In other words, the NetBeans Platform supports a loose coupling of modules within an application.

To optimize the encapsulation of code within modules, which is necessary within a modular system, the NetBeans Platform provides its own *classloader system*. Each module is loaded by its classloader and, in the process, makes a separate independent unit of code available. As a result, a module can explicitly make its packages available, with specific functionality being exposed to other modules. To use functionality from other modules, a module can declare dependencies on other modules. These dependencies are declared in the module's manifest file and resolved by the NetBeans runtime container, ensuring that the application always starts up in a consistent state. More than anything else, this loose coupling plays a role in the declarative concept of the NetBeans Platform. By that I mean that as much as possible is defined in description and configuration files, in order to avoid a hard-wired connection of these concepts with the Java source code.

A module is described by its manifest file's data together with the data specified in related XML files and therefore does not need to be explicitly added to the NetBeans Platform. Using XML files, the NetBeans Platform knows the modules that are available to it, as well as their locations and the contracts that need to be satisfied for them to be allowed to be loaded. These dependencies are declared in the module's manifest file and resolved by the NetBeans runtime container, ensuring that the application always starts up in a consistent state. The NetBeans Platform itself is formed from a group of core modules (see Figure 2-2), which are needed for starting the application and for defining its user interface. To this end, the NetBeans Platform makes many API modules and service provider interface (SPI) modules available, simplifying the development process considerably. Included in this group (shown in Figure 2-2) are, for example, the Actions API, which makes available the often needed action classes; the powerful Nodes API; and the Options SPI, which helps your own options dialogs to be easily integrated into the application. In addition to these, there are also complete reusable components in the NetBeans Platform, such as the Output Window and the Favorites module.

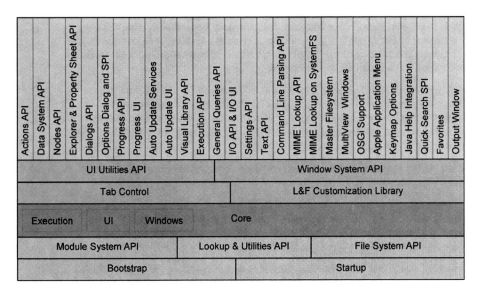

Figure 2-2. *NetBeans Platform architecture*

NetBeans Platform Distribution

Normally you do not need to separately download a distribution of the NetBeans Platform, because the NetBeans Platform is already a basic part of the NetBeans IDE, which is a rich client application itself. Developing your application in the NetBeans IDE, the Platform is extracted from the NetBeans IDE. However, there is the possibility of also adding multiple NetBeans Platforms to the NetBeans IDE. To that end, you can download a separate distribution of the NetBeans Platform from the official site, at http://netbeans.org/features/platform.

Now let's take a closer look at the important parts of the NetBeans Platform distribution:

- The modules org.netbeans.bootstrap, org.netbeans.core.startup, org-openide-filesystems, org-openide-modules, org-openide-util, and org-openide-util-lookup comprise the NetBeans runtime container, which is the core of the platform and is responsible for the development of all other modules.

- The NetBeans Platform also supports OSGi technology. The modules needed for this are org.netbeans.libs.felix, org.netbeans.core.osgi, org.netbeans.core.netigso, and org.netbeans.libs.osgi.

- The modules org-netbeans-core, org-netbeans-core-execution, org-netbeans-core-ui, and org-netbeans-core-windows provide basic functionalities for the API modules.

- org-netbeans-core-output2 is a complete application module which can be used as a central output window.

- The module org-netbeans-core-multiview is a framework for MultiView Windows, (e.g., the form editor window) and provides an API for it.

- The module `org-openide-windows` contains the Window System API, which is the API that is probably used most. It includes basic classes for developing windows and the windows manager, among others. From the windows manager you can access information about all existing windows.

- The update functionality of an application is implemented by the module `org-netbeans-modules-autoupdate-services`. This module provides the complete functionality for finding, downloading, and installing modules. The module `org-netbeans-modules-autoupdate-ui` provides the Plugin Manager, which enables the user to manage and control modules and updates.

- With the `org-netbeans-modules-favorites` module you can display random data and directory structures and thereby influence their actions via the Data Systems API.

- The `org-openide-actions` module provides a set of frequently used actions, such as copy, cut, and print. The functionality of these actions can be implemented in a context-sensitive manner.

- A very powerful module is `org-openide-loaders`, which contains the Data Systems API. This can be used to create dataloaders that can be linked with certain types of files and then create data objects for it. A special behavior can be added to these data objects in a simple way.

- The Nodes API of the module `org-openide-nodes` is a very central feature of the NetBeans Platform. Nodes can, for example, be displayed in an explorer view; by doing so, nodes can provide actions and property sheets for data objects.

- The `org-openide-explorer` module provides a framework to develop explorer views as used, for example, in the projects or file view of the NetBeans IDE.

- The `org-netbeans-modules-editor-mimelookup` module provides an API to find MIME type–specific settings, services, and other objects, such as an SPI to implement your own MIME type–specific data provider. The `org-netbeans-modules-editor-mimelookup-impl` module is a special implementation of this SPI which is responsible for finding objects in the directory structure of the System Filesystem.

- `org-netbeans-modules-javahelp` contains the JavaHelp runtime library and provides an implementation to the modules API, which makes it possible for application modules to integrate their own helpsets by means of the JavaHelp technology.

- The QuickSearch SPI for implementing and providing your own providers is located in the module `org.netbeans.spi.quicksearch`.

- The master filesystem module `org-netbeans-modules-masterfs` provides an important wrapper filesystem.

- The module `org-netbeans-modules-options-api` provides an option dialog and an SPI, making it easy to add your own option panels.

- Long-running tasks can be managed centrally by the module `org-netbeans-api-progress`. The module `org-netbeans-modules-progress-ui` provides a visualization of this with which it is possible to stop separate tasks.

- `org-netbeans-modules-queries` provides a general query API with which modules can query information about files. An SPI is also provided to supply your own query implementations.

- `org-netbeans-modules-sendopts`, this module provides a *Command Line Parsing API* and an SPI with which your own handlers can become registered for command lines.

- The `org-netbeans-modules-settings` module provides an API to save module-specific settings in a user-defined format. It also provides several useful setting formats.

- The `org-openide-awt` module includes the *UI Utilities API*, by which the different help classes for creating the user interface are provided.

- In the module `org-openide-dialogs` an API for displaying standard and application-specific dialogs is provided. The Wizard Framework is located in this module.

- `org-openide-execution` provides an API for executing long-running asynchronous tasks.

- `org-openide-io` provides an API and an SPI for the input and output of files. This module also provides a standard implementation with which you can write on the Output Window module.

- The Text API in the module `org-openide-text` provides an extension of the `javax.swing.text` API.

- The modules `org-netbeans-swing-plaf` and `org-netbeans-swing-tabcontrol` are responsible for the adaptation of the look and feel and displaying the tabs. The module `org-jdesktop-layout` is a wrapper module of the Swing layout extenstion library.

- The Visual Library API is provided by the module `org-netbeans-api-visual`.

Furthermore, it is possible to add modules out of the IDE distribution to the listed modules.

NetBeans Runtime Container

The basis of the NetBeans Platform and its modular architecture is called *NetBeans Runtime Container*. It consists of the following five modules:

- *Bootstrap*: This module is executed initially. It executes all registered command-line handlers, creates a boot classloader which loads the startup module, and then executes it.

- *Startup*: This module deploys the application by initializing the module system and the file system.

- *Module System API*: This API is responsible for the management of the modules and for their settings and dependencies.

- *File System API*: This API provides a virtual file system which provides a platform-independent access . It is mostly used for loading resources of the modules.

- *Lookup & Utilities API* : This component provides an important base component which is used for the intercommunication of the modules. The Lookup API is located in an independent module, so it can be used independently of the NetBeans Platform.

The arrows in Figure 2-3 show the dependencies of these five basic modules.

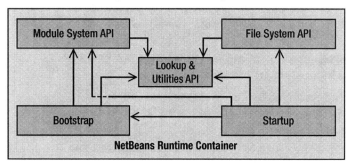

Figure 2-3. *NetBeans runtime container*

The runtime container is the minimal form of a rich client application and can be executed as such without further modules. If there are no tasks to do, the runtime container would directly shut down again after starting up. It is interesting to note that, on the one hand, the Netbeans Platform can create applications with an extensive user interface, and on the other, can also use this runtime container for a modular command-line application. Starting the runtime container, it finds all available modules and creates an internal registry out of them. Usually, one module is just loaded when needed. First, it is registered as existing. However, a module has the possibility to do tasks right at the start. This is done by the Module Installer, which will be discussed in Chapter 3. The runtime container also facilitates dynamic loading, unloading, installing, and uninstalling of modules during runtime. This functionality is especially necessary for users when updating an application (with the auto update function). It is also necessary for deactivating unneeded modules within an application.

For a complete understanding of the process of a rich client application, it is also important to mention that the Bootstrap module (the first module executed) is started by a platform-specific launcher. This launcher is also responsible for identifying the Java Runtime Environment. The launcher is part of the NetBeans Platform and is operating system (or OS) specific, so that, for example, on Windows systems it is an .exe file.

NetBeans Classloader System

The NetBeans classloader system is part of the NetBeans runtime container and a precondition for encapsulating the module and the structure of a modular architecture. This system consists of three different types of classloaders. These are the *module classloader,* the *system classloader,* and the *original classloader.*

- Most classes are loaded by the module classloader.

- The system classloader is only used in certain cases, such as when resources must be accessed outside a module.

- The original classloader loads resources out of the class path of the launcher of the application.

The module classloader and the system classloader are multiparent classloaders; they can have not just one classloader as parent, as usual, but any number of parents. Figure 2-4 shows the connections of the single classloader types.

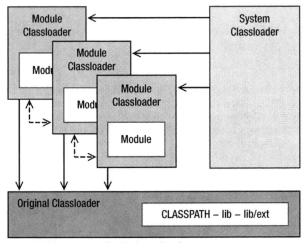

- - - = optional, according to dependencies

Figure 2-4. NetBeans classloader system

Module Classloader

For each module registered in the Module System, an instance of the module classloader is created, by means of which every module obtains its own namespace. This classloader primarily loads classes from the module's JAR archive, but it may load from multiple archives, as often happens with library wrapper modules. You will learn more about this in Chapter 3.

The original classloader is implicitly a parent classloader of every module classloader, and is the first on the parent's list. Further parents are those of related modules, on which dependencies have been set. How dependencies are set is described in Chapter 3.

This multiparent module classloader enables classes to be loaded from other modules, while avoiding namespace conflicts. The loading of classes is delegated to the parent classloader, rather than the modules themselves. In addition to the classes of the module JAR archive, this classloader is also responsible for loading the Locale Extension Archive (see Chapter 34) from the subdirectory locale, as well as the patch archives under the subdirectory patches, if these are available.

System Classloader

The system classloader is, by default, a multiparent classloader. It owns all the instantiated module classloaders as its parents. As a result, it is theoretically possible to load everything provided by a module with this classloader. Access to the system classloader can be obtained in one of two different ways: via Lookup (about which you will read much more later), as well as the context classloader of the current thread. This is the default (insofar as you have not explicitly set other context classloaders) of the system classloader.

```
ClassLoader cl = (ClassLoader) Lookup.getDefault().lookup(ClassLoader.class);
```

or

```
ClassLoader cl = Thread.currentThread().getContextClassLoader();
```

Original Classloader

The original (application) classloader is created by the launcher of the application. It loads classes and other resources on the original CLASSPATH and from the lib directories and their ext subdirectories as well. If a JAR archive is not recognized as a module (that is, the manifest entries are invalid), it is not transferred to the module system. Such resources are always found first: if the same resource is found here as in the module JAR archive, those found in the module are ignored. This arrangement is necessary for the branding of modules, for example, as well as for the preparation of multiple language distributions of a particular module. As before, this classloader is not used for loading all related resources. It is much more likely to be used for resources that are needed in the early start phase of an application, such as for the classes required for setting the look and feel classes.

Summary

This chapter examined the structure of the NetBeans Platform beginning with a look at its architecture, the core of which is provided by its runtime container. The runtime container provides the execution environment of applications created on top of the NetBeans Platform and also provides an infrastructure for modular applications. The NetBeans classloader system, which ensures the encapsulation of modules, was introduced and explained. Aside from the runtime container, many modules form parts of the NetBeans Platform and this chapter looked briefly at each of these, finally noting that the NetBeans IDE is itself a rich client application consisting of modules reusable in your own applications.

CHAPTER 3

The NetBeans Module System

The *NetBeans Module System* is responsible for managing all modules. This means it is responsible for tasks such as creating the classloader, loading modules, or activating or deactivating them. The NetBeans module system was designed using standard Java technologies, as much as possible. The basic idea for the module format originates from the Java extension mechanism. The fundamental ideas of the package versioning specification are used to describe and manage dependencies between application modules and applications of system modules.

Basic properties, such as the description of a module and the dependencies on another module, are described in a manifest file. This file uses the standard manifest format with additional NetBeans-specific attributes. The Java Activation Framework and Java Development Kit (JDK) internal functions (such as the support of executable JAR archives) were models for the module specification. Most modules do not need a special installation code, except of the attributes in the manifest file, meaning they are declaratively added to the Platform. An XML file, the *layer.xml* file, provides user-specific information and defines the integration of a module into the Platform. In this file everything is specified that a module wants to add to the Platform, ranging from actions to menu items to services, among others.

Structure of a Module

A module is a simple JAR archive which usually consists of the following parts:

- Manifest file (*manifest.mf*)

- Layer file (*layer.xml*)

- Class files

- Resources like icons, properties bundles, helpsets, etc.

Only the manifest file is obligatory, because it identifies a module. All other content depends on its modules task. For example, if the module just represents a library, no layer file is needed. The structure of a module is shown in Figure 3-1.

Figure 3-1. *NetBeans module*

Furthermore, an XML configuration file (`com-galileo-netbeans-module.xml`), which is located outside the JAR archive, belongs to each module. This is the first file read by the module system; that is, it announces the module to the Platform.

Configuration File

Each module is declared in the module system by an XML configuration file, located outside the module in the directory *config/Modules* of a cluster. This directory is read by the module system when the application is started. The modules are loaded according to this information. In this configuration file the name, version, and the location of the module are defined and whether and how a module is loaded is defined. This file has the following structure, as shown in Listing 3-1.

Listing 3-1. Module configuration file: com-galileo-netbeans-module.xml

```
<module name="com.galileo.netbeans.module">
    <param name="autoload">false</param>
    <param name="eager">false</param>
    <param name="enabled">true</param>
    <param name="jar">modules/com-galileo-netbeans-module.jar</param>
    <param name="reloadable">false</param>
    <param name="specversion">1.0</param>
</module>
```

The enabled attribute defines whether a module is loaded, and therefore whether it is provided to the application. There are three ways to determine at which point a module should be loaded:

- *Regular:* Most application modules are this type. They are loaded when starting the application. The application loading time is extended by the time of module initialization. Therefore, it is recommended to keep the module initialization very short. Normally, it is not necessary to run anything during module loading, because many tasks can be defined declaratively.

- *Autoload:* These modules are just loaded, when another module requires them. Autoload modules correspond to the principle of *Lazy-Loading*. This mode is usually used for those modules acting as libraries.

- *Eager:* Eager modules are only loaded when all dependencies are met. This is another possibility for minimizing the starting time. For example, if a module X depends on the modules A and B which are actually not even available, it makes no sense to load module X.

If the value of both attributes `autoload` and `eager` is `false`, a module is type Regular. If one of these values is `true`, the module type is Autoload or Eager. The module type is defined in the API Versioning section of the modules Properties (see Figure 3-7). Regular mode is used, by default.

Manifest File

Each module running within the NetBeans Platform has a manifest file. This file is a textual description of the module and its environment. When loading a module, the manifest file is the first file read by the module system. A NetBeans module is recognized if the manifest file contains the `OpenIDE-Module` attribute. This is the only mandatory attribute. Its value can be any identifier (typically the code name is the base of the used module—for example, `com.galileo.netbeans.module`). Therefore, conflicts cannot occur between modules, even if created by various developers. This identifier is used to clearly distinguish a non-ambiguous module which is necessary for upgrades or dependency definitions, for example.

Attributes

In the following, frequently used manifest attributes are listed. A module can be textually described with those manifest attributes. Additionally, those attributes determine the integration of a module into the Platform.

- *OpenIDE-Module*: This attribute defines a unique name for the module used for recognition as a module by the module system. Defining this attribute is obligatory.

  OpenIDE-Module: com.galileo.netbeans.module

- *OpenIDE-Module-Name*: This defines a displayable name of the module which is also displayed in the plugin manager.

  OpenIDE-Module-Name: My First Module

- *OpenIDE-Module-Short-Description*: A short functionality description by the module.

  OpenIDE-Module-Short-Description:
      This is a short description of my first module

- *OpenIDE-Module-Long-Description*: With this attribute the functionality of the module can be better described. This text is also displayed in the plugin manager. Thus, it makes sense to always use this attribute, to inform the user about the module's features.

  OpenIDE-Module-Long-Description:
  ```
  Here you can put a longer description with more than one
  sentence. You can explain the capability of your module.
  ```

- *OpenIDE-Module-Display-Category*: With this attribute, modules can be grouped to a virtual group so it can be presented to the user as a functional unit.

  OpenIDE-Module-Display-Category: My Modules

- *OpenIDE-Module-Install:* A module installer class can be registered with this attribute (see the section Lifecycle), in order to execute actions at certain points of time of the module life cycle.

  OpenIDE-Module-Install: com/galileo/netbeans/module/Installer.class

- *OpenIDE-Module-Layer*: This is one of the most important attributes. With it the path of the layer file is specified (see the section *Layer File*). The integration of a module into the Platform is described by the layer file.

  OpenIDE-Module-Layer: com/galileo/netbeans/module/layer.xml

- *OpenIDE-Module-Public-Packages*: To support encapsulation, accessing classes in other modules is denied by default. With this attribute, packages can be explicitly declared as public so other modules can access it. This is especially essential with libraries.

  OpenIDE-Module-Public-Packages:
  ```
  com.galileo.netbeans.module.actions.*,
  com.galileo.netbeans.module.util.*
  ```

- *OpenIDE-Module-Friends*: If only certain modules can access the packages which are declared as public with the attribute OpenIDE-Module-Public-Packages then those may be stated here.

  OpenIDE-Module-Friends:
  ```
  com.galileo.netbeans.module2,
  com.galileo.netbeans.module3
  ```

- *OpenIDE-Module-Localizing-Bundle*: Here, a properties file can be defined that is used as a localizing bundle (see Chapter 8).

  OpenIDE-Module-Localizing-Bundle:
  ```
  com/galileo/netbeans/module/Bundle.properties
  ```

Versions and Dependencies

Different versions and dependencies can be defined with the following attributes. In the section *Versioning and Dependencies* you find a detailed description of the application and of the whole functionality of these attributes.

- *OpenIDE-Module-Module-Dependencies*: With this attribute the dependencies between modules are defined, and the least-needed module version can also be specified.

  OpenIDE-Module-Module-Dependencies:
  ```
      org.openide.util > 6.8.1,
      org.openide.windows > 6.5.1
  ```

- *OpenIDE-Module-Package-Dependencies*: A module may also depend on a specific package. Such dependencies are defined with this attribute.

  OpenIDE-Module-Package-Dependencies: com.galileo.netbeans.module2.gui > 1.2

- *OpenIDE-Module-Java-Dependencies*: If a module requires a specific Java version, it can be set with this attribute.

  OpenIDE-Module-Java-Dependencies: Java > 1.5

- *OpenIDE-Module-Specification-Version*: This attribute indicates the specification version of the module. It is usually written in the Dewey-Decimal format.

  OpenIDE-Module-Specification-Version: 1.2.1

- *OpenIDE-Module-Implementation-Version*: This attribute sets the implementation version of the module, usually by a timestamp. This number should change with every change of the module.

  OpenIDE-Module-Implementation-Version: 200701190920

- *OpenIDE-Module-Build-Version:* This attribute has only an optional character and is ignored by the module system. Typically, a timestamp is given.

  OpenIDE-Module-Build-Version: 20070305

- *OpenIDE-Module-Module-Dependency-Message*: Here, a text can be set. This text is displayed if a module dependency cannot be resolved. In some cases, it can be quite normal to have an unresolved dependency. In this case, it is a good idea to show the user a helpful message, informing them where the required modules can be found or why none are needed.

  OpenIDE-Module-Module-Dependency-Message:
  ```
      The module dependency is broken. Please go to the
      following URL and download the module.
  ```

- *OpenIDE-Module-Package-Dependency-Message*: The message defined by this attribute is displayed if a necessary reference to a package fails.

  OpenIDE-Module-Package-Dependency-Message:
  ```
      The package dependency is broken. The reason could be…
  ```

- *OpenIDE-Module-Deprecated*: Use this to mark an old module which is no longer supported. A warning is displayed if the user tries to load the module into the Platform.

  OpenIDE-Module-Deprecated: true

- *OpenIDE-Module-Deprecation-Message*: Use this attribute to add optional information. Both the information and the deprecated warning are displayed in the application log so, for example, you can tell the user which module to use instead. Note that this message will only be displayed if the attribute OpenIDE-Module-Deprecated is set to true.

  OpenIDE-Module-Deprecation-Message:
      Module 1 is deprecated, use Module 3 instead.

Service Interfaces and Service Implementations

The following attributes are used to define certain service provider interfaces and implementations. Further information on this topic can be found in Chapter 5.

- *OpenIDE-Module-Provides*: Use this attribute to declare a service interface to which this module furnishes a service provider.

  OpenIDE-Module-Provides: com.galileo.netbeans.spi.ServiceInterface

- *OpenIDE-Module-Requires*: Here, a service interface can be declared for which the module needs a service provider. It does not matter which module provides an implementation of the interfaces.

  OpenIDE-Module-Requires: org.openide.windows.IOProvider

- *OpenIDE-Module-Needs*: This attribute is an understated version of the require attribute and does not need any specific order of modules. This may be useful with API modules which require a specific implementation.

  OpenIDE-Module-Needs: org.openide.windows.IOProvider

- *OpenIDE-Module-Recommends*: Using this attribute, you can realize an optional dependency. For example, if there is a module which provides a java.sql.Driver implementation, this module is activated and access is granted. Nevertheless, if no provider of this token is available, the module defined by the optional dependency can be executed.

  OpenIDE-Module-Recommends: java.sql.Driver

- *OpenIDE-Module-Requires-Message*: Like the two previous attributes, a message can be defined with this attribute. This message is displayed if a required token is not found.

  OpenIDE-Module-Requires-Message:
      The required service provider is not available. For more
      information go to the following website.

OPERATING SYSTEM-DEPENDENT MODULES

The manifest attribute `OpenIDE-Module-Requires` allows you to define modules that tend to be used on a specific operating system. This attribute is used to check the presence of a particular token. The following tokens are available:

```
org.openide.modules.os.Windows
org.openide.modules.os.Linux
org.openide.modules.os.Unix
org.openide.modules.os.PlainUnix
org.openide.modules.os.MacOSX
org.openide.modules.os.OS2
org.openide.modules.os.Solaris
```

The module system ensures that the tokens are only available on the appropriate operating systems. For example, a module that is automatically activated by the module system using a Windows system would automatically be deactivated with all others. To provide a module that automatically loads on Windows systems but automatically deactivates on other operating systems, set the module type to `eager` and add the following entry to the manifest file:

OpenIDE-Module-Requires: `org.openide.modules.os.Windows`

Visibility

With the following attributes, the visibility of modules within the plugin manager is controlled. This way, modules can be hidden, which are not important to the end user of your application.

- *AutoUpdate-Show-In-Client*: This attribute determines whether a module is displayed in the plugin manager. It can be set to `true` or `false`.

    AutoUpdate-Show-In-Client: `true`

- *AutoUpdate-Essential-Module*: With this attribute you can mark modules that are part of your application. A module which is marked like this cannot be deactivated or uninstalled in the plugin manager by the user. It can be set to `true` or `false`.

    AutoUpdate-Show-In-Client: `true`

In conjunction with these two attributes, so-called *kit* modules were introduced in the NetBeans Platform. Each visible module (`AutoUpdate-Show-In-Client: true`) is treated as a kit module in the plugin manager. All modules on which the kit module defines a dependency are treated the same way, except for invisible modules which belong to other kit modules, too. This means if a kit module is deactivated, all dependent modules will be deactivated as well.

This way you can build wrapper modules to several logically related modules. Then you can display them to the end user as a unit. You can create an empty module in which the `AutoUpdate-Show-In-Client` attribute is set to `true`, while defining a dependency on all modules which belong to this kit module. Then you set the attribute `AutoUpdate-Show-In-Client` to `false` in the dependent modules so they are not displayed separately.

Example

Listing 3-2 shows a manifest file with some typical attributes.

Listing 3-2. Example of a Manifest File

```
OpenIDE-Module: com.galileo.netbeans.module
OpenIDE-Module-Public-Packages: -
OpenIDE-Module-Module-Dependencies:
    com.galileo.netbeans.module2 > 1.0,
    org.jdesktop.layout/1 > 1.4,
    org.netbeans.core/2 = 200610171010,
    org.openide.actions > 6.5.1,
    org.openide.awt > 6.9.0,
OpenIDE-Module-Java-Dependencies: Java > 1.6
OpenIDE-Module-Implementation-Version: 200701100122
OpenIDE-Module-Specification-Version: 1.3
OpenIDE-Module-Install: com/galileo/netbeans/module/Install.class
OpenIDE-Module-Layer: com/galileo/netbeans/module/layer.xml
OpenIDE-Module-Localizing-Bundle: com/galileo/netbeans/module/Bundle.properties
OpenIDE-Module-Requires:
    org.openide.windows.IOProvider,
    org.openide.modules.ModuleFormat1
```

Layer File

In addition to the manifest file of a module with which mainly the interfaces and the environment of a module are described, there is also a *Layer* file. This is the central configuration file, in which virtually everything is defined what a module adds to the Platform. So, the layer file is the interface between the module and the NetBeans Platform, declaratively describing the integration of a module into the Platform. Firstly, the attribute OpenIDE-Module-Layer makes public if a layer file exists in the manifest file. During that process the path of the file is defined, usually using layer.xml as the file name.

```
OpenIDE-Module-Layer: com/galileo/netbeans/module/layer.xml
```

This file format is a hierarchical file system containing folders, files, and attributes. Starting the application, all existing layer files are summarized to one virtual file system. This is the so-called *System Filesystem* which is the runtime configuration of the NetBeans Platform.

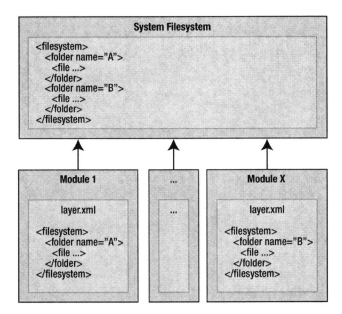

Figure 3-2. *System Filesystem*

This layer file contains certain default folders. They are defined by different modules which are extension points. So, there is the default folder Menu, for example, which looks like Listing 3-3.

Listing 3-3. *Default Folder of the Layer File*

```
<folder name="Menu">
    <folder name="Edit">
        <file name="MyAction.shadow">
            <attr name="originalFile"
                    stringvalue="Actions/Edit/com-galileo-netbeans-module-MyAction.instance"/>
        </file>
    </folder>
</folder>
```

In this example, the action class MyAction is added to the Edit menu. Do not worry about the exact syntax at this point; it is explained in the context of respective standard folders in later chapters. First of all, we elaborate this basic structure of the layer file. In addition, the NetBeans Platform provides practical features for working with the layer file, as shown in subsequent chapters, when our first module will be created. You can also find an index with the most important extension points in this book's appendix.

Every module is able to add new menu items or create new toolbars. Since each layer file of a module is merged to the System Filesystem, the entire menu bar content is assembled. The window system, which is responsible for generating the menu bar, now has to read the Menu folder in order to gain the content of the entire menu bar.

This System Filesystem also contributes significantly to the fact that modules can be added or removed at runtime. Listeners can be registered on this System Filesystem. This is done by the window system, too, for example. If any changes occur because of an added module, the window system or the menu bar itself can update its content.

Order of Folders and Files

The order in which the entries are read out of the layer file (and the order they are displayed in the menu bar), can be determined by a position attribute as shown in Listing 3-4.

Listing 3-4. Defining the Order of Entries in the Layer File

```
<filesystem>
  <folder name="Menu">
    <folder name="Edit">
      <file name="CopyAction.shadow">
        <attr name="originalFile"
              stringvalue="Actions/Edit/org-openide-actions-CopyAction.instance"/>
        <attr name="position" intvalue="10"/>
      </file>
      <file name="CutAction.shadow">
        <attr name="originalFile"
              stringvalue="Actions/Edit/org-openide-actions-CutAction.instance"/>
        <attr name="position" intvalue="20"/>
      </file>
    </folder>
  </folder>
</filesystem>
```

Thus, the copy action would be shown before the cut action. If necessary, you can also use this attribute to define the order of the folder elements. In practice, positions are chosen with greater distance. This simplifies the subsequent insertion of additional entries. Should the same position be assigned twice, a warning message is logged while running the application.

In order to easily position the layer content, the NetBeans IDE offers a layer tree in the projects window, in which all entries of the layer files are shown. There, their order can be defined by drag-and-drop. The respective entries in the layer file are then handled by the IDE. Where exactly to find these layer trees is already explained in the section *Creating Modules* after creating our first module. You can determine the order of actions with the wizard of the NetBeans IDE (see Chapter 6). The respective attributes are then created by the wizard.

Should positions of entries in the layer tree be changed, some entries will be added to the layer file. These entries overwrite the default positions of the entries affected by the change. The position of an entry (also of an entry of a NetBeans Platform module) is overwritten as follows:

```
<attr name="Menu/Edit/CopyAction.shadow/position" intvalue="15"/>
```

Use the complete file path of the affected entry in front of the attribute name position.

File Types

There are different file types provided within the System Filesystem. You will be confronted with them at some points again, when developing your application. For example, registering actions and menu entries in the layer file. I want to explain two frequently used file types in the following sections.

instance Files

Files of the type .*instance* in the System Filesystem describe objects of which instances can be created. The filename typically describes the full class name of a Java object (for example, `com-galileo-netbeans-module-MyClass.instance`), which makes a default constructor or static method create an instance.

```
<filesystem>
   <file name="com-galileo-netbeans-module-MyClass.instance"/>
</filesystem>
```

An instance is created by using the File Systems and Data Systems API, as follows:

```
FileObject o = FileUtil.getConfigFile(name);
DataObject d = DataObject.find(o);
InstanceCookie c = d.getLookup.lookup(InstanceCookie.class);
c.instanceCreate();
```

If you want a more convenient name for an instance, the full class name can be defined by using the instanceClass attribute. This enables much shorter names to be used:

```
<file name="MyClass.instance">
   <attr name="instanceClass" stringvalue="com.galileo.netbeans.module.MyClass"/>
</file>
```

In classes that do not have a parameterless defauld contructor, create the instance via a static method defined by the instanceCreate attribute.

```
<file name="MyClass.instance">
   <attr name="instanceCreate" methodvalue="com.galileo.netbeans.module.MyClass.getDefault"/>
</file>
```

Doing so, the FileObject of the entry is passed to the getDefault() method, if declared so in the factory method signature. With this FileObject you can read self-defined attributes, for example. Assuming, you want to define the path of an icon or any other resource in the layer file as an attribute:

```
<file name="MyClass.instance">
   <attr name="instanceCreate" methodvalue="com.galileo.netbeans.module.MyClass.getDefault"/>
   <attr name="icon" urlvalue="nbres:/com/galileo/icon.gif"/>
</file>
```

The getDefault() method with which an instance of the MyClass class can be created could thus look like the following:

```
public static MyClass getDefault(FileObject obj) {
   URL url = (URL) obj.getAttribute("icon");
   ...
   return new MyClass(...);
}
```

As you will recognize, I specified the path with a urlvalue attribute type. Therefore, a URL instance is directly delivered. In addition to the already known attribute types stringvalue, methodvalue, and urlvalue there are several others. We will take a closer look at them in the section *Layer File*.

One or more instances of a certain type can also be generated by a Lookup rather than via an InstanceCookie, as previously shown. Contrary to what was shown previously, you can easily produce multiple instances of a certain type and create the Lookup for a particular folder of the System

Filesystem. Using the lookup() or the lookupAll() method, one or more instances (if several have been defined) can be delivered.

```
Lookup lkp = Lookups.forPath("MyFolder");
Collection<? extends MyClass> c = lkp.lookupAll(MyClass.class);
```

Such a Lookup is used in Chapter 10 to extend the content menu of the top component with your own actions defined in the layer file. The basic class or the interface can be user defined by the instanceOf attribute in the layer file. This allows a more efficient working of Lookup and avoids Lookup having to initiate each object in order to determine from which base class the class will inherit, or which interface it implements. This way, the Lookup can directly create only the desired object type instances.

If the class MyClass from the prior entry implements, for example, the MyInterface interface, we can complete the entry as follows:

```
<file name="com-galileo-netbeans-module-MyAction.instance">
   <attr name="instanceOf" stringvalue="com.galileo.netbeans.module.MyInterface"/>
</file>
```

shadow Files

.shadow files are a kind of link of reference to an *.instance* file. They are mainly used when singleton instances of objects, as with actions, are used. These are defined by an .instance file in the Actions folder. An entry in the Menu or Toolbars folder then refers to the action by using the .shadow file. A .shadow file refers to files in the System Filesystem as well as to files on disk. This way, the Favorites module stores its entries. The path to the .instance file is specified by the attribute originalFile (see Listing 3-5).

Listing 3-5, Connecting a .shadow File with an .instance File

```
<folder name="Actions">
  <folder name="Window">
    <file name="com-galileo-netbeans-module-MyAction.instance"/>
  </folder>
</folder>
<folder name="Menu">
  <folder name="Window">
    <file name="MyAction.shadow">
      <attr name="originalFile"
            stringvalue="Actions/Window/com-galileo-netbeans-module-MyAction.instance"/>
    </file>
  </folder>
</folder>
```

Attribute Values

Mostly, file entries are expanded by attributes in the System Filesystem. The attributes can have quite different meanings, though. For example, the name of a registered action is defined by the attribute. It is possible to define class names or factory methods by attributes elsewhere. The System Filesystem provides a series of types with which the attribute values become available; with those attributes, the different attribute values can be read out. The most common types and their meaning are shown in Table 3-1. All types are listed in the Filesystem DTD (see Appendix).

Table 3-1. Types of Attribute Values and Their Meanings

Type	Meaning / Usage
intvalue	Specification of numerical values, e.g., for the location of files and folders by the position attribute.
boolvalue	Specification of true or false, e.g., for defining whether an action shall be executed asynchronously by the asynchronous attribute.
stringvalue	Specification of textual constants, e.g., naming an action.
urlvalue	Specification of paths, e.g., assigning an icon of an action as follows: nbres:/com/galileo/netbeans/module/icon.gif
methodvalue	With this you can define a factory method with which a class shall become instantiated. To get there, specify the code name base, the class name, and the method as follows: com.galileo.netbeans.module.MyClass.getDefault
newvalue	Use this type when a class shall be instantiated with its default constructor. Specify the class name with code name base: com.galileo.netbeans.module.MyClass
bundlevalue	Using this type, the attribute value is read from a properties bundle. This is very helpful with names of actions, for example. Like this, you can outsource text constants so they can be localized easier. The key follows the complete name of the bundle, separated by the # symbol: com.galileo.netbeans.Bundle#CTL_MyFirstAction

A factory method which is indicated by the type methodvalue has different signatures:

```
static MyClass factoryMethod();
static MyClass factoryMethod(FileObject fo);
static MyClass factoryMethod(FileObject fo, String attrName);
static MyClass factoryMethod(Map attrs);
static MyClass factoryMethod(Map attrs, String attrName);
```

You get access on the according entry in the System Filesystem by the FileObject parameter in a simple way. With this object you can access the referring attributes (compare the section *File Types*). You directly get the attributes when using a Map as parameter of your factory method.

Accessing System Filesystem

Of course it it possible that your own module folder, files, and attributes are used from the layer file to provide module extension points to others. You get access on the System Filesystem by the following call for reading entries:

```
FileUtil.getConfigRoot();
```

This call provides the root of the System Filesystem as `FileObject`. From there, you can access the whole content. You can also use the following method if you want to access a certain path in the System Filesystem:

```
FileUtil.getConfigFile(String path);
```

In Chapter 10 I will show you an example of how to define your own entries in the layer file, read them, and thus provide an extension point to other modules.

Creating Modules

Now it is time to create your first module. A good introduction to module development is also offered by the sample applications already integrated in the NetBeans IDE. For simplicity's sake, you will just design a single module here.

First, create a NetBeans Platform Application or a Module Suite. This way you will be able to execute and test the module easier, and you can define dependencies to your own modules and libraries (see the "Defining Dependencies" section). Afterward, you can even create an independent rich client distribution (see Chapter 35).

The NetBeans IDE provides a wizard to help you apply a NetBeans Platform Application project.

1. Start the NetBeans IDE and then select *File ➤ New Project…* in the menu.
    Different project categories are displayed in the dialog that appears on the left
    side. Select *NetBeans Modules* there. Then choose the project type *NetBeans
    Platform Application* on the right side (see Figure 3-3).

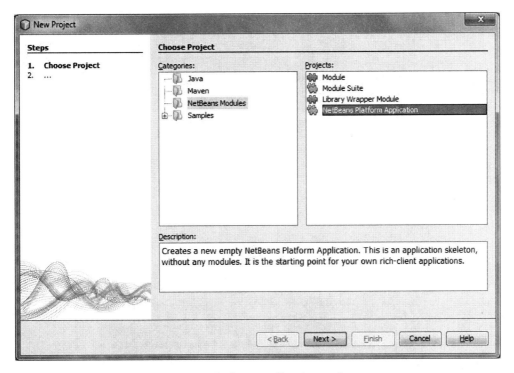

Figure 3-3. Creating a new NetBeans Platform application project

2. On the next page, name the application (for example, My Application) and choose the location where the project is to be saved. The remaining fields can be left blank.

3. Click the *Finish* button to create the NetBeans Platform application project.

4. Now the first module can be created; another wizard is available for this task. Open the *File* ➤ *New Project …* menu. Choose the category *NetBeans Modules*, and then the project type *Module* on the right side.

5. Click the *Next* button to go to the next page, for naming the project. Enter here, for example, My Module, and then select the option *Add to Module Suite*, and select the previously created NetBeans Platform Application or Module Suite from the list.

6. On the last page, define the Code Name Base and a module display name. The default value for the Localizing Bundle can be kept. To make it complete, activate the option *Generate XML Layer* due to create a layer file. If it is not needed, it can be deleted later, together with the referring entry in the manifest file.

7. Click the *Finish* button and let the wizard generate the module, as shown in Figure 3-4.

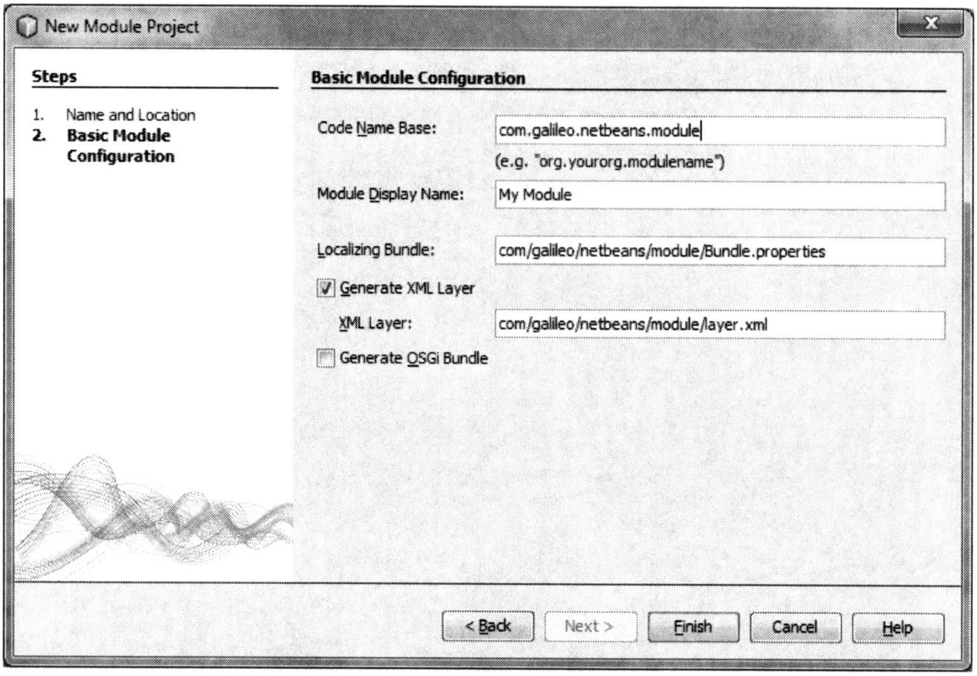

Figure 3-4. Configuration of a new module

Looking at the module in the Projects window, you see the folder *Source Packages*. At the moment, this folder contains only the files *Bundle.properties* and *layer.xml*. The file *Bundle.properties* only provides a localizing bundle for the information registered in the manifest file. The so-called *Layer Tree*, a special view, which you can find in the folder *Important Files*, is provided for the *layer.xml* file. It provides two different views. On the one hand, there is the folder *<this layer>*, in which only the content of your layer file is displayed. On the other hand, there is the folder *<this layer in context>*, in which the entries of the layer files of the modules (belonging to your NetBeans Platform application) are displayed. This view is represented as System Filesystem, too, as provided to the Platform during the runtime.

In this view entries of the module (in which you look at the folders) are displayed in bold. This gives you an overview of the most important default folders, and you can directly move, delete, or add entries. Furthermore, you can find the manifest file, which was also created by the wizard, in the folder *Important Files (see Figure 3-5).*

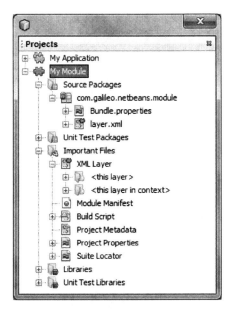

Figure 3-5. Module in the projects window

You can already start the created module as a rich client application. To do so, call *Run ➤ Run Main Project (F6)* in the menu or *Run* in the context menu of your NetBeans Platform application project. (See Figure 3-6.)

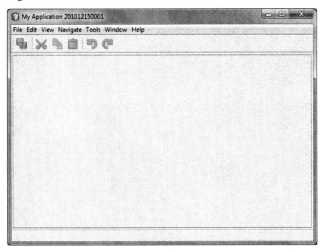

Figure 3-6. The basic structure of your NetBeans Platform application

We applied the basic structure of a NetBeans Platform application in just a few steps. In the following chapters, we will equip our module with functionalities, such as windows and menu entries, step by step. In this way we will enrich the rich client application.

Versioning and Dependencies

To ensure that a modular system remains consistent and maintainable, it is crucial that the modules within the system prescribe the modules they need to use. To that end, the NetBeans Platform allows definition of dependencies on other modules. Only by defining a dependency can one module access the code from another module. Dependencies are set in the manifest file of a module. That information is then read by the module system when the module is loaded.

Versioning

To guarantee compatibility between dependencies, you must define versions; for example, the *Major Release Version*, the *Specification Version*, and the *Implementation Version*. These versions are based on the Java Package Versioning Specification and reflect the basic concepts of dependencies. You can define and edit dependencies in the Properties dialog of your module, which you can access via *Properties* ➤ *API Versioning* (see Figure 3-7).

First, define the *Major Release Version* in this window. This is the version notifying the user of incompatible changes, compared to the previous version of the module. Here, the slash is used to separate the code name base from the version within the manifest file:

OpenIDE-Module: com.galileo.netbeans.module**/1**

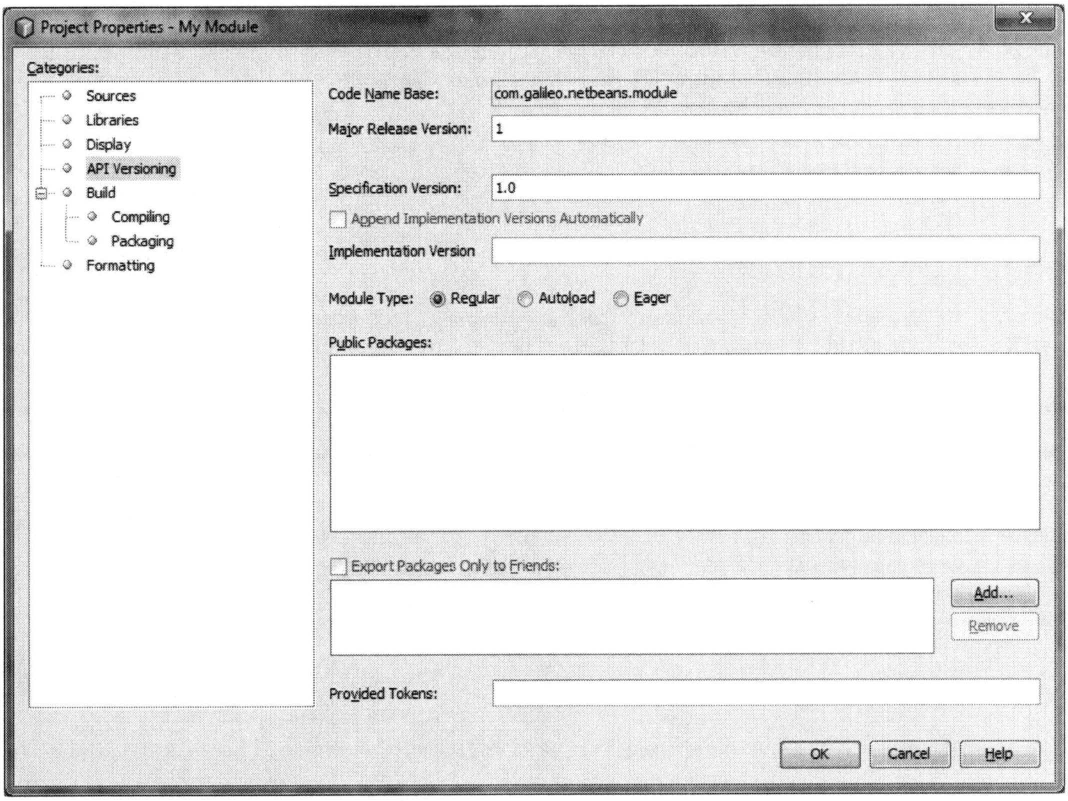

Figure 3-7. *Setting the module version*

The most important version is the *Specification Version*. The Dewey-Decimal-Format is used to define this version:

OpenIDE-Module-Specification-Version: 1.0.4

The *Implementation Version* is freely definable text. Typically, a timestamp is used, providing the date and time. In that way, you determine it is unique. If not explicitly set in the Properties dialog of the module, the IDE adds the implementation version when the module is created, using the current timestamp, set within the manifest file:

OpenIDE-Module-Implementation-Version: 200701231820

On the other hand, if you define your own implementation version in the Properties dialog, the IDE adds the OpenIDE-Module-Build-Version attribute with the current timestamp.

In the list of Public Packages, all packages in your module are listed. To expose a package to other modules, check the box next to the package you want to expose. In doing so, you define the API of your module. Exposed packages are listed as follows in the manifest file:

OpenIDE-Module-Public-Packages:
```
com.galileo.netbeans.module.*,
com.galileo.netbeans.module.model.*
```

To restrict access to the public packages (for example, to allow only your own modules to access the public packages), you can define a module's *Friends*. You define them beneath the list of public packages in the API Versioning section of the Properties dialog. These are then listed as follows in the manifest file:

OpenIDE-Module-Friends:
```
    com.galileo.netbeans.module2,
    com.galileo.netbeans.module3
```

Defining Dependencies

Based on these various versions, define your clear dependencies. To that end, three different types of dependencies are available: a module depends on a module, a package, or a version of Java.

NO ACCESS WITHOUT DEPENDENCIES

To use classes from another module, including the NetBeans Platform's own modules, you must first define a dependency, as described in the following sections. That means, if you use a NetBeans Platform class in your module and the code editor cannot find the desired class, the problem can normally be fixed by simply setting a dependency on the module that provides the class.

Module Dependencies

You define and edit module dependencies via *Properties* ➤ *Libraries*, as shown in Figure 3-8.

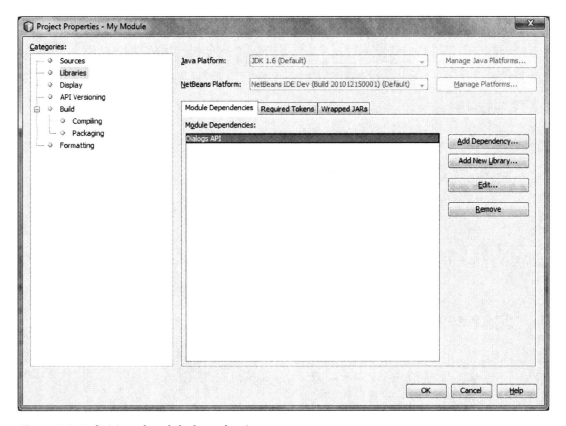

Figure 3-8. *Definition of module dependencies*

In this window, use *Add Dependency…* to add dependencies to your module. The NetBeans module system offers different methods to connect dependencies to a particular module.

In the simplest case, no version is required. That means there should simply be a module available, though not a particular version (although, where possible, you still specify a version):

OpenIDE-Module-Module-Dependencies: com.galileo.netbeans.module2

In addition, you may require a certain specification version. In this case, the module version should be greater than version 7.1. This is the most common manner of defining dependencies:

OpenIDE-Module-Module-Dependencies: org.openide.dialogs **> 7.1**

If the module on which you want to depend has a major release version, it must be specified via a slash after the name of the module:

OpenIDE-Module-Module-Dependencies: org.netbeans.modules.options.api**/1** > 1.5

Additionally, you may also specify a range of major release versions:

OpenIDE-Module-Module-Dependencies: com.galileo.netbeans.module3**/2-3** > 3.1.5

To create tight integration to another module it is possible to set an *Implementation Dependency*. The main difference and the reason for this approach is to make use of all the packages in the module, regardless of whether the module has exposed them or not. A dependency of this kind must be set with care, since it negates the principle of encapsulation and the definition of APIs. To enable the system to guarantee the consistency of the application, the dependency must be set precisely on the version of the given implementation version. However, this version changes with each change to the module.

OpenIDE-Module-Module-Dependencies: com.galileo.netbeans.module2 = **200702031823**

Select the required dependency in the list (see Figure 3-8) and click the *Edit...* button. As shown in Figure 3-9 you can set various types of dependencies.

Figure 3-9. Editing module dependencies

Java Package Dependency

NetBeans lets you set a module dependency on a specific Java package. A dependency of this kind is set in the manifest file:

OpenIDE-Module-Package-Dependencies: javax.sound.midi.spi > 1.4

Java Version Dependency

If your module depends on a specific Java version, such as Java 6, you can also specify that in the module properties under *Properties ➤ Sources*, using the *Source Level* setting. Aside from that, you can require a specific version of the Java Virtual Machine:

OpenIDE-Module-Java-Dependencies: Java > 1.6 VM > 1.0

You can require an exact version using the equal sign or require a version that is greater than the specified version.

Lifecycle

You can implement a so-called *Module Installer* to influence the lifecycle of a module and thus react on certain events. The Module System API provides the `ModuleInstall` class, from which we derive our own module installer class. Doing so, the following methods of the desired events can be overwritten. The following methods or events are available:

- *validate()*: This method is called before a module is installed or loaded. If necessary, certain load sequences, such as the verification of a module license, are set here. Should the sequence not succeed and the module not be loaded, an `IllegalStateException` can be thrown. This exception prevents loading or installing the module.

- *restored()*: This method is always called when an installed module is loaded. Here, actions can be initialized starting a module.

- *uninstalled()*: This method is called when a module is removed from the application.

- *closing()*: Before a module is ended, this method is called. Here, you can also test whether the module is ready to be removed or if there are still activities to be executed. If the return value is `false`, the module and the whole application is not ended, because this method is always called before ending a module. The application is just ended when all modules are set `true`. You can, for example, show the user a dialog to confirm whether the application should really be closed.

- *close()*: If all modules are ready to end, this method is called. Here, you can call the actions before shutting down a module.

▓ **Note** Using these methods, consider whether the actions you are calling could be set declaratively instead. However, always check if the desired action could go a declarative way. In particular, in the cases of the methods `validate()` and `restored()`, consider that these methods influence the startup time of the whole application. For example, when services are registered, you could either use entries in the layer file or the Java Extension Mechanism (see Chapter 5). This way they are loaded at their first usage and doesn't extend the startup time of the application as a whole.

Listing 3-6 shows the structure of a module installer class.

Listing 3-6. Structure of a Module Installer Class

```
public class Installer extends ModuleInstall {
    public void validate() throws IllegalStateException {
        // e. g. check for a license key and throw an
```

```
            // IllegalStateException if this is not valid.
    }
    public void restored() {
        // called when the module is loaded.
    }
    public void uninstalled() {
        // called when the module is deinstalled.
    }
    public boolean closing() {
        // called to check if the module can be closed.
    }
    public void close() {
        // called before the module will be closed.
    }
}
```

To record the state of the module installer class over different sessions, overwrite the methods readExternal() and writeExternal() from the Externalizable interface, which is implemented by the ModuleInstall class. There you store and retrieve necessary data. When doing so, it is recommended to first call the methods to be overwritten on the superclass. To let the module system know at startup if a module provides a module installer, and where to find it, register it in the manifest file:

OpenIDE-Module-Install: com/galileo/netbeans/module/Installer.class

Now you want to create your first module installer. The NetBeans IDE provides a wizard to create this file (see Figure 3-10). Go to *File ➤ New File...* and choose the file type *Installer / Activator* in the category *Module Development.*

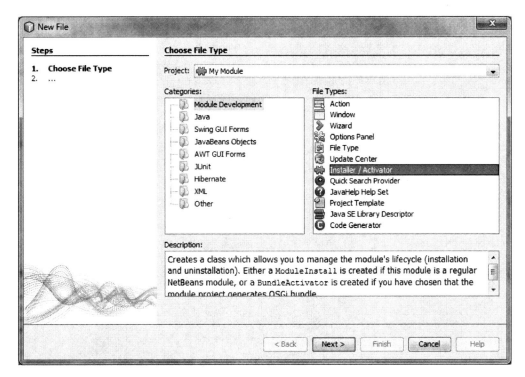

Figure 3-10. Creating a module installer

Click *Next* and then click *Finish* on the next page to complete the wizard. Now the module installer class is created in the specified package and registered in the manifest file. You just need to overwrite the required methods of this class. For example, you can overwrite the closing() method to show a dialog confirming whether the application should really be shut down. You can implement this as shown in Listing 3-7.

Listing 3-7. Dialog for Shutting Down the Application

```java
import org.openide.DialogDisplayer;
import org.openide.NotifyDescriptor;
import org.openide.modules.ModuleInstall;

public class Installer extends ModuleInstall {
    public boolean closing() {
        NotifyDescriptor d = new NotifyDescriptor.Confirmation(
            "Do you really want to exit the application?",
            "Exit",
            NotifyDescriptor.YES_NO_OPTION);
        if (DialogDisplayer.getDefault().notify(d) == NotifyDescriptor.YES_OPTION) {
            return true;
        } else {
            return false;
```

41

```
      }
    }
}
```

Be aware that this module requires a dependency on the Dialogs API to be able to use the NetBeans dialog support. Defining dependencies was described previously in the section *Versioning and Dependencies*, while information about the Dialogs API can be found in Chapter 13.

To try this new functionality, invoke *Run ➤ Run Main Project (F6)*. When the application shuts down, the dialog is shown and you can confirm whether or not the application should actually be shut down.

Module Registry

Modules do not normally need to worry about other modules. Nor should they need to know whether other modules exist. However, it might sometimes be necessary to create a list of all available modules. The module system provides a ModuleInfo class for each module, where all information about modules is stored. The ModuleInfo objects are available centrally via the Lookup, and can be obtained there as follows:

```
Collection<? extends ModuleInfo> modules = Lookup.getDefault().lookupAll(ModuleInfo.class);
```

The class provides information such as module name, version, dependencies, current status (activated or deactivated), and the existence of service implementations for the current module. Use the getAttribute() method to obtain this information from the manifest file. To be informed of changes, register a PropertyChangeListener, which informs you both of the activation and deactivation of modules in the system (ModuleInfo object). You can also register a LookupListener that informs you of the installation and uninstallation of modules. For example, a listener could be defined as shown in Listing 3-8.

Listing 3-8. Reacting on Changes in the Module System

```
Lookup.Result<ModuleInfo> result = Lookup.getDefault().lookupResult(ModuleInfo.class);
result.addLookupListener(new LookupListener() {
    public void resultChanged(LookupEvent lookupEvent) {
        Collection<? extends ModuleInfo> c = result.allInstances();
        System.out.println("Available modules: " + c.size());
    }
});
result.allItems(); // initialize the listener
```

Using Libraries

When developing rich client applications, you will more than likely need to include external libraries in the form of JAR archives within your application. Since the whole application is based on modules, it is desirable to integrate the external JAR file in the form of a module. That has the advantage of setting dependencies on the module, enhancing the consistency of the application as a whole. You can also bundle multiple JAR files into a single module, after which you will no longer need to put the physical JAR files on the application classpath, as is normally done when developing applications.

Library Wrapper Module

To achieve the scenario just outlined, create a *Library Wrapper Module*. The NetBeans IDE provides a project type and a wizard for this purpose.

1. To create a new library wrapper project, go to *File ➤ New Project…*, and use the dialog shown in Figure 3-11 to choose the category *NetBeans Modules*, followed by the project type *Library Wrapper Module*.

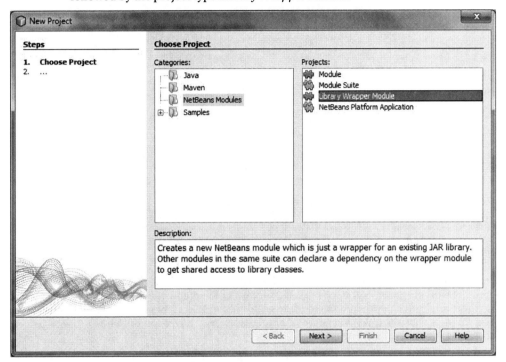

Figure 3-11. Creating a library wrapper module

2. Click *Next* to choose the required JAR files. You can choose one or more JAR files here (hold down the Ctrl key to select multiple JAR files). You are also able to add a license file for the JAR you are wrapping as a module.

3. In the next step, provide a project name, as well as a location to store the new module. Specify the Module Suite or Platform Application to which the library wrapper module belongs.

4. Click *Next* again to fill out the *Basic Module Configuration* dialog, as shown in Figure 3-12.

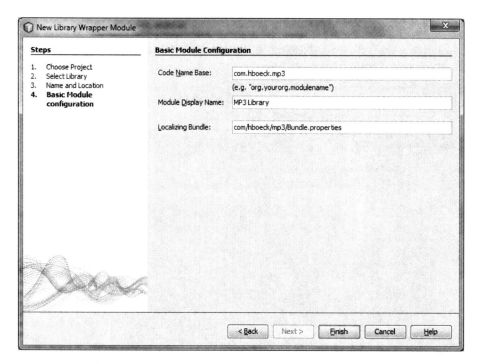

Figure 3-12. Library wrapper module configuration

5. This is where you can define the code name base. Normally this field is prefilled with the name of the selected JAR archive of the read code name base. Furthermore, you can provide the module with a name and a Localizing Bundle to localize the module manifest information. With a click on the *Finish* button, you create the new project.

When you are looking at the newly created library wrapper module in the *Projects* window, and you additionally open the *Source Packages* folder, you will see that the *Bundle.properties* file of the manifest file is located here. The library, which is encapsulated by the module, was copied in the directory *release/modules/ext* of the project folder.

To understand how a library wrapper module works, take a look at the related manifest file which is found in the projects structure in the folder *Important Files.* Note that the manifest information, which is depicted in the Listing 3-9, may not be found directly in the manifest file. Certain information, such as the public packages, are just written when you build the module (when calling *Build Project*). To see the entire manifest file, create the module and then open the manifest file within the created module JAR archive (located in the *build/cluster/modules* directory of your NetBeans Platform application. You can see which packages are exposed in the properties of your library wrapper module under *API Versioning.* There, you can delete packages from the *Public Packages* list later.

Listing 3-9. Manifest File of a Library Wrapper Module

```
Manifest-Version: 1.0
Ant-Version: Apache Ant 1.7.0
```

```
Created-By: 1.6.0-b105 (Sun Microsystems Inc.)
OpenIDE-Module: com.hboeck.mp3
OpenIDE-Module-Public-Packages:
    com.hboeck.mp3.*,
    com.hboeck.mp3.id3.*,
    ...
OpenIDE-Module-Java-Dependencies: Java > 1.4
OpenIDE-Module-Specification-Version: 1.0
OpenIDE-Module-Implementation-Version: 101211
OpenIDE-Module-Localizing-Bundle:
    com/hboeck/mp3/Bundle.properties
OpenIDE-Module-Requires: org.openide.modules.ModuleFormat1
Class-Path: ext/com-hboeck-mp3.jar
```

Two very important things have been accomplished by the wizard. On the one hand, it marked all packages of the library with the attribute **OpenIDE-Module-Public-Packages**, making all these packages publicly accessible. This is useful because a library is supposed to be used by other modules, too. On the other hand, the wizard marked the library (located in the distribution in the directory *ext/*) with the **Class-Path** attribute, putting it on the module class path. This way, the classes of the library can be loaded by the module classloader. The type *Autoload* was automatically assigned to the library wrapper module (see the section *Configuration File*). This way, it is just loaded when needed.

Adding a Library to a Module

It is advisable to always use a library wrapper module when integrating a library into an application, as seen in the preceding section. Creating a new module in this way for a third-party library adds to the value and maintainability of the application as a whole, because you can then set dependencies on the library with the module that wraps it. In some cases, it can be desirable to add a library to the existing module (your own application module). To do this is simple and works similarly to creating a library wrapper module.

To add a library, open the features of the desired module with *Properties* in the context menu. In the category *Libraries*, in which dependencies on other modules are defined, you find the tab *Wrapped JARs* on the right side. There you can add the wanted library with the *Add JAR* button.

Doing so, a class-path-extension entry is added to the *Project Metadata* file for each library. The path defined by the runtime-relative-path attribute is the path within which the library is located in the distribution (this is where it is automatically copied when creating the module). The location where the original of the library is located is specified by the binary-origin attribute. As you can see, it is the same directory as with the library wrapper modules. (See Listing 3-11.)

Listing 3-11. Project Metadata File with Class Path Extension

```
<class-path-extension>
    <runtime-relative-path>ext/com-hboeck-mp3.jar</runtime-relative-path>
    <binary-origin>release/modules/ext/com-hboeck-mp3.jar</binary-origin>
</class-path-extension>
```

With this entry into the project metadata file the library is copied into the *ext/* directory and is added to the manifest of the module with the entry Class-Path: ext/com-hboeck-mp3.jar when creating the module. In contrast to a library wrapper module, the packages of the library are not exposed. As a result, they can only be used by the module. (In most cases, this is the reason for the direct addition of the library: it should not be made public). It is also possible to define the packages of the library as being public, which is automatically the case with a library wrapper module.

WHEN TO USE WHICH APPROACH?

Bear in mind that you should create a library wrapper module of a library whenever possible rather than directly adding libraries because of modularity and maintainability. As a rule, only add a library to a module directly, when the library is solely used by this module and if it is not a problem to distribute the library together with the module that uses it. Furthermore, note that you cannot load the same library from two different modules with the Class-Path. This could lead to unforeseen problems. Also, do not try to use the Class-Path attribute to refer to the module JAR archives or to libraries found in the NetBeans *lib/* directory.

Reusing Modules

Usually, you create a NetBeans platform application project for applications which are not that big, then add the whole logic of the application to this project in the form of modules. In case you then want to implement, for example, a big application for enterprises in a team, it can be useful to break down the application into multiple parts, each containing an amount of modules. For this purpose, the NetBeans IDE offers the opportunity to add both a single module or a complete cluster (folder with NetBeans modules) as dependency. So if you develop, for example, a series of base modules, whose functionality you want to use in multiple applications, it is best to use a module suite.

You can create a module suite with *File* ➤ *New Project…* ➤ *NetBeans Modules*. Within this module suite you can develop and test your base modules encapsulated from special application modules. Starting the build process of your modules, all modules are stored in a cluster. Then you can add this cluster to another NetBeans Platform project as follows: call *Properties* ➤ *Libraries* in the desired application. There, you find the button *Add Cluster…* (see Figure 3-13) with which you can select the cluster of the module suite.

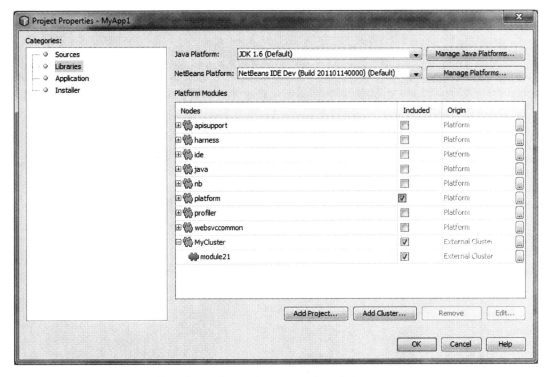

Figure 3-13. *Adding a complete cluster for reusing external modules.*

If you did not select a real cluster, the NetBeans IDE asks you to select the desired modules of the folder, and then creates a respective cluster. This means the NetBeans IDE automatically creates a cluster from a folder with modules.

Now, you can access further NetBeans modules from different NetBeans Platform applications with the possibility of reusing modules, as described. This way, you can, for example, implement your generic modules centrally, independent from special applications.

MODULE SUITE VS. NETBEANS PLATFORM APPLICATION

This book is primarily about developing independent applications based on the NetBeans Platform. This is why it constantly uses the *NetBeans Platform Application* project type to create an application in the following chapters. For this project type only the NetBeans Platform modules are provided, by default, since it will become an independent application and not an extension of the NetBeans IDE. However, you have the possibility of accessing any modules of the NetBeans IDE. For this purpose, call *Properties ➤ Libraries* in your NetBeans Platform application project. There you can activate the desired modules. Your own modules can only define dependencies on modules which are activated there. You can switch between a NetBeans Platform application and a module suite anytime under *Properties ➤ Libraries*. The branding support and creating an installer are logically just provided with a NetBeans Platform application.

Summary

In this chapter you learned how the underlying module system of NetBeans Platform applications is structured and how it functions. The module system is part of the runtime container. First, we looked at the structure of a NetBeans module. You learned about the many configuration options that are defined in the manifest file. In addition to the manifest file, a module optionally provides a layer file. You learned how to make contributions to the whole application, via registration entries in a module layer file.

You created your first module, learned how modules use code from other modules, and explored the lifecycle of modules and how third-party libraries integrate in a module via a library wrapper module. Finally, you discovered how those kinds of modules work, and you got some hands on experience with them.

CHAPTER 4

The OSGi Framework

The OSGi Framework provides a modular runtime environment. An application built on the OSGi Framework is developed in a modular way—in the form of *bundles*—so the OSGi Framework is comparable to the module system of the NetBeans Platform. An OSGi bundle matches the principle of a NetBeans module. The OSGi Framework has been widely adopted because of its standardization by a consortium of companies. By now, it is accepted as an official dynamic component model for Java through the Java community process as JSR 291.

However, this chapter will not discuss the OSGi Framework in too much detail (there is plenty of information specific to OSGi already available). Instead, it will demonstrate the possibilities of OSGi connected with the NetBeans Platform.

OSGi and the NetBeans Platform

Because of the importance of OSGi—especially to companies—the NetBeans Platform has been extended so that OSGi bundles can now be executed in a NetBeans Platform application. To do so, bundles must not be executed by a NetBeans module system but by an integrated OSGi runtime container (Felix or Equinox). This means you are able to develop hybrid applications in which NetBeans modules and OSGi bundles can run in parallel. A special adapter layer must establish the connection between both module systems; as a result, NetBeans modules are able to define dependencies on OSGi bundles and refer to their APIs. It is also possible the other way around: OSGi bundles can define dependencies on and refer to NetBeans modules.

Furthermore, it is possible to execute a whole NetBeans Platform application in an OSGi runtime container. For this purpose all NetBeans Platform modules are converted into OSGi bundles while creating an application. The NetBeans IDE naturally supports this as well as the development of bundles. Because the two module systems are quite similar, it is possible for both systems to interact as well as convert NetBeans modules into OSGi bundles.

OSGi Bundle Format

In Chapter 3 you learned about the basic structure of a NetBeans module and the special importance of the manifest file in that structure. In the manifest file, you define features and interfaces of a module. An OSGi bundle is also depicted by a manifest file; most attributes correspond to an attribute of the NetBeans module system. The basic structure of an OSGi bundle is shown in Figure 4-1.

Figure 4-1. *Components of an OSGi bundle*

Table 4-1 lists the most important NetBeans module attributes together with the corresponding OSGi bundle attributes.

Table 4-1. *Comparison of the Attributes of NetBeans Modules and OSGi Bundles*

NetBeans Module Attribute	OSGi Bundle Attribute
OpenIDE-Module	Bundle-SymbolicName
OpenIDE-Module-Name	Bundle-Name
OpenIDE-Module-Specification-Version	Bundle-Version
OpenIDE-Module-Public-Packages	Export-Package
OpenIDE-Module-Module-Dependencies	Require-Bundle
OpenIDE-Module-Localizing-Bundle	Bundle-Localization
OpenIDE-Module-Install	Bundle-Activator
OpenIDE-Module-Java-Dependencies	Bundle-RequiredExecutionEnvironment

Each of the following Listings (Listing 4-1 and Listing 4-2) shows the manifest file of a simple NetBeans module and of an equally structured OSGi bundle. As you can see, the differences between the two files are negligible.

Listing 4-1. Manifest File of a NetBeans Module

```
OpenIDE-Module: com.galileo.netbeans.module
OpenIDE-Module-Specification-Version: 1.0
OpenIDE-Module-Name: My Module
OpenIDE-Module-Localizing-Bundle: com/galileo/netbeans/module/Bundle.properties
OpenIDE-Module-Install: com/galileo/netbeans/module/Installer.class
OpenIDE-Module-Public-Packages: com.galileo.netbeans.module.api.*
OpenIDE-Module-Module-Dependencies: com.galileo.netbeans.library > 1.0
OpenIDE-Module-Java-Dependencies: Java > 1.6
```

Listing 4-2. Manifest File of an OSGi Bundle

```
Bundle-SymbolicName: com.galileo.osgi.bundle
Bundle-Version: 1.0
Bundle-Name: My Bundle
Bundle-Localization: com/galileo/osgi/bundle/Bundle
Bundle-Activator: com.galileo.osgi.bundle.Installer
Export-Package: com.galileo.osgi.bundle.api
Require-Bundle: com.galileo.netbeans.library;bundle-version="[1.0,100)"
Bundle-RequiredExecutionEnvironment: JavaSE-1.6
```

Defining a localizing bundle with the attribute OpenIDE-Module-Localizing-Bundle or Bundle-Localization, remember that the file extension is not given in an OSGi bundle. Defining a dependency on another module or bundle by the attribute Require-Bundle indicates the needed version with bundle-version. To define a minimum requirement on the runtime environment you can specify a tag list with the attribute Bundle-RequiredExecutionEnvironment. Expecting Java 6, use JavaSE-1.6. Other examples of tags are J2SE-1.5 or OSGi/Minimum-1.1.

Creating New OSGi Bundles

Creating a new OSGi bundle in the NetBeans IDE is easy. To do this use the wizard for creating a new NetBeans module and indicate that it should become a bundle that is OSGi conformant, as shown in Figure 4-2.

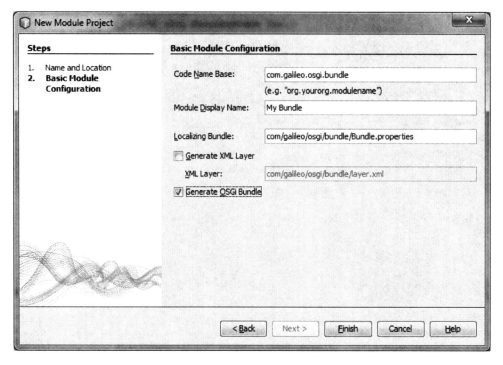

Figure 4-2. Creating an OSGi bundle with the NetBeans wizard

Choose the type Module with *File ➤ New Project…* in the category *NetBeans Modules.* Then activate the option *Generate OSGi Bundle* under *Basic Module Configuration* (see Figure 4-2). Further usage of the module or bundle is completely transparent then, meaning you can define dependencies or add features to the bundle with the NetBeans wizard as usual. It is especially interesting that you can also add a layer file to an OSGi bundle. This layer file is integrated in the layer files of the NetBeans modules in the System Filesystem, too.

Within a NetBeans Platform application, please bear in mind that OSGi bundles are actually executed by an OSGi container—by default the Apache Felix OSGi implementation—not by the NetBeans module system. In connection with this, please also bear in mind that the following modules are activated and hence included in your platform application:

- OSGi Specification

- Apache's Felix OSGi Implementation

- NetBeans OSGi Integration

Bundle Lifecycle

Similar to a Module Installer for a NetBeans module, which was covered in Chapter 3, the OSGi Framework offers a possibility for OSGi bundles that you can refer to certain events in the lifecycle of a bundle. Such a class that implements the interface BundleActivator is called an activator (see Listing 4-3). It provides the methods start() and stop().

Listing 4-3. Activator Class of an OSGi Bundle

```
import org.osgi.framework.BundleActivator;
import org.osgi.framework.BundleContext;

public class Activator implements BundleActivator {
    public void start(BundleContext c) throws Exception {
    }
    public void stop(BundleContext c) throws Exception {
    }
}
```

It is possible to create such a class with the same NetBeans wizard with which a Module Installer is created, too. If you call this wizard for an OSGi bundle with *File* ➤ *New File* ➤ *Modules Development* ➤ *Installer / Activator* an Activator class will automatically be created.

Integrating Existing OSGi Bundles

One important advantage of supporting OSGi bundles by the NetBeans Platform is definitely the reusability of already existing components that exist as OSGi bundles.

Adding a whole folder of bundles, called a *cluster*, to a Platform application is very easy. For this purpose just activate the category *Libraries* in the *Properties* dialog of the referring project. You can add bundles with the *Add Cluster...* button, which is where you can choose the modules which are provided by the NetBeans Platform, too. (See Figure 4-3.) Choose the referring directory in the following dialog. The wizard will point out that it is not a cluster. The wizard will list all JAR files (bundles and modules) if you click *Next*. Then you can choose the desired bundles and finish the wizard with the *Finish* button.

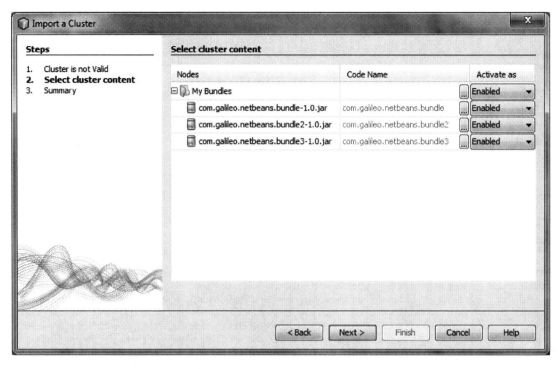

Figure 4-3. Creating and importing bundle clusters

Now you can define dependencies from among the previously added bundles in your modules.

NetBeans Platform in OSGi Runtime Container

The preceding sections were about executing OSGi bundles within (or more precisely parallel to) the NetBeans Platform; NetBeans Platform modules were still executed by the NetBeans Platform system. Now, if you want to develop an application plainly based on OSGi, it is possible to treat the whole NetBeans Platform as OSGi bundles.

To do this, click *OSGi ➤ Build Bundles* in the context menu of your NetBeans Platform application. The whole application, meaning all necessary NetBeans Platform modules plus your self-created modules, is created in the directory *build/osgi* as OSGi-conformant bundles. Furthermore, it is possible that your applications will be executed directly out of the NetBeans IDE in the OSGi runtime container, Felix. To do so, click on *OSGi ➤ Run in Felix* in the context menu; the bundles are automatically created and started with Felix.

Summary

In this chapter you learned some basics about the OSGi framework. You looked at the structure of an OSGi bundle and compared the manifest file attributes of NetBeans modules with those of OSGi bundles. You also learned how you can create OSGi-compatible modules with the NetBeans IDE. The last part of this chapter explained the bundle lifecycle and how you integrate existing bundles in a NetBeans Platform application.

CHAPTER 5

Lookup Concept

The Lookup concept is as important as it is simple. Used in many places within NetBeans Platform applications, it allows modules to communicate with each other. This chapter shows typical use cases and how the Lookup concept works.

Functionality

The *Lookup* is a central component and a commonly used concept in the NetBeans Platform for the management of object instances. Simplified, the Lookup is a Map, with Class objects as keys and instances of those Class objects as values.

The main idea behind the Lookup is decoupling components. I let modules communicate with each other, which plays an important role in component-based systems, such as applications based on the NetBeans Platform. On the one hand, modules can provide objects; on the other hand, modules can search and use objects with the Lookup.

Note The Lookup concept is implemented in the module Lookup API. It provides a very simple and clear interface. The Lookup API module is used quite often within the NetBeans Platform (often indirectly, too); it is the cornerstone of the modular concept of the NetBeans Platform. By the way, the Lookup API module works completely innocently and has no dependencies on other modules at all. That is to say, you can use the Lookup API module in any Java application, even if it was not developed on the basis of the NetBeans Platform.

The advantage of the Lookup is its type safety, achieved by using Class objects instead of strings as keys. With this, the key defines the type of the retrieved instance. So it is impossible to request an instance whose type is unknown in the module. This pattern results in a more robust application, since errors like ClassCastException do not occur. The Lookup is also used to retrieve and manage multiple instances for one key, which is to say of one type. This central management of specific instances is used for different purposes. The Lookup is used to discover service providers for which declarative adding and lazy-loading of instances is supported. In addition to this, you may pass instances via Lookup from one module to another, without the modules knowing each other. In this way a kind of inter-module communication is established. Even context-sensitive actions are realized using the Lookup component.

To clear up a common misunderstanding, within a single application it is possible to have more than one Lookup. The most commonly used Lookup is global, provided by default in the NetBeans Platform. In addition, there are components, such as TopComponent, that have their own Lookup. These are local Lookups. As described in the "Inter-module communication" section, it is possible to create your own Lookups and equip your components with a Lookup.

The Lookup concept is simple, efficient and convenient. Once you are familiar with this pattern, you will find it applies to many different areas. In the following sections, the usage of the Lookup in its main use cases is shown.

Services and Extension Points

A main application of the Lookup is the discovery and provision of services. The role of the Lookup in this scenario is a function of a dynamic service locator, allowing separation of the service interface and the service provider. A module makes use of functionality without knowing anything about implementation. In this way, loose coupling is achieved between modules.

Using the Lookup and a service interface, it is simple to define extension points for graphic components. A good example is the NetBeans status bar, defining the interface `StatusLineElementProvider`. With this interface and a service provider registration, the status bar is extended with user-defined components (an example of this is described in the "Status Bar" section of Chapter 5) without the status bar knowing about or having a dependency on those components.

For a dynamic and flexible provision and exchange of services, these are added declaratively to the Lookup, rather than programmed in the source code. This is achieved by either of two methods: adding the implementation of a service using the Service Provider Configuration file in the *META-INF/services* directory, or using the layer file of your module. Both are shown in the "Registering Service Providers" section later in this chapter.

The NetBeans Platform provides a global Lookup, which is retrieved using the static method `Lookup.getDefault()`. This global Lookup is used to discover services, added by using one of the available declarative registrations. Use this approach to register more than one implementation for a single service. The declarative registration allows instantiation of implementations on the first request. This pattern is known as lazy loading.

To achieve a better understanding of this pattern for providing and requesting services, and to get a more practical perspective, this chapter will illustrate the creation of a search list for MP3 files.

Defining the Service Interface

Module A is a module providing a user interface allowing the user to search for MP3 files by special search criteria. The search results are shown in a list. To remain independent of the search algorithm and ensure the dynamic use of multiple search variants (which may be switched at runtime), you specify the service interface `Mp3Finder` in module A. This service defines the search interface for MP3 files. The actual search algorithm is implemented in a separate module, module B, provided via declarative registration.

Loose Service Provisioning

Module B is a service provider for implementation of the interface `Mp3Finder`. In this example, assume the module is searching for MP3 files in a database. This allows multiple implementations of the service provider to be registered. All implementations can be in either one or more than one separate modules. To create an `Mp3DatabaseFinder` implementation of the interface `Mp3Finder` from module A, module B must define a dependency on module A. However, module A, the search list user interface, needs no dependency on module B. This is because the Lookup provides the service based on the interface (living in module A as well) rather than the implementation (residing in module B). Thus, module A is completely independent of the implementation of the service (see Figure 5-1) and can use it transparently.

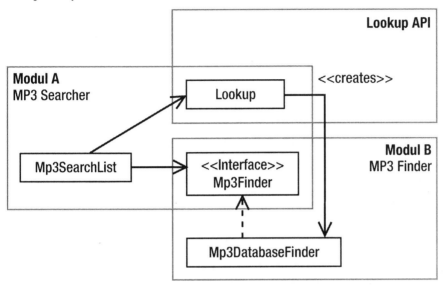

Figure 5-1. Service Lookup pattern

In module A, the service interface Mp3Finder is specified and a user interface is implemented for search and display of MP3 files (see Listing 5-1). A service provider is retrieved by passing the Class object of the interface Mp3Finder to Lookup, returning an instance matching the requested type. The interface Mp3Finder is also known as an extension point of module A. Any module can register implementations for it.

Listing 5-1. Module A: MP3 Searcher

```
public interface Mp3Finder {
    public List<Mp3FileObject> find(String search);
}
public class Mp3SearchList {
    public void doSearch(String search) {
        Mp3Finder finder =
            Lookup.getDefault().Lookup(Mp3Finder.class);
        List<Mp3FileObject> list = finder.find(search);
    }
}
```

Module B provides a service provider allowing the search of a database for MP3 files. This is done by implementing the interface Mp3Finder, specified by module A (see Listing 5-2). So, module B is an extension of module A at the extension point Mp3Finder.

The newly created service provider must be registered, so it can be discovered with Lookup. For this purpose you use the ServiceProvider annotation.

Listing 5-2. Module B: MP3 Finder

```
import org.openide.util.Lookup.ServiceProvider;
...
@ServiceProvider(service = Mp3Finder.class)
public class Mp3DatabaseFinder implements Mp3Finder {
    public List<Mp3FileObject> find(String search) {
        // search in database for mp3 files
    }
}
```

Providing Multiple Service Implementations

It is useful to be able to register multiple MP3 search implementations. This is easy. Simply create further implementations of the interface Mp3Finder. Again these have to be registered with an annotation. Such an implementation could be, for example, as follows:

```
import org.openide.util.Lookup.ServiceProvider;
...
@ServiceProvider(service = Mp3Finder.class)
public class Mp3FilesystemFinder implements Mp3Finder {
    public List<Mp3FileObject> find(String search) {
        // search in local filesystem for mp3 files
    }
}
```

To use all registered implementations of a service, discovery of the services using Lookup must be adopted. Rather than using the Lookup() method to retrieve a single implementation, use LookupAll() to retrieve all registered implementations of the service. Call the find() method of all discovered services as follows:

```
public class Mp3SearchList {
    public void doSearch(String search) {
        Collection<? extends Mp3Finder> finder =
            Lookup.getDefault().LookupAll(Mp3Finder.class);
        List<Mp3FileObject> list = new ArrayList<Mp3FileObject>();
        for(Mp3Finder f : finder) {
            list.addAll(f.find(search));
        }
    }
}
```

Ensuring Service Availability

A search module is of no use to the user if no search service is available allowing a search for MP3 files. To enable module A, ensuring that at least one implementation of a service is available, the NetBeans module system provides two attributes: OpenIDE-Module-Provides and OpenIDE-Module-Requires, which allow definition in the manifest file of a module if a special service implementation is provided or required. These and further attributes of the manifest file are described in more detail in the "Module Manifest" section of Chapter 3.

Within the manifest file of module A, the existence of at least one provider of the Mp3Finder service is required, with the following entry:

OpenIDE-Module-Requires: com.galileo.netbeans.modulea.Mp3Finder

To inform the module system during loading of the modules that module B provides the service Mp3Finder, add the following entry to the manifest file of module B:

OpenIDE-Module-Provides: com.galileo.netbeans.modulea.Mp3Finder

If no module declares such an entry in its manifest file (that is, there is no service provider available), the module system announces an error and does not load module A.

Global Services

Global services—services that can be used by multiple modules and are only provided by one module—are typically implemented using abstract (singleton) classes. With this pattern, the services manage the implementation on their own and provide an additional trivial implementation (as an inner class) in case there is no other implementation registered in the system. This has the advantage that the user always gets a valid reference to a service and never a null value.

An example would be an MP3 player service (see Listing 5-3), used by different modules—for example, a search list or playlist. The implementation of the player should be exchangeable.

Listing 5-3. MP3 Player As a Global Service in Module MP3 Services

```
public abstract class Mp3Player {
    public abstract void play(Mp3FileObject mp3);
    public abstract void stop();
    public static Mp3Player getDefault() {
        Mp3Player player =
            Lookup.getDefault().Lookup(Mp3Player.class);
        if(player == null) {
            player = new DefaultMp3Player();
        }
        return player;
    }
    private static class DefaultMp3Player extends Mp3Player {
        public void play(Mp3FileObject mp3) {
            // send file to an external player or
            // provide own player implementation or
            // show a message that no player is available
        }
        public void stop() {}
    }
}
```

This service, implemented as an abstract class, specifies its interface via the abstract methods, and at the same time provides access to the service via the static method getDefault().The advantage of this pattern is that there is no need for users of the service to know anything about the Lookup API. This keeps the application logic lean, as well as independent from the Lookup API.

The abstract class should normally be part of a module, which is, in turn, part of the standard distribution of the application (in the example, this would be the module MP3 Services). The service provider (that is, the classes that contain the real code for playing MP3 files) can be encapsulated in a separate module (see Listing 5-4). In the example, this is the class MyMp3Player, for which you subsequently create a skeleton and add it to module C.

Listing 5-4. *MP3 Player Service Provider in Module MP3 Player*

```
public class MyMp3Player extends Mp3Player {
    public void play(Mp3FileObject mp3) {
        // play file
    }
    public void stop() {
        // stop player
    }
}
```

Now the MyMp3Player service provider must be registered. For this purpose you can use the ServiceProvider annotation which looks like the following:

```
@ServiceProvider (service = Mp3Player.class)
public class MyMp3Player extends Mp3Player { ...
```

The relationships and dependencies of the modules are shown in Figure 5-2.

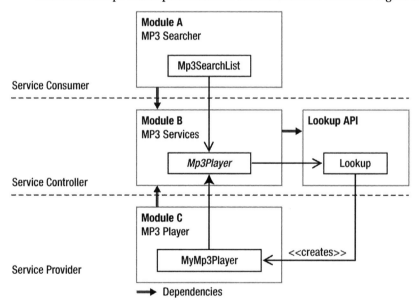

Figure 5-2. *Dependencies and relationships of global service, service provider, and application module*

Good examples for global services inside the NetBeans Platform are StatusDisplayer and IOProvider. The class IOProvider grants access to the Output window. The service provider actually writing the data to the Output window is in a separate class, NbIOProvider, in a separate module. If the module is available and the service provider registered, its implementation is retrieved via the static method IOProvider.getDefault(). If the module is not available, the default implementation is provided, which writes the output data to the default output (System.out and System.err).

Registering Service Providers

To allow a dynamic and flexible registration of service providers, even after delivering the application, and to ensure those are loaded only if needed, the registration is done declaratively, using configuration files.

Services which shall be available through the Lookup within a NetBeans Platform-based application can be registered and made public to the system in different ways. These different possibilities will be described in the following sections.

Annotation

The Lookup API provides the ServiceProvider annotation for the registration of a service provider. This is the easiest and the most transparent way to make your provider class known to the Lookup. So, when creating your application, a service provider configuration file is applied automatically, as you will see in the section *Service Provider Configuration File*. Thus, if you do not want to use an annotation, you can directly jump to that section. In the example shown in Listing 5-5, you see the attribute of this annotation.

Listing 5-5. Registering a Service Provider with the @ServiceProvider Annotation

```
import com.galileo.netbeans.mp3object.Mp3FileObject;
import java.util.List;
import org.openide.util.Lookup.ServiceProvider;

@ServiceProvider(
    service = Mp3Finder.class,
    path = "Mp3FinderServices",
    position = 10,
    supersedes={"com.galileo.netbeans.module.DefaultMp3Finder"})
public class Mp3DatabaseFinder implements Mp3Finder {
    @Override
    public List<Mp3FileObject> find(String what){
        ...
    }
}
```

In Listing 5-5 the class Mp3DatabaseFinder is registered with the ServiceProvider annotation as implementation of the service Mp3Finder. The only mandatory attribute is the service attribute, with which you determine which service you want to provide. You can influence the order, how the Lookup delivers multiple service providers, by the position attribute. With supersedes you can indicate a list of already registered service providers wich are substituted in this registration. This way, you can, for example, delete a registered standard implementation of a service. Finally, there is also the path attribute. With it you can indicate a name or a whole path (for example, *MyServices/Mp3Services*) under which the service provider configuration file is applied. However, in this case, the directory *META-INF/namedservices* is used instead of *META-INF/services*. So in the example of Listing 5-5, the configuration file would be stored in the directory *META-INF/namedservices/Mp3FinderServices*. Like this, the implementation can be accessed by a Lookup which you can create with Lookups.forPath().

Service Provider Configuration File

Service provider can also be registered by a *Service Provider Configuration* file. Such a file is actually created using the ServiceProvider annotation in the background.

This approach is part of the Java JAR File Specification. A file is named after its service and lists in its content all service providers. The file must be placed in the *META-INF/services* directory, which is part of the *src/* directory of a module, or in other words, it must be part of the class path of a module.

```
src/META-INF/services/com.galileo.netbeans.module.Mp3Finder
        com.galileo.netbeans.module.Mp3DatabaseFinder
        com.galileo.netbeans.module.Mp3FilesystemFinder
```

In this example, two service providers are registered for the service (that is, the interface or abstract class, Mp3Finder). The global Lookup, which is to say, the standard Lookup (Lookup.getDefault()) discovers the services in the *META-INF/services* directory and instantiates the providers. A successful service instantiation requires that each service provider have a default constructor so that creation from Lookup is possible.

As already described, you can make your service implementation public under a certain name; thus, it can be accessed more quickly. To do this, create the configuration file in the *META-INF/namedservices* directory. A subfolder of this directory indicates the name, for example *META-INF/namedservices/Mp3FinderServices*. You get the services which are registered there by a Lookup created with Lookups.forPath("Mp3FinderServices").

Based on the original specification of the service provider configuration file, the NetBeans Platform provides two extensions, allowing the removal of existing service providers and changing the order of the registered providers. To make these additions comply with the original Java specification, the add-ons are prefixed with the comment sign #. So, these lines are ignored by the JDK implementation.

Removal of a Service Provider

It is possible to remove a service provider registered by another module. This feature can be used to substitute the standard implementation of a service of the NetBeans Platform with your own implementation.

A service provider is removed by adding the following entry in your service provider configuration file. At the same time, you can provide your own implementation.

```
# remove the other implementation (by prefixing the line with #-)
#-org.netbeans.core.ServiceImpl
# provide my own
com.galileo.netbeans.module.MyServiceImpl
```

Order of Service Providers

The order in which service providers are returned from Lookup is controlled using a position attribute for each provider entry. For example, this is necessary to control the order of additional entries in the status bar (see Chapter 11) or to ensure that your own implementation is called before the NetBeans Platform implementation. Also, it is allowed to specify a negative value for the position attribute. The NetBeans Platform orders instances by ascending positions, so that instances with smaller numbers are returned before instances with larger numbers. For that purpose, the following entry is added to the service provider configuration file:

```
com.galileo.netbeans.module.MyServiceImpl
#position=20
com.galileo.netbeans.module.MyImportantServiceImpl
#position=10
```

It is recommended that position values are assigned in larger intervals, as shown in the example. This simplifies adding further implementations later on.

Services Folder

Another way to provide a service implementation is registration using the Services folder in the module layer file, as shown in Listing 5-6.

Listing 5-6. Registration of Service Providers in a Layer File

```
<folder name="Services">
    <folder name="Mp3Services">
        <file name="com-galileo-netbeans-module-Mp3DatabaseFinder.instance">
            <attr name="instanceOf" stringvalue="com.galileo.netbeans.module.Mp3Finder"/>
        </file>
    </folder>
</folder>
```

If a service is requested using the default Lookup, implementations are discovered by searching the Services folder and its subdirectories for instances, which can be assigned to the requested service interface. So, services can be grouped using arbitrary folders, as shown with the folder Mp3Services in our example.

In contrast to the registration using the service provider configuration file, the service provider need not provide a default constructor if registered in the layer file. With the layer file, specifying a static method in the instanceCreate attribute is possible, creating an instance of the service provider. Let's assume the already created provider Mp3DatabaseFinder has a static method getDefault() that returns the instance. The declaration can be changed by adding the following attribute:

```
<attr name="instanceCreate"
    methodvalue="com.galileo.netbeans.module.Mp3DatabaseFinder.getDefault"/>
```

With this attribute declaration, the service provider instance is not created using the default constructor, but rather by calling the static method getDefault() (more detailed information regarding this attribute and the corresponding *.instance* files are described in Chapter 3).

Also, using the registration via the Services folder allows removing existing service providers and controlling the order of the providers. Both mechanisms are achieved using default features of the layer file. A service provider can be removed by adding the suffix _hidden to its name, as it is done for menu entries (see Chapter 9).

```
<file name="com-galileo-netbeans-module-ServImp.instance_hidden">
```

The order in which service providers are returned is controlled using the position attribute, which is the same strategy as used for other entries in the layer file (see Chapter 3).

```
<folder name="Services">
    <file name="com-galileo-netbeans-module-ServImp.instance">
        <attr name="position" intvalue="10"/>
    </file>
    <file name="com-galileo-netbeans-module-ServImp2.instance">
```

```
        <attr name="position" intvalue="20"/>
    </file>
</folder>
```

In this example, the `position` attributes ensure that the service provider `ServImp` will be returned before `ServImp2`.

Inter-Module Communication

In addition to the global Lookup, which is provided by the NetBeans Platform and allows access to all registered services, it is possible to equip your own components with a local Lookup. The Lookup API offers a factory to create Lookups and an opportunity to listen to changes in Lookups. Using the class `ProxyLookup`, a user can create a proxy combining multiple Lookups into one. Using this feature of the Lookup API and SPI, you enable communication between components of different modules without making them interdependent.

A typical use case for the communication of loosely coupled modules is the visualization of detailed information for a selected object. The selection of objects and visualization of information is done in separate modules. As an example, imagine a list displaying the search results for MP3 files. Selecting an entry in the list provides the selected entry via Lookup, so other parts of the application can access the entry and display the required detailed information. This pattern is similar to the observer pattern. The module providing the objects—in this case the search list—is the subject, and the information display module is the observer. This allows multiple modules to display the data or detailed information in various ways. Again, the advantage is loose coupling of the modules: they are completely independent of each other. The only thing they have in common is the provided object (or, to be more precise, its interface), which is the source of the information to be processed. This loose coupling is achieved by using a proxy object, which acts as a substitute for the subject in the registration process of the observer. So, the observer is registered with the proxy component (in this case the Lookup), not the subject.

Figure 5-3 shows the example implemented in the following paragraphs. Both windows are in a separate module, each independent of the other (both can be exchanged or new ones can be added arbitrarily).

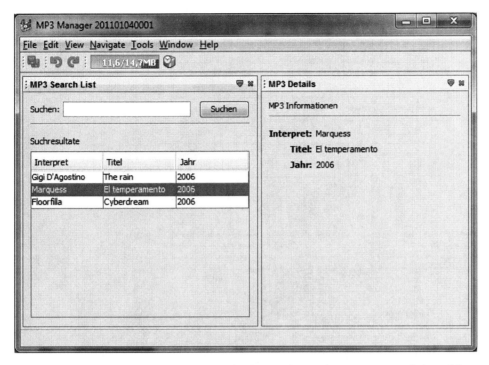

Figure 5-3. *Typical application example of a data exchange between two modules, without interdependency*

The structure of this concept is shown in Figure 5-4. The class Mp3SearchList in module A represents a list of search results. A search result entry is represented by the class Mp3FileObject, residing in a separate module, since this class is the most common denominator of all modules. If an entry is selected in the list, the Mp3FileObject instance is added to the local Lookup. A broker (that is, a proxy component depicted as the interface ContextGlobalProvider) is needed to decouple modules A and B. This proxy component provides the local Lookup of module A to module B, which contains the currently selected instance. To enable the centralized proxy component to access the local Lookup of the class Mp3SearchList, the Lookup API provides the interface Lookup.Provider. This interface must be implemented from the class Mp3SearchList.

With the getLookup() method, the local Lookup can be provided. The Lookup.Provider interface is already implemented by the class TopComponent, which is the superclass of all visible NetBeans window system components, as well as the Mp3SearchList. The NetBeans window system already provides an instance of the central proxy component, the class GlobalActionContextImpl. This class provides a proxy Lookup, which has access to the local Lookup of the focused TopComponent. This Lookup can be obtained easily by calling the static utility method Utilities.actionsGlobalContext(). So, there is no need to care about the ContextGlobalProvider instance, but you already have access to the global proxy Lookup. If you are interested in more details and want to know more about this concept, it may be worthwhile to investigate the sources for the classes and methods mentioned.

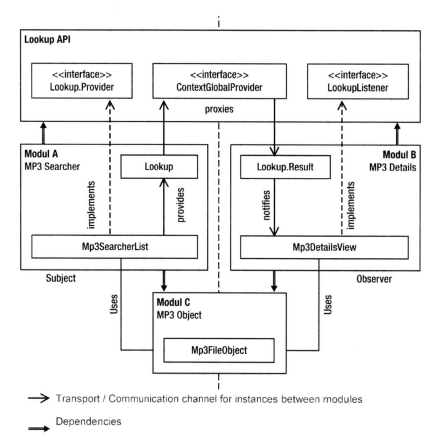

Figure 5-4. *Structure of the intermodule communication concept using a local Lookup via a proxy component to decouple subject and observer*

The class Mp3DetailsView gains access to the local Lookup of the Mp3SearchList by calling Utilities.actionsGlobalContext(). Based on the global proxy Lookup, you create a Lookup.Result for the class Mp3FileObject. An instance of the class Lookup.Result provides a subset of a Lookup for a special type of class. The main advantage is that the user can listen for changes in this subset by using a LookupListener. So, the component will be notified as soon as another Mp3FileObject is selected in the Mp3SearchList, or if the window showing the Mp3SearchList loses focus. As an example, no detailed MP3 information will be displayed.

Following, you find the classes of this example application. Only the important parts of the classes are shown.

First, there is the class Mp3SearchList, which represents a window, and because of this, extends from the base class TopComponent. To enable listening to selection changes in the result list, you also implement the ListSelectionListener interface. As a private member, you have a data model that manages the data in the table. For demonstration purposes, a simple data model has been chosen, creating three example objects of the class Mp3FileObject in the constructor and adding them to the model. This data would normally be provided using the search algorithm. The second private member object is an instance of InstanceContent. This enables you to dynamically change the content of the Lookup. In the constructor of the Mp3SearchList, you can now create a local Lookup, using the class AbstractLookup and passing the InstanceContent object into its constructor. Using the method associateLookup(), your local Lookup is set as the Lookup of the TopComponent, so that it will be returned from the getLookup() method.

In the method valueChanged(), which gets called if a data set is selected in the table, you get the data set from the data model, wrap it into a collection, and pass it to the InstanceContent instance (see Listing 5-7), which is the data storage for the Lookup. So, the selected element is always part of the local Lookup.

Listing 5-7. Mp3SearchList Displays the Search Results in a Table and Adds the Actual Selected Data Set to the Local Lookup.

```
public class Mp3SearchList extends TopComponent
    implements ListSelectionListener {
    private Mp3SearchListModel model = new Mp3SearchListModel();
    private InstanceContent content = new InstanceContent();
    public Mp3SearchList() {
        initComponents();
        searchResults.setModel(model);
        searchResults.getSelectionModel().
            addListSelectionListener(this);
        associateLookup(new AbstractLookup(content));
    }
    public void valueChanged(ListSelectionEvent event) {
        if(!event.getValueIsAdjusting()) {
            Mp3FileObject mp3 =
                model.getRow(searchResults.getSelectedRow());
            content.set(Collections.singleton(mp3), null);
        }
    }
}
```

Here, the data model Mp3SearchListModel of the table with the search results is just an example and kept quite simple (see Listing 5-8). Three objects of the type Mp3FileObject are directly created in the constructor.

Listing 5-8. Simplified Data Model Managing and Providing the Data for the Result List

```
import javax.swing.table.AbstractTableModel;
...
public class Mp3SearchListModel extends AbstractTableModel {
    private String[] columns = {"Interpret", "Titel", "Jahr"};
    private List<Mp3FileObject> data = new ArrayList<Mp3FileObject>();

    public Mp3SearchListModel() {
        data.add(new Mp3FileObject("Gigi D'Agostino", "The rain", "2006"));
        data.add(new Mp3FileObject("Marquess", "El temperamento", "2006"));
        data.add(new Mp3FileObject("Floorfilla", "Cyberdream", "2006"));
    }
    public Mp3FileObject getRow(int row) {
        return data.get(row);
```

```
    }
    @Override
    public Object getValueAt(int row, int col) {
        Mp3FileObject mp3 = data.get(row);
        switch(col) {
            case 0: return mp3.getArtist();
            case 1: return mp3.getTitle();
            case 2: return mp3.getYear();
        }
        return "";
    }
}
```

The class Mp3DetailsView is the window showing detailed information of the selected entry of the Mp3SearchList. To get notification of changes in the Lookup—in case of selection changes, for example—the LookupListener interface is implemented. A Lookup.Result, which enables us to react to changes for a specific type (in our case Mp3FileObject), is used as a private member. Opening a window triggers the method componentOpened(). Use this callback to obtain the Lookup of the proxy component, using the method Utilities.actionsGlobalContext(), which returns a Lookup that always delegates to the local Lookup of the active TopComponent. Based on this proxy Lookup, you now create a Lookup.Result for the type Mp3FileObject and register a LookupListener to listen to changes on this result. If a TopComponent now gains the focus, which has one or more instances of this type in its local Lookup, the method resultChanged() gets called. With this, you only need to retrieve the instances and display the information accordingly as shown in Listing 5-9.

Listing 5-9. The Window Mp3DetailsView Shows the Information of the Mp3FileObject, Which is Selected in the Mp3SearchList.

```
public class Mp3DetailsView extends TopComponent implements LookupListener {
    private Lookup.Result<Mp3FileObject> result = null;

    public Mp3DetailsView() {
        initComponents();
    }
    public void componentOpened() {
        result = Utilities.actionsGlobalContext().LookupResult(Mp3FileObject.class);
        result.addLookupListener(this);
    }
    public void resultChanged(LookupEvent event) {
        Collection<? extends Mp3FileObject> mp3s = result.allInstances();
        if(!mp3s.isEmpty()) {
            Mp3FileObject mp3 = mp3s.iterator().next();
            artist.setText(mp3.getArtist());
            title.setText(mp3.getTitle());
            year.setText(mp3.getYear());
        }
    }
}
```

The information provided via Mp3SearchList and displayed using Mp3DetailsView is part of the class Mp3FileObject (see Listing 5-10). This class should be implemented in a separate module to achieve the best possible encapsulation and reuse; in this example, it is module C. To grant modules A and B access to this class, they must declare a dependency on module C. If the class Mp3FileObject is provided only via module A, it is possible to move the class to module A.

Listing 5-10. Mp3FileObject Provides the Data

```java
public class Mp3FileObject {
    private String artist;
    private String title;
    private String year;

    public Mp3FileObject(String artist, String title, String year) {
        this.artist = artist;
        this.title  = title;
        this.year   = year;
    }
    public String getArtist() {
        return this.artist;
    }
    public String getTitle() {
        return this.title;
    }
    public String getYear() {
        return this.year;
    }
}
```

As a proxy component, this example uses the global proxy Lookup provided by the NetBeans Platform, which delegates to the local Lookup of the active TopComponent. In Figure 5-4, this is depicted with the interface ContextGlobalProvider. This global proxy Lookup can also be easily substituted by your own implementation. This implementation only has to provide the local Lookup of the component containing the subject to the observer.

Dynamic Lookup

We already dealt with a typical use case for the Lookup in the section *Registering Service Providers*. There, you learned how to add instances of your own classes to a Lookup by an InstanceContent object. In this paragraph, I will show you how to use the advantages of the Lookup API for general application purposes with a small helper class. To get there, you create a Lookup class based on the AbstractLookup class. This class will be centrally provided and thus implemented by a singleton pattern. (See Listing 5-11.)

Listing 5-11. Dynamic Lookup to Which Central Objects Can Be Added or Deleted Again

```java
import org.openide.util.Lookup.AbstractLookup;
import org.openide.util.Lookup.InstanceContent;

public class DynamicLookup extends AbstractLookup {
    private static DynamicLookup Lookup = new DynamicLookup();
    private InstanceContent content = new InstanceContent();

    private DynamicLookup() {
```

```
    }
    public void add(Object instance) {
        content.add(instance);
    }
    public void remove(Object instance) {
        content.remove(instance);
    }
    public static DynamicLookup getDefault(){
        return Lookup;
    }
}
```

This simple Lookup class contains the InstanceContent object, which you already used in the section *Registering Service Providers*; it manages the objects you want to add. By the getDefault() method you deliver the central instance of the dynamic Lookup. With the two other methods add() and remove() you can add and access objects from any location; a multidirectional communication emerges easily.

Of course, there is the possibility for this Lookup to register a listener (LookupListener) (see the section *Registering Service Providers*) and so to react on the presence of a certain object, for example.

Java Service Loader

Since Java 6, a similar API to Lookup is available: ServiceLoader. This class loads service providers, which are registered over the *META-INF/services* directory. With this functionality, the ServiceLoader class equals the NetBeans standard Lookup that can be obtained using Lookup.getDefault(). A ServiceLoader is created for a special type using the Class object of the service interface or the abstract service class. A static factory method is used for creating a ServiceLoader instance. Depending on the classloader used to load the service providers, three methods for creating service loaders are available.

By default, service providers are loaded using the context classloader of the current thread. Inside the NetBeans Platform, this is the system classloader (for more details on the NetBeans classloader system, see Chapter 2). This allows the user to load service providers from all modules. Such a service loader is created with the following call:

```
ServiceLoader<Mp3Finder> s = ServiceLoader.load(Mp3Finder.class);
```

You may want to use a special classloader to load service providers, such as the module classloader to restrict loading of service providers to classes from your own module. To obtain such a ServiceLoader, the classloader to be used is passed to the factory method:

```
ServiceLoader<Mp3Finder> s = ServiceLoader.load(
    Mp3Finder.class, this.getClass().getClassLoader());
```

In addition to this, it is possible to create a service loader that only returns installed service providers—for example, a service provider from JAR archives located in the *lib/ext* directory or in the platform-specific extension directory. Other service providers found on the class path are ignored. This service loader is created using the loadInstalled() method:

```
ServiceLoader<Mp3Finder> s = ServiceLoader.loadInstalled(Mp3Finder.class);
```

The service provider can be obtained using an iterator. The iterator triggers dynamic loading of the provider on first access. The loaded providers are stored in a local cache. The iterator returns the cached providers before loading the remaining previously unloaded providers. If necessary, the internal cache can be cleared using the method reload(). This ensures that all providers are reloaded.

```
Iterator<Mp3Finder> i = s.iterator();
if(i.hasNext()) {
   Mp3Finder finder = i.next();
}
```

If a provider cannot be instantiated, it does not match the indicated type, or the configuration file is incorrect. In that case, a ServiceConfigurationError is triggered.

Summary

In this chapter, you learned one of the most interesting and important concepts of the NetBeans Platform: Lookup. This chapter examined the functionality of Lookups and familiarized you with the service interfaces and service providers. You learned to create service interfaces and use them within service providers, as well as how service providers are discovered in a loosely coupled way. To that end, you began to use the various registration mechanisms.

However, Lookups do a lot more than simply discover services. In fact, they also function to enable intermodular communication. This chapter showed you an example, in which information is shared between windows without them knowing about each other. Finally, the exploration of this topic was broadened by relating it to the JDK 6 ServiceLoader class.

CHAPTER 6

Actions

The treatment of actions of the NetBeans Platform is based on the *Swing Action Framework*. Consequently, each action is based on the Swing interface `ActionListener` or `Action`. The benefit of the NetBeans Platform is that it provides an infrastructure for different recurring types of actions. Previously actions had to be derived from a special class depending on the type of action; since NetBeans Platform7 all actions have the same form and just need to implement the `ActionListener` interface. In addition to the fact that actions are now easier to use, the implementation of actions has become more transparent for you as a developer. Now the NetBeans Platform does the hard work for you in the background.

ENORMOUSLY EASIER: ACTIONS IN THE NETBEANS PLATFORM 7

Just implement your action logic via an `ActionListener` interface. Meta information, such as ID, name, or the icon of the action, is simply added with annotations. The NetBeans Platform does the rest for you.

Not only is it possible to create rudimentary action classes which execute their logic encapsulated (`AlwaysEnabled`), but actions can be created which dynamically transfer available actions (`Callback`) or actions which are able to include their logic in a certain context (`ContextAware`). Figure 6-1 gives an overview of these three main types of actions again with their most important features.

AlwaysEnabled
- Standard action that is always active
- Does not contain context
- Directly contains the actions logic

Callback
- Proxy action which can forward to another action
- Can provide a fallback implementation

ContextAware
- Context-dependent action
- Gets delivered the current context
- Action logic can access the context

Figure 6-1. Different types of actions within the NetBeans Platform

The registration of actions is centrally done in the layer file of your standard folder `Actions`. This central registration can then be referred to from other places. This has one great advantage: actions can be used at different places at once, for example in the menu bar, in the toolbar, and in an application module itself connected with a control element. So just one instance of the action class is created by the platform. A further reason for the central declaration of the actions is the possibility of adapting the toolbar user specifically. Like this, all available actions can be shown to the user and can be assigned to any toolbar. If the user removes an entry from the toolbar, the action is not lost because only the reference is deleted and not the action itself.

To simplify the registration and the assignment of actions the NetBeans Platform 7 has something new, too. Now, annotations are used instead of the manual registration and assignment in the layer file. With this information the referring layer entries are automatically generated creating the application. You are not forced to use annotations, though. You can still create the layer entries directly in the layer file.

In the following sections I will explain how to simply create actions, how to build them, and how to register them via annotations or by a manual layer entry. To create action classes you use the wizard that is provided by the NetBeans IDE. You will learn that action classes are so simple that you do not even need the wizard.

Always Enabled Actions

Choose *File* ➤ *New File...* ➤ *Module Development* ➤ *Action* to call the wizard for creating a new action class. In the first step you can choose the type of action. Doing so you can choose between an *Always Enabled* action and a *Conditionally Enabled* action. You want to create an action that is always provided and so you should choose *Always Enabled*. In the next step you can integrate your action class into the menu bar and the toolbar and you can also define a short cut (see Figure 6-2). Right now you're concerned with the actions so you deactivate these options and just assign the action to create to the existing or a new category.

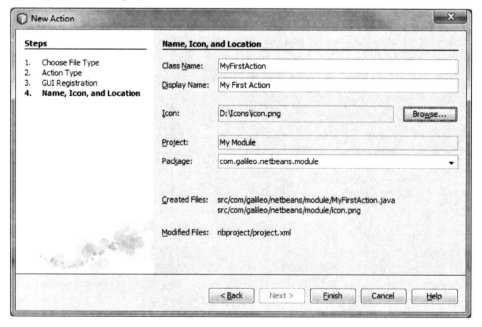

Figure 6-2. Creating an action class with the NetBeans wizards

Press the *Next* button to get to the last step. You can define the name of the action class, which will be shown in the menu, there. Furthermore you can or must choose an icon for the action. This icon should typically have a size of 16×16 pixels. You should provide the same icon sized 24×24 pixels. Like this, the user has the possibility of depicting the toolbar in two different sizes. You do not have to especially select it, it should only be in the same folder and named the same with *24* attached. If the 16×16 pixels icon is called *icon.gif,* the 24×24 pixels icon has to be called *icon24.gif.* Furthermore, you can provide the icons *icon_pressed.gif, icon_disabled.gif, icon_rollover.gif* for the referring conditions. Then press the *Finish* button to close the wizard and to generate the action class. Now let's look at the action class, shown in Listing 6-1.

Listing 6-1. Example of an Action Class—although the Assignment and the Provision Occur by Meta Information via Annotations

```
import java.awt.event.ActionEvent;
import java.awt.event.ActionListener;
import org.openide.awt.ActionID;
import org.openide.awt.ActionRegistration;
import org.openide.awt.ActionReferences;

@ActionID(
    id = "com.galileo.netbeans.MyFirstAction",
    category = "File")
@ActionRegistration(
    displayName = "#CTL_MyFirstAction",
    iconBase = "com/galileo/netbeans/icon.gif")
@ActionReferences({})
public final class MyFirstAction implements ActionListener {
    public void actionPerformed(ActionEvent e) {
        // TODO implement action body
    }
}
```

First, you should give each action a unique identifier by means of the `ActionID` annotation. You do so by specifying a unique string with the `id` parameter. I suggest using the classname in connection with its code name base. This way the ID is really unique. Moreover, the action has to be assigned to a category; that can either be an already existing category or a new category.

The action is registered by the `ActionRegistration` annotation. The action is registered at the identifier which is assigned by the `ActionID`. The display name is read by the assignment of the key `#CTL_MyFirstAction` from the *Bundle.properties* file. The advantage of this is that the name can be localized easily (the name can be adjusted to another language). Besides, an icon with the `iconBase` parameter is specified.

■ **Note** For the time being I will ignore the `ActionReferences` annotation, which is automatically created by the wizard. This way, an action is assigned to a menu or to a toolbar. I will get to this in Chapter 9.

The action class itself is quite simple. Only the `actionPerformed()` method of the `ActionListener` inferface has to be implemented. The action that you intend will be executed by this method.

As already mentioned at the beginning of the chapter, the registration of actions via annotations is the normal method. However, you do not have to use it. It is equally good to introduce your actions to the NetBeans Platform by referring entries in the layer file since, in principle, it is not really different using annotations. The only difference is that these entries are created when automatically creating your application out of the information of the annotations. To register an always enabled action class without annotations, create the following `.instance` element in the `Actions` folder, as shown in Listing 6-2.

Listing 6-2. Registration of an Always Enabled Action by a Direct Entry in the Layer File

```
<file name="com-galileo-netbeans-MyFirstAction.instance">
  <attr name="displayName" bundlevalue=
    "com.galileo.netbeans.Bundle#CTL_MyFirstAction"/>
  <attr name="iconBase"
    stringvalue="com/galileo/netbeans/icon.gif"/>
  <attr name="instanceCreate"
    methodvalue="org.openide.awt.Actions.alwaysEnabled"/>
  <attr name="delegate"
    newvalue="com.galileo.netbeans.MyFirstAction"/>
</file>
```

The attributes with names, which correspond to the annotation parameters, refer to its meaning. These and other necessary attributes and their values are explained in Table 6-1.

Table 6-1. Attributes of an .instance Element to Register an Always Enabled Action

Attribute	Meaning
displayName	Name under which the action is displayed, e.g., in the menu (*stringvalue*). Can also be read out of a *Bundle.properties* file (*bundlevalue*).
iconBase	Path to an icon which is used, e.g., in the menu or in the toolbar.
instanceCreate	Assigns a factory method which will create the action. This is `org.openide.awt.Actions.alwaysEnabled` for an always enabled action.
delegate	Assigns the implementation of your action out of which the real action is created by the above mentioned factory method.

In addition to these attributes two more optional attributes are provided. These are presented in Table 6-2.

Table 6-2. *Optional Attributes of an .instance Element for the Registration of an Always Enabled Action*

Attribute	Meaning
noIconInMenu	Determines that no icon is displayed in the menu. If you have not defined an icon with iconBase there is also no placeholder.
asynchronous	Can be set to true or false. This way, it is possible to simply execute actions asynchronously. That means the action is executed out of the Event Dispatch thread and so does not block the GUI.

Callback Actions

A callback action is different from an always enabled action since a callback action is able to delegate to another action which typically depends on the context. Typically, a callback action does not contain action logic, but delegates further to a so called *Action Performer*. In case no action performer exists, you can add a so-called fallback implementation within the callback action. Callback actions are mainly used for global actions, meaning actions that follow different logics depending on the context. These are actions such as search, copy, or paste. Such global actions are also already provided in multiples by the actions API of the NetBeans Platform. Action performers are provided by a Java ActionMap. During that process, the action performer and the key of the callback action are registered within this map. All classes, which transfer from JComponent, have an ActionMap by default. The NetBeans Platform base class also has a TopComponent by default. It is used for windows that will be displayed within a NetBeans Platform application (more about this in Chapter 10). This ActionMap is provided by a Lookup. It is the task of a callback action class to check if an ActionMap exists in the global proxy Lookup. And if there is one, the task is to check whether an action performer was registered for your own action. In this case, action representers, such as menu and toolbar entries, are automatically activated. If no action performer and no fallback implementation are provided, the action representers are deactivated.

The NetBeans IDE does not provide a special wizard to create a callback action. If you want to create a callback action with a fallback implementation, just use the wizard for an always enabled action class as described in the section "Always Enabled Actions." Then you just have to add another parameter to the ActionRegistration annotation. It is even easier if you do not want a fallback implementation. Then just add the ActionID and the ActionRegistration annotation to the key. In this case, a class is not even necessary anymore.

In Listing 6-3, an action with fallback implementation will be created to be able to refresh. It will execute a different action depending on which window has the focus. Create an action class named RefreshAction with the wizard for an always enabled action and add it to a menu or a toolbar. The class which was already extended with the key parameter should then look like Listing 6-3.

Listing 6-3. *Callback Action with Fallback Implementation*

```
import java.awt.event.ActionEvent;
import java.awt.event.ActionListener;
import org.openide.awt.ActionRegistration;
import org.openide.awt.ActionReference;
```

```
import org.openide.awt.ActionReferences;
import org.openide.awt.ActionID;

@ActionID(
    category = "File",
    id = "com.galileo.netbeans.RefreshAction")
@ActionRegistration(
    iconBase = "com/galileo/netbeans/icon.gif",
    displayName = "#CTL_RefreshAction"
    key = "RefreshAction")
@ActionReferences({
    @ActionReference(path = "Menu/File", position = 900),
    @ActionReference(path = "Toolbars/File", position = 300)
})
public final class RefreshAction implements ActionListener {
    public void actionPerformed(ActionEvent e) {
        // TODO fallback implementation
    }
}
```

The only difference with an always enabled action is that a callback action uses the additional parameter key. This way you can assign a random identifier by which an action performer is linked.

The class RefreshAction itself functions as a fallback implementation. If you do not need such a class, you just have to annotate a key as shown in Listing 6-4.

Listing 6-4. Callback Action Without Fallback Implementation

```
@ActionID(
    category = "File",
    id = "com.galileo.netbeans.RefreshAction")
@ActionRegistration(
    iconBase = "com/galileo/netbeans/icon.gif",
    displayName = "#CTL_RefreshAction")
public static final String REFRESH_ACTION = "RefreshAction";
```

Now if you start the application and neither a fallback implementation nor an action performer is provided, the action is deactivated in the menu as well as in the toolbar. Listing 6-5 conventionally explains how to provide an action performer since it assumes a window which derives from the class TopComponent. You will create such a window in Chapter 10. As soon as you have created it, you can also test this action class practically.

Listing 6-5. Registration of an Action Performer for a Callback Action

```
public final class MyTopComponent extends TopComponent {
    public MyTopComponent() {
        ...
        getActionMap().put("RefreshAction",
                            new AbstractAction() {
            public void actionPerformed(ActionEvent event) {
                // refresh content of top component
            }
        });
```

```
  }
}
```

Give the action map of the top component by the method getActionMap(), which is defined by the class JComponent. Then add an instance of the actions implementations connected with the key of the RefreshAction. Now the action, which is created by the class AbstractAction, is in the context of MyTopComponent. You can add each action class to the action map which implements the interface Action.

As soon as the window MyTopComponent is focused, the RefreshAction is active. Confirming the action, the method actionPerformed() provided by MyTopComponent is executed. For a comprehensive understanding it makes sense to know how a callback class gets to the action performer, since the action performer is not provided to the RefreshAction class just by adding it to the action map. The connection between those two parts is still missing. The Lookup concept is responsible for that connection. In this case the Lookup concept means a local Lookup of the top component and a global proxy Lookup which facilitates access of the callback action to the local Lookup. The top component has to ensure that its action map is located in its Lookup. Then, a callback action can find an action performer. By default, the action map is already in the local Lookup of the top component; you do not have to worry about it anymore, except for setting another local Lookup with the method associateLookup() or overwriting the getLookup() method. Just know that you will need to add the action map again. But that is enough about the Lookup concept; you can find more information about it in Chapter 5.

You are now able to add any number of action performers, which are automatically executed, depending on the current concept, to a callback action. You might be asking yourself how to use actions provided by the NetBeans Actions API such as the CopyAction, the CutAction, or the DeleteAction classes, which at least are already integrated in the menu and so can be used. These classes are all callback actions and can be used just by providing an action performer, as explained before by means of the class RefreshAction.

If you do not want to use annotations for your callback action you can also register them in the folder Actions via the entries shown in Listing 6-6.

Listing 6-6. *Registration of a Callback Action via an Entry in the Layer File*

```
<file name="com-galileo-netbeans-RefreshAction.instance">
  <attr name="displayName"
    bundlevalue="com.galileo.netbeans.Bundle#CTL_RefreshAction"/>
  <attr name="iconBase"
    stringvalue="com/galileo/netbeans/icon.gif"/>
  <attr name="instanceCreate"
    methodvalue="org.openide.awt.Actions.callback"/>
  <attr name="fallback"
    methodvalue="org.openide.awt.Actions.alwaysEnabled" />
  <attr name="delegate"
    newvalue="com.galileo.netbeans.RefreshAction"/>
  <attr name="key" stringvalue="RefreshAction"/>
</file>
```

The attributes displayName and iconBase correspond to the attributes of an always enabled action explained in the section "Always Enabled Actions". The special attributes for a callback action are listed and explained in Table 6-3.

The optional attributes of an always enabled action (see Table 6-2) are also provided using a callback action.

Table 6-3. Attributes of an .instance Element to Register a Callback Action

Attribute	Meaning
instanceCreate	Indicates a method which will create the action. For a callback action this would be `org.openide.awt.Actions.callback`
fallback	Indicates either a factory method (`methodvalue`), which creates the fallback action, or the fallback action as `Action` instance (`newvalue`).
delegate	Indicates the fallback implementation (`newvalue`) out of which the already named factory method creates the fallback action.
key	Key with which an action performer is registered in an action map.
surviveFocusChange	Optional attribute which defines whether the action is still active when the focus is not on the context any more (if the action had been activated before because of a certain context).

Context Aware Actions

Actions of this type work in a particular context—a file, for example. The special thing about this type of action is that such actions are only active when the referring context in the application is active, too. In the example, the file is opened in the application. The context is automatically transferred to the action by the NetBeans Platform, so the action can execute the referring action on the context, such as edit a file, for example. Typically, connecting the context and the action by a so-called *Context Interface* (also called a *Cookie*), which is implemented by the context.

We want to use a node class as context in the following example. A node is the representation of certain data. In practice, a node can be a file which is depicted in a tree structure or which is opened in an editor, for example. You will learn more about this concept, which is frequently used within the NetBeans Platform, in Chapters 7 and 12.

To create a context aware action you can use the action wizard again (*File ➤ New File… ➤ Module Development ➤ Action*). However in this case you should choose the type *Conditionally Enabled*. Specify the context interface then and choose whether the action should be even active when multiple instances of the context interface exist. We use the context interface `Editable` in this example and specify that the action will only work on one context instance. On the following page of the wizard you can then integrate the action into the menubar and the toolbar (see the "Always Enabled Action" section). After completing the wizard, your action class should about look like Listing 6-7.

Listing 6-7. Action Class of the Type Context Aware Which Becomes Active When an Instance of the Context Interface Editable Exists

```java
import java.awt.event.ActionListener;
import java.awt.event.ActionEvent;
import org.netbeans.api.actions.Editable;
import org.openide.awt.ActionID;
import org.openide.awt.ActionRegistration;
import org.openide.awt.ActionReferences;

@ActionID(
    category = "Edit",
    id = "com.galileo.netbeans.MyContextAction")
@ActionRegistration(
    iconBase = "com/galileo/netbeans/icon.gif",
    displayName = "#CTL_MyContextAction")
@ActionReferences({})
public final class MyContextAction implements ActionListener {
    private final Editable context;
    public MyContextAction(Editable context) {
        this.context = context;
    }
    public void actionPerformed(ActionEvent ev) {
        // do something with context
        context.edit();
    }
}
```

Now looking at the created action class, you will quickly recognize that it hardly differs from an always enabled action. A context aware action is registered the same way with `ActionID` and `ActionRegistration` annotations.

A context aware action has a constructor unlike an always enabled action. A constructor gets the desired context as parameter. In the `actionPerformed()` method you can then access this context. If you define that the action should be active even when the majority of the context instances are active, creating the action (or afterwards), a list of context instances is transferred to the constructor. You do not have to define other parameters when registering. Only the following section changes:

```java
private final List<Editable> context;
public MyContextAction(List<Editable> context) {
    this.context = context;
}
```

What we still need now is a node with which the action will be active. As an example, I created the class `MyNode` which derives from the `Node` subclass `AbstractNode`. In a real application, such a node class could represent a file of a certain type, for example. The class in this example will only clarify the connection of a context aware action with a certain context. In the action class, you defined that the node has to implement the interface `Editable`. So you have to do this now. This context interface specifies the method `edit()`, which you just created by an empty implementation. The method is later called in by the action class; it represents the context dependent action logic. The Actions API provides a series of frequently used context interfaces such as `Openable` or `Closable`. Because you do not need a certain super interface, though, you can just use any interface as context interface. (See Listing 6-8.)

Listing 6-8. Node That Implements the Context Interface Editable and So Represents the Context of the Action

```
import org.netbeans.api.actions.Editable;
import org.openide.nodes.AbstractNode;
import org.openide.nodes.Children;

public class MyNode extends AbstractNode implements Editable {
    public MyNode() {
        super(Children.LEAF);
    }
    public void edit() {
        // edit something depend on the data, this node represents
    }
}
```

Now you just have to set the active node in your top component, which could be a file editor, for example, in which that file which is represented by the node is opened. To get there, you just have to add the node to the local Lookup of the top component. (See Listing 6-9.)

Listing 6-9. Set Active Node. By Doing So, the Action Becomes Active, When Implementing the Referring Context Interface of this Node.

```
public final class MyTopComponent extends TopComponent {
    public MyTopComponent() {
        MyNode node = new MyNode();
        ...
        associateLookup(Lookups.fixed(node, getActionMap()));
    }
}
```

If the focus in your application is on this top component, the NetBeans Platform ensures that the local Lookup (in which there is now a MyNode instance) is provided to the action as global context. In this case, even the action in the menubar and/or in the toolbar is automatically activated by the NetBeans Platform.

Finally, regarding a context aware action, Listing 6-10 shows how to register such an action class without annotation by a direct entry in the layer file.

Listing 6-10. Registration of a Context Aware Action by a Direct Entry in the Layer File

```
<file name="com-galileo-netbeans-MyContextAction.instance">
  <attr name="displayName" bundlevalue=
    "com.galileo.netbeans.Bundle#CTL_MyContextAction"/>
  <attr name="iconBase"
    stringvalue="com/galileo/netbeans/icon.gif"/>
  <attr name="instanceCreate"
    methodvalue="org.openide.awt.Actions.context"/>
  <attr name="delegate"
    methodvalue="org.openide.awt.Actions.inject"/>
  <attr name="injectable"
    stringvalue="com.galileo.netbeans.MyContextAction"/>
```

```
  <attr name="type"
    stringvalue="org.netbeans.api.actions.Editable"/>
  <attr name="selectionType" stringvalue="EXACTLY_ONE"/>
</file>
```

The attributes displayName and iconBase refer to the attributes of an always enabled action depicted in the"Always Enabled Actions" section. In Table 6-4, the special attributes for a context aware action are listed and explained. The optional attributes of an always enabled action from Table 6-2 are provided with a context aware action.

Table 6-4. Attributes of an .instance Element for Registering a Context Aware Action.

Attribute	Meaning
instanceCreate	Defines a factory method which will create the action. For a context aware action this is org.openide.awt.Actions.context
delegate	The method of the Actions API shown here: org.openide.awt.Actions.inject cares about the transfer of your action to the constructor.
injectable	With this you define your own action class which will be registered.
type	With this attribute you define the desired context interface.
selectionType	Defines whether the action just expects one (EXACTLY_ONE) or more (ANY) context instances.
surviveFocusChange	Optional attribute which defines whether the action is even active when the context is not focused anymore (if it had been activated before because of a certain context).

Summary

This chapter discussed actions. You learned how to quickly and efficiently create actions via a wizard in NetBeans IDE. You also saw the various types of actions that are available and learned how to make effective use of them. For example, some actions are always available, while others are only available within specific contexts. You learned how easy it is to register and assign actions with annotations.

CHAPTER 7

Data and Files

The NetBeans Platform provides a very substantial concept for creating, managing, manipulating, and presenting data. This concept mainly embraces the File Systems API and the Data Systems API. Additionally, there is the Nodes API and the Explorer API. Each of these APIs is located on its own abstraction level. This system can be divided into four levels together with the concrete data outside the NetBeans Platform application, as shown in Figure 7-1.

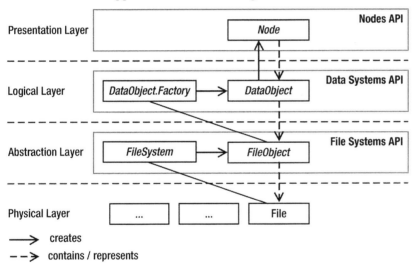

Figure 7-1. Architecture for managing data and files within the NetBeans Platform

A data system is initially abstracted using the FileSystem class. Doing so, the physical data, which lie below, can be present in any form. The FileSystem class lets users address physical data from different sources in the same way—for example, a local file system, a file system in the form of an XML file (similar to how the System Filesystem is built, too) or a JAR file. Only an implementation of the abstract FileSystem class has to be provided in the desired form. This way, the File Systems API abstracts from the concrete data and provides it within the application in a virtual file system. Thus access is possible independent from the origin of the data. The abstracted data on the abstraction layer in the form of a FileObject class do not have information yet about what kind of data to manage. So this layer does not contain data-specific logic. Building upon this layer, there is the Data Systems API in the logical layer. There are objects, which represent the data of a very specific type. These objects build upon the

DataObject class. For each of the desired data types there exists a DataObject.Factory which is responsible for creating objects. The NodesAPI is the top layer in this concept (it is on the presentation layer). So a node is responsible for the type-specific representation of data. In this respect, a Node represents a DataObject, which itself is responsible for creating the node. In Chapter 12, I will explain in detail how to represent your data by means of nodes and the explorer.

File Systems API

The NetBeans Platform provides transparent access to files and folders by means of the File Systems API. In this process, access is very abstract; it works the same way, whether the data are present, for example, as a virtual XML file system (such as the System Filesystem), or if they are in a JAR archive or a normal directory. The general interfaces of a file system are described in the abstract class FileSystem. The abstract class AbstractFileSystem implements some of the tasks of a file system. Thus it is helpful as a base class for special file system implementations. The concrete implementation LocalFileSystem, JarFileSystem, and XMLFileSystem derive from this class. The class MultiFileSystem represents a proxy for multiple file systems; it is mostly used as a base class. The file system class hierarchy is shown in Figure 7-2.

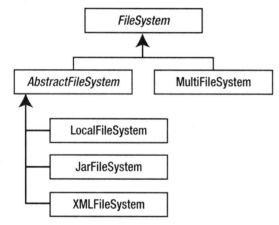

Figure 7-2. Class hierarchy of the file systems

The File Object

Files within a filesystem—directories and files—are represented by the class FileObject.This is an abstract wrapper class for the File class of the Java Platform. The implementation of a FileObject is provided by the concrete file system. Apart from the standard file operations, the class FileObject also provides the possibility of supervising changes of files or directories. The following sections will describe the operations of the class FileObject.

Creating

If you want to create a FileObject for an existing file in your local file system, you can do this with the helper class FileUtil:

```
FileObject obj = FileUtil.toFileObject(new File("C:/file.txt"));
```

If you want to create a FileObject out of a concrete FileSystem object, you can indicate the complete paths with the method findResource():

```
FileSystem fs = ...
FileObject obj = fs.findResource("folder/file");
```

Here is how to create new files or directories based on a File object:

```
File file   = new File("E:/newfolder/newfile.txt");
File folder = new File("E:/newfolder2");
FileObject fo1 = FileUtil.createData(file);
FileObject fo2 = FileUtil.createFolder(folder);
```

If you already have a directory in the form of a FileObject, you can create a file or a directory in its file system as follows:

```
FileObject folder    = ...
FileObject file      = folder.createData("newfile.txt");
FileObject subfolder = folder.createFolder("newfolder");
```

Renaming

If you want to rename a file or a directory, you first have to ensure that the FileObject cannot be edited by just anybody. You do this by means of a FileLock object. After renaming, you release this FileLock again in a finally block.

```
FileObject myfile = ...
FileLock lock = null;
try {
   lock = myfile.lock();
} catch (FileAlreadyLockedException e) {
   return;
}
try {
   myfile.rename(lock, "newfilename", myfile.getExt());
} finally {
   lock.releaseLock();
}
```

Deleting

Deleting files or directories is very easy, because the method delete() is concerned with reserving and opening a FileLock itself. Consequently, deleting only requires the following line:

```
FileObject myfile = ...
myfile.delete();
```

Furthermore, a variant of the method is provided. It enables you to pass your own FileLock, analogous to the renaming of a FileObject.

Removing

A `FileObject` cannot just be removed by renaming as you can do it with a `File`. The `FileUtil` class provides the `moveFile()` method for removing a `FileObject`. This method copies the file or the directory into a destination directory, deletes the source, and in doing so, automatically reserves the needed `FileLock` objects and releases them again.

```
FileObject fileToMove = ...
FileObject destFolder = ...
FileUtil.moveFile(fileToMove, destFolder, fileToMove.getName());
```

Reading and Writing Data

As with Java, reading and writing a `FileObject` works by streams. For this purpose, the `FileObject` class provides the `InputStream` and the `OutputStream`. You pack them in a `BufferedReader` for simple and performant reading and in a `PrintWriter` for writing, as shown in Listing 7-1.

Listing 7-1. Reading and Writing a FileObject

```
FileObject myFile = ...
BufferedReader input = new BufferedReader(new InputStreamReader(myFile.getInputStream()));
try {
    String line = null;
    while((line = input.readLine()) != null) {
        // process the line
} finally {
    input.close();
}
PrintWriter output = new PrintWriter(
    myFile.getOutputStream());
try {
    output.println("the new content of myfile");
} finally {
    output.close();
}
```

Optionally, you can transfer your own `FileLock` to the method `getOutputStream()`.

The `FileObject` class itself provides two simple methods for the easy reading of a text-based `FileObject`. On the one hand, it is possible to get the complete content of a file at once with the method `asText()`. On the other hand, you can get a list with all separate lines with the method `asLines()`. You can add a special encoding (such as UTF-8) as parameter to both methods, alternatively.

```
FileObject myFile = ...
for (String line : fo.asLines()) {
    // process the line
}
```

Monitoring Changes

The class `FileObject` enables you to react on changes of files within a filesystem because you can register a `FileChangeListener` for that case, as shown in Listing 7-2

Listing 7-2. Reacting on Changes of a Data Object

```
File file = new File("E:/NetBeans 7/file.txt");
FileObject fo = FileUtil.toFileObject(file);
fo.addFileChangeListener(new FileChangeListener(){
    public void fileFolderCreated(FileEvent fe) {
    }
    public void fileDataCreated(FileEvent fe) {
    }
    public void fileChanged(FileEvent fe) {
    }
    public void fileDeleted(FileEvent fe) {
    }
    public void fileRenamed(FileRenameEvent fre) {
    }
    public void fileAttributeChanged(FileAttributeEvent fae) {
    }
});
```

The methods fileFolderCreated() and fileDataCreated() are called when creating a directory or when calling a file. These methods only make sense when the supervised FileObject is a directory. Changing a file, the event is always triggered for the file itself and for the parent directory. This means the methods are informed about changes of data, even when supervising the parent directory. If you are not interested in all events of the FileChangeListener interfaces, you can instead use the adapter class FileChangeAdapter.

■ **Caution** Remember that you can only be informed about events that are executed within your application on the concrete FileObject. You cannot be informed when renaming a file outside of the application in the Windows Explorer, for example.

The classes FileSystem, FileObject, and FileUtil provide numerous very helpful methods. So, in this respect, it is totally worthwhile to take a closer look at the documentation of the File Systems API.

Data Systems API

The Data Systems API provides a logical layer which is based on the File Systems API. While a FileObject manages its data regardless of the type, a DataObject is a wrapper for a FileObject of a really specific type. A DataObject expands a FileObject with type-specific features and functionalities. These functionalities are specified by interfaces or abstract classes, the so-called context interfaces. Implementations of the functionalities are provided by the DataObject via the local Lookup. Due to this mechanism, the abilities of a DataObject can be adapted dynamically and flexibly and they can be called from outside. Since a DataObject knows the type of its managed data, it is able to represent the data accordingly. That means, a DataObject is responsible itself for creating a Node which accordingly represents the data on the user interface. A DataObject is created by a special DataObject.Factory which is exactly responsible for one type of data.

The coherence of this system is easily demonstrated. In the following example it becomes quite clear how the APIs of the three layers work together and build upon each other. In this regard, the NetBeans IDE does quite a lot of work and provides a wizard.

Now you want to use this wizard to add a data file for MP3 files to a module.

1. To do so, select File ➤ New File… and File Type in the category Module Development.

2. For the moment, you can determine the MIME type; type in audio/mpeg, for this example. The file type is recognized on the basis of the ending; it is also possible with XML files that the type of the content is recognized by means of the root element. Here, you want the files to be recognized by the ending mp3. Accordingly, you fill this in (see Figure 7-3). Optionally, you can define multiple file endings, each separated by a comma. So for video files, mpg or mpeg would make sense.

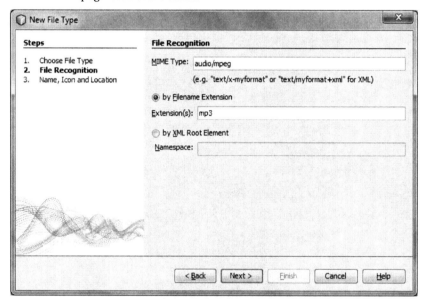

Figure 7-3. Creating a new file type for MP3 files with the NetBeans wizard

3. To get to the last page, press Next. Type in Mp3 as class name prefix and choose any icon sized 16×16 pixels, too.

4. Then press the Finish button so the wizard creates the data object class.

The Data Object

In principle, a data object is specified by the abstract class DataObject. Usually, the subclass MultiDataObject is used as base class. On the one hand, it already implements most abstract methods of DataObject; this is why your own data object class remains very small. On the other hand, a multidata object can contain one or more file object. A data object always has a file object which is called a primary file. Furthermore, a multidata object can optionally contain one or more files, which are called secondary files. Secondary files typically occur with related data—as, for example, with the form editor. In the editor, the files *myform.java, myform.form, myform.class* are represented by a data object. In this example, the file *myform.java* is the primary file and the files *myform.class* and *myform.form* are the secondary files. A file object within a data object is managed by the class MultiDataObject.Entry. Here the subclass FileEntry is mostly used. The standard file operations, such as removing or deleting, are executed via this class. Look at the class Mp3DataObject which was created by the wizard, shown in Listing 7-3.

Listing 7-3. Data Object Class for a File Object Type Mp3. This Class Provides the Logic for the MP3 Files.

```java
import java.io.IOException;
import org.openide.filesystems.FileObject;
import org.openide.loaders.DataNode;
import org.openide.loaders.DataObjectExistsException;
import org.openide.loaders.MultiDataObject;
import org.openide.loaders.MultiFileLoader;
import org.openide.nodes.Node;
import org.openide.nodes.Children;
import org.openide.util.Lookup;

public class Mp3DataObject extends MultiDataObject {
    public Mp3DataObject(FileObject pf, MultiFileLoader loader)
        throws DataObjectExistsException, IOException {
        super(pf, loader);
    }
    protected Node createNodeDelegate() {
        return new DataNode(this, Children.LEAF, getLookup());
    }
    public Lookup getLookup() {
        return getCookieSet().getLookup();
    }
}
```

As you already know, a data object is normally created by a data object factory. This factory is responsible for the creation of a certain data object type. The constructor of the Mp3DataObject class contains two parameters. First, the primary file, which contains or represents the actual MP3 files. Second, it contains the factory instance in form of a MultiFileLoader object, which is responsible for the data object. You just hand these parameters over to the base class constructor which does the management. A data object cares about the creation of according nodes, because the object knows the type of its data. The nodes are used to represent data objects on the user interface. You do this with the method createNodeDelegate() which creates an instance of the node class DataNode and returns. This is the interface with the Nodes API which is located on the presentation layer (see Figure 7-1). You will learn more about this in Chapter 12.

The main difference between a file object and a data object is that a data object knows which data it contains. This means that a data object is characterized by being able to provide features and functionalities for this type of data—in this case an MP3 file. The functionalities, which provide a data object for its files, are described by interfaces or by abstract classes. These are the context interfaces. Instances of these interfaces are managed by the data object in a local Lookup. Because the interfaces are not necessarily implemented by DataObject itself, but are managed by the Lookup, a data object is able to provide its capabilities dynamically. This means it can offer a playing MP3 file during the runtime, for example. This is provided as long as the MP3 file is playing. Furthermore, it is possible to flexibly expand a data object with further functionalities. The Lookup offers type-safe access on these interfaces per se.

Now, the basic structure of your Mp3DataObject is finished. The contructor gets the file object to manage from the lower abstraction layer by the corresponding factory. The abstraction layer delivers a representative for the upper presentation layer and finally abandons its functionalities to the environment by a Lookup. The base classes DataObject and MultiDataObject provide numerous methods for using a data object. Here a look at the API documentation can be very helpful.

Implementing Context Interfaces

First, you specify the functionality which will receive your Mp3DataObject by an interface. You should now call it PlayInterface and so specify the method play() with which the corresponding Mp3DataObject can be played:

```
public interface PlayInterface {
    public void play();
}
```

Of course, you then need an implementation of the desired functionality which you have specified by the context interface. You might imagine that you implement the interface directly by the class Mp3DataObject; however, it is better to do this by a separate class, a *Support* class. That way the functionality can be flexibly added to the Mp3DataObject and deleted again. Furthermore, multiple context interfaces can be grouped semantically and the Mp3DataObject class remains very small.

```
public class PlaySupport implements PlayInterface {
    private Mp3DataObject mp3 = null;
    public PlaySupport(Mp3DataObject mp3) {
        this.mp3 = mp3;
    }
    public void play() {
        System.out.println("Play: " + mp3.getPrimaryFile().getName());
    }
}
```

Furthermore, it is only necessary to add an instance of this support class to the Lookup of the Mp3DataObject class. You do this with the method getCookieSet().assign() and in doing so indicate that it is the type PlayInterface. Of course, you could also indicate PlaySupport.class, but this way, you are independent of the implementation.

```
public class Mp3DataObject extends MultiDataObject {
    public Mp3DataObject(FileObject pf, MultiFileLoader loader)
        throws DataObjectExistsException, IOException {
        super(pf, loader);
        getCookieSet().assign(PlayInterface.class, new PlaySupport(this));
    }
}
```

You finally expanded your Mp3DataObject with a functionality in three steps. This functionality can be used from outside in the local Lookup which is available through getLookup().

Using Context Interfaces

Finally, the question remains how to access the functionalities of a data object. I want to answer this question by means of a context aware action class. To do this, you create a new class with the wizard by *File ➤ New File… ➤ Module Development ➤ Action.* You now use Mp3DataObject as context. This way, the action only becomes active when a Mp3DataObject, meaning its node, is selected. As you already know from Chapter 6, the context is transferred to the constructor of a context aware class:

```
public final class MyContextAction implements ActionListener {
    private final Mp3DataObject context;
    public MyContextAction(Mp3DataObject context) {
        this.context = context;
    }
    public void actionPerformed(ActionEvent ev) {
        // do something with context
        PlayInterface p = context.getLookup().Lookup(PlayInterface.class);
        p.play();
    }
}
```

If an Mp3DataObject is now selected in your application, the context aware action automatically becomes active through the NetBeans Platform. You can then access the context, which is the Mp3DataObject instance, in the actionPerformed() method. As you already know, the features of the data object are managed in a Lookup. So you catch this Lookup and deliver the implementation of the PlayInterface by the Lookup() method. You can now access the implementation of the PlaySupport class and you can execute its methods.

You can test everything with the *Favorites* module.

1. To do this, ensure that the module Favorites is activated in your NetBeans Platform application under *Properties ➤ Libraries* in the cluster platform.

2. Next start your application and open the Favorites window with *Window ➤ Favorites.*

3. Right-click the window and choose *Add to Favorites.*

4. Then select an MP3 file or a directory with MP3 files in the selection dialog and press *Add* to add the selected entry from the Favorites window. The shown MP3 files are represented by a data node instance which was created by the Mp3DataObject itself. The object was created by a data loader when you added the MP3 files to the Favorites window.

If you selected an MP3 file and you now execute the action—looking at the output of the play() method—you see that you can directly access the selected data by the context class of this action.

Providing Context Interfaces Dynamically

In the following example (Listing 7-4), I will show you how to change the functionalities provided by an Mp3DataObject during the runtime of the application. This way, you can also implicitly control the actions which are available to the user. You already created a context interface and a support class for playing an MP3 file. Now, you want to apply the same just for stopping an MP3 file. Furthermore, the support classes and the method playing() now set the current playing status of the Mp3DataObject.

Listing 7-4. Context Interfaces and Support Class for Playing Mp3DataObject

```
public interface PlayInterface {
   public void play();
}
public class PlaySupport implements PlayInterface {
   private Mp3DataObject mp3 = null;
   public PlaySupport(Mp3DataObject mp3) {
      this.mp3 = mp3;
   }
    public void play() {
       System.out.println("play");
       mp3.playing(true);
    }
}
public interface StopInterface {
   public void stop();
}
public class StopSupport implements StopInterface {
   private Mp3DataObject mp3 = null;
   public StopSupport(Mp3DataObject mp3) {
      this.mp3 = mp3;
   }
   public void stop() {
      System.out.println("stop");
      mp3.playing(false);
   }
}
```

You create both support classes in the constructor. First, you can assume that the MP3 file is not played, and so you add the PlaySupport with the assign() method to the Lookup. You change the context interfaces, which are in the context interfaces. You do this in the playing() method which is called by the support classes by corresponding parameters. If only the file is playing, delete all instances of the type by only passing the type PlayInterface and no instances to the assign() method and add an instance of StopInterface (see Listing 7-5). If the file is stopped, it works the other way around.

Listing 7-5. Dynamically Adding and Deleting Instances of Context Interfaces

```
public class Mp3DataObject extends MultiDataObject {
   private PlaySupport playSupport = null;
   private StopSupport stopSupport = null;
   public Mp3DataObject(FileObject pf, MultiFileLoader loader)
      throws DataObjectExistsException, IOException {
      super(pf, loader);
      playSupport = new PlaySupport(this);
      stopSupport = new StopSupport(this);
      getCookieSet().assign(PlayInterface.class, playSupport);
   }
   public synchronized void playing(boolean value) {
```

```
    if(value) {
        getCookieSet().assign(PlayInterface.class);
        getCookieSet().assign(StopInterface.class, stopSupport);
    } else {
        getCookieSet().assign(StopInterface.class);
        getCookieSet().assign(PlayInterface.class, playSupport);
    }
  }
}
```

To complete the example, you need another two action classes with which you can start and stop the MP3 file. These should be two ContextAware classes which use PlayInterface and StopInterface as context. Then, the menu or tool entries are automatically activated or deactivated, depending on which context interface or which support class is provided by the selected MP3 file (see Listing 7-6).

Listing 7-6. Context-Sensitive Actions Which Are Active When the Selected Mp3DataObject Provides an Instance of the According Context Interface

```
public final class PlayAction implements ActionListener {
    private final PlayInterface context;
    public PlayAction(PlayInterface context) {
        this.context = context;
    }
    @Override
    public void actionPerformed(ActionEvent ev) {
        context.play();
    }
}
public final class StopAction implements ActionListener {
    private final StopInterface context;
    public StopAction(StopInterface context) {
        this.context = context;
    }
    @Override
    public void actionPerformed(ActionEvent ev) {
        context.stop();
    }
}
```

Data Object Factory

Data Objects are created by a data object factory. A factory is responsible for exactly one type. A factory can recognize the type of a file either because of the file ending or with an XML root element. Factories are registered in the layer and automatically created by the NetBeans Platform, which manages all existing factories and can find the corresponding file for the respective file type. A factory is specified by the interface DataObject.Factory. The class MultiFileLoader represents an implementation which is used by default (see Listing 7-6).

The factory, responsible for creating data objects of the type Mp3DataObject, has also been registered in the layer file by the NetBeans wizard. A look into the layer file (Listing 7-7) reveals how such a factory registration is built.

Listing 7-7. Registration of a Data Object Factory in the Layer File

```
<folder name="Loaders">
    <folder name="audio">
        <folder name="mpeg">
            <folder name="Factories">
                <file name="Mp3DataLoader.instance">
                    <attr name="SystemFileSystem.icon" urlvalue=
                     "nbresloc:/com/galileo/netbeans/module/mp3.png"/>
                    <attr name="dataObjectClass" stringvalue=
                     "com.galileo.netbeans.module.Mp3DataObject"/>
                    <attr name="instanceCreate" methodvalue=
                     "org.openide.loaders.DataLoaderPool.factory"/>
                    <attr name="mimeType" stringvalue="audio/mpeg"/>
                </file>
            </folder>
        </folder>
    </folder>
</folder>
```

In the standard folder Loaders subfolders are created according to the defined MIME type (in this example audio/mpeg). Under them is the standard folder Factories in which our special data object factory is registered with the name Mp3DataLoader.instance. An icon for this file type is specified by the attribute SystemFileSystem.icon. With the attributes mimeType and dataObjectClass you determine for which type of data which data object type shall be produced by the factory. This means, here, that only the MIME type, not the file ending is determined. This determination is also made in the layer file in the standard folder Services/MIMEResolver. Finally, the now-registered special factory for your Mp3DataObject class is created by the method DataLoaderPool.factory().

When you created the MP3 file type at the beginning of this chapter, the file *Mp3Resolver.xml* was created besides the Mp3DataObject class by the NetBeans wizard. This file determines that the file extension *.mp3* is assigned to the MIME type audio/mpeg (see Listing 7-8).

Listing 7-8. MIME Resolver-Datei

```
<!DOCTYPE MIME-resolver PUBLIC
    "-//NetBeans//DTD MIME Resolver 1.0//EN"
    "http://www.netbeans.org/dtds/mime-resolver-1_0.dtd">
<MIME-resolver>
    <file>
        <ext name="mp3"/>
        <resolver mime="audio/mpeg"/>
    </file>
</MIME-resolver>
```

This file is also registered in the layer file. For this purpose, the already mentioned standard folder Services/MIMEResolver is used, as shown in Listing 7-9.

Listing 7-9. Registration of a MIME Type

```
<folder name="Services">
    <folder name="MIMEResolver">
```

```
    <file name="Mp3Resolver.xml" url="Mp3Resolver.xml">
        <attr name="displayName" bundlevalue=
                "com.galileo.netbeans.module.Bundle#Services/MIMEResolver/Mp3Resolver.xml"/>
    </file>
  </folder>
</folder>
```

Manually Creating Data Object

Usually, a data object does not have to be created explicitly, but is created by a factory on demand. However, you have the possibility of creating a DataObject for a given FileObject with the static find() method of the DataObject class:

```
FileObject myFile = ...
try {
    DataObject obj = DataObject.find(myFile);
} catch(DataObjectNotFoundException ex) {
    // no loader available for this file type
}
```

In that process, the FileObject is passed. A factory is searched for its file type. If one is found, it creates a DataObject and returns it. Otherwise, a DataObjectNotFoundException is thrown, in case no factory is registered for this file type.

Summary

In this chapter, you learned about two of the four most important NetBeans APIs, together with their dependencies. You learned about these by means of an example with MP3 files. Of the four, the File Systems API is found on the lowest level, as a generic abstraction layer over any kind of data. On top of that, the Data Systems API handles the logic relating to the data abstracted by the File Systems API; for example, you can use the Data Systems API to connect an MP3 file with the functionality that plays it.

C H A P T E R 8

Tips and Tricks

This chapter will cover two topics of general importance. The first section will introduce you to the possibilities for doing tasks on specific NetBeans Platform lifecyle events. The second section will look at how logging is typically done within a NetBeans Platform application.

Lifecycle of the NetBeans Platform

The NetBeans Platform provides different opportunities to react on certain events of the lifecycle and to trigger them yourself.

Tasks on Starting the Platform

The NetBeans Platform offers an extension point named WarmUp for executing asynchronous tasks when starting applications:

```
<folder name="WarmUp">
   <file name="com-galileo-netbeans-module-MyWarmUpTask.instance"/>
</folder>
```

You can add any instances (that implement the Runnable interface) to this extension point in your layer file:

```
public class MyWarmUpTask implements Runnable {
   public void run() {
      // do something on application startup
   }
}
```

Critical tasks—for example, tasks that are necessary as module-starting conditions—must not be started here. These tasks are executed asynchronously at the start of applications, which means there is no guarantee about when the task is started or finished. In this case, a module installer should be used (see Chapter 3).

Tasks on Ending the Platform

When a NetBeans Platform application is shut down, all user-specific settings (such as the information about open top components, application window size, and toolbars) are saved to the application user directory. In addition, all modules that implement a module installer (see Chapter 3) are asked if the application can be shut down. Thus, an application is not only closed, but it is shut down properly.

Usually, an application is closed using the menu or the close button in the title bar. In some cases, you might close an application programmatically. This could be an option if wrong data is entered in a login dialog, and the application should then be closed. In this case, you must not or cannot—as usual in Java applications—close the application using System.exit().The process for shutting down an application is specified by the Utilities API in the global service LifecycleManager. The NetBeans Core module offers a service provider for that purpose, responsible for executing the tasks mentioned earlier. This standard implementation of the LifecycleManager can be obtained by calling the getDefault() method. Close an application by calling the following line:

```
LifecycleManager.getDefault().exit();
```

Since this LifecycleManager is implemented as a service, you can provide your own implementation of this abstract class. This does not mean that the standard implementation of the NetBeans Platform is no longer available—you simply need to call it. This way, it is possible to execute custom tasks while the application is closed. Listing 8-1 demonstrates how to call the standard implementation after executing custom tasks and shut down applications properly.

Listing 8-1. A Custom LifecycleManager Implementation, Which Calls the Standard Implementation

```java
import org.openide.LifecycleManager;

public class MyLifecycleManager extends LifecycleManager {
    @Override
    public void saveAll() {
        for(LifecycleManager manager :
            Lookup.getDefault().lookupAll(LifecycleManager.class)) {
            if(manager != this) { /* skip our own instance */
                manager.saveAll();
            }
        }
    }
    @Override
    public void exit() {
        // do application specific shutdown tasks
        for(LifecycleManager manager :
            Lookup.getDefault().lookupAll(LifecycleManager.class)) {
            if(manager != this) { /* skip our own instance */
                manager.exit();
            }
        }
    }
}
```

This implementation must be registered as a service provider. It is important to note that a position must be declared to ensure that the custom implementation is delivered and called first by the Lookup. The standard LifecycleManager would be called only if this were not done. We register the class with the following annotation:

```
@ServiceProvider(service=LifecycleManager.class, position=1)
```

Restart of the Platform

You can not only finish, but also restart your application by means of the lifecycle manager of the NetBeans Platform. For this purpose, the LifecycleManager class offers the method markForRestart(). If this is called before finishing, a restart is realized:

```
LifecycleManager.getDefault().markForRestart();
LifecycleManager.getDefault().exit();
```

Logging

A very important and helpful (but often disregarded) topic is logging. Logging is the practice of recording status, warning, and error messages. Logging in the NetBeans Platform is based on the Java Logging API.

Logger

Log output is recorded by the Logging API using a Logger object. Typically, different Logger instances are used for specific   components. You get an instance of a Logger via the factory method getLogger(). You can also use a global logger, but you should use a named component-specific logger whenever possible. This way, different loggers can be individually turned on or off, which is very helpful when searching for bugs. A named logger is obtained by the following call:

```
Logger log = Logger.getLogger(MyClass.class.getName());
```

Typically, the full name of the class that creates the log output is used as the name for the logger. This name is obtained from the Class method getName(). If a logger already exists for this name, it is returned. The global logger can be obtained using the name Logger.GLOBAL_LOGGER_NAME.

Record log output (of a defined Level) using the log() methods in the Logger class. The following log levels are provided in the Level class:

- FINEST
- FINER
- FINE
- CONFIG
- INFO
- WARNING
- SEVERE

For convenience, the methods finest(), finer(), fine(), config(), info(), warning(), and severe() are also provided; these record the given message at the declared level.

LogManager

The Java Logging API specifies a central LogManager. This manager controls a hierarchical namespace holding all named loggers. That is why it is reasonable to use the full names of classes (that hold the hierarchical package structure) for logger names. For access to this manager, use the following:

```
LogManager manager = LogManager.getDefault();
```

The LogManager provides all names of all loggers. As a result, you can detect the name of a NetBeans Platform logger whose level may be changed for debugging purposes, for example. A list of all loggers can be retrieved as follows:

```
LogManager manager = LogManager.getLogManager();
for(String name : Collections.list(manager.getLoggerNames())) {
    System.out.println(name);
}
```

Configuration

Besides the loggers, the manager also administers configuration files, which are initially loaded from the lib/logging.properties file in the Java Platform directory. You can load special configuration files from a specific file by setting their file name to the system property java.util.logging.config.file. Configuration data may be loaded from a database, for example. For this purpose, implement a class that extracts the data from the database. Then register this class with the system property java.util.logging.config.class. Registration causes it to be automatically instantiated. Within this class, you provide the configuration data for the LogManager via an InputStream for the readConfiguration(InputStream) with the LogManager method.

Register Handler implementations in the configuration file so they output log data to the console (ConsoleHandler) or into a file (FileHandler). You can register your own implementations like the handler from the NetBeans Platform that display log messages graphically. The logging system comes with a root logger. All other loggers forward their logs to this root logger. Register a handler for this root logger, with the following property:

```
handlers = java.util.logging.ConsoleHandler
```

Multiple handlers can be listed using commas. To disable forwarding logs to the root logger, do so by using the following:

```
<logger name>.useParentHandlers = false
```

In this case, you can or must define a handler especially for this logger in order to obtain log output:

```
<logger name>.handlers = java.util.logging.FileHandler
```

Finally, setting the log level is important in the configuration. A log level defines which kind of log is recorded. This way, you can hide simple status messages and just show warning and error messages when searching errors. On the one hand, you can globally define the log level with the following feature:

```
.level = WARNING
```

On the other hand, you can overwrite a single logger's log level by using its name as a prefix:

```
<logger name>.level = INFO
```

Configuration data is not only set in the configuration file, but also as system properties. Set it at runtime using the System.setProperty() method. Doing so, make sure to call the LogManager's readConfiguration() method in order to apply the new configuration data. Alternatively, determine the configuration right at the application's startup using command-line parameters. During development in NetBeans, set your Module Suite start parameters in the *Project Properties* file (under *Important Files*) using the property run.args.extra . For example, use the following:

```
run.args.extra = -J-Dcom.galileo.netbeans.myclass.level=INFO
```

For distribution of your application, set command-line parameters using the property default_options in the *etc/<application>.conf* file.

Error Reports

The NetBeans Platform implements and registers a special log handler that displays recorded error messages for the user in a dialog. Therefore, use either the SEVERE or WARNING log level, and pass the Exception directly to the log() method.

```
Logger logger = Logger.getLogger(MyClass.class.getName());
try {
    ...
} catch(Exception e) {
    logger.log(Level.SEVERE, null, e);
    // oder
    logger.log(Level.WARNING, null, e);
}
```

Summary

In this chapter you learned how to execute tasks on starting and finishing a NetBeans Platform application. You can register any Runnable instances as tasks. You can also restart your application with the lifecycle manager. The second part of this chapter dealt with the important topic of logging, including the different kinds of log output and how you can configure them.

PART 2

Look & Feel: Developing User Interfaces

CHAPTER 9

Menu Bar and Toolbar

In addition to managing your own windows, a status bar, and a progress bar, the application window of a NetBeans Platform application manages a menu bar and a toolbar by default. The following sections will cover how to use the menu bar and the toolbar.

Tip Creation and registration of menus, menu entries, and toolbar actions has been quite simplified with NetBeans Platform 7. In connection with the annotations for actions described in Chapter 6, menu entries and toolbar actions are easily created.

Menu Bar

The menu bar of an application based on the NetBeans Platform is built by the Platform itself via the System Filesystem. Every menu (as well as the menu entries) is defined in the module layer file. This allows each module to declaratively add its menu entries to the menu bar. With NetBeans Platform 7 this is even easier. Just implement the action performed when selecting a menu entry; that way, this action is supplied with an annotation and the corresponding layer entries are automatically created out of these annotations.

In Chapter 6, you learned how to create and annotate action classes. In this section you will learn how to integrate actions into the menu bar.

Creating and Positioning Menu and Menu Entries

When creating an action with the action wizard of the NetBeans IDE (see Chapter 6) you can easily assign it to a menu and position it in the desired location via the wizard GUI. So you know what happens meanwhile in the background—to change something later or to be able to get by without the support of the NetBeans IDE—I will explain the process of creating menu entries for your own actions.

For example, say you want to add a menu entry to the *Edit* menu. To do this, use the simple action class mentioned in the "Always Enabled Actions" section in Chapter 6. You have not assigned the action to a menu or toolbar there yet—so far, we have ignored the ActionReferences annotation, which has automatically been created by the action wizard. Now, you need exactly this annotation to assign an action to a menu (see Listing 9-1).

Listing 9-1. Assign Actions to a Menu with Annotations

```
@ActionID(
    category = "Edit",
    id = "com.galileo.netbeans.module.MyFirstAction")
@ActionRegistration(
    iconBase = "com/galileo/netbeans/module/icon.png",
    displayName = "#CTL_MyFirstAction")
@ActionReferences({
    @ActionReference(
        path = "Menu/Edit",
        position = 1200)
})
public final class MyFirstAction implements ActionListener {
    public void actionPerformed(ActionEvent e) {
        // TODO implement action body
    }
}
```

In Listing 9-1 you see that the ActionReferences annotation is a list of assignments. An assignment is done by the ActionReference annotation. Specify with the path attribute where the action will be displayed. Menu is a standard folder in the System Filesystem in which the complete menu bar of your application is managed. The menu is determined by the name that follows Menu/. In this example, the action is displayed in the Edit menu. The name of the menu entry is given by the action itself; it is the value determined by displayName. Additionally, define the position of your action within the menu with the position attribute.

Listing 9-2 shows the effects of this annotation: a correspondent entry is generated in the layer file when creating the software. If you do not want to use an annotation, you can create this entry yourself and assign your action to a menu this way, too.

Listing 9-2. Assigning Action to a Menu by Direct Layer Entry

```
<filesystem>
  <folder name="Menu">
    <folder name="Edit">
      <file name="MyFirstAction.shadow">
        <attr name="originalFile"
          stringvalue="Actions/Edit/com-galileo-netbeans-module-MyFirstAction.instance"/>
        <attr name="position" intvalue="1200"/>
      </file>
    </folder>
  </folder>
</filesystem>
```

You assigned the menu Edit with the folder element in the standard folder Menu. The menu entry is added by the file element. Now, referencing on the action class, which must be defined in the standard folder Actions, follows with the attribute originalFile. Since the module system brings together all layer files, the menu entries of all modules, which are set below the folder Edit, are displayed in the *Edit* menu. So a menu is only created by the definition with the folder element. Thus, you have created your first menu entry. So far, we have assumed that the *Edit* menu is already present. However, this must not be the case. Since menus do not have to be explicitly applied, they are automatically created by the

NetBeans Platform. This way, you can easily create menus in any combination. So, for example, to move the action above into a submenu of *Edit*, you just have to modify the path attribute of the ActionReference annotation:

```
@ActionReference(
    path = "Menu/Edit/My Submenu",
    position = 1200)
```

This leads to another folder My Submenu in the layer file which represents the content of the submenu, as shown in Listing 9-3 and Figure 9-1.

Listing 9-3. *Creating a Submenu*

```
<folder name="Menu">
  <folder name="Edit">
    <folder name="My Submenu">
      <file name="MyFirstAction.shadow">
        <attr name="originalFile"
          stringvalue="Actions/Edit/com-galileo-netbeans-module-MyFirstAction.instance"/>
        <attr name="position" intvalue="1200"/>
      </file>
    </folder>
  </folder>
</folder>
```

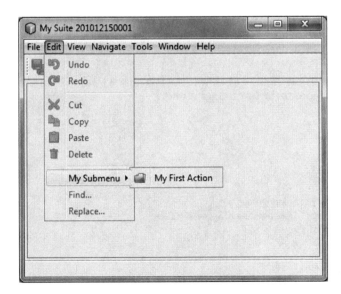

Figure 9-1. *Menu ➤ Submenu ➤ Menu entry*

You can look at the order of menus or menu entries in the layer tree (see Chapter 3) before executing your application. In the preceding examples, you learned how to determine the position of a menu entry by the position attribute (either with the ActionReference annotation or directly in the layer file). Since menus and submenus are implicitly applied when creating a menu entry, you cannot determine the order via annotation. So when assigning a new menu or submenu which you want to position exactly, you must assign the menu before using it in the layer file. There you can determine the position as shown in Listing 9-4. For more information see Chapter 3.

Listing 9-4. Determining the Position of a Menu or Submenu

```
<folder name="Menu">
  <folder name="Edit">
    <folder name="My Submenu">
      <attr name="position" intvalue="800"/>
    </folder>
  </folder>
</folder>
```

Insert Separator

You can determine seperators, which will be displayed between the menu entries, when defining a menu entry with the ActionReference annotation. For this purpose, the attributes separatorBefore and separatorAfter are provided. This is when you enter their absolute position. To add a separator in front of the example menu entry in Listing 9-1, extend the annotation of the action as shown in Listing 9-5.

Listing 9-5. Adding Separator via Annotation Attribute

```
@ActionReference(
    path = "Menu/Edit",
    position = 1200,
    separatorBefore = 1190)
```

Furthermore, there is an opportunity to define separators directly in the layer file. The layer entry would look like that shown in Listing 9-6, analogous to the previous example.

Listing 9-6. Adding Separator via Layer Entry

```
<folder name="Menu">
  <folder name="Edit">
    <folder name="My Submenu">
      <file name="MyFirstAction.shadow"> ... </file>
      <file name="MyFirstAction-separatorBefore.instance">
        <attr name="instanceCreate" newvalue="javax.swing.JSeparator"/>
        <attr name="position" intvalue="1190"/>
      </file>
    </folder>
  </folder>
</folder>
```

Hiding Present Menu Entries

You also have the possibility of hiding preexisting menus or menu entries, which either derive from Platform modules or were added by other application modules. This is quite easy because of the layer tree. To do so, open the folder *Important Files* ➤ *XML Layer* ➤ *<this layer in context>* in your module.

The entries you defined are shown there, as well as those from other modules of your application or from Platform modules. Below the *Menu Bar* folder you see all menus and menu entries. Choose the desired entry here and delete it via the context menu. They will not actually be deleted now, but just set as invisible in your layer file, assuming you deleted the *View* menu and the menu entry *Edit ➤ Find....* In this case, the entries in Listing 9-7 are added to your layer file.

Listing 9-7. Hiding of Menu Entries

```
<folder name="Menu">
  <folder name="View_hidden"/>
  <folder name="Edit">
    <file name="org-openide-actions-FindAction.shadow_hidden"/>
  </folder>
</folder>
```

So the suffix _hidden is added to the according entry. If you now want to add a deleted (i.e. a hidden) entry again, just remove the suffix from your layer file.

Shortcuts and Mnemonics

Shortcuts are defined and managed centrally in the layer file. This is why the standard folder Shortcuts exists. The shortcut is defined by the file element and is referred on an action class as an attribute from the central Actions folder. So a shortcut is not created for a menu entry, but for an action. A shortcut consists of one or more modifiers and an identifier, separated by a minus sign:

```
modifier-identifier
```

The following keys can be used as modifiers which are represented by a letter (code) in the layer file:

- C – (Ctrl)

- A – (Alt)

- S – (Shift)

- M – (Cmd)/(Meta)

Furthermore, there are two wildcard codes that ensure that the shortcuts are independent from the operating system; these should be used:

- D – (Ctrl) or (Cmd)/(Meta) (with Mac OS)

- O – (Alt) or (Ctrl) (with Mac OS)

All constants, which are defined by the Java class KeyEvent, can be used as identifier. For example, for KeyEvent.VK_M, just omit the prefix VK_, so the identifier would be M.

As mentioned at the beginning of this section, shortcuts are managed in the layer file,even though you can create them with an ActionReference annotation in a simple manner. This means, creating a shortcut is analogous to creating a menu entry. For example, using the shortcut (Ctrl) + (M) concerning the action MyFirstAction, you add the annotation shown in Listing 9-8.

Listing 9-8. Definition of a Shortcut with Annotations

```
@ActionID(
    category = "Edit",
    id = "com.galileo.netbeans.module.MyFirstAction")
@ActionRegistration(
    iconBase = "com/galileo/netbeans/module/icon.png",
    displayName = "#CTL_MyFirstAction")
@ActionReferences({
    @ActionReference(path = "Menu/Edit", position = 100),
    @ActionReference(path = "Shortcuts", name = "D-M")
})
public final class MyFirstAction implements ActionListener {
    ...
}
```

This annotation leads to a layer entry as shown in Listing 9-9. This means, defining shortcuts, you have the option of using a direct layer entry if you do not want to use annotations that represent the preferred variant (see Listing 9-9).

Listing 9-9. Definition of Shortcuts in the Layer File

```
<folder name="Shortcuts">
    <file name="D-M.shadow">
        <attr name="originalFile"
              stringvalue="Actions/Edit/com-galileo-netbeans-module-MyFirstAction.instance"/>
    </file>
</folder>
```

In this context, it can be helpful to look at the Javadocs of the functions `Utilities.keyToString()` and `Utilities.stringToKey()`, which are used to encode the shortcuts. Some possible combinations are listed in Table 9-1 as an example. If you do not know the spelling for a certain key, you can also use the action wizard (see Chapter 6).

Table 9-1. Examples of Shortcuts and the Corresponding Entries in the Layer File

Shortcut	Entry in the Layer File
(Ctrl)+(+)	`<file name="D-PLUS.shadow">`
(Ctrl)+(Shift)+(S)	`<file name="DS-S.shadow">`
(F3)	`<file name="F3.shadow">`
(Alt)+(Enter)	`<file name="O-ENTER.shadow">`
(Alt)+(O)	`<file name="O-O.shadow">`
(Alt)+(Shift)+(S)	`<file name="OS-S.shadow">`

Mnemonics are inserted directly by setting an ampersand (&) before the corresponding character in the name of an action. This can also take place in the action class or in a properties file:

```
CTL_OpenMyWindow=Open MyWind&ow
```

bear in mind that the mnemonics are displayed only when holding the (Alt) key.

Creating Your Own Menu Bar

If you want to create your own menu bar to use within a module, you can easily use the features of the NetBeans APIs. The Data Systems API actually provides a subclass of the JMenubar class with the class MenuBar. This class can create a DataFolder object out of its content, so you can define your own menu like the standard menu in the layer file of your module.

Now, only a DataFolder object needs to be created, too. To do this, you need to get access to the root folder of our menu by the method FileUtil.getConfigFile(). In this example it is called MyModuleMenu. For this module you create a DataFolder object and transfer this directly to the MenuBar constructor with the static method findFolder(), as shown in Listing 9-10.

Listing 9-10. Creating Your Own Menu Bar That Reads Its Content out of the System Filesystem

```
FileObject menu = FileUtil.getConfigFile("MyModuleMenu");
MenuBar    bar  = new MenuBar(DataFolder.findFolder(menu));
```

Toolbar

Creating Toolbar and Toolbar Actions

You can add actions to the toolbar the same way you add actions to the menu bar. You can use the existing toolbar or create any number of custom toolbars to group your toolbar buttons. Toolbars are defined in the standard folder Toolbars in the layer file. As described in the "Menu Bar" section, use the ActionReference annotation to add an action to a toolbar. You want to add the action class to the MyFirstAction toolbar, as shown in Listing 9-11.

Listing 9-11. Adding an Action to a Toolbar with Annotations

```
@ActionID(
    category = "Edit",
    id = "com.galileo.netbeans.module.MyFirstAction")
@ActionRegistration(
    iconBase = "com/galileo/netbeans/module/icon.png",
    displayName = "#CTL_MyFirstAction")
@ActionReferences({
    @ActionReference(
        path = "Toolbars/MyToolbars",
        position = 100)
})
public final class MyFirstAction implements ActionListener {
    public void actionPerformed(ActionEvent e) {
        // TODO implement action body
    }
```

```
}
```

As you see in Listing 9-11, a toolbar only differentiates from a menu entry by the corresponding path specification. A menu entry refers to an action in the standard folder Menu with the ActionReference annotation, while for a toolbar action the standard folder Toolbars is used. Remember that for a toolbar action the action class is provided with a corresponding icon by the iconBase attribute.

Analogous to the menu bar, such an annotation leads to an automatically created layer entry. If you do not want to use annotations, you can also add your toolbar actions by direct entries into the layer file of a toolbar. An entry that matches Listing 9-9 would look like that shown in Listing 9-12.

Listing 9-12. *Adding an Action to a Toolbar with Direct Layer Entry*

```
<folder name="Toolbars">
  <folder name="MyToolbar">
    <file name="MyFirstAction.shadow">
      <attr name="originalFile"
            stringvalue="Actions/Edit/com-galileo-netbeans-module-MyFirstAction.instance"/>
    </file>
  </folder>
</folder>
```

Toolbar Configurations

Which toolbars are displayed in what order is saved in a toolbar configuration in XML format. (Please find the corresponding DTD in the appendix.) The toolbars, which the NetBeans Platform entails by default, are defined by the configuration *Standard.xml* in the Core-UI module. This looks like Listing 9-13.

Listing 9-13. *Standard Platform Toolbar Configuration: Standard.xml*

```
<Configuration>
  <Row>
    <Toolbar name="File"/>
    <Toolbar name="Clipboard"/>
    <Toolbar name="UndoRedo"/>
    <Toolbar name="Memory"/>
  </Row>
</Configuration>
```

You have the option to create your own configurations and set them dynamically during the runtime, so you show and hide your toolbars dependent on the context. Now, you create your own configuration, in which you want to show the already created toolbar named MyToolbar and the standard toolbar Edit, while the toolbar File will be hidden. The configuration could look like Listing 9-14.

Listing 9-14. Configuration of Your Own Toolbar

```
<!DOCTYPE Configuration PUBLIC
  "-//NetBeans IDE//DTD toolbar//EN"
  "http://www.netbeans.org/dtds/toolbar.dtd">
<Configuration>
  <Row>
    <Toolbar name="UndoRedo"/>
    <Toolbar name="MyToolbar"/>
  </Row>
  <Row>
    <Toolbar name="File" visible="false"/>
  </Row>
</Configuration>
```

You can save this newly created configuration with any name. You now add it to the layer file to make the configuration public in the Platform. To do so, define the location of the configuration relative to the layer file with the url attribute, as shown in Listing 9-15.

Listing 9-15. Registering Toolbar Configuration

```
<folder name="Toolbars">
  <file name="MyToolbarConfig.xml" url="toolbars/MyToolbarConfig.xml"/>
</folder>
```

To display the desired toolbar and to activate the configuration, you just have to add a line in your source code at the place you want it. For this purpose, the UI Utilities module provides a helpful API:

```
ToolbarPool.getDefault().setConfiguration("MyToolbarConfig");
```

This call could occur, for example, when activating a window, to display a context-independent toolbar to the user. For this chapter you want to set this up as soon as you create your first window.

The class ToolbarPool is responsible for managing toolbars that are registered in the System Filesystem. The getDefault() method delivers the ToolbarPool object which is produced by the system and which cares about the toolbars that were defined in the standard folder Toolbars. You also have the option to create your own ToolbarPool object which manages toolbars that were defined in your own folder. To do so, you just have to pass a DataFolder object to the constructor. I will show you how this works in the section "Creating Your Own Toolbars."

The class ToolbarPool provides some useful functions, as shown in Table 9-2.

Table 9-2. Useful Methods of the ToolbarPool Class

Methode	Function
findToolbar(String name)	Returns a certain toolbar.
getToolbars()	Returns all available toolbars in this pool.
getConfiguration()	Returns the name of the currently active configuration.

getConfigurations()	Returns an array with all available configurations.
setConfiguration(String c)	Changes the current toolbar configuration.
setPreferredIconSize(int s)	With it you can define the icon size of the toolbar buttons. The values 16 and 24 pixels are supported.

Adaptation by the User

Pressing the right mouse button, a context menu is displayed on the toolbars in your application. The user can use it to show and hide separate toolbars. The toolbars can also be configured by the user via *Customize…* during the runtime. Add or delete single actions via drag-and-drop, as shown in Figure 9-2.

Figure 9-2. User-specific toolbars setting

Creating Your Own Toolbars

As with the menu bar, you have the possibility of creating your own toolbar or a pool of toolbars. Then you can use these toolbars within your top component, for example. For this purpose, the ToolbarPool class and the Menubar class provide a constructor to which you can pass a DataFolder object that represents a folder of the toolbars in the System Filesystem, as shown in Listing 9-16. You can define your toolbars exactly as you do with the standard toolbars.

Listing 9-16. Creating Your Own Toolbars Which Read Their Content out of the System Filesystem

```
FileObject  tbs  = FileUtil.getConfigFile("MyToolbars");
ToolbarPool pool = new ToolbarPool(DataFolder.findFolder(tbs));
```

You will find more information about which components you can add to the toolbars via the System Filesystem in the API documentation of the class `ToolbarPool`.

Using Your Own Controls

Your actions are displayed as an icon in the toolbar, by default. Over and above that you can equip your toolbar actions with a certain control element, such as a combo box. You do not need a special action class for that. You can use a standard action as used in the previous sections. Instead of implementing the `ActionListener` interface, this class must inherit of `AbstractAction`. We implement the `Presenter.Toolbar` interface so the action can always provide its special control element. Furthermore, it makes sense to implement a standard constructor for the initialization of the control element.

Combo Box in Toolbar

As an example, I want to show you an action class which has a combo box as control element with which you can edit a zoom, for example.

Listing 9-17. User-Specific Control Elements for a Toolbar Action

```
@ActionID(
    category = "View",
    id = "com.galileo.netbeans.module.MyComboboxAction")
@ActionRegistration(displayName = "#CTL_MyComboboxAction")
@ActionReferences({
    @ActionReference(path="Toolbars/MyToolbar")
})
public final class MyComboboxAction extends AbstractAction implements Presenter.Toolbar {
    JComboBox box = new JComboBox(new String[]{"100%", "200%"});

    public MyComboboxAction() {
        box.setMaximumSize(box.getPreferredSize());
        box.setAction(this);
    }

    @Override
    public void actionPerformed(ActionEvent e) {
        System.out.print("Adjust zoom to: ");
        System.out.println(box.getSelectedItem());
    }

    @Override
    public Component getToolbarPresenter() {
        return box;
```

```
        }
    }
```

The action class is usually registered by the annotations, and thus assigned to a toolbar. You add your own control element as a private field. You want to avoid having the combo box taking the whole width, so you set the maximal width of the combo box on the preferred width in the constructor. The connection of control element and action is very important. You achieve this by the setAction() method of the combo box to which you pass the reference on your own class by the this operator. If the combo box is now operated, this action is executed. Finally, you just have to implement the getToolbarPresenter() method and return the combo box with it. The combo box you created is displayed instead of the standard button.

Drop-down Menu in Toolbar

The NetBeans Platform provides a special factory class for creating a drop-down button with popup menu (see Figure 9-3). You can integrate such a button into the toolbar the same way as the combo box that was previously shown. So first, you create an action class and add a toolbar to it. It must inherit from the class AbstractAction to be able to implement the Toolbar.Presenter interface. In the getToolbarPresenter() method, you then produce a popup menu which you fill with the actions of the layer file. Then you produce the corresponding button by the method DropDownButtonFactory.createDropDownButton() and return it, as shown in Listing 9-18.

Listing 9-18. Creating a Drop-down Button

```
@ActionID(
    category = "File",
    id = "com.galileo.netbeans.module.MyDropDownButton")
@ActionRegistration(
    iconBase = "com/galileo/netbeans/module/icon.png",
    displayName = "#CTL_MyDropDownButton")
@ActionReferences({
    @ActionReference(path = "Toolbars/File", position = 300)
})
public final class MyDropDownButton extends AbstractAction implements Presenter.Toolbar {
    final String EXTENSION_POINT = "MyDropDownActions";
    JPopupMenu popup = new JPopupMenu();

    @Override
    public void actionPerformed(ActionEvent e) { }

    @Override
    public Component getToolbarPresenter() {
        for (Action a: Utilities.actionsForPath(EXTENSION_POINT))
            popup.add(a);
        return DropDownButtonFactory.createDropDownButton(
                ImageUtilities.loadImageIcon("com/galileo/netbeans/module/icon.png", false),
                popup);
    }
}
```

If you look at the source code in Listing 9-17 you see that only a few lines are necessary to create a flexible extendable drop-down button with popup menu. Besides the factory method that creates the button, the actionsForPath() method of the Utilities class is important. It provides a list of all actions which are registered in a certain folder. You can register them there by an ActionReference annotation, by default, like this:

```
@ActionReference(path = "MyDropDownActions", position = 100)
public final class MyDropDownAction1 implements ActionListener
```

Thus, the action MyDropDownAction1 is registered in the System Filesystem in the folder MyDropDownActions. It works the same way as adding an action to the menu bar or the toolbar. You see, the System Filesystem is not just helpful for standard components, such as the menu bar or the toolbar, but you can also take advantage of it for your own components.

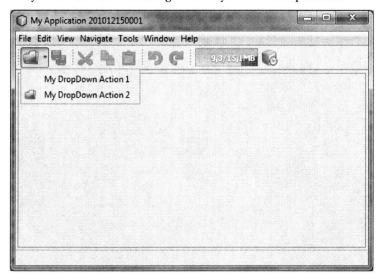

Figure 9-3. Drop-down button with popup menu in the toolbar

Summary

This chapter covered the menu bar and the toolbar of a NetBeans Platform application. You learned how a menu is structured, how to set your own toolbar, and, most important, how to simply add your actions to a toolbar or to a menu.

CHAPTER 10

Window System

The *Window System* is a framework provided by the NetBeans Platform. It is responsible for the administration and display of all application windows and allows the user to customize the layout of the user interface.

▨ **Tip** The registration of windows now works with annotations, making the development of NetBeans Platform applications not just easier, but also more independent of the NetBeans IDE.

The basic structure of the visual window system is document based . That means the central section—that is, the editor section—is all about the display of several files in tabs. Different windows can be placed in variant areas around the editor area, the view areas (see Figure 10-1). Usually, these are supporting windows that offer edit functionality to the documents. In the case of the NetBeans IDE, for example, these windows provide the structure of the project, the Properties dialog, and the Output window. These three are located around the editor area.

By default, all windows are displayed in the NetBeans main application window. Moreover, undocking windows by using the context menu or dragging the window from the application window is possible (*Dock/Undock*). What that looks like is shown in Figure 10-2, where the project window is undocked. Docking and undocking allows for flexible window positioning. The so-called *Floating Windows* feature is especially useful when you are using multiple monitors.

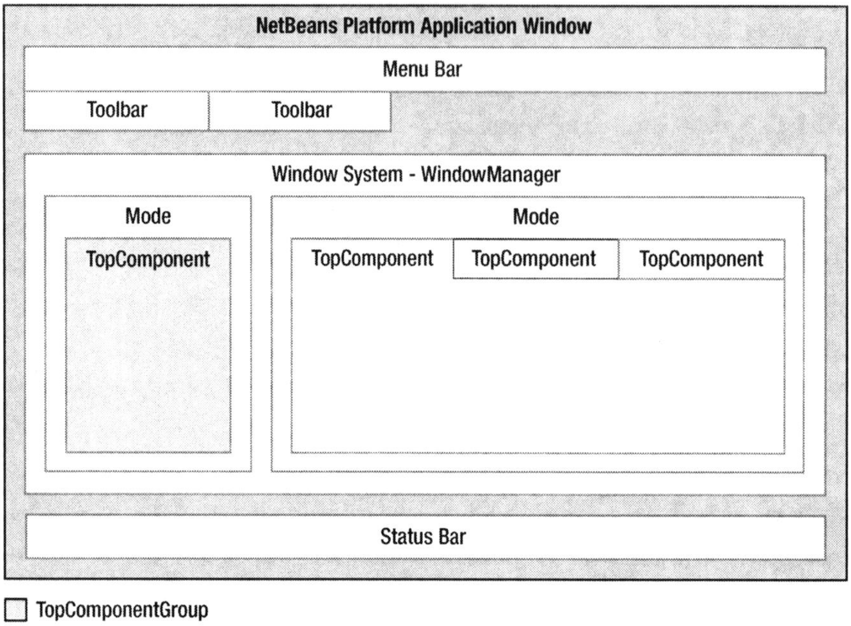

☐ TopComponentGroup

Figure 10-1. Structure of the NetBeans Platform application window

The window system is comprised of modes. A *mode* is a container in which windows can be displayed like a tab. The windows must be subclasses of TopComponent. All displayed windows are managed by the WindowManager. It is also possible to group windows. The assembly of the window system is declaratively described in the layer file. This assembly entails a description of the available modes, the windows that are displayed within them, and a definition of which window belongs to what group of windows. This information is also provided to the window system via the System Filesystem. In the following sections, the separate parts of the window system are described in detail; I will also show you how to use them in your module.

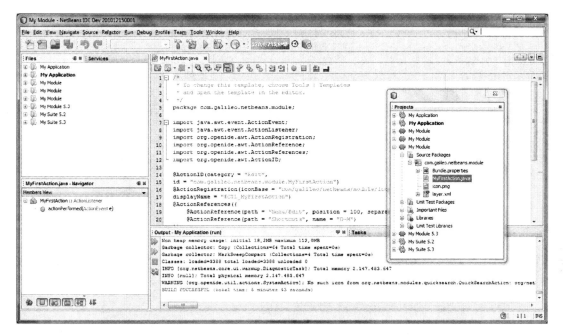

Figure 10-2. NetBeans window system with floating windows

Configuration

A module configures its windows, modes, and groups in the layer file, within the folders `Components`, `Modes`, and `Groups` within the standard folder `Windows2`. This way, a module can define its available windows, associate them with modes, and group them.

This configuration is the default configuration a module defines. The default configuration is used by the window system upon the first start. When exiting the application, any changes made to the layout of the application (e.g., moving a window to another mode or closing a window group) are stored within the user directory in the folder `config/Windows2Local` in a hierarchy identical to the layer file. Upon restarting, the application settings are read first. Only if no configuration files exist in the user directory (as is the case when starting the application for the very first time), are the settings read from the layer file.

Window: Top Component

The Window System API provides the class `TopComponent` for creating windows that integrate into the NetBeans Platform. This is a subclass of the Java class `JComponent` and it provides optional support for window interactions with the window system. A `TopComponent` always exists inside a mode and, as such, is dockable, is automatically managed by the `WindowManager`, and receives lifecycle events.

Creating a Top Component

The NetBeans IDE provides a helpful wizard for creating TopComponents. This wizard creates the complete basic skeleton. It is started by calling *File ➤ New File...,* and selecting the category *Module Development* and file type *Window.* On the following page, *Basic Settings,* you can edit a series of settings for your top component, as shown in Figure 10-3.

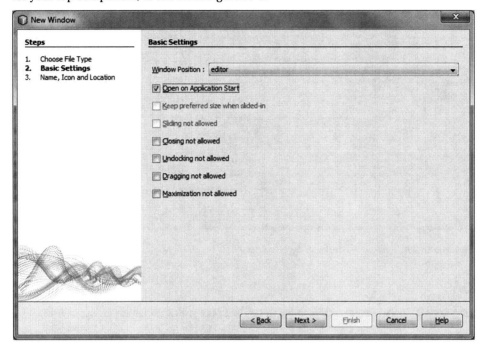

Figure 10-3. *Creating a top component: Basic Settings*

First, define the *Window Position,* meaning the mode in which your top component is supposed to be displayed. For the moment, you can only select the modules that the NetBeans Platform provides. However, later you can substitute it with a self-defined mode. Furthermore, you can define the behavior of the top component to create on this wizard page. I will explain the meaning of this option later in the "Behavior" section.

Press *Next* to get to the last page of the wizard. There, you can determine a prefix for the class name and an icon for the top component, as shown in Figure 10-4.

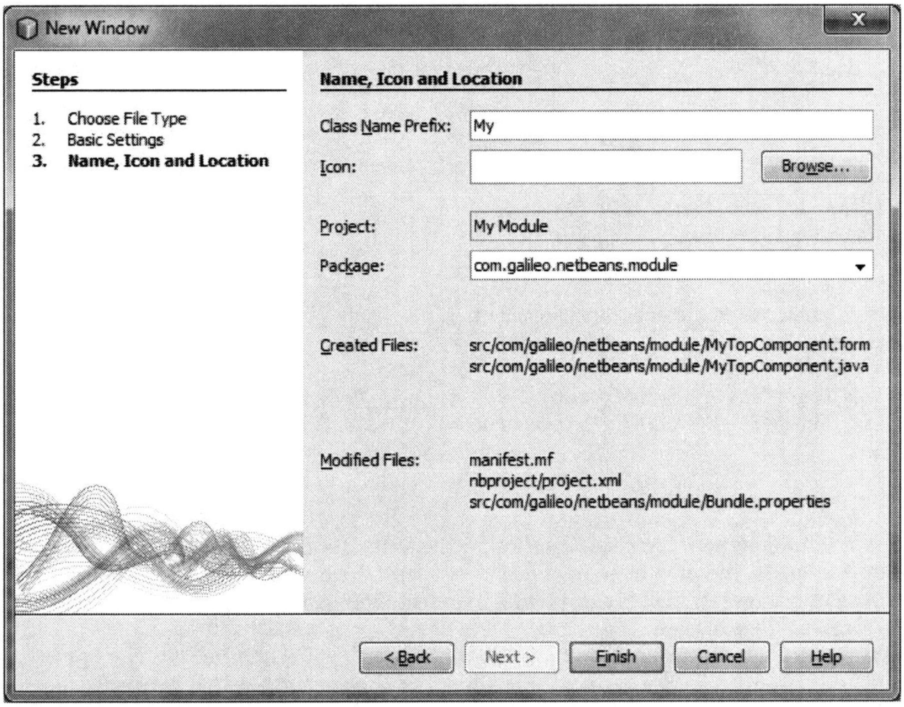

Figure 10-4. Creating a top component: Name, Icon and Location

Press the *Finish* button to end the wizard and to create the top component. The wizard has already done everything you need for you. Now you can edit the top component and equip it with the desired functionality with the Form Editor. You can test everything with *Run ➤ Run Main Project*.

Now let's take a look at the class which has been created by the wizard. This class is now marked by a series of annotations whose meaning is explained in Listing 10-1.

Listing 10-1. Basic Structure of a Top Component with Annotations

```
import org.openide.util.NbBundle;
import org.openide.windows.TopComponent;
import org.netbeans.api.settings.ConvertAsProperties;
import org.openide.awt.ActionID;
import org.openide.awt.ActionReference;

@ConvertAsProperties(
    dtd = "-//com.galileo.netbeans.module//My//EN",
    autostore = false)
@TopComponent.Description(
    preferredID = "MyTopComponent",
    iconBase = "com/galileo/netbeans/module/icon.png",
    persistenceType = TopComponent.PERSISTENCE_ALWAYS)
```

```
@TopComponent.Registration(
    mode = "editor",
    openAtStartup = true)
@ActionID(
    category = "Window",
    id = "com.galileo.netbeans.module.MyTopComponent")
@ActionReference(
    path = "Menu/Window" /*, position = 333 */)
@TopComponent.OpenActionRegistration(
    displayName = "#CTL_MyAction",
    preferredID = "MyTopComponent")
public final class MyTopComponent extends TopComponent {
    public MyTopComponent() {
        initComponents();
        setName(NbBundle.getMessage(MyTopComponent.class, "CTL_MyTopComponent"));
        setToolTipText(NbBundle.getMessage(MyTopComponent.class, "HINT_MyTopComponent"));
    }
    ...
}
```

The top component is marked with basic information by the annotation TopComponent.Description. A unique identifier (preferredID), the path to an icon (iconBase), and the determination whether the top component will be saved or not (persistenceType) belong to this basic information. The possibilities are described in the next section, "Persistence".

You add the top component to a mode by the TopComponent.Registration annotation. The mode determined by the attribute mode must already exist. You can either choose a mode that is already defined by the NetBeans Platform or you can create one yourself. In the section "Creating a Mode" you will learn how to do this. With the openAtStartup attribute you can determine whether your top component will be automatically opened when starting the application. Finally, the optional attribute position is provided for determining the order of multiple top components within a mode.

The NetBeans Platform does a lot of work in the background with the annotation TopComponent.OpenActionRegistration. This annotation causes the registration of an action to open the annotated top component in the layer file. In this respect, it is interesting that not only the registration occurs, but the action is also automatically provided. This means, no corresponding action class exists in your module anymore. The action class is created in the background by means of the transferred parameters with the factory method TopComponent.openAction(). You define the name of the action by the displayName attribute. Using # you can determine a key for a text constant out of a properties bundle (see Chapter 6). With the preferredID attribute you can easily determine whether only one or more instances can be produced by your top component. For this purpose use the already defined identifier of your top component. That way, only a singleton instance is created. Omitting the attribute, a new instance of the top component is opened when executing the action.

The two attributes ActionID and ActionReference are connected to the TopComponent.OpenActionRegistration annotation. As described in Chapter 6, with ActionID, a unique identifier is added to the open action with a category. With the ActionReference annotation you determine where and in which menu the action will be displayed (see Chapter 9). While using the annotation as described is considerably easier than registering a top component, I will explain (see Listing 10-2)—its use is not mandatory, however. You also have the possibility here of directly specifying the necessary information in the layer file. First, the top component is defined in the standard folder Windows2/Components in the layer file. The assignment to a mode occurs in the standard folder Windows2/Modes.

Listing 10-2. Definition and Assignment of a Top Component in the Layer File

```
<folder name="Windows2">
    <folder name="Components">
        <file name="MyTopComponent.settings" url="MyTopComponentSettings.xml"/>
    </folder>
    <folder name="Modes">
        <folder name="editor">
            <file name="MyTopComponent.wstcref" url="MyTopComponentWstcref.xml"/>
        </folder>
    </folder>
</folder>
```

A *Settings* file is needed for defining a top component in the folder Windows2/Components. The complete class name of the top component is named in this file. Thus, the window system is able to create an instance of the top component. (See Listing 10-3.)

Listing 10-3. Settings File to Declaratively Add a Top Component

```
<!DOCTYPE settings PUBLIC
 "-//NetBeans//DTD Session settings 1.0//EN"
 "http://www.netbeans.org/dtds/sessionsettings-1_0.dtd">
<settings version="1.0">
    <instance class="com.galileo.netbeans.module.MyTopComponent"/>
</settings>
```

Mapping a top component to a mode is done using a *Top Component Reference* file, as shown in Listing 10-4. In this file a unique identifier of the top component is defined. Additionally, it is defined by the opened attribute of the state element, whether the window is opened starting the application.

Listing 10-4. Top Component Reference File Mapping a Top Component to a Mode

```
<!DOCTYPE tc-ref PUBLIC
 "-//NetBeans//DTD Top Component in Mode Properties 2.0//EN"
 "http://www.netbeans.org/dtds/tc-ref2_0.dtd">
<tc-ref version="2.0" >
    <tc-id id="MyTopComponent"/>
    <state opened="true"/>
</tc-ref>
```

If you chose the declarative way instead of the annotations, you should finally overwrite the two methods preferredID() and getPersistenceType() of your top component class and thus deliver the corresponding values.

Behavior

A top component's behavior can be adapted by a series of features, shown in Table 10-1. You edit the settings of these features with the NetBeans window wizard. Otherwise, you can also adapt these features which are set in the constructor of a top component later.

Table 10-1. *Features of a Top Component Which Can Be Adapted User Specifically*

Feature	Description
CLOSING_DISABLED	Top component cannot be closed by the user. Close symbol and menu entry are hidden in the context menu.
DRAGGING_DISABLED	Drag-and-drop of the top component is deactivated. This means the top component cannot be removed in another mode.
MAXIMIZATION_DISABLED	Top component cannot be maximized. A corresponding entry is hidden in the context menu.
SLIDING_DISABLED	Deactivates marginal minimizing of a top component. The minimize button as well as the context menu entry are hidden. This feature is not provided with a top component in the editor mode.
UNDOCKING_DISABLED	Undocking the top component is not possible. This means the window cannot be detached by dragging. The corresponding context menu entry is deactivated, too.
KEEP_PREFERRED_SIZE_WHEN_SLIDED_IN	The top component is displayed in the original size. This feature is not provided with a top component in the editor mode.

These features can be prepended by PROP_ with the following method within a top component:

```
putClientProperty(
    TopComponent.PROP_CLOSING_DISABLED,
    Boolean.TRUE);
```

States

A top component can have several states, listed in Table 10-2.

Table 10-2. *Different States of a Top Component*

State	Condition
Opened	A top component has the state opened when it is displayed in a tab inside one of the window system modes.
Closed	A top component has the state closed either after it is closed or if it has not yet been opened. Even closed, a top component continues to exist.

Visible	If a top component is alone in its mode or is in top position, it remains in the visible state.
Invisible	If one top component is covered by another one inside a mode, it changes to the invisible state.
Active	A top component is in the active state when it or one of its components is focused. In this state, the global selection context is provided by the top component.
Inactive	A top component that is unfocused is in the inactive state.

Entering a specific state is announced via a call to one of the methods shown in Table 10-3. If a window has to perform an action in a specific state, simply override the corresponding method.

Table 10-3. Methods for the Different States

State	Method
opened	protected void **componentOpened()**
closed	protected void **componentClosed()**
visible	protected void **componentShowing()**
invisible	protected void **componentHidden()**
active	protected void **componentActivated()**
inactive	protected void **componentDeactivated()**

Chapter 9 showed how to create toolbar configurations and how to use them to display application-specific toolbars. Use two previously described methods that inform us about the state of the top component to display the currently active top component, as shown in Listing 10-5.

Listing 10-5. Displaying and Hiding Toolbars Based on Context

```
public class MyTopComponent extends TopComponent {
    private String origConfig = "Standard";
    private String myConfig   = "MyToolbarConfig";

    protected void componentActivated() {
        origConfig = ToolbarPool.getDefault().getConfiguration();
        ToolbarPool.getDefault().setConfiguration(myConfig);
    }
```

```
    protected void componentDeactivated() {
        ToolbarPool.getDefault().setConfiguration(origConfig);
    }
}
```

If the top component is focused, the method componentActivated() is called. The current configuration is stored for later reactivation. Then, you set your own toolbar configuration MyToolbarConfig (created in Chapter 9). If another top component is selected, this top component loses focus and the method componentDeactivated() is called. The stored configuration is set in this method to restore previous toolbars.

Context Menu

When right-clicking the title bar of a top component, a context menu is displayed, with actions such as *Undock Window* or *Close Window*. These actions are obtained from the TopComponent class via its getActions() method. To add your own actions to this context menu, you can override this method (see Listing 10-6). When doing so, it is useful to add the actions declaratively. In Chapter 3, I mentioned that it is possible to add your own folders and extension points to the layer file. That is exactly what you want to use here. The actions are declared in the layer file and read it on demand in the getActions() method.

Listing 10-6. Reading Actions for a Context Menu from the Layer File

```
public class MyTopComponent extends TopComponent {
    private List<Action> ca = null;

    @Override
    public Action[] getActions() {
        if (ca == null) {
            ca = new ArrayList<Action>(Arrays.asList(super.getActions()));
            ca.add(null); /* add separator */
            Lookup lkp = Lookups.forPath("ContextActions/MyTC");
            ca.addAll(lkp.lookupAll(Action.class));
        }

        return ca.toArray(new Action[ca.size()]);
    }
}
```

First, the superclass's getActions() method is called in order to obtain default actions. With the help of the method Lookups.forPath() you can easily create a Lookup for the declared folder ContextActions/MyTC. The method lookupAll() then obtains all registered actions that implement the Action interface. When creating the menu, a null value is automatically replaced by a separator by the Platform. The assembled list of actions is returned as an array. Finally, you just have to create references on the actual action definitions (usually in the standard folder Actions). You can realize the references either elegantly via annotation in the respective action class itself or by a direct entry in the layer file. The necessary annotation would look like the following:

```
@ActionReference(path = "ContextActions/MyTC")
```

The corresponding entry in the layer file in the self-defined folder could look like Listing 10-7, for example.

Listing 10-7. Defining Context Menu Actions in the Layer File

```
<folder name="ContextActions">
  <folder name="MyTC">
    <file name="MyAction1.shadow">
      <attr name="originalFile"
            stringvalue="Actions/Edit/com-galileo-netbeans-module-MyAction1.instance"/>
    </file>
    <file name="MyAction2.shadow">
      <attr name="originalFile"
            stringvalue="Actions/Edit/com-galileo-netbeans-module-MyAction2.instance"/>
    </file>
  </folder>
</folder>
```

You have now created an extension point. Other modules can easily add actions to the context menu of your top component by defining this action in their layer file in the folder `ContextActions/MyTC`. Thus, the context menu can be flexibly extended by any other module without any dependency.

Persistence

The window system is capable of storing opened top components upon exiting the application and restoring them upon restart. However, there are use cases where storing the top component is not desirable. Determining whether a top component will be stored or not is done via the value that is delivered by the method `getPersistenceType()`. You can determine this value with the `persistenceType` attribute of the `TopComponent.Description` annotation. If you do not use annotations, though, the named method should always be overridden. The constants listed in Table 10-4 are available as return values.

Table 10-4. Possible Persistence Types of a Top Component

Constant	Property
PERSISTENCE_ALWAYS	The top component is always stored.
PERSISTENCE_ONLY_OPENED	This constant defines a top component stored only when opened in a mode.
PERSISTENCE_NEVER	With this constant, the top component is never stored.

The window system calls the methods `writeProperties()` and `readProperties()` upon storing or restoring a top component. The window system then calls the methods when saving and loading a top component. You can use these methods in order to save or load your top component-specific data. For this purpose you always get a `Properties` object as parameter. The data that is saved there is saved by the NetBeans Platform in the user directory as an XML file. From there it is loaded, too.

Registry

All top components of the NetBeans window system are centrally managed in a registry. The interface of this registry is specified by the TopComponent.Registry interface. An instance of this registry is obtained either directly via the TopComponent class by calling

```
TopComponent.Registry registry = TopComponent.getRegistry();
```

or via the WindowManager:

```
TopComponent.Registry registry = WindowManager.getDefault().getRegistry();
```

This registry will return, for example the currently activated top components via getActivated() or all opened top components via getOpened(). Furthermore, a PropertyChangeListener can be registered on the registry in order to globally react to state changes of the top component, for example (see Table 10-5).

Table 10-5. Publicly Accessing a Top Component's State

Property	Condition
PROP_ACTIVATED	If a top component is being activated
PROP_TC_CLOSED	If a top component has been closed
PROP_TC_OPENED	If a top component has been opened

In the following example, a listener is added to the registry. This listener reacts when a top component is opened (see Listing 10-8).

Listing 10-8. Track Changes of Top Component States Globally

```
public class MyTopComponent extends TopComponent implements PropertyChangeListener {

    public MyTopComponent() {
        TopComponent.Registry reg = TopComponent.getRegistry();
        reg.addPropertyChangeListener(WeakListeners.propertyChange(this, reg));
    }

    public void propertyChange(PropertyChangeEvent evt) {
        if(evt.getPropertyName().equals(TopComponent.Registry.PROP_OPENED))
            // Top Component opened
    }
}
```

Docking Container: Mode

The entire window system of the NetBeans Platform comprises sections, where multiple components can be displayed docked in tabs. These sections are the previously mentioned editor and view sections. Such a section is called a mode. However, a mode as such is not a displayed component, but acts as controller and container for those components displayed therein. These components are of the type

TopComponent, as mentioned in the previous section. A mode is specified by the interface Mode of the Window System API.

Creating a Mode

A mode is not a fixed section, but it can be defined individually via an XML file. Some important sections (such as the central editor section or the section where the NetBeans IDE usually opens the project view) are already defined in NetBeans Platform modules. You can also define and add your own modes. A configuration file for a mode has the structure shown in Listing 10-9.

Listing 10-9. Mode Configuration File: MyMode.wsmode

```
<!DOCTYPE mode PUBLIC
 "-//NetBeans//DTD Mode Properties 2.3//EN"
 "http://www.netbeans.org/dtds/mode-properties2_3.dtd">
<mode version="2.3">
    <module name="com.galileo.netbeans.module" spec="1.0"/>
    <name    unique="MyMode"/>
    <kind    type="view"/>
    <state   type="joined"/>
    <constraints>
        <path orientation="vertical" number="0" weight="0.2"/>
        <path orientation="horizontal" number="0" weight="1.0"/>
    </constraints>
    <empty-behavior permanent="true"/>
</mode>
```

First, with the module attribute you define the module to which the mode belongs. The most important element is the name element. The value of the name element must be a unique identifier and also has to match the file name (uppercase and lowercase, too). Additionally, by the kind element you can define the way the mode displays its components. There are three mode types: editor, view, and sliding. Figure 10-5 displays the appearance of each of the three via the NetBeans IDE.

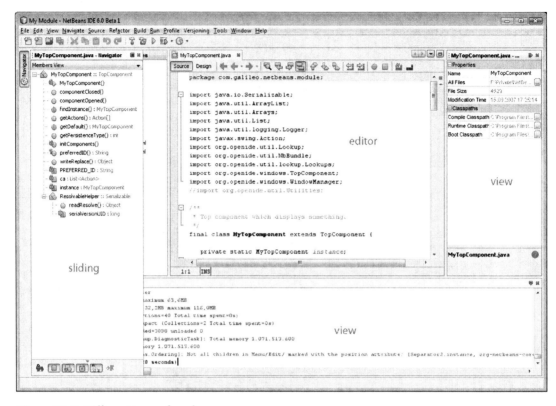

Figure 10-5. *Different types of modes*

A mode of the type editor is for the most part centrally arranged in an application, like the Editor Mode which is specified by the Core Windows module by a *wsmode* file (as the name of the mode already reveals). The top components, arranged surrounding this editor mode, are typically displayed in modes of the type view.

These windows are often also called helper windows, because they offer features to, for example, edit documents. Aside from differently displaying the tabs in the modes, the editor and view modes differ in so far as the editor type has control elements in the top-right corner for easier navigation between documents and the top components. Furthermore, there is also the mode of the type sliding. The window system gives you the possibility of moving or minimizing top components to the right, left, or bottom border of the application window. This is often useful when working with windows that are seldom or sporadically used. When hovering with the mouse above the button of the minimized top component, it opens above the opened windows and hides automatically again when exiting the control element. These windows are in a mode of the type sliding.

A mode of the type sliding can also define the element slidingSide. It selects borders (left, right, bottom) upon which the mode will be located. Concerning this, the following values are allowed:

```
<slidingSide side="left"/>

<slidingSide side="right"/>

<slidingSide side="bottom"/>
```

The element state defines whether the mode is docked in the application window or undocked in a separate window. The admissible values are joined for the docked mode and separated for the undocked representation. For example, when a top component is undocked, its mode changes to separated.

The constraints element allows the definition of dimension and position in relation to other modes. The preceding example would display the mode on the top border of the application window, for example. If it is on the bottom border, a bigger number (e.g., 30) is put into the attribute number. Since this number controls the position of all modes, it is helpful to take a look at the configuration files of the predefined modes for the NetBeans Platform. Some of them are in the module *Core-UI*.

We now add this configuration file to the Platform via the module's layer file. For this purpose, we refer the *.wsmode* file in the folder Windows2/Modes (see Listing 10-10).

Listing 10-10. Adding a New Mode to the Layer File

```
<folder name="Windows2">
    <folder name="Modes">
        <file name="MyMode.wsmode" url="MyMode.wsmode"/>
        <folder name="MyMode">
            <file name="MyTopComponent.wstcref" url="MyTopComponentWstcref.xml"/>
        </folder>
    </folder>
</folder>
```

The top component is added to the new mode via the top component reference file which the wizard created. This allows for flexible declarative changes in the arrangement of top components. As you can see, you can flexibly change the arrangement of your components because of the declarative assignment.

A top component can be maximized by double-clicking the title bar in the application window. By default, all other components are changed to a sliding mode. If a component must stay in place and not move to the border, an attribute can be added to the corresponding top component reference file (*.wstcref*), as follows:

```
<docking-status maximized-mode="docked">
```

Direct Docking

It is also possible to directly dock a top component into a certain mode, as shown in Listing 10-11.

Listing 10-11. Programmatically Adding a Top Component to a Certain Mode

```
TopComponent tc = new MyTopComponent();
Mode m = WindowManager.getDefault().findMode("explorer");
if(m != null)
    m.dockInto(tc);
tc.open();
tc.requestActive();
```

For this purpose use the findMode() method of the WindowManager class. The mode is returned because of the unique name, in case it exists. With the dockInto() method you can then dock your instance to a top component directly in the mode.

Modifying a Mode

At runtime, the user retains the ability to move the top components to other modes or change the dimension of a mode. These changes of data are stored in the user directory and restored upon restarting the application. Configurations are read from the layer file and the module's configuration files only if no data was stored in the user directory. This is why it is often helpful to clean and build the project (*Clean & Build Project*) when changing configuration files during development.

Groups of Windows: Top Component Group

Frequently, multiple windows are required at once for certain tasks. One such case is creating a GUI within the NetBeans IDE. The Inspector, Palette, and Properties windows are displayed in this case. Upon leaving the Form Editor mode, these windows are hidden. For this purpose, the NetBeans Platform provides the ability to assemble top components into a group that enables toggling the visibility of them all. The Window System API provides the interface TopComponentGroup for this purpose. However, a group does not change the layout of the windows, meaning the assembly or dimension of modes, but it is responsible for opening and closing the groups' windows.

Behavior of a Top Component Group

Groups manage their windows in accordance with the user settings, allowing the following cases:

- When a group is being opened, all windows that have not already opened will be opened, if the open attribute is set to true (if no window has been opened, yet).

- Upon closing a group, all windows will be closed that were not open prior to opening the group, and their close attribute will be set to true. That means the windows the user had open prior to opening the group will remain open.

- Closing a group (if one of the windows has already been opened before opening the group), only those windows are closed in which the close attribute is true and whose attributes have not been opened before opening the group. This means the windows the user opened before opening the group itself stay open.

- If a window of a group is closed by the user, the open attribute is set to false when closing the group. When the group is reopened, the window will thus not be opened.

- If during the time a group is open, the user opens a window from the group that was previously closed, the open attribute is set to true, opening the window when the group is reopened.

So, the user is able to influence the content of a group. Even if you found the descriptions of the preceding cases somewhat confusing, the best way of digging these logic groups is to directly explore them.

Creating a Top Component Group

Groups are defined via a *Group Configuration* file and groups are declared in the layer file in the folder *Windows2/Groups*, announcing its existence to the platform. This file has the structure shown in Listing 10-12.

Listing 10-12. The Group Configuration File: MyGroup.wsgrp

```
<!DOCTYPE group PUBLIC
 "-//NetBeans//DTD Group Properties 2.0//EN"
 "http://www.netbeans.org/dtds/group-properties2_0.dtd">
<group version="2.0">
   <module name="com.galileo.netbeans.module" spec="1.0"/>
   <name unique="MyGroup"/>
   <state opened="false"/>
</group>
```

By the optional `module` attribute you declare the name of the module that this group belongs to. The name attribute defines unique identifiers that must correspond to the file name. Whether the group is currently displayed or not is set in the `state` attribute. Now you create the group in the layer file and refer it to the *Group Configuration* file (see Listing 10-13).

Listing 10-13. Adding a Group to the Layer File

```
<folder name="Windows2">
   <folder name="Groups">
      <file name="MyGroup.wsgrp" url="MyGroup.wsgrp"/>
      <folder name="MyGroup">
         <file name="MyTopComponent.wstcgrp" url="MyTopComponent.wstcgrp"/>
      </folder>
   </folder>
</folder>
```

As you see, I already added your first top component to the newly created group. This is done by declaring a *Group Reference Configuration* file (*.wstcgrp*), where the behavior of the top component inside the group is declared (as shown in Listing 10-14).

Listing 10-14. Group Reference Configuration: MyTopComponent.wstcgrp

```
<!DOCTYPE tc-group PUBLIC
 "-//NetBeans//DTD Top Component in Group Properties 2.0//EN"
 "http://www.netbeans.org/dtds/tc-group2_0.dtd">
<tc-group version="2.0">
   <module name="com.galileo.netbeans.module" spec="1.0"/>
   <tc-id id="MyTopComponent"/>
   <open-close-behavior open="true" close="true"/>
</tc-group>
```

This file references a top component via its unique identifier. The `TopComponent` must be declared in the layer file in the folder `Windows2/Components` with a *.settings* file (as occurs automatically when using the wizard to create a top component. See the section "Creating a Top Component"). Further, the behavior of the window is defined considering opening and closing. (Those attributes are discussed in the previous section.)

For each window that you now want to add to the group, create such a file and make an entry in the folder of your group in the layer file. You can easily use the group via the Window Manager. The Window Manager also provides a method for finding a group, as shown in Listing 10-15.

Listing 10-15. Opening and Closing a Top Component Group

```
TopComponentGroup group = WindowManager.getDefault().findTopComponentGroup("MyGroup");
if(group != null) { /* group found */
    group.open();
}
```

Administration: Window Manager

The Window Manager is the central component of the window system. It manages modes, windows, and groups, and provides an API to access its administrated components. For this purpose, the methods for locating components (see Table 10-6) are very helpful.

Table 10-6. Methods Locating Components of the Window System

Method	Description
findMode(String name)	Find a mode via its name.
findMode(TopComponent tc)	Find the mode into which the TopComponent is docked.
findTopComponent(String id)	Find a top component via its unique ID.
findTopComponentID(TopComponent tc)	Get a top component's unique ID.
findTopComponentGroup(String name)	Find a top component group via its name.

A PropertyChangeListener can be added to the Window Manager, for example to become informed when a mode is activated. Additionally, a set of all available modes in the window system can be obtained via a call to getModes(). The main application window is accessed via the following call:

```
Frame main = WindowManager.getDefault().getMainWindow();
```

The architecture of the window system classes is summarized in Figure 10-6.

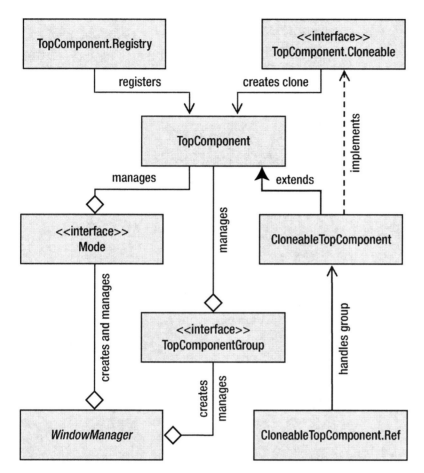

Figure 10-6. *Architecture of NetBeans window system*

MultiViews

Use the *MultiViewAPI* to internally divide a top component across multiple containers or components. Typically, as the name suggests, this approach is used to provide more than one view for a single data object. The most common example of this is the NetBeans Form Editor, in which the user can switch between the Source view and the Design view. Both views have as their basis the same *.java* and *.form* file. However, a relationship between the views is not mandatory. That means you can integrate any components into the container that are completely independent of each other, displaying different data. The MultiView SPI can, as a result, be used as a generic framework.

The button bar provided by a multiview top component allows the user to switch between the different views. Optionally, one of the views, consisting of any kind of JComponent, provides a toolbar displayed next to the drop-down list (see Figure 10-7).

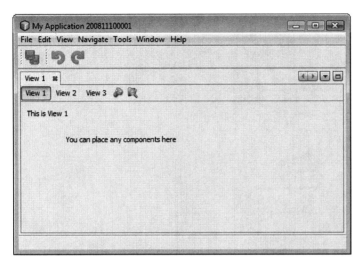

Figure 10-7. Multiview top component with three views/components

Each view consists of an independent component, which must be a subclass of JComponent. Typically, the base class JPanel is used. However, nothing prevents you from using the class TopComponent, allowing integration of one or more windows into a multiview. To allow a component to be a view in a multiview top component, implement the MultiViewElement interface. The meaning of the methods, specified by this interface, can best be illustrated via a simple example, as follows:

```
public class MultiViewPanel1 extends JPanel implements MultiViewElement {
    private JToolBar toolbar = new JToolBar();
    private MultiViewElementCallback callback = null;

    public MultiViewPanel1() {
        initComponents();
        toolbar.add(new Panel1ToolbarAction1());
        toolbar.add(new Panel1ToolbarAction2());
    }
```

The view initially receives a MultiViewElementCallback via the setMultiViewElementCallback() method in order to access the top component (that it is embedded in). For example, via this object you obtain the multiview top component or—as you will see—you can adapt the name of the multiview top component. To use this callback object in your class, save the data as a private element. The instance of the view is obtained via the getVisualRepresentation() method. This method is called whenever the view is activated, meaning that creating the component in this method should be avoided. Normally, use this to deliver the current component. The toolbar of the current view is obtained via the getToolbarRepresentation() method. It is also repeatedly called. For this purpose, you should also provide an already created toolbar. Actions in the context menu of the multiview top component are obtained from the currently active view, via the getActions() method. First, use this method to access the standard actions of a top component via the MultiViewElementCallback object. Next, you can add your own actions to the set of standard actions. Use getLookup() to provide a Lookup which gets part of the multiview top component's Lookup and thus is also part of the global context.

```
public void setMultiViewCallback(MultiViewElementCallback c) {
    callback = c;
}

public JComponent getVisualRepresentation() {
    return this;
}

public JComponent getToolbarRepresentation() {
    return toolbar;
}

public Action[] getActions() {
    if(callback != null) {
        return callback.createDefaultActions();
    } else {
        return new Action[]{};
    }
}

public Lookup getLookup() {
    return Lookups.singleton(this);
}
```

The next methods should be familiar, since they were covered in discussions concerning the TopComponent class. Via these methods you are informed about the various states of the view and the multiview top component. In this example you want to name the title of the top component dynamically (like the name of the view), whenever the view is opened or activated. The title can be changed via the MultiViewElementCallback object, using the updateTitle() method.

```
public void componentOpened() {
    callback.updateTitle("View 1");
}

public void componentClosed() {}
public void componentShowing() {}
public void componentHidden() {}

public void componentActivated() {
    callback.updateTitle("View 1");
}

public void componentDeactivated() {}
```

Each view offers its own undo/redo functionality, via the getUndoRedo() method. (How to implement undo/redo via the NetBeans API is discussed in Chapter 15.) If this support is unwanted, provide UndoRedo.NONE, as shown in the following:

```
public UndoRedo getUndoRedo() {
    return UndoRedo.NONE;
}
```

Finally, implement the canCloseElement() method. This method is called on each of the views when the multiview top component closes. Only if all the views have provided CloseOperationState.STATE_OK is the top component closed. If your view is not immediately closed because (for example) changed data has not yet been saved, provide a CloseOperationState object, created via the MultiViewFactory.createUnsafeCloseState() method. However, this makes sense only when CloseOperationHandler has been implemented, which is passed when the multiview top component is created, since this handler is responsible for resolving the CloseOperationState objects of all views. For example, within this handler, a dialog can then be shown to the user.

```
    public CloseOperationState canCloseElement() {
        return CloseOperationState.STATE_OK;
    }
}
```

For creating and describing each view component you need one MultiViewDescription. The main point of this class is the instantiation of graphic view components, which are just created on demand by the createElement() method. The method is called only once, when the user opens the view for the first time. The method getPersistenceType() is used to specify how the top component is saved. Use the constants of the TopComponent class (discussed in the "Persistence" section). See Listing 10-16.

Listing 10-16. Description and Factory of a View

```
public class MultiViewPanel1Description implements MultiViewDescription, Serializable {

    public MultiViewElement createElement() {
        return new MultiViewPanel1());
    }

    public String preferredID() {
        return "PANEL_1";
    }

    public int getPersistenceType() {
        return TopComponent.PERSISTENCE_NEVER;
    }

    public String getDisplayName() {
        return "View 1";
    }

    public Image getIcon() {
        return null;
    }

    public HelpCtx getHelpCtx() {
        return HelpCtx.DEFAULT_HELP;
    }
}
```

Finally, there remains the creation of a multiview top component from independently created views. To that end, the *MultiView SPI* provides a factory: the MultiViewFactory class. This class contains methods permitting the creation of a TopComponent or of a CloneableTopComponent, depending on need.

```
MultiViewDescription dsc[] = {
    new MultiViewPanel1Description(),
    new MultiViewPanel2Description(),
    new MultiViewPanel3Description()};
TopComponent tc = MultiViewFactory.createMultiView(dsc, dsc[0]);
tc.open();
```

First, create an array with the instances of the MultiViewDescription classes of your views. Then, pass this array to the createMultiView() method. As second parameter you determine the initial active view. Optionally, you can pass an implementation of the CloseOperationHandler as third parameter. This handler is responsible for processing the CloseOperationState objects that are created of the views via the canCloseElement() method when closing the multiview top component. Thus, the multiview top component is created, and you just have to open and display this component via the open() method. To also get access to the views from outside, you can use the static method MultiViews.findMultiViewHandler() in oder to create a MultiViewHandler for a view top component. Via this handler, you can then get the currently selected view or all available views at once.

Summary

The NetBeans Platform window system definitely represents a central part of the graphical user interface with which you implement and manage your user-specific GUI in separate windows. In this chapter you learned about the basic structure of the window system. You looked at the operation and the features of top components, modes, and groups. Finally, you also learned how to use the MultiView API combining multiple top components.

CHAPTER 11

Status Bar and Progress Bar

The status bar enables you to give information directly to the user of your application. At the same time, it is possible to extend the status bar with your own components. In addition to the status bar, a progress bar that is able to manage and display multiple tasks at once is integrated in the application. In the following sections you will learn how to use these two components.

Status Bar

A status bar is already integrated in the application window of the NetBeans Platform. You access this status bar via the abstract class `StatusDisplayer`. You get the standard implementation of the status bar (this is the standard NetBeans Platform status bar if no other is provided) via the `getDefault()` method. It is also possible to provide your own implementation of the status bar. (Chapter 5 describes how to create your own implementation for a service, such as the status bar.)

Using the Status Bar

You can output a text on the status bar via the method `setStatusText()`:

```
StatusDisplayer.getDefault().setStatusText("my first status");
```

There is a variant belonging to this method. With this variant you can determine the importance of the displayed text via an additional parameter. This means the status message is displayed until a new message (with the same or higher importance) is set. Additionally, you have the option to delete the message yourself. For this purpose, the `setStatusText()` method returns a handle:

```
StatusDisplayer.Message setStatusText(String t, int importance)
```

You can delete the corresponding message after a parameterizable number of milliseconds. You can do this via a handle in the form of a `StatusDisplayer.Message` instance by the method `clear(int timeInMillis)`.

You can register a `ChangeListener` via the method `addChangeListener()` to react to these changes (changes of the text) of the status bar. If you want to use the status bar, you must ensure that your module defines a dependency on the UI Utilities module.

Extending the Status Bar

You can extend the status bar (if there is enough space) very simply. The UI Utilities API provides the service interface `StatusLineElementProvider`. This interface specifies the method `getStatusLineElement()`, with which the component that will be added to the status bar is returned.

You add your implementation via the ServiceProvider annotation. More information about how a service provider provides its implementation and how to determine the position of your component in the status bar is provided in Chapter 5. As an example, Listing 11-1 shows adding a clock to the status bar (see Figure 11-1).

Listing 11-1. Extending the Status Bar with a Clock

```
import org.openide.awt.StatusLineElementProvider;

public class MyStatusLineClock implements StatusLineElementProvider {
    private static final DateFormat format = DateFormat.getTimeInstance(DateFormat.MEDIUM);
    private static JLabel time = new JLabel(" " + format.format(new Date()) + " ");
    private JPanel panel = new JPanel(new BorderLayout());

    public MyStatusLineClock() {
        Timer t = new Timer(1000, new ActionListener() {
            public void actionPerformed(ActionEvent event) {
                time.setText(" " + format.format(new Date()) + " ");
            }
        });
        t.start();
        panel.add(new JSeparator(SwingConstants.VERTICAL), BorderLayout.WEST);
        panel.add(time, BorderLayout.CENTER);
    }

    public Component getStatusLineElement() {
        return panel;
    }
}
```

Now, the implementation must be published to be found by the status bar. For this purpose, add the following annotation to the class:

```
import org.openide.util.lookup.ServiceProvider
@ServiceProvider(service = StatusLineElementProvider.class)
public class MyStatusLineClock implements StatusLineElementProvider { … }
```

Thus, your clock is declaratively added to the Lookup. Consequently, it can be found by the status bar which then adds the component.

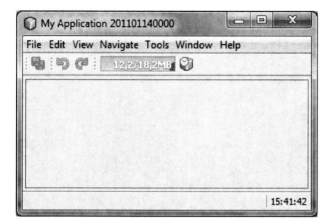

***Figure 11-1.** Extending the Status Bar with Your Own Components*

Notifications

Besides the display of static text on the left side of the status bar, you can also display notifications in the form of a balloon on the right (see Figure 11-2). Not only can messages be displayed more conspicuously to the user, but the user can also trigger an action by clicking the message. This kind of notification is used by the Plugin Manager, for example, from which you can download or install new modules. This way the user can directly start the process with one click.

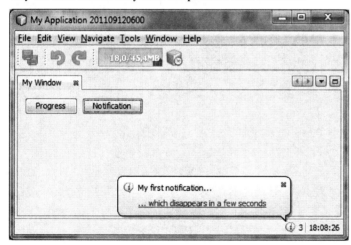

***Figure 11-2.** Displaying Notifications As Balloons Within the NetBeans Platform*

The displayed balloon is hidden again after a few seconds. However, the icon remains in the status bar so the user still has the option to call the notification later (see Listing 11-2).

Listing 11-2. Displaying a Notification in the Status Bar

```
Notification noti = NotificationDisplayer.getDefault().notify(
    "My first notification...",
    ImageUtilities.loadImageIcon("com/galileo/netbeans/module/info16.png", true),
    "... which disappears in a few seconds",
    Lookups.forPath("NotificationActions").lookup(ActionListener.class));
```

Pass a title, an icon, a detailed description, and an action to the notify() method (in the example, an action is used via the Lookup of the System Filesystem), as shown in Listing 11-2. Or instead, you can just pass null if no action will be provided. Optionally, you can determine the priority of the message with NotificationDisplayer.Priority. The values HIGH, LOW, NORMAL and SILENT are provided; however, SILENT means that only the icon is displayed in the status bar. When clicking this icon, the balloon appears. If the message will consist of more than one string you can also use a JComponent instance both for the detailed description in the balloon and for displaying it in the notification list. You can use a variant of the notify() method for this.

The message remains visible in the status bar in the notification list until it is closed by the user. You also have the option of closing the notification by the clear() method over the handle Notification, which the notify() method returns as return value.

Progress Bar

By default, the NetBeans status bar has an integrated progress bar. It is used via the Progress API. There are classes available for visualizing the progress of simple tasks as well as for monitoring multiple tasks that have their progress displayed as one. The progress of separate tasks can be monitored as well.

Displaying the Progress of Separate Tasks

There are three variants of displays available that you can set depending on the information about the task in progress, as shown in Figure 11-3:

- A finite display of percentile progress until completion, if the number of required steps is known.

- A finite display of remaining seconds until completion, if the number of required steps and their total duration are known.

- An infinite display if neither the number nor the total duration of required steps is known.

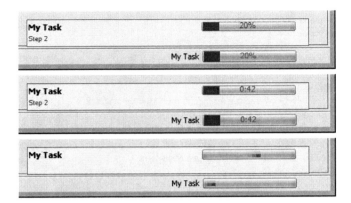

Figure 11-3. *Different Kinds of Progress Display*

The most basic use case entails the use of ProgressHandleFactory, creating an instance of ProgressHandle for a specific task (see Listing 11-3). The ProgressHandle provides control of the progress display.

Listing 11-3. *Using the Progress Bar for Separate Tasks*

```
Runnable run = new Runnable() {
    public void run() {
        ProgressHandle p = ProgressHandleFactory.createHandle("My Task");
        p.start(100);
            // do some work
        p.progress("Step 1", 10);
            // do next work
        p.progress(100);
        p.finish();
    }
};

Thread t = new Thread(run);
t.start(); // start the task and progress visualisation
```

Table 11-1 lists the methods used to start different display types.

Table 11-1. *Methods Starting the Different Display Types*

Method	Display
start()	Lets the progress bar run until a call to the finish() method is made
start(int workunits)	Displays the progress of execution in percentiles
start(int workunits, long sec)	Displays the remaining time in seconds

The methods shown in Table 11-2 allow switching between finite and infinite progress bars during runtime, including displaying percentile or seconds.

Table 11-2. Methods for Changing the Display Type

Method	Description
switchToDeterminate(int workunits)	Switches to percentile progress display

switchToDeterminate(
    int workunits,
    long estimate)
	Switches to time progress display with the remaining seconds

switchToIndeterminate()	Switches to infinite mode

▪ **Caution** a common error working with progress bars concerns the real task performed in the event dispatch thread that is responsible for updating the GUI. Executing the task there blocks the thread, which in turn blocks displaying the progress bar, because this step is already finished until the event dispatch thread comes into play again updating the GUI. To separately execute the task, the SwingWorker class of the Java API can be used, for example. Its use is shown via an asynchronous initialization in Chapter 15. In this context, the class ProgressUtils also provides useful functions.

There are several methods for creating a ProgressHandle with the ProgressHandleFactory. One of these methods allows passing the Cancellable service interface, allowing the user to abort the task with a button displayed next to the progress bar (see Figure 11-3).

createHandle(String displayName, **Cancellable** allowToCancel)

With the suspend(String message) method you can pause the progress bar and display a corresponding message.

Displaying the Progress of Multiple Related Tasks

Additionally, the Progress API provides an extended method for monitoring progress. An AggregateProgressHandle can be created via the AggregateProgressFactory. With the help of this handle, you can assemble the progress of multiple tasks and display them in a single progress bar. For this purpose, the class ProgressContributor is additionally required. Every task requires an instance of it to communicate current progress to the AggregateProgressHandle.

The following example shows the use of this type of progress display. For this purpose, we want to create a number of tasks with different durations of execution and then display its progress in the progress bar.

For this purpose, we firstly create the abstract class AbstractTask that inherits from the class Thread. This allows the parallel execution of tasks from the list. It is also possible not to derive from Thread and start the tasks sequentially. This abstract class shall take care of creating and managing the ProgressContributor class and it shall communicating current progress.

```
public abstract class AbstractTask extends Thread {
    protected ProgressContributor p = null;

    public AbstractTask(String id) {
        p = AggregateProgressFactory.createProgressContributor(id);
    }

    public ProgressContributor getProgressContributor() {
        return p;
    }
}
```

You now create an example task that takes ten steps to finish via the class MyTask. You just have to implement the run() method, in which the task is executed and progress is communicated.

```
public class MyTask extends AbstractTask {
    public MyTask(String id) {
        super(id);
    }

    public void run() {
        p.start(10);
        //do some work
        p.progress(5);
        //do some work
        p.progress(10);
        p.finish();
    }
}
```

The class MyTask2 is an additional example task that takes more steps to finish than the class MyTask1.

```
public class MyTask2 extends AbstractTask {
    public MyTask2(String id) {
        super(id);
    }

    public void run() {
        p.start(30);
        //do another work
        p.progress(2);
        //do another work
        p.progress(15);
        p.finish();
    }
}
```

Located in the MyProgram class is a list of the tasks and the processTaskList() method to execute the tasks. As an example, you store three tasks in the constructor and add them to your task list. By calling the method processTaskList() (which could, for example, be called by a button), an array for the

ProgressContributor is created, and every task's ProgressContributor is added to that array. Then, you pass this array to the AggregateProgressFactory (which creates an AggregateProgressHandle) via the createHandle() method (see Listing 11-4). When starting this handle, the progress bar is displayed and ready to receive progress notifications from the tasks. What remains is to start the tasks. The progress bar automatically terminates when the last task is finished.

Listing 11-4. Executing a List of Tasks

```
public class MyProgram {
   private List<AbstractTask> tasks = new ArrayList<AbstractTask>();

   public MyProgram() {
      tasks.add(new MyTask("Task1"));
      tasks.add(new MyTask2("Task2"));
      tasks.add(new MyTask2("Task3"));
   }

   public void processTaskList() {
      ProgressContributor cps[] = new ProgressContributor[tasks.size()];
      int i = 0;
      for(AbstractTask task : tasks) {
         cps[i] = task.getProgressContributor();
         i++;
      }

      AggregateProgressHandle aph = AggregateProgressFactory.createHandle(
            "MyTasks", // displayed name
            cps,       // progress contributors
            null,      // not canceable
            null);     // no output
      aph.start();
      for(AbstractTask task : tasks) {
         task.start();
      }
   }
}
```

If you want to be informed about the separate events of all tasks, a monitor can be passed to the instance of AggregateProgressHandle. To do so, you just have to implement the interface ProgressMonitor at the desired position and pass an instance of it to the AggregateProgressHandle (see Listing 11-5).

Listing 11-5. Supervising Events of Separate Tasks via a Monitor

```
public class MyProgressMonitor implements ProgressMonitor {
   public void started(ProgressContributor pc) {
      System.out.println(pc.getTrackingId() + " started");
   }

   public void progressed(ProgressContributor pc) {
      System.out.println(pc.getTrackingId() + " progressed");
   }
```

```
    public void finished(ProgressContributor pc) {
        System.out.println(pc.getTrackingId() + " finished");
    }
}

AggregateProgressHandle aph = AggregateProgressFactory.create...
aph.setMonitor(new MyProgressMonitor());
```

Integrating a Progress Bar into Your Component

For integrating a progress bar into a component, both ProgressHandleFactory and
AggregateProgressFactory offer three methods to get a label with the name, a label with the details, and
the progress bar for a certain ProgressHandle or AggregateProgressHandle:

```
JLabel      createMainLabelComponent(ProgressHandle ph)
JLabel      createDetailLabelComponent(ProgressHandle ph)
JComponent  createProgressComponent(ProgressHandle ph)
```

Summary

Besides the menu bar, the toolbar, and the window system, a status bar and a progress bar are integrated
into the application window of the NetBeans Platform. In this chapter you got to know both of them. In
the first part you saw how you can use and extend the status bar. You also looked at the support to
display notifications in the form of a balloon. In the second part you learned about the various methods
for showing the progress of more or less ongoing tasks.

CHAPTER 12

Nodes and Explorer

In Chapter 7 you learned that the NetBeans Platform provides a very substantial concept for creating, managing, editing, and presenting data. You then looked at the File Systems API and the Data Systems API. This chapter is about the presentation of data in the form of nodes. Nodes can be provided with actions and displayed in an explorer view. So, a node is responsible for the type-specific representation of the data. In this context, a `Node` represents a `DataObject` that is itself responsible for creating the nodes (see Chapter 7).

Nodes API

The *Nodes API* is the third and uppermost layer in the NetBeans Resource Management System. In this context, the role of the Nodes API is the visual representation of data. Closely connected to this API is the *Explorer API*, which is used for displaying and managing nodes. A node is used to present data to the user interface of an application, as well as to give the user actions, functionalities, and properties for interacting with underlying data. However, a node does not need to merely present data, but can also be used for many other things as well. For example, an action hiding beneath a node could be invoked when the node is double-clicked. Besides, a node is not typically concerned with business logic, but focuses on providing a presentation layer, delegating user interaction to action classes and, where applicable, to its related data object.

Node Classes

The general interfaces and features are described by the abstract base class `Node` (see Figure 12-1). All subclasses of `Node` can be managed and displayed in an explorer view, the possibilities for which are covered in the "Explorer API" section.

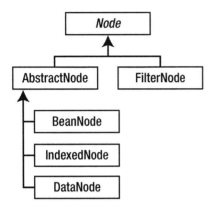

Figure 12-1. Hierarchy of the node base classes

The two classes AbstractNode and FilterNode derive from Node. The class AbstractNode represents the simplest form of a node by providing the abstract methods of the base class with a standard implementation. So, starting from this class, you can directly create an instance. A proxy node can be realized by the class FilterNode that delegates its method calls to the original node. This kind of node is typically used when a data set will be visualized at multiple positions. The class BeanNode is used for representing a JavaBean. The child element of the node can be classified with an Index via the class IndexedNode. Finally, there is also the subclass DataNode which is the most commonly used; with this kind of node, data objects are represented. In the simplest case, this class is used directly; this was also the case in Chapter 7 with the MP3 file type. This class is instantiated by the method createNodeDelegate() of the Mp3DataObject. This object is responsible for providing the corresponding node itself.

Besides the reference to the data object, the Lookup of the Mp3DataObject is also passed to the constructor. With this Lookup, a data object can, in a way, provide its actions to the user or bring its actions to the surface. For example, an action that is executed on the node gets the features of the node via the getLookup() method and thus gets the Lookup of the data object below. So, the node just forwards the Lookup. However, a node itself —as well as a data object—can possess and provide functionalities in the form of context interfaces. These functionalities are associated—exactly as with the data object—by the node via getCookieSet().assign() and also called from outside via the getLookup() method. In this case, no Lookup must be passed to the node constructor, because the constructor uses its own Lookup.

If a node will not display a data object, but something special—as, for example, with a root node— you create your own node class that directly derives from AbstractNode. Using this base class, you also implement the folder nodes in the subsequent example.

Node Container

Each node has its own Children object, representing a container for child nodes, which are the node's subnodes. In this context, the container is responsible for adding, deleting, and structuring the child nodes. Each node that is located in this container gets the node (the owner of the container) as parent. For those nodes that do not have child nodes—as, in this case, the DataNode of the Mp3DataObject— an empty container can be passed via Children.LEAF. There are multiple variants of the abstract base class Children. Usually, you should not derive from this base class. The most common class is the Children.Keys<T> class, where mostly a one-to-one relationship is given between key and node. In the example shown in Figure 12-2 the key for a node is a file object. However, you do not directly use the class, but instead derive from the class `ChildFactory` and create a `Children` object via the factory method `Children.create()`. This enables you to simply create the child nodes in the background (if, for example, it would otherwise block the GUI for too long).

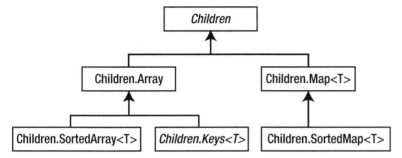

Figure 12-2. *Hierarchy of the different children container classes*

Node Icons

You use the method `setIconBaseWithExtension()` to set the path to a set of icons (displayed for a node), depending on the node's current state. You define the base name of four different icons via this method. For example, if you indicate *com/galileo/netbeans/module/icon.png,* the following icons (which should already be provided) are automatically found:

- com/galileo/netbeans/module/icon.png

- com/galileo/netbeans/module/iconOpen.png

- com/galileo/netbeans/module/icon32.png

- com/galileo/netbeans/module/iconOpen32.png

Node Context Menu

A node provides a context menu to the user over which context-independent actions can be provided. A `DataNode` gets its entries or respective actions for its context menu by the factory of the data object that is managed by the node. In turn, the node class provides the actions via the `getActions()` method. As you already learned in Chapter 7, it is possible in this respect to register actions in the standard folder `Loaders` below a MIME type–specific folder. If the MIME type is, for example, `audio/mpeg`, as in Chapter 7, the actions are registered in `Loaders/audio/mpeg/Actions`. Of course, you can use the mechanisms of the Actions API (described in Chapter 6) for this purpose. The actions are automatically read and added to the context menu of the node. To explain this, I will continue with the example of the MP3 data object from Chapter 7. Only the following additional annotation is needed to add the action `PlayAction` to the node context menu of the `Mp3DataObject`.

```
@ActionReferences({
    ...
    @ActionReference(
        path = "Loaders/audio/mpeg/Actions",
        position = 50, separatorAfter=60)
})
```

```
public final class PlayAction implements ActionListener { ...
```

Thus, the play functionality also appears in the context menu of an MP3 file (see Figure 12-3). Of course, with the context sensitivity implemented in Chapter 7 (see also Chapter 6). This means if the file is being played, the play action is deactivated in the context menu, too.

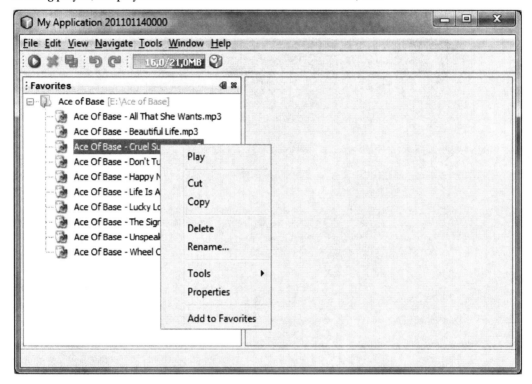

Figure 12-3. *Adding actions to the context menu of a node*

A node delivers the action that is executed when double clicking via the getPreferredAction() method. If this method is not overridden, the first action of the array is used by getActions().

Event Handling

To react on the events of a node, you can install a PropertyChangeListener as well as a NodeListener. You can use the PropertyChangeListener to monitor the properties that a node supplies via the getPropertySet() method. With the NodeListener you can be informed about internal node changes such as the name, the parent node, and also the child nodes, for example. For this purpose, the node class provides a series of public property keys, such as PROP_NAME or PROP_LEAF. The NodeListener provides the methods shown in Table 12-1.

***Table 12-1.** Methods of the NodeListener Interface*

Method	Event
childrenAdded(NodeMemberEvent evt)	Triggered when child nodes are added
childrenRemoved(NodeMemberEvent evt)	Triggered when child nodes are deleted
childrenReordered(NodeReorderEvent evt)	Triggered when the order of the child nodes changes
nodeDestroyed(NodeEvent evt)	Triggered when the monitored node itself is deleted
propertyChange(PropertyChangeEvent evt)	Occurs when node features change (for example, the name)

If you do not want to become informed about or implement all events, you can use the adapter class NodeAdapter instead of the NodeListener interface.

Example

Next I will show you an example of how to use the Nodes API to create your own node classes and build a children container. Doing so, you will also see that there cannot only be files behind a node. In this example, the nodes will be used for representing actions in a tree structure while you want to define the content via the layer file. This way, the content can be flexibly adapted and an extension point is offered to other modules. To display the nodes in a tree structure, use the Explorer API (discussed in the next section). The complete example will result in an explorer window like the one shown in Figure 12-4.

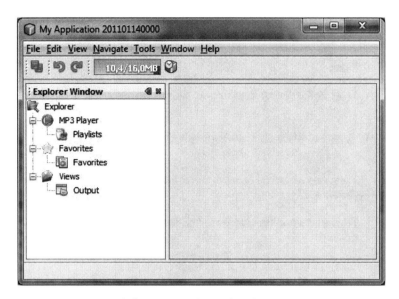

Figure 12-4. Example for using nodes and explorer views

You determine the context of the explorer window in a separate folder in the layer file. We will call this folder Explorer; it represents the extension point of the window or of the module, respectively. Actions, which are represented by nodes in the tree structure of the explorer window, can be registered in any subfolder there (see Listing 12-1). The content of the layer file looks like the example shown in Figure 12-4.

Listing 12-1. Extension Point in the Layer File; All Entries in the Explorer Folder Are Displayed in the Explorer Window.

```
<folder name="Explorer">
  <attr name="icon" stringvalue="com/galileo/netbeans/module/explorer.png"/>
  <folder name="MP3 Player">
    <attr name="icon" stringvalue="com/galileo/netbeans/module/player.png"/>
    <file name="PlaylistAction.shadow">
      <attr name="originalFile"
            stringvalue="Actions/Edit/com-galileo-netbeans-module-PlaylistAction.instance"/>
    </file>
  </folder>
  <folder name="Views">
    <attr name="icon" stringvalue="com/galileo/netbeans/module/views.png"/>
    <file name="OutputAction.shadow">
      <attr name="originalFile"
            stringvalue="Actions/Window/org-netbeans-core-io-ui-IOWindowAction.instance"/>
    </file>
  </folder>
  <folder name="Favorites">
    <attr name="icon" stringvalue="com/galileo/netbeans/module/favorites.png"/>
```

```
  <file name="FavoritesAction.shadow">
    <attr name="originalFile"
          stringvalue="Actions/Window/org-netbeans-modules-favorites-View.instance"/>
  </file>
 </folder>
</folder>
```

You can see that the actions—which are registered at this point via shadow files—refer to already registered actions. Moreover, you want to be able to assign an icon to a folder by the self-defined attribute icon. The references can, of course, also be created by corresponding annotations (see Chapter 6). To display this structure with nodes you need a node class and a child factory class for each action . Start with the node class which represents the content of a folder. Call it ExplorerFolderNode and derive it from the node standard implementation AbstractNode. Thus, for now, you do not need anything other than a constructor. You pass the FileObject to the constructor of this node. The FileObject represents a folder entry of the layer file and a Children object that is responsible for creating the child elements. You pass this object to the base class constructor. Then you set the name and the icon base path of the node via the values of the layer file. (See Listing 12-2.)

Listing 12-2. Node Class for Representing a Folder

```java
import org.openide.filesystems.FileObject;
import org.openide.nodes.AbstractNode;
import org.openide.nodes.Children;

public class ExplorerFolderNode extends AbstractNode {

    public ExplorerFolderNode(FileObject node, Children ch) {
        super(ch);
        setDisplayName(node.getName());
        String iconBase = (String) node.getAttribute("icon");
        if(iconBase != null) {
            setIconBaseWithExtension(iconBase);
        }
    }
}
```

You create a ChildFactory class for the Children object. This class will be called ExplorerFolderFactory. The nodes will be created by means of a FileObject, which means you derive from ChildFactory<FileObject> (see Listing 12-3).

Listing 12-3. Child Factory for Elements of the Type ExplorerFolderNode

```java
import org.openide.filesystems.FileObject;
import org.openide.nodes.ChildFactory;
import org.openide.nodes.Children;
import org.openide.nodes.Node;

public class ExplorerFolderFactory extends ChildFactory<FileObject> {
    private FileObject folder = null;
```

```
   public ExplorerFolderFactory(FileObject folder) {
      this.folder = folder;
   }

   @Override
   protected boolean createKeys(List<FileObject> toPopulate) {
      toPopulate.addAll(Arrays.asList(folder.getChildren()));
      return true;
   }

   @Override
   protected Node createNodeForKey(FileObject key) {
      return new ExplorerFolderNode(key,
         Children.create(new ExplorerChildFactory(key), false));
   }
}
```

You pass the FileObject of the parent node to the constructor of the factory class (which is depicted in Listing 12-3). You want to load and manage all entries here, located below this node. The createKeys() method is automatically called when the parent node is opened. This means the child nodes are just created then on demand. You read all subordinate folders from there, and add them to the list toPopulate. This list is managed by the ChildFactory class. The createNodeForKey() method is called for each key, added within this method. So, this is where you create the ExplorerFolderNode object. In turn, such an object will contain the action. Thus, you pass an ExplorerChildFactory instance to the object. Listing 12-4 shows the implementation of the object in the context of the ExplorerLeafNode class.

Listing 12-4. Node Class for the Representation of an Action

```
import org.openide.awt.Actions;
import org.openide.nodes.AbstractNode;
import org.openide.nodes.Children;

public class ExplorerLeafNode extends AbstractNode {
   private Action action = null;

   public ExplorerLeafNode(Action action) {
      super(Children.LEAF);
      this.action = action;
      setDisplayName(Actions.cutAmpersand((String)action.getValue(Action.NAME)));
   }

   @Override
   public Action getPreferredAction() {
      return action;
   }

   @Override
   public Image getIcon(int type) {
      ImageIcon img = (ImageIcon) action.getValue(Action.SMALL_ICON);
      if(img != null) {
         return img.getImage();
      } else {
```

```
        return null;
    }
  }
}
```

You derive the node classes (shown in Listing 12-4) that will each represent an action, from `AbstractNode`, too. The constructor gets delivered the actual action by the child factory. Of course, those nodes are not supposed to have further child nodes, so you pass an empty container with `Children.LEAF`. Moreover, set the name and the icon of the node. You overwrite the `getPreferredAction()` method in order to deliver the action which is behind this node. When you double-click this node, the corresponding action is actually executed.

Listing 12-5 shows how these kinds of nodes are created by the class `ExplorerChildFactory`.

Listing 12-5. *Child Factory for Elements of the Type ExplorerLeafNode*

```java
import org.openide.filesystems.FileObject;
import org.openide.nodes.ChildFactory;
import org.openide.nodes.Node;
import org.openide.util.lookup.Lookups;

public class ExplorerChildFactory extends ChildFactory<Action> {
    private FileObject folder = null;

    public ExplorerChildFactory(FileObject folder) {
        this.folder = folder;
    }

    @Override
    protected boolean createKeys(List<Action> toPopulate) {
        for(Action action : Lookups.forPath(folder.getPath()).lookupAll(Action.class)) {
            toPopulate.add(action);
        }
        return true;
    }

    @Override
    protected Node createNodeForKey(Action key) {
        return new ExplorerLeafNode(key);
    }
}
```

The child elements of the type `ExplorerLeafNode` will be created via an action instance, so you derive from `ChildFactory<Action>`. Pass the corresponding parent element to the constructor in the form of a `FileObject` instance. In the `createKeys()` method you can now access the parent element and create a Lookup for the the parent element. This offers a very elegant way to get to all actions that are registered there. Finally, you create the node object for the actions via the `createNodeForKey()` method.

So far you have learned how to implement your own node classes and how to create instances of them. With these classes, you are able to completely depict the defined structure in the layer file. But you still need another view to depict the nodes in a tree structure in a window. The Explorer API accomplishes representing the nodes. To illustrate this, the following sections offer a short introduction to the Explorer API, after which we will finish with the example already begun.

Explorer API

With the Explorer API you can visually display and manage your nodes in different variants. For this purpose, the API provides a set of explorer views with which you can display your nodes in typical structures. The class hierarchy of these views is shown in Figure 12-5. For example, the class ChoiceView presents its nodes in a combo box, while the MenuView presents it in a menu structure of any depth. The most commonly used view—and probably the most popular one—is the BeanTreeView which presents its nodes in a tree structure. Besides representing nodes and processing actions (such as cutting out, inserting, deleting, or dragging and dropping nodes), those views are responsible for displaying the context menu of a node. The view gets the actions of a node via the getActions() method of a node.

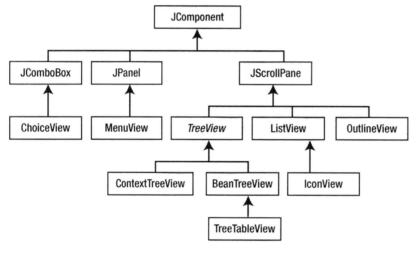

Figure 12-5. Class hierarchy of the different explorer views

Managing an explorer view is always done by the ExplorerManager class. An instance of this manager must be provided by the component that contains the explorer view. In most cases, this is its top component.

The remarkable thing about this is that the manager does not have to be connected to the view, since, the view automatically searches for a manager in the component hierarchy, which is to say, in the parent components. The parent component must implement the interface ExplorerManager.Provider, so this manager can be found. This interface specifies the getExplorerManager() method, by which the view determines the manager. In the course of this, multiple different views can use the same manager.

One of the main tasks of the explorer manager is to monitor the selection of nodes in a view. The manager always provides the selected node and its Lookup. You proceed as follows, so the current context can be accessed by another top component or even by another module from outside (from an action class). With the helper class ExplorerUtils you can create a Lookup that always represents the selected node (or several nodes, delivered by the explorer manager) via the method createLookup(). Using the associateLookup() method you define the Lookup (that was created this way) as local Lookup of your top component. Thus, the Lookup can be accessed from outside via the global proxy Lookup (which you get when calling Utilities.actionsGlobalContext()).

In the previous section, you created the necessary node classes and child factory classes for the explorer example. What is still missing at this point is a window with an explorer view that can display the nodes. By means of this still missing step, I will explain the usage of a view and the manager. First, you create the top component ExplorerTopComponent by the window wizard of the NetBeans IDE. Then you provide it with an explorer manager. For this purpose, you have to implement the interface ExplorerManager.Provider and apply an instance of the ExplorerManager as private data element. With the getExplorerManager() method you return this manager. In the next step, you add a BeanTreeView to the top component; this is most easily done by dragging a scroll pane on the window by the Form Editor and entering new BeanTreeView() in the properties in the category *Code* at *Custom Creation Code*. Then, your initComponents() method should look like the example. As already mentioned, the view finds the explorer manager itself, so you do not have to make further steps to connect the view and the manager. Every view, respectively every manager, is based on a root element from which all the other nodes originate. You set this root element with setRootContext() in the initTree() method. You also pass an instance of the node class ExplorerFolderNode to the just-named method. From this node, the creation of all other nodes is initiated. Of course, you only create this node if the folder Explorer exists in the System Filesystem (meaning, if any module added the entry to the folder Explorer in its layer file). See Listing 12-6.

Listing 12-6. Explorer Window Which Displays the Nodes by a BeanTreeView. The Nodes Are Managed by an Explorer Manager.

```
public final class ExplorerTopComponent extends TopComponent
    implements ExplorerManager.Provider {

    private static final String ROOT_NODE = "Explorer";
    private final ExplorerManager manager = new ExplorerManager();

    public ExplorerTopComponent() {
        initComponents();
        initTree();
        initActions();
        associateLookup(ExplorerUtils.createLookup(manager, getActionMap()));
    }

    private JScrollPane jScrollPane1;

    private void initComponents() {
        jScrollPane1 = new BeanTreeView();
        setLayout(new BorderLayout());
        add(jScrollPane1, BorderLayout.CENTER);
        ...
    }

    private void initTree() {
        FileObject root = FileUtil.getConfigFile(ROOT_NODE);
        if(root != null) { /* folder found */
            manager.setRootContext(
                new ExplorerFolderNode(root, Children.create(
                new ExplorerFolderFactory(root), false)));
        }
    }

    private void initActions() {
```

```
        CutAction cut = SystemAction.get(CutAction.class);
        getActionMap().put(cut.getActionMapKey(), ExplorerUtils.actionCut(manager));
        CopyAction copy = SystemAction.get(CopyAction.class);
        getActionMap().put(copy.getActionMapKey(), ExplorerUtils.actionCopy(manager));
        PasteAction paste = SystemAction.get(PasteAction.class);
        getActionMap().put(paste.getActionMapKey(), ExplorerUtils.actionPaste(manager));
        DeleteAction delete = SystemAction.get(DeleteAction.class);
        getActionMap().put(delete.getActionMapKey(), ExplorerUtils.actionDelete(manager, true));
    }

    public ExplorerManager getExplorerManager() {
        return manager;
    }

    protected void componentActivated() {
        ExplorerUtils.activateActions(manager, true);
    }

    protected void componentDeactivated() {
        ExplorerUtils.activateActions(manager, false);
    }
}
```

As a next step, you connect the standard actions (cut, copy, paste, and delete) provided by the Platform with the actions of the explorer manager in the initActions() method. The actions of the explorer manager are provided by the ExplorerUtils class which you register by the action map key in the action map of your top component. You create a proxy Lookup (which provides the respectively selected node with its Lookup) by means of the ExplorerUtils.createLookup method, so the respectively selected nodes of a view can be accessed via the Lookup of the top component. You define this proxy Lookup as local Lookup of your top component via the associateLookup() method. The action map also has to be located in the Lookup of the top component, so the previously registered actions (registered in the action map) are actually active. Practically, you can directly pass the action map to the createLookup() method, which makes the action map available via the proxy Lookup.

To save resources, you can switch on or switch off the listener of the explorer manager actions (which you previously connected to the system actions) in the methods componentActivated() and componentDeactivated(), which are called when activating and deactivating your windows. This way, they are not notified of events in the clipboard, for example, if the window is not even active.

At this point, I should mention the many interesting examples and tutorials available on the NetBeans website at http://netbeans.org/kb/trails/platform.html. The tutorials are easy to understand and the examples concerning the Nodes, Explorer, and Property Sheet API are particularly useful.

Summary

With the Nodes and Explorer API the NetBeans Platform provides a universal framework for displaying very different data. In this chapter you learned the basics about the different node classes and the functionality of a node container. Using an example, you created your own node classes and container and used the Explorer API to display some data defined in an XML file.

CHAPTER 13

Dialogs and Wizards

The *Dialogs API* helps you create and display dialogs and wizards. The dialogs are based on the Java `Dialog` class. Using the Dialogs API, you can display standard dialogs, as well as custom dialogs tailored to specific business needs. In addition, the API integrates well with the NetBeans window system, as well as the NetBeans help system. Wizards can be seen as a special kind of dialog and are therefore part of the Dialogs API.

Standard Dialogs

Use the `NotifyDescriptor` class to define the properties of a standard dialog. Provide a message in the form of a `String`, an `Icon`, or a `Component`, which will be displayed with the dialog. Optionally, use an array to display multiple messages in varying situations. Different types of messages can be specified, giving control over the icon displayed. Define the type via the predefined constants in the `NotifyDescriptor`, as listed in Table 13-1.

Table 13-1. Constants to Determine the Message Type

Constant	Message Type/Symbol
PLAIN_MESSAGE	The message is displayed neutrally, without a symbol.
INFORMATION_MESSAGE	The default information symbol is displayed with the message.
QUESTION_MESSAGE	The question symbol is displayed with the message.
WARNING_MESSAGE	The warning symbol is displayed with the message.
ERROR_MESSAGE	The error symbol is shown with the message.

An option type defines which buttons are displayed in the dialog, for which the constants shown in Table 13-2 are provided.

Table 13-2. Constants Defining Dialog Buttons

Constants	Buttons Displayed
DEFAULT_OPTION	The standard buttons are displayed according to the dialog type. For example, an information dialog only has an *OK* button, while an entry dialog has an *OK* button as well as a *Cancel* button.
OK_CANCEL_OPTION	*OK* and *Cancel* buttons are displayed.
YES_NO_OPTION	*Yes* and *No* buttons are displayed.
YES_NO_CANCEL_OPTION	*Yes*, *No*, and *Cancel* buttons are displayed.

Additionally, you can use the constructor or the setAdditionalOptions() method to pass in an Object array whose components are added to the buttons of the dialog in the form of JButton objects. Typically, String objects are passed here, though you can also use Component or Icon objects. However, if you want to omit the default buttons, only custom buttons can be provided via the setOptions() method or by passing them in to the constructor. Here, too, the classes String, Component, and Icon are used:

```
NotifyDescriptor d = new NotifyDescriptor(
    "Text",  // Dialog message
    "Title", // Dialog title
    NotifyDescriptor.OK_CANCEL_OPTION,    // Buttons
    NotifyDescriptor.INFORMATION_MESSAGE, // Symbol
    null,    // Own buttons as Object[]
    null);   // Additional buttons as Object[]
```

Dialog description, such as the one defined previously, is passed in to the notify() method of the DialogDisplayer class, which is responsible for the creation and display of dialogs, and also gives a return value when the dialog closes. The DialogDisplayer is designed as a global service, whose provider is supplied by the getDefault() method via the Lookup.

```
Object retval = DialogDisplayer.getDefault().notify(d);
```

You can identify the buttons the user clicked by comparison with the constants listed in Table 13-3.

Table 13-3. Dialog Return Value Constants

Constant	Returned When
OK_OPTION	The *OK* button is clicked.
YES_OPTION	The *Yes* button is clicked.
NO_OPTION	The *No* button is clicked.
CANCEL_OPTION	The *Cancel* button is clicked.

| CLOSED_OPTION | The dialog is closed without any button having been clicked. |

For the most common dialog types, the Dialogs API provides three subclasses of the NotifyDescriptor class, so you only need to define a few parameters. We will take a closer look at these classes with examples in the following sections.

Information Dialog

Create an information dialog via the NotifyDescriptor.Message class. Pass the text to be displayed to the constructor, as well as an optional message type. By default, the dialog shows the information symbol, as shown in Figure 13-1.

```
NotifyDescriptor nd = new NotifyDescriptor.Message("Information");
```

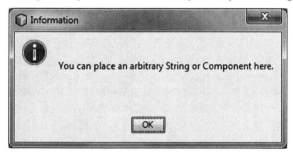

Figure 13-1. *Information dialog*

Question Dialog

Should the user be enabled to answer a question posed in the dialog (see Figure 13-2), use the NotifyDescriptor.Confirmation class. To that end, a range of constructors is available for passing in the message, title, message type, and additional option types.

```
NotifyDescriptor d = new NotifyDescriptor.Confirmation(
    "You can place any String or Component here",
    "That's a question");
```

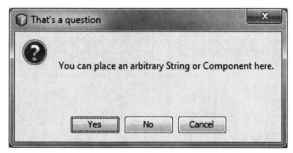

Figure 13-2. *Question dialog*

Input Dialog

An input dialog is easily created via the NotifyDescriptor.InputLine class. Define the text and title to be displayed in the input area of the dialog (see Figure 13-3). Optionally, pass in an option type and message type so that the desired buttons and symbols are shown.

```
NotifyDescriptor d = new NotifyDescriptor.InputLine(
    "First and last name: ",
    "Please enter your name");
```

Figure 13-3. Input dialog

Access text entered by the user via the getInputText() method. Optionally, enter text into the field via the setInputText() method.

Custom Dialogs

Custom dialogs are created via the DialogDescriptor class. This class is an extension of the NotifyDescriptor class. Pass in a Component object to be displayed, while also defining dialog modality and a related ActionListener that reacts when the buttons are clicked. Optionally, pass in a HelpCtx object, providing the ID of a help topic so that a Help button is automatically displayed on the dialog. For the DialogDescriptor, create a Dialog object via the DialogDisplayer's createDialog() method. Alternatively, display the dialog directly, via the notify() or notifyLater() methods.

Displaying Notifications

Creating your own dialogs, for example, in order to query certain data from the user, you can display notifications to the user (see the section *Wizards*), equivalent to a wizard. The notification line, which is automatically integrated by the Dialogs API, can be created if needed via the createNotificationLineSupport() method of your NotifyDescriptor instance. Thus, the notification line is created in the form of a NotificationLineSupport instance at the bottom of the dialog (see Figure 13-4). You can display information with the following methods in that line:

```
setInformationMessage(String msg)
setWarningMessage(String msg)
setErrorMessage(String msg)
```

Each of these methods also sets a corresponding icon in front of the displayed notification. You can read the respectively displayed notification via the corresponding get methods. With the clearMessages() method you can delete a displayed notification again.

Figure 13-4. Dialog with integrated notification line

Example

The following example illustrates creation of a Login dialog via the `DialogDescriptor` class. It is important that the dialog is displayed at the appropriate time: when the application starts. The application should be blocked until the login details are correctly entered. Two approaches are supported, as discussed in the following paragraphs.

As mentioned, a `Component` object can be passed in to the `DialogDescriptor`, displaying it in the dialog. In the example shown in Figure 13-5, this approach is used to integrate two text fields into the dialog so that the user can enter a username and password. The panel provides the username and password via its `getUsername()` and `getPassword()` methods. To display the dialog at application startup, a Module Installer is needed (see Chapter 3). In the `restored()` method of the Module Installer you create the `DialogDescriptor` to display the Login dialog.

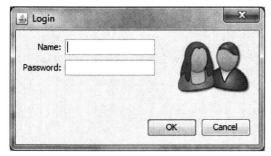

Figure 13-5. Login dialog created via DialogDescriptor and an additional panel

Because you need to execute the dialog asynchronously—otherwise the dialog would be displayed during the initialization phase—it is necessary to register an `ActionListener` to react to user button clicks. The actual login process is executed in the `actionPerformed()` method. If the entered values are incorrect, exit the application via the `LifecycleManager` class (see Chapter 8).

To allow reaction when users click the Close button (on the upper-right side of the dialog), register a `PropertyChangeListener`, in which the application is shut down. To display the dialog immediately after the initialization phase—that is, directly after the splash screen—use the `notifyLater()` method, as shown in Listing 13-1.

Listing 13-1. Login Dialog Displayed When the Application Starts, Blocking the Application Until the Username and Password Are Successfully Entered

```
public class Installer extends ModuleInstall
    implements ActionListener {
    private LoginPanel panel = new LoginPanel();
    private DialogDescriptor d = null;
    @Override
    public void restored() {
        d = new DialogDescriptor(panel, "Login", true, this);
        d.setClosingOptions(new Object[]{});
        d.addPropertyChangeListener(new PropertyChangeListener() {
            public void propertyChange(PropertyChangeEvent e) {
                if(e.getPropertyName().equals(DialogDescriptor.PROP_VALUE)
                && e.getNewValue()==DialogDescriptor.CLOSED_OPTION) {
                    LifecycleManager.getDefault().exit();
                }
            }
        });
        DialogDisplayer.getDefault().notifyLater(d);
    }
    public void actionPerformed(ActionEvent event) {
        if(event.getSource() == DialogDescriptor.CANCEL_OPTION) {
            LifecycleManager.getDefault().exit();
        } else {
            if(!SecurityManager.login(panel.getUsername(), panel.getPassword())) {
                panel.setInfo("Wrong user name or password");
            } else {
                d.setClosingOptions(null);
            }
        }
    }
}
```

Another way to display the dialog uses the notify() method, which is executed in a separate thread, as soon as the application is available. Do this via the invokeWhenUIReady() method provided by the WindowManager class. The difference between this approach and notifyLater() is that the dialog is only displayed when the application window is completely loaded.

```
WindowManager.getDefault().invokeWhenUIReady(new Runnable(){
    public void run() {
        DialogDisplayer.getDefault().notify(d);
    }
});
```

Finally, a complete dialog can be built from scratch, by extending JDialog. To that end, use the related NetBeans IDE wizard available via *File ➤ New File… ➤ Java GUI Forms ➤ JDialog Form*. If you need the main application window as a parent for your dialog, you can obtain it via the Window Manager, like this:

```
Frame f = WindowManager.getDefault().getMainWindow();
```

Wizards

Aside from support for dialogs, the Dialogs API includes a wizard framework to create step-by-step procedures that help users work through a particular process. Wizards of this kind are familiar within the NetBeans IDE itself, such as those used to create new windows or actions. For each step, provide a panel appropriate to the related data entry required for the step. Coordination between steps is handled by the wizard framework. We will use this wizard for the following example by which I will show you the possibilities for designing a wizard and its architecture, in particular. In this example you will make a wizard for creating playlists. The wizard provides two steps. The first step allows users to describe the playlist, as shown in Figure 13-6, while the second allows music titles to be chosen and added to the playlist.

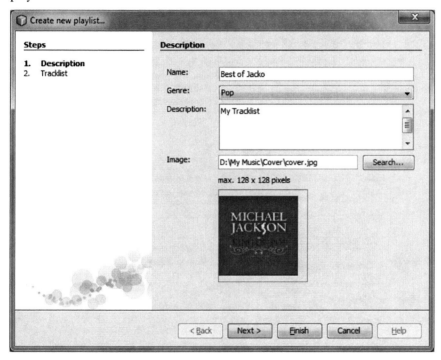

Figure 13-6. First step in the example wizard for playlist creation

Wizard Architecture

The WizardDescriptor class describes and configures a wizard in principle. The class is a subclass of the DialogDescriptor class, explained in the previous section. The DialogDescriptor class, in turn, is a subclass of NotifyDescriptor. The WizardDescriptor contains and manages all panels in the wizards and is responsible for central tasks such as controlling the action buttons and displaying the table of contents. In other words, the WizardDescriptor is the controller of the entire wizard. Typically, the WizardDescriptor also provides the data model, from which data collected over various steps is saved as properties. But you can also provide your own data model.

For each step in the wizard, a panel has to be provided. Typically, a panel is built out of two separate classes. The first class implements the GUI. This class is known as the *Visual Panel*, and normally extends JPanel. The second class, handling the management and validation of the panel, is known as the *Wizard Panel*. This class extends the WizardDescriptor.Panel<Data> class. It creates the Visual Panel on demand and makes it available to the wizard. In terms of the MVC (Model-View-Controller) paradigm, the Visual Panel is the view, and the Wizard Panel is the controller. The Visual Panel only contains the user interface implementation and provides the user-entered data via get and set methods. The Visual Panel should not include business logic and, in particular, does not deal with any wizard-specific classes or calls. As a result, the panel is completely reusable and can also be used outside of the wizard. In this way, the panel is reusable—for example, in a dialog for later editing of a playlist. The relationship between WizardDescriptor, WizardPanel, and VisualPanel is illustrated again in Figure 13-7.

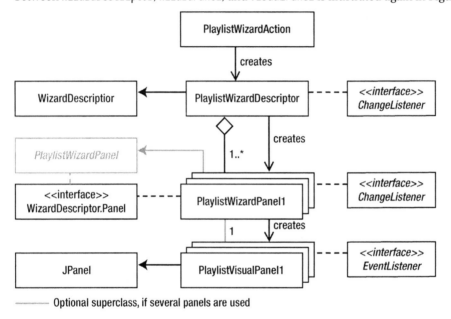

Figure 13-7. *Architecture of a wizard*

Creating Panels

The skeleton of a wizard is created in the NetBeans IDE. Go to *File ➤ New File…* and, in the *Module Development* category, choose the *Wizard* file type. In the next step, choose *Custom* as the Registration Type, and set the Wizard Step Sequence to *Static*. Enter *2* for the number of panels to be created. In the final step, provide a prefix for the name of the classes created. For this example, use Playlist as the prefix. Finally, click *Finish*. The IDE then creates the skeleton of two panels, both with a Visual Panel and a Wizard Panel. However, you will adapt the content of some predefined methods.

First, create the user interface of the first panel—this is the class PlaylistVisualPanel1—in the NetBeans Form Editor. Add several fields with which the user can describe the playlist. The user must be able to assign a name to the playlist, while choosing a genre and providing a description and image. The completed panel should look like Figure 13-6, whereby the panel is already shown integrated into the wizard. The panel is a normal Swing component, extending JPanel; however, you should bear in mind the following implementation details:

- For each piece of data requested from the user, a public property constant is defined. These are constants for the name of the playlist, the genre, a description, and an image. In particular, these constants are needed later to save and load data into the data model.

- In the constructor, a listener is added to each field to be monitored. In the example, you want to ensure that the name has at least three characters, the chosen image has a maximum size of 128 × 128 pixels, and a warning message is shown when no image has been selected. To that end, you register a DocumentListener for the two text fields playlistName and imagePath.

- It is important to override the getName() method. Thus you provide the names of the panels displayed in the headers of the steps in the wizard.

- For each field, add a getter method which the wizard panel uses to access data entered by the user.

- In the DocumentListener methods changedUpdate(), insertUpdate(), and removeUpdate(), use the firePropertyChange() method to notify all registered PropertyChangeListeners. The interaction between the three layers of a wizard is discussed in detail in the next section.

Listing 13-2 shows a section from the Visual Panel PlaylistWizardPanel1. Notice the panel is completely free from any wizard logic. The complete source code of this class as well as the complete example project can be downloaded from the Source Code/Download area for this book on the Apress web site.

Listing 13-2. Visual Panel of the First Wizard Step

```
public final class PlaylistVisualPanel1 extends JPanel
    implements DocumentListener {
    public static final String PROP_PLAYLIST_NAME = "playlist";
    public static final String PROP_GENRE        = "genre";
    public static final String PROP_DESCRIPTION  = "description";
    public static final String PROP_IMAGE_PATH   = "imagePath";
    public PlaylistVisualPanel1() {
        initComponents();
        playlistName.getDocument().addDocumentListener(this);
        imagePath.getDocument().addDocumentListener(this);
    }
    public String getName() {
        return NbBundle.getMessage(PlaylistWizardPanel1.class, "Panel1.Name");
    }
    public String getPlaylistName() {
        return playlistName.getText();
    }
    public String getGenre() {
        return (String)genre.getSelectedItem();
    }
    public String getDescription() {
        return description.getText();
    }
```

```
    public String getImagePath() {
        return imagePath.getText();
    }
    public void changedUpdate( DocumentEvent e ) {
        if (playlistName.getDocument() == e.getDocument()) {
            firePropertyChange(PROP_PLAYLIST_NAME, 0, 1);
        } else if(imagePath.getDocument() == e.getDocument()) {
            firePropertyChange(PROP_IMAGE_PATH, 0, 1);
        }
    }
}
```

Look at the content of the related Wizard Panel, providing the controller for the Visual Panel. The class implements the `WizardDescriptor.Panel<Data>` interface, defining the interface of wizard panels. As a template, you can define a class that will be used as a data model. Since you need no special custom data model, typically the class `WizardDescriptor` is used to define the wizard panel. In addition, implement a `PropertyChangeListener`, allowing reaction to changes in the visual panel.

A wizard panel has a status: valid or invalid. Validity depends on your individual requirements. In this case, a panel is only valid when the name has at least three characters. The status is saved via the private data element isValid.

```
import java.beans.PropertyChangeEvent;
import java.beans.PropertyChangeListener;
import javax.swing.event.ChangeEvent;
import javax.swing.event.ChangeListener;
import javax.swing.event.EventListenerList;
import org.openide.WizardDescriptor;
...
public class PlaylistWizardPanel1 implements
    WizardDescriptor.Panel<WizardDescriptor>, PropertyChangeListener {
    private PlaylistVisualPanel1 view  = null;
    private WizardDescriptor      model = null;
    private boolean isValid = false;
    private ResourceBundle bundle = NbBundle.getBundle(PlaylistWizardPanel1.class);
```

The getComponent() method is a factory method with which you create the visual panel on demand. The method is called from the `WizardDescriptor` when the panel is first created in the wizard. The method is called from the `WizardDescriptor` when the panel in the wizard should be displayed for the first time. Thus not all panels need to be created at the very start of a wizard. This will significantly improve the performance of wizards that provide many different steps. Therefore, be very careful when using the getComponent() method. For example, do not call it in the getName() method, which is called when the wizard is created. After creating the Visual Panel, you set some properties that influence display of components in the wizard.

- Use PROP_CONTENT_SELECTED_INDEX to provide the number of the panel (shown in the table of contents on the left side of the wizard), enabling the user to see the number of the current step.

- Set the property PROP_AUTO_WIZARD_STYLE to true, which creates wizards with the typical components, such as a contents section as well as a header. Setting this to false makes sense when the wizard has only one step, so only the panel and the buttons are displayed.

- Via the properties PROP_CONTENT_DISPLAYED and PROP_CONTENT_NUMBERED, specify that names and numbers of wizard steps are shown on the left side of the wizard.

```
public PlaylistVisualPanel1 getComponent() {
    if (view == null) {
        view = new PlaylistVisualPanel1();
        view.putClientProperty(WizardDescriptor.PROP_CONTENT_SELECTED_INDEX, new Integer(0));
        view.putClientProperty(WizardDescriptor.PROP_AUTO_WIZARD_STYLE, Boolean.TRUE);
        view.putClientProperty(WizardDescriptor.PROP_CONTENT_DISPLAYED, Boolean.TRUE);
        view.putClientProperty(WizardDescriptor.PROP_CONTENT_NUMBERED, Boolean.TRUE);
    }
    return view;
}
```

With the getName() method, you provide the name to be displayed in the header of the wizard. With the getHelp() method, you first return HelpCtx.DEFAULT_HELP. This means the *Help* button is disabled in the wizard. Return a HelpCtx object if you want to provide help for your panel. (Further information about the HelpCtx class and the NetBeans help system are described in Chapter 16.) The status of panels, discussed earlier (in the section on defining whether the wizard step is valid or not), is provided via the isValid() method. This method is called from the WizardDescriptor when a panel is called or via notifications received from the ChangeListener. Only when the method returns the value true are the *Next* or *Finish* buttons of the wizard activated. The setMessage() method is a helper method for which a notification is displayed to the user. The notification line of the wizard is provided by default and displayed underneath a panel in the wizard window. This line is represented by the class NotificationLineSupport. You get access via the getNotificationLineSupport() method of the WizardDescriptor.

Then, set the text via the method setErrorMessage(). If a text is set this way and the isValid() method delivers the value false, an error symbol is displayed. If the isValid() method delivers the value true, though, only a warning sign is shown. If you want to constantly display a warning sign or an info sign, you can use the methods setWarningMessage() or setInformationMessage().

```
public String getName() {
    return bundle.getString("Panel1.Name");
}
public HelpCtx getHelp() {
    return HelpCtx.DEFAULT_HELP;
}
public boolean isValid() {
    return isValid;
}
private void setMessage(String message) {
    model.getNotificationLineSupport().setInformationMessage(message);
}
```

The data model is accessed via the readSettings() and storeSettings() methods. The type of the data model depends on the template, specified via the WizardDescriptor.Panel interface in the class signature. In this case, the class in question is WizardDescriptor. The readSettings() method is called when the panel is opened. Here, values from a previous panel can be read in, for example. Register a PropertyChangeListener on the Visual Panel, informing you of user activities in the panel. Register it here to make sure the WizardDescriptor is available. The storeSettings() method is called when panels are exited. Save the user-entered values in the WizardDescriptor via the property names defined in the

Visual Panel. In this way, the values are immediately passed from panel to panel until they can be read from the WizardDescriptor after completion of the wizard.

```java
public void readSettings(WizardDescriptor model) {
    this.model = model;
    getComponent().addPropertyChangeListener(this);
}
public void storeSettings(WizardDescriptor model) {
    model.putProperty(PlaylistVisualPanel1.PROP_PLAYLIST_NAME,
                    getComponent().getPlaylistName());
    model.putProperty(PlaylistVisualPanel1.PROP_GENRE,
                    getComponent().getGenre());
    model.putProperty(PlaylistVisualPanel1.PROP_DESCRIPTION,
                    getComponent().getDescription());
    model.putProperty(PlaylistVisualPanel1.PROP_IMAGE_PATH,
                    getComponent().getImagePath());
}
```

When discussing the Visual Panel, I have already said that values entered by the user must be validated. More specifically, you want to make sure the user has entered a name consisting of at least three characters and that the size of the chosen image doesn't exceed 128 pixels in width and height. To be informed about changes made to the visual panel—that is, when the user enters a name or chooses an image—you register a PropertyChangeListener on the Visual Panel in the readSettings() method. You need to implement the propertyChange() method. There, the values entered in the wizard can be validated via the checkValidity() method, which examines the relevant criteria, possibly displays a message, and returns the corresponding return value. We now need to inform the parent WizardDescriptor about the changes so that relevant buttons can be activated or deactivated. The user can only proceed to the next step when the entered data are validated and the WizardDescriptor is notified of that fact. Achieve this via the fireChangeEvent() method.

```java
public void propertyChange(PropertyChangeEvent event) {
    boolean oldState = isValid;
    isValid = checkValidity();
    fireChangeEvent(this, oldState, isValid);
}
private boolean checkValidity() {
    if(getComponent().getPlaylistName().trim().length() < 3) {
        setMessage(bundle.getString("Panel1.Error1"));
        return false;
    } else if(getComponent().getImagePath().length() != 0) {
        ImageIcon img = new ImageIcon(getComponent().getImagePath());
        if(img.getIconHeight()>128 || img.getIconWidth()>128) {
            setMessage(bundle.getString("Panel1.Error2"));
            return false;
        }
    } else if(getComponent().getImagePath().length() == 0) {
        setMessage(bundle.getString("Panel1.Warning1"));
        return true;
    }
    setMessage(null);
    return true;
}
```

To register a WizardDescriptor with a wizard panel, the WizardDescriptor.Panel interface specifies the addChangeListener() and removeChangeListener() methods. Implement these in the class. Use the fireChangeEvent() method to inform all registered listeners. For performance reasons, first verify whether the status of panels has changed, so that the WizardDescriptor is notified only when changes occur. If the isValid() method returns true, indicating that the panel has valid status, you can implement the methods with an empty body. The fireChangeEvent() method would even by omitted completely in this case. This scenario applies to the second panel of the example, which always returns true.

```
private final EventListenerList listeners =
    new EventListenerList();
public void addChangeListener(ChangeListener l) {
    listeners.add(ChangeListener.class, l);
}
public void removeChangeListener(ChangeListener l) {
    listeners.remove(ChangeListener.class, l);
}
protected final void fireChangeEvent(
    Object source, boolean oldState, boolean newState) {
    if(oldState != newState) {
        ChangeEvent ev = new ChangeEvent(source);
        for (ChangeListener listener : listeners.getListeners(ChangeListener.class)) {
            listener.stateChanged(ev);
        }
    }
}
}
```

SHARING A BASE PANEL BETWEEN MULTIPLE WIZARD STEPS

If the wizard consists of multiple panels, it is advisable to create a base class which handles the listener logic and provides helper methods such as the setMessage() method. This base class implements the WizardDescriptor.Panel<Data> interface, so specific panels only need to derive from the base class. This approach is also considered in Figure 13-7.

Creating a Wizard from Panels

So far, you've learned about constructing a panel that represents a step in a wizard. You saw how the tasks of view and controller are distributed and, above all, clearly separated. Only one small step remains before the entire wizard is completed. A wizard is represented by the WizardDescriptor class, which manages the individual panels. One option now is to instantiate your own panels and pass them to a WizardDescriptor. The action class—which is created automatically when using the IDE to create the panels—works that way. In the interest of encapsulation, a clearer structuring, and reusability, it is a good idea to create an individual wizard descriptor, extending the WizardDescriptor class. Thus this class can even take care of the creation of panels and their properties. Action classes, when starting a wizard, only need to create an instance of the wizard descriptor. This one can be directly passed to the DialogDisplayer. In this way, your wizard can be called fully transparent.

Therefore, for this example, create the PlaylistWizardDescriptor class, extending the WizardDescriptor class (see Listing 13-3). Use the setPanelsAndSettings() method to pass in both panels, which are declared as private fields. The panels must be passed with an iterator instance; such an iterator class is responsible for the order of the panels. Use the default ArrayIterator. The second parameter for setPanelsAndSettings() is a data model, which is passed to the panels via the readSettings() and storeSettings() methods. In this data model the data collected by the wizard are stored. Pass this as a reference to the PlaylistWizardDescriptor, which you want to use as data model. Finally, carry out a few configuration tasks.

Listing 13-3. Wizard Descriptor, Which Assembles the Panels to a Wizard

```
public class PlaylistWizardDescriptor extends WizardDescriptor {

    private PlaylistWizardPanel1 p1 = new PlaylistWizardPanel1();
    private PlaylistWizardPanel2 p2 = new PlaylistWizardPanel2();

    public PlaylistWizardDescriptor() {
        List<Panel<WizardDescriptor>> panels = new ArrayList<Panel<WizardDescriptor>>();
        panels.add(p1);
        panels.add(p2);
        this.setPanelsAndSettings(new ArrayIterator<WizardDescriptor>(panels), this);
        this.setTitleFormat(new MessageFormat("{0}"));
        this.setTitle(NbBundle.getMessage(PlaylistWizardDescriptor.class, "Wizard.Name"));

        putProperty(WizardDescriptor.PROP_CONTENT_DATA,
            new String[]{panel1.getName(), panel2.getName()});
        putProperty(WizardDescriptor.PROP_AUTO_WIZARD_STYLE,
            Boolean.TRUE);
        putProperty(WizardDescriptor.PROP_CONTENT_DISPLAYED,
            Boolean.TRUE);
        putProperty(WizardDescriptor.PROP_CONTENT_NUMBERED,
            Boolean.TRUE);
    }
}
```

Simpler than the WizardDescriptor itself is the action class that starts the wizard. Create a simple instance of the PlaylistWizardDescriptor class and immediately pass it to the createDialog() method, as illustrated in the "Custom Dialogs" section earlier in the chapter. This creates a Dialog object, which contains a wizard displayed as usual, via the setVisible() method (see Listing 13-4). After completing the wizard, you can determine which button the user has pressed with the getValue() method. The most important point here is how the data is analyzed. Since the WizardDescriptor itself is your data model, you can read the data directly from it. The best approach is to use the getProperties() method, providing a Map with all the properties that have been saved.

Listing 13-4. Action Class That Creates and Calls a Wizard

```
@ActionID(
    category = "Tools",
    id = "com.galileo.netbeans.module.PlaylistWizardAction")
@ActionRegistration(
```

```
    displayName = "#CTL_PlaylistWizardAction",
    iconBase = "com/galileo/netbeans/module/wizard.png")
@ActionReference(path = "Menu/Tools", position = 1200)
public final class PlaylistWizardAction implements ActionListener {
    @Override
    public void actionPerformed(ActionEvent e) {
        PlaylistWizardDescriptor descriptor = new PlaylistWizardDescriptor();
        Dialog dialog = DialogDisplayer.getDefault().createDialog(descriptor);
        dialog.setVisible(true);
        dialog.toFront();
        if(descriptor.getValue()==WizardDescriptor.FINISH_OPTION) {
            Map<String, Object> props = descriptor.getProperties();
            //Create the playlist with the data stored in props
        }
    }
}
```

Event Handling

In this section, I will again explain in overview the concept of interaction between the three layers—wizard descriptor, wizard panel and visual panel—and how events and notifications are received and processed. In the sequence diagram in Figure 13-8, both scenarios—the initialization of a wizard and the interaction between the various parts of the wizard as the user enters data—are displayed.

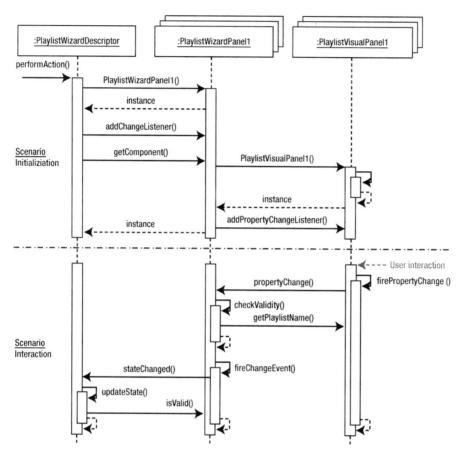

Figure 13-8. *Interaction between the wizard descriptor, wizard panel, and visual panel.*

In the `actionPerformed()` method of the action class to start the wizard, an instance of the `PlaylistWizardDescriptor` is created. This descriptor generates its panels and registers a `ChangeListener` for each, so that it is notified whenever the status of the panel changes. The visual panels are then obtained via the `getComponent()` method of the wizard panels. This method creates the visual panel on demand and registers a `PropertyChangeListener`, informing of changes made by the user. The wizard descriptor observes the status of its panels via a `ChangeListener`, which in turn observes the status of the visual panels via a `PropertyChangeListener`.

When the user types data into a field that is monitored by the view with a listener, a `PropertyChangeEvent` is fired, notifying the wizard panel that data has changed. The wizard panel retrieves the data via the getters and then verifies received data. Depending on the result of the verification, status of the panel is set.

If the status changes, a `ChangeEvent` is fired, notifying the wizard descriptor, which verifies the panel status, calling the `isValid()` method. Depending on the value of the `isValid()` method, the wizard descriptor activates or deactivates the buttons in the wizard.

Ending a Wizard Prematurely

Depending on the use case, it may be useful to allow the user to end the wizard prematurely. Normally the *Finish* button is only activated in the last panel. To allow the user to end the wizard in an earlier panel, implement the interface WizardDescriptor.FinishablePanel on the corresponding panel. This specifies the method isFinishPanel() with which you can return the value true, if the wizard can be finished. In the example, it is conceivable to implement this interface in the first panel, allowing the user to end the wizard already after entering the data without adding tracks to the playlist.

Additional Validation of Data

A panel announces the validity of its data to the wizard descriptor via the isValid() method. The method is called on opening a panel and on notification via the ChangeListener. Should additional verifications be done when the user clicks *Next* or ends the wizard, implement the WizardDescriptor.ValidatingPanel interface. This interface specifies the validate() method, in which detailed verifications can be performed. Errors identified in this way are announced with a WizardValidationException. The constructor of this exception class receives a JComponent, which obtains the focus, in order to show the user the wrong place. In addition, a failure message can be added, which is then shown in the wizard.

Rather than using the validate() method of the WizardDescriptor.ValidatingPanel interface, which is executed asynchronously in the event dispatch thread (EDT) (where no long-running tasks should be performed, or else the complete user interface is blocked), use the WizardDescriptor.AsynchronousValidatingPanel interface to asynchronously handle verification. Using this interface, the validate() method is automatically executed in a separate thread. As a result, the user interface is available to the user, enabling use of the *Cancel* button to end the process. Since the asynchronous method is not carried out in the EDT, you should not access GUI components to read data from them. To that end, the interface specifies the prepareValidation() method, which is called in the EDT, allowing access to data in the GUI components while disallowing further change. Accomplish your checks on these data using the validate() method.

Iterators

Within a wizard descriptor the panels are managed by an iterator. This iterator is responsible for the order of the panels. The interface of an iterator of this kind is described by the WizardDescriptor.Iterator class. A standard implementation of this interface provides the WizardDescriptor.ArrayIterator class, providing panels in a sequential order. This class is also used when passing panels as an array to the WizardDescriptor class. However, when giving the user the choice to skip one or more panels, based on the chosen or entered data, assign your own iterator implementation to the WizardDescriptor, which handles the dynamic order of the panels. The skeleton of such an interator can also be created via a wizard in the NetBeans IDE. Returning to the first step of the *Wizard* wizard, you set the *Wizard Step Sequence* to *Static*. However, if you set *Dynamic* at this point, the IDE will create an iterator class.

Based on the WizardDescriptor.Iterator interface there are a few extensions. Use the WizardDescriptor.InstantiatingIterator interface and its instantiate() method to create a Set of objects. An extension is the WizardDescriptor.AsynchronousInstantiatingIterator, with its instantiate() method, which is performed asynchronously outside the EDT, when the user clicks the *Finish* button. Finally, use the WizardDescriptor.ProgressInstantiatingIterator interface to show the user a progress bar when the wizard ends, while the instantiate() method is processing. In this case, the instantiate() method is called in a separate thread, receiving a ProgressHandle. The status is shown via this class, as is done with the standard progress bar (see Chapter 11).

Summary

The NetBeans Platform provides a professional API for creating dialogs and wizards. In this chapter you learned both how to quickly create simple standard dialogs and how to create complex dialogs that are adapted to your special needs. Additionally, you learned how to implement clearly structured wizards by the Dialogs API, in order to guide the user through a complex world of facts.

CHAPTER 14

Visual Library

The NetBeans *Visual Library API* is a generic library for visualizing very different structures. It is particularly well suited to graph-oriented representations. The Visual Library API is part of the standard NetBeans Platform and is used by the NetBeans IDE itself in numerous modules and areas, such as the visual modeling of midlets in a Java Micro Edition (JME) application, as shown in Figure 14-1. To use the Visual Library API, you just need to define a dependency on the module (under *Libraries* within your module's *Properties)*, as previously noted with respect to other modules.

Structure of the Visual Library API

The components of the Visual Library API, like Swing, are structured and managed as a tree. The superclass of all graphic components is the Widget class. If you consider Figure 14-1, then the three components (*Mobile Device, form,* and *loginScreen*), as well as the edges connected to the components, are all widgets. A widget can also be a container for more widgets. Each widget has a position that is determined relative to its parent widget. The Widget superclass is responsible for presenting the border and background of a widget in addition to managing properties such as color and transparency. Like a Swing container, a widget has a certain layout responsible for positioning its child widgets. Widgets can also depend upon each other in order to be notified about changes. A widget enables a series of actions (which are executed when specific user events occur) to be linked.

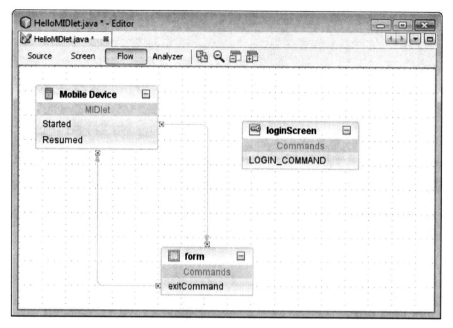

Figure 14-1. Visual model of a graph-oriented structure using the Visual Library API

The Widget Classes

All graphic components of the Visual Library API are subclasses of the Widget class, which manages and provides basic features and functionalities such as layout, background, and font. So, a Widget is a graphic primitive, equivalent to the JComponent class in Swing. From Widget, numerous classes are derived, which provide a Widget implementation for the respective purpose. This inheritance hierarchy is represented in Figure 14-2, and the meanings of these various widget classes are listed in Table 14-1. The most important of these classes are dealt with in more detail in the following sections. For a more exhaustive description of these classes, see the Visual Library API documentation, found within the JavaDoc page of the Visual Library.

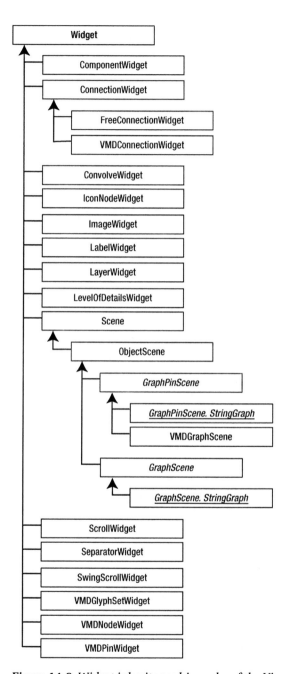

Figure 14-2. Widget inheritance hierarchy of the Visual Library API

Table 14-1 provides an overview of the features and functionalities of various widget implementations.

Table 14-1. The Meanings of the Different Widget Subclasses

Class	Description
ComponentWidget	Using a ComponentWidget, AWT/Swing components can be used within a Scene. In this respect, that widget serves as a placeholder and is responsible for displaying and updating the contained component.
ConnectionWidget	A ConnectionWidget is used to connect two points determined by anchors. Thus, it is responsible for the presentation of the connecting line, as well as for the presentation of control points, endpoints, and anchors. Control points, resolved by a Router, specify the path of a connecting line.
ConvolveWidget	A ConvolveWidget applies a convolve filter to a child element.
ImageWidget	With an ImageWidget, images can be represented within a Scene.
LabelWidget	With this widget, text can be displayed. Thus, the text can be represented in four different horizontal and vertical alignments.
LayerWidget	A LayerWidget is a transparent widget, whose function is similar to a JGlassPane. For example, a Scene uses several such layers to organize different types of widgets.
LevelOfDetailsWidget	A LevelOfDetailsWidget just serves as container for its child widgets, depending on the zoom factor of the Scene.
Scene	The Scene widget is the root element of the current hierarchy of widgets to display. In this respect, it is responsible for the control and representation of the whole rendered area. This class makes a view of the Scene available in the form of a JComponent instance, which can then be embedded into any Swing component. We will look at this important class in more detail in the section "The Scene."s
ScrollWidget	A ScrollWidget is a scrollable container whose functionality corresponds to a JScrollPane. The scroll bars are only shown when needed.
SeparatorWidget	This widget represents a separator whose thickness and orientation can be set.
SwingScrollWidget	This widget, like a ScrollWidget, also represents a scrollable area;

Class	Description
	the JScrollBar class is used for the scroll bars, though.
IconNodeWidget	An IconNodeWidget represents both an image and a label that can alternatively be placed below the image or on the right side of the image.

Dependencies

Dependencies can be defined between individual widgets. You are thereby able to respond to changes in position or size of other widgets. This dependency is realized by a listener that is registered on the widget. For this purpose, the Widget class provides two methods, addDependency() and removeDependency(). With these two methods, a listener can be added or removed. A listener is specified by the interface Widget.Dependency. Doing so, the listener must implement the method revalidateDependency(), which is called by the respective widget when there is a change of position or size. In this method you should call the revalidate() method of your widget, meaning the widget that depends on another widget.

Border

Each widget has a border. By default, this is an empty border, represented by the class EmptyBorder. You can determine another border with the setBorder() method. A border is specified by the interface Border. This interface is implemented by numerous border classes. Besides the EmptyBorder class, these are the classes LineBorder, BevelBorder, DashedBorder, ImageBorder, ResizeBorder, RoundedBorder and SwingBorder. A ResizeBorder adds eight points to the edges of your widget, which are used to change its size. Beyond the class SwingBorder you can use any Swing javax.swing.border.Border implementation. Finally, the CompositeBorder class is provided, to which you can pass any amount of the already mentioned Border instances in order to combine multiple different borders.

However, the borders are not created directly, but via a factory. This is the BorderFactory class that provides numerous methods with which you can create various border types. You can also use instances produced by this factory for multiple widgets at once. So, if you wish to use the same border for several widgets, you just need to create one instance of it.

Layout

A widget (like a Swing container) has a special layout, managed and determined by a layout manager. A layout is specified by the interface Layout and is responsible for the arrangement of the child widgets. Four different variants of layouts are available. You create them via the LayoutFactory class and add them to a widget via the setLayout() method.

- *AbsoluteLayout*: With the AbsoluteLayout, child widgets are arranged according to the coordinates that are supplied by getPreferredLocation(). The size of child widgets corresponds to the proportions provided by getPreferredBounds(). If both methods supply null, the position becomes (0, 0) or the size (0, 0, 0, 0) is used. By default, this layout is used by a widget. This layout is generated with

  ```
  Layout al = LayoutFactory.createAbsoluteLayout();
  ```

- *FlowLayout*: The FlowLayout arranges its widgets in sequential order in a horizontal or vertical direction. Doing so, four different alignments can be selected: left top, center, right bottom, and justified. Furthermore, the gap between individual widgets can be determined. The size of the widgets corresponds to the value that getPreferredBounds() returns. The following methods are available for the creation of this layout; alternatively, supply the alignment as a LayoutFactory.SerialAlignment type along with the gap:

  ```
  Layout hfl = LayoutFactory.createHorizontalFlowLayout();
  Layout vfl = LayoutFactory.createVerticalFlowLayout();
  ```

- *CardLayout*: A CardLayout always shows the currently active widget only, which is determined by the method setActiveCard(). The size of the active widget is determined by getPreferredBounds(). All other widgets are represented in the size (0, 0, 0, 0), so are practically invisible. Determine the currently active widget by the method getActiveCard(). You can create the layout with the following:

  ```
  Layout cl = LayoutFactory.createCardLayout();
  ```

  and specify the active widget by the following call:

  ```
  LayoutFactory.setActiveCard(Widget parent, Widget act);
  ```

  You can switch to another widget using the SwitchCardAction class.

- *OverlayLayout*: The OverlayLayout determines the minimum area containing all child widgets. Both the widget that contains this layout and all child widgets are set to the size of this determined area and arranged on top of each other. The last child widget is displayed on top. You create this layout as follows:

  ```
  Layout ol = LayoutFactory.createOverlayLayout();
  ```

A widget knows its position, size, and content, but it does not get information about its behavior. The behavior of a widget is influenced by actions added arbitrarily to a widget. These actions are specified by the interface WidgetAction, which defines a number of event methods. These methods are called by corresponding events, such as clicking a mouse button on the widget the action is assigned to. The implementation of the action class then executes the desired behavior such as moving a widget by drag and drop.

Like borders and layouts, actions are created by a factory. This is the ActionFactory class. These actions are managed within a widget by the WidgetAction.Chain class. This class receives the user events and forwards them to the appropriate actions that are managed by this class. Each widget has an instance of this class, which is obtained by the getAction() method. With the methods addAction() and removeAction() of the WidgetAction.Chain class you can add or remove actions to your widget.

Some of the factory methods of the ActionFactory class require a provider as parameter. A provider implements a specific behavior of an action. In some cases (for example, the EditAction), a provider implementation (which is executed when double-clicking the respective widget) must be specified. For other actions, such as the MoveAction, you can optionally specify a provider if you wish the behavior to deviate from the default. These providers are each specified through a special interface such as EditProvider or HoverProvider.

The possibility of grouping is the real advantage or purpose of managing a widget's actions in a WidgetAction.Chain class. In some applications, you may only want to permit certain actions for a Scene. So, for example, it will only be possible to move widgets, but not to edit them. You determine the current status of a Scene using the setActiveTool() method in the Scene class. Now, the Widget class can manage a separate WidgetAction.Chain instance concerning different states. Previously, access was gained to actions via the getAction() method. This method supplied the default WidgetAction.Chain instance, which is also used if no status is set (setActiveTool(null)). Now you can use a variant of the getActions(String tool) method (to which you supply the name of the tool and obtain the relevant WidgetAction.Chain instance), in order to get an instance for a specific status.

AcceptAction

This action is for the treatment of drag-and-drop operations. Thus, an AcceptProvider implementation must be provided when creating the action. The AcceptProvider interface specifies the method isAcceptable(), which allows specifying whether a drop operation on this widget is allowed, as well as the method accept(), with which you accomplish the drop operation.

```
ActionFactory.createAcceptAction(AcceptProvider p);
```

ActionMapAction

This action creates a context menu, displayed by right-clicking the widget. Connected to this, it is possible to create the action using the default method without parameters, whereby actions for the menu are inferred from the ActionMap of the Scene view. Additionally, there is an option to supply the method with an InputMap and ActionMap used for creating the menu.

```
ActionFactory.createActionMapAction();
ActionFactory.createActionMapAction(InputMap i, ActionMap a);
```

AddRemoveControlPointAction

This action can only be used by FreeConnectionWidget widgets. You can add or remove control points by double-clicking them. Optionally, you can also indicate the sensitivity used.

```
ActionFactory.createAddRemoveControlPointAction();
ActionFactory.createAddRemoveControlPointAction(
    double createSensitivity,
    double deleteSensitivity);
```

MoveAction/AlignWithMoveAction

With the MoveAction, a Widget can be moved by drag-and-drop. Please note that this action only works if the parent widget has an AbsoluteLayout. The AlignWithMoveAction behaves similarly to the MoveAction. In contrast with the MoveAction, in the AlignWithMoveAction an additional "snapping" with other widgets occurs, though. You can check which widgets will be aligned or respectively checked either by a list with an AlignWithWidgetCollector instance or by a LayerWidget. In the second case, the alignment of all child widgets within each layer is checked.

```
ActionFactory.createMoveAction();
ActionFactory.createMoveAction(
    MoveStrategy          strategy,
    MoveProvider          provider);
ActionFactory.createAlignWithMoveAction(
    AlignWithWidgetCollector collector,
    LayerWidget              interactionLayer,
    AlignWithMoveDecorator   decorator);
```

```
ActionFactory.createAlignWithMoveAction(
    LayerWidget            collectionLayer,
    LayerWidget            interactionLayer,
    AlignWithMoveDecorator decorator);
```

ResizeAction/AlignWithResizeAction

With the ResizeAction, you change the size of widgets. Additionally, the AlignWithResizeAction checks
the alignment of other widgets. You can pass widgets that need their alignment checked against others
either by an AlignWithWidgetCollector or by a LayerWidget.

```
ActionFactory.createResizeAction();
ActionFactory.createResizeAction(
    ResizeStrategy            strategy,
    ResizeProvider            provider);
ActionFactory.createResizeAction(
    ResizeStrategy            strategy,
    ResizeControlPointResolver resolver,
    ResizeProvider            provider);
ActionFactory.createAlignWithResizeAction(
    AlignWithWidgetCollector  collector,
    LayerWidget               interactionLayer,
    AlignWithMoveDecorator    decorator);
ActionFactory.createAlignWithResizeAction(
    LayerWidget               collectionLayer,
    LayerWidget               interactionLayer,
    AlignWithMoveDecorator    decorator);
```

ZoomAction/CenteredZoomAction

With these actions, you can change the zoom of the whole scene with the mouse wheel. So you do not
add these actions to a widget, but directly to a scene.

```
ActionFactory.createZoomAction();
ActionFactory.createZoomAction(double zoom, boolean animated);
ActionFactory.createCenteredZoomAction(double zoomMultiplier);
```

ConnectAction/ExtendedConnectAction/ReconnectAction

With a ConnectAction instance, you check the source and the target widgets on the desired connection
and you can then establish this connection. Optionally, you can indicate a user-specific connection
element by a ConnectDecorator. With the ExtendedConnectAction, a connection can only be established
as long as the *Ctrl* key is pressed. This action is meant for those cases where conflicts with other actions
occur—for example, if you want to use the ConnectAction and the MoveAction at the same time. In those
cases, use the ExtendedConnectAction.

```
ActionFactory.createConnectAction(
    LayerWidget       interactionLayer,
    ConnectProvider   provider);
ActionFactory.createConnectAction(
    ConnectDecorator  decorator,
```

```
    LayerWidget         interactionLayer,
    ConnectProvider     provider);
ActionFactory.createExtendedConnectAction(
    LayerWidget         interactionLayer,
    ConnectProvider     provider);
ActionFactory.createExtendedConnectAction(
    ConnectDecorator    decorator,
    LayerWidget         interactionLayer,
    ConnectProvider     provider);
ActionFactory.createReconnectAction(
    ReconnectProvider   provider);
ActionFactory.createReconnectAction(
    ReconnectDecorator decorator,
    ReconnectProvider   provider);
```

CycleFocusAction/CycleObjectSceneFocusAction

With CycleFocusAction and CycleObjectSceneFocusAction you can shift the focus between widgets of a scene using the *Tab* key, either forward or backward. With CycleFocusAction you specify the behavior, i. e. the preceding or following widget to set the focus on, using a CycleFocusProvider. In the case of CycleObjectSceneFocusAction, which can be applied to an ObjectScene, the order of the focusing is determined by the return value of getIdentityCode().

```
ActionFactory.createCycleFocusAction(CycleFocusProvider p);
ActionFactory.createCycleObjectSceneFocusAction();
```

EditAction/InplaceEditorAction

To edit a widget by double-clicking, add an EditAction to the widget. You implement the behavior that this will trigger by means of an EditProvider. Moreover, you can also supply an in-place editor that is displayed upon double-clicking. For this purpose, use the InplaceEditorAction, with which the editor can be any JComponent subclass. For example, with an IconNodeWidget or a LabelWidget, this would typically be a JTextField.

```
ActionFactory.createEditAction(
    EditProvider           provider);
ActionFactory.createInplaceEditorAction(
    InplaceEditorProvider  provider);
ActionFactory.createInplaceEditorAction(
    TextFieldInplaceEditor editor);
ActionFactory.createInplaceEditorAction(
    TextFieldInplaceEditor editor,
    EnumSet                expansionDirections);
```

ForwardKeyEventsAction

Wih this action, you can forward keyboard events to other widgets.

```
ActionFactory.createForwardKeyEventsAction(
    Widget forwardToWidget,
    String forwardToTool);
```

HoverAction

With the HoverAction, you can react when the mouse pointer is moved above your widget. How the widget behaves is specified by a HoverProvider or a TwoStateHoverProvider.

```
ActionFactory.createHoverAction(HoverProvider p);
ActionFactory.createHoverAction(TwoStateHoverProvider p);
```

MoveControlPointAction/FreeMoveControlPointAction/OrthogonalMoveControlPointAction

These actions move the control points of the connecting line of a ConnectionWidget. The OrthogonalMoveControlPointAction is used when a ConnectionWidget has an OrthogonalSearchRouter. The FreeMoveControlPointAction has no restrictions at all on positioning the points.

```
ActionFactory.createMoveControlPointAction(MoveControlPointProvider provider);
ActionFactory.createFreeMoveControlPointAction();
ActionFactory.createOrthogonalMoveControlPointAction();
```

PanAction

If the view of a scene is contained within a JScrollPane, the PanAction allows scrolling the view of a scene by moving the mouse while the middle button is pressed. So, this action is added to a scene:

```
ActionFactory.createPanAction();
```

PopupMenuAction

Use the PopupMenuAction to provide a widget with a context menu. This requires implementing a PopupMenuProvider with which you provide a JPopupMenu instance.

```
ActionFactory.createPopupMenuAction(PopupMenuProvider provider);
```

SelectAction/RectangularSelectAction

The SelectAction is similar to the EditAction, but this event is the result of just a single click. The logic implementation for the click event is provided by a SelectProvider. With this provider you can also determine whether a widget may even be selected. Usually, the RectangularSelectAction is added to an ObjectScene or to a LayerWidget with which you select widgets by drawing rectangles around them.

```
ActionFactory.createSelectAction(SelectProvider provider);
ActionFactory.createRectangularSelectAction(
    ObjectScene              scene,
    LayerWidget              interactionLayer);
ActionFactory.createRectangularSelectAction(
    RectangularSelectDecorator decorator,
    LayerWidget                interactionLayer,
    RectangularSelectProvider  provider);
```

SwitchCardAction

This action is required for switching between widgets that are in a CardLayout:

```
ActionFactory.createSwitchCardAction(Widget cardLayoutWidget);
```

The Scene: The Root Element

As you already know, the components of the Visual Library API—that is, the widgets—are arranged and managed in a hierarchical tree structure. In turn, this means widgets can contain other widgets. The Scene class, which is itself a widget, represents the container for the subsequent elements and therefore is the root element of the tree hierarchy (see Figure 14-2). Graphically, a scene is represented by a view, which is a simple JComponent instance. This is then typically added to a JScrollPane. You always start with creating a scene, to which you then add further widgets in hierarchical arrangement, depending on the application's purpose. Listing 14-1 illustrates this.

Listing 14-1. Creating a Scene and Adding Widgets

```
import org.netbeans.api.visual.action.ActionFactory;
import org.netbeans.api.visual.action.WidgetAction;
import org.netbeans.api.visual.widget.ImageWidget;
import org.netbeans.api.visual.widget.LayerWidget;
import org.netbeans.api.visual.widget.Scene;
...
public final class SceneTopComponent extends TopComponent {
    private JScrollPane scenePane = new JScrollPane();
    private Scene sc = new Scene();

    public SceneTopComponent() {
        scenePane.setViewportView(sc.createView());
        LayerWidget layer1 = new LayerWidget(sc);
        sc.addChild(layer1);
        ImageWidget w1 = new ImageWidget(sc,
            ImageUtilities.loadImage("com/galileo/netbeans/module/node.gif"));
        layer1.addChild(w1);
        ImageWidget w2 = new ImageWidget(sc,
            ImageUtilities.loadImage("com/galileo/netbeans/module/node.gif"));
        layer1.addChild(w2);
        LayerWidget layer2 = new LayerWidget(sc);
        sc.addChild(layer2);
        ImageWidget w3 = new ImageWidget(sc,
            ImageUtilities.loadImage("com/galileo/netbeans/module/node2.gif"));
        layer2.addChild(w3);
        WidgetAction ma = ActionFactory.createMoveAction();
        w1.getActions().addAction(ma);
        w2.getActions().addAction(ma);
        w3.getActions().addAction(ma);
    }
}
```

The scene was created as a private data element. With the createView() method you can create a view for this scene which is of the type JComponent, which can thus be embedded into any Swing containers. Add this to a JScrollPane, so the scene or the view is not limited to a certain size. Now, you can hierarchically add widgets to the scene after creating a LayerWidget that acts like a JGlassPane and to which you can then add two ImageWidgets. To illustrate the grouping and alignment of widgets, you create another LayerWidget instance and add an additional ImageWidget. So, you add each of the ImageWidgets to a LayerWidget which in turn are assigned to the scene. We add it to a MoveAction instance, so the widgets can be moved within the scene. The move action instance is created with the `ActionFactory` and you can use it repeatedly. This example is shown in Figure 14-3.

Satellite View

In order to keep the overview and to enable fast navigation within larger scenes, a scene offers an overview in the form of an interactive `JComponent`. This is a *Satellite View* created using the `createSatelliteView()` method. If the view of your scene is embedded in a `JScrollPane` and the scene is larger than the displayed area at the same time, you can navigate the scene by moving the gray frame present in the overview to update the view (see Figure 14-3).

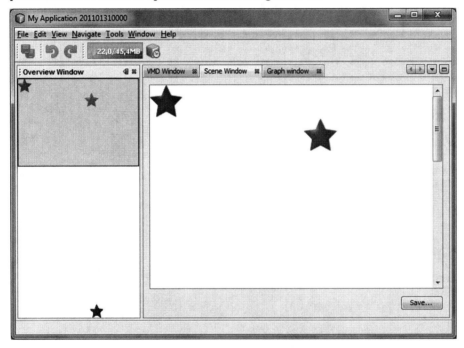

Figure 14-3. An overview for a scene can be created that can be used for navigation at the same time.

Exporting a Scene

In a few steps and with the assistance of some Java utilities, you can export a scene, generated with the Visual Library API, into an image within a PNG file. To this end, you first create a `BufferedImage` object into which you can write the graphic data. Specify the size of this `Image` instance using the current size of the view of the respective scene, to ensure that the complete content is stored. From this object, you get the `Graphics2D` context with which you feed data into the buffer of the `BufferedImage` object. Next, you must supply this context to the `paint()` method of the scene. Then the scene writes its content on the buffer of the `BufferedImage` instance rather than on the screen (see Listing 14-2). Following this, dispose of the context so that the resources can be released. With a `JFileChooser`, you request a file name and, if necessary, append the appropriate suffix. Once this is done, you utilize the `ImageIO` class that looks for an

ImageWriter for PNG files, using the ImageWriter to write the data of the BufferedImage object into the selected file.

Listing 14-2. Exporting a Scene into a PNG File

```
private Scene sc = new Scene();

public void exportScene() {
    BufferedImage img = new BufferedImage(
        sc.getView().getWidth(),
        sc.getView().getHeight(),
        BufferedImage.TYPE_4BYTE_ABGR);

    Graphics2D graphics = img.createGraphics();
    sc.paint(graphics);
    graphics.dispose();

    JFileChooser chooser = new JFileChooser();
    chooser.setFileFilter(new FileNameExtensionFilter(
        "Portable Network Graphics (.png)", "png"));

    if(chooser.showSaveDialog(sc.getView()) == JFileChooser.APPROVE_OPTION) {
        File f = chooser.getSelectedFile();
        if (!f.getName().toLowerCase().endsWith(".png")) {
            f = new File(f.getParentFile(), f.getName() + ".png");
        }
        try {
            ImageIO.write(img, "png", file);
        } catch (IOException e) {
            Logger.getLogger(getName()).warning(e.toString());
        }
    }
}
```

ObjectScene – Model-View Relation

The Visual Library API provides only the constituent components of a view. That means a widget has only information about the kind of presentation or flow of data. What a widget does not have is a data model. This is where the ObjectScene class comes into play, representing an extension of the Scene class. The function (or extension) of this class is to manage the mapping between the view (i.e., the widget) and an associated data model, which can be any object. The class ObjectScene provides methods allowing the assignment of a data model or of multiple widgets. Furthermore, it is possible to determine the data model registered to a widget or vice versa. Besides representing the data model and the widgets, the ObjectScene class also provides information about the current state (represented by the ObjectState class) of a widget or of a data model.

Data models are stored internally in a Map. For identification and comparison purposes, the equals() method of the data models is used. Ensure that your data model contains a useful implementation of this method and note additionally that each unique data model can only be added once (because of the unique identification). Thus, if the data model, d1, is in an ObjectScene and you add a second data model, d2, whereby d1.equals(d2) == true applies, an exception is raised.

Table 14-2 summarizes the most important methods of the ObjectScene class and their functions.

Table 14-2. The Most Important Methods of the ObjectScene Class

Method	Description

void addObject(
    Object   model,
    Widget... widgets)
	With the addObject() method, several widgets and their associated data models are added to a scene.

void removeObject(Object model)	You can remove a known data model with the removeObject() method. In this respect, note that the associated widget is not removed, but eliminated separately via the removeChild() method.
Object findObject(Widget widget)	Use the findObject() method to find the data model belonging to a certain Widget.
Widget findWidget(Object model)	This method is the counterpart to findObject() and finds the widget to a given data model.
List<Widget> findWidgets(Object model)	If multiple widgets are assigned to a model, these can be called with findWidgets().
ObjectState getObjectState(Object model)	To receive the current state of a model, use the getObjectState() method. If the state of a data model changes, the state of the widget is changed accordingly. The opposite does not occur, though. The status of a widget is determined via the getState() method.

Graphs

To simplify creating graphs—that is, the creation of nodes and associated edges—the API based on the ObjectScene class (which was introduced in the previous section) provides the classes GraphScene and GraphPinScene. Listing 14-3 illustrates the practical meaning of the ObjectScene class for these classes, again.

Both GraphScene and GraphPinScene are abstract classes, whose only task is the management of data models and widgets. Creating widgets is done by subclasses that create widgets depending on the data model. This is achieved by the abstract attach methods which must be overridden by the subclasses. The types of data models are defined by templates and can vary in each case for nodes, edges, and pins. In the simplest case, as in this example, you use the type String. For the nodes and edges, you must provide a separate LayerWidget to each and add them to the scene.

Listing 14-3. Implementation of a GraphPinScene Class

```
public class MyGraphPinScene extends GraphPinScene<String, String, String> {
    private LayerWidget mainLayer;
    private LayerWidget connectionLayer;

    public MyGraphPinScene() {
        mainLayer = new LayerWidget(this);
        addChild(mainLayer);
        connectionLayer = new LayerWidget(this);
        addChild(connectionLayer);
    }
```

The attachNodeWidget() method is responsible for creating nodes. For this purpose, this example uses the IconNodeWidget class. (The ImageWidget class could also be used.) Practically, you can also manage the accompanying pins with the IconNodeWidget class. This is done by using LabelWidget, which is accessed by the getLabelWidget() method. A FlowLayout is defined for this widget, so that the pins can be arranged and presented correctly. To move the node, add a MoveAction instance. Finally, add the node to the mainLayer and return it.

```
    protected Widget attachNodeWidget(String node) {
        IconNodeWidget widget = new IconNodeWidget(this);
        widget.setImage(ImageUtilities.loadImage("com/galileo/netbeans/module/node.gif"));
        widget.getLabelWidget().setLayout(
            LayoutFactory.createHorizontalFlowLayout(LayoutFactory.SerialAlignment.JUSTIFY, 5));
        widget.getActions().addAction(ActionFactory.createMoveAction());
        mainLayer.addChild(widget);
        return(widget);
    }
```

The attachEdgeWidget() method is responsible for creating edges. For this purpose, you want to use the ConnectionWidget class. Use a router so that you do not just draw the edges between the nodes in a straight line (eventually intersecting other nodes or edges). You can pass a series of LayerWidgets to a router. Doing so, the widgets of the LayerWidgets are not crossed. Accordingly, the router determines a path for the edges, so that no intersections occur. You can create such a router with the RouterFactory. Then, we add the configured edges to the ConnectionLayer and return them.

```
    protected Widget attachEdgeWidget(String edge) {
        ConnectionWidget widget = new ConnectionWidget(this);
        widget.setTargetAnchorShape(AnchorShape.TRIANGLE_FILLED);
        widget.setRouter(RouterFactory.createOrthogonalSearchRouter(mainLayer,connectionLayer));
        connectionLayer.addChild(widget);
        return widget;
    }
```

Pins are created with the attachPinWidget() method. A pin is an input or output of a node, to which an edge can be connected (the red points in Figure 14-4 represent the pins). So, a pin is assigned to a node; this node may possess multiple pins. You receive the data model for the pin and for the node to which the pin will be added as data model. Via the findWidget() method you can determine the widget of the node. Afterward, you can add the created pin to this widget.

```
    protected Widget attachPinWidget(String node, String pin) {
```

```
    ImageWidget widget = new ImageWidget(this,
        ImageUtilities.loadImage("com/galileo/netbeans/module/pin.gif"));
    IconNodeWidget n = (IconNodeWidget) findWidget(node);
    n.getLabelWidget().addChild(widget);
    return widget;
}
```

Finally, you must override the attachEdgeSourceAnchor() and attachEdgeTargetAnchor() methods. With these methods, the starting point and the endpoint of an edge are specified. In this respect, you first determine the pin to which the edge is to be connected via the findWidget() method. Then, you create an anchor point for this pin via the AnchorFactory. Afterward, you add this pin to the edge that you already traced by the findWidget().

```
    protected void attachEdgeSourceAnchor(String edge, String oldPin, String pin) {
        ConnectionWidget c = (ConnectionWidget) findWidget(edge);
        Widget widget = findWidget(pin);
        Anchor a = AnchorFactory.createRectangularAnchor(widget);
        c.setSourceAnchor(a);
    }

    protected void attachEdgeTargetAnchor(String edge, String oldPin, String pin) {
        ConnectionWidget c = (ConnectionWidget) findWidget(edge);
        Widget widget = findWidget(pin);
        Anchor a = AnchorFactory.createRectangularAnchor(widget);
        c.setTargetAnchor(a);
    }
}
```

Analogously, you could also create an implementation for the GraphScene class, which has no pins. There, edges are connected directly to the node rather than to a pin. The advantages of the just-created implementation now become apparent when using it (see Listing 14-4). As with a normal scene, you create an instance and add its view to a JScrollPane. Now, you do not need to create separate widgets. You just need to supply the data model (which is a string in this case) to the methods addNode(), addPin(), or addEdge(). Then, these methods internally call the attach methods that you implemented for creating the widgets—plus they create the mapping of the widget on the passed data model.

Listing 14-4. Usage of a GraphPinScene

```
import org.netbeans.api.visual.graph.layout.GridGraphLayout;
import org.netbeans.api.visual.layout.LayoutFactory;
import org.netbeans.api.visual.layout.SceneLayout;
...
public final class GraphTopComponent extends TopComponent {
    public GraphTopComponent() {
        MyGraphPinScene scene = new MyGraphPinScene();
        scenePane.setViewportView(scene.createView());
        scene.addNode("Node 1");
        scene.addNode("Node 2");
        scene.addNode("Node 3");
        scene.addPin("Node 1", "p1");
        scene.addPin("Node 2", "p2");
```

```
        scene.addPin("Node 2", "p3");
        scene.addPin("Node 3", "p4");
        scene.addEdge("Edge 1");
        scene.addEdge("Edge 2");
        scene.setEdgeSource("Edge 1", "p1");
        scene.setEdgeTarget("Edge 1", "p2");
        scene.setEdgeSource("Edge 2", "p3");
        scene.setEdgeTarget("Edge 2", "p4");

        GridGraphLayout<String, String> layout = new GridGraphLayout<String, String>();
        SceneLayout sceneLayout = LayoutFactory.createSceneGraphLayout(scene, layout);
        sceneLayout.invokeLayout();
    }
}
```

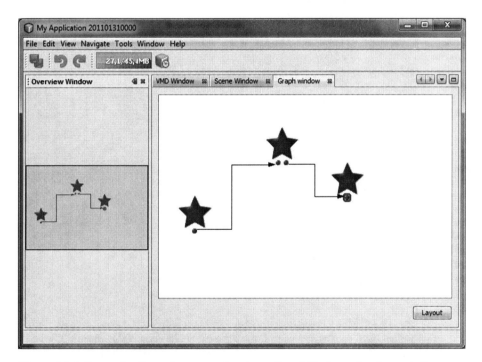

Figure 14-4. Example of creating a graph using a GraphPinScene implementation

VMD: Visual Mobile Designer

The implementation of graphs using the VMD classes is even easier. In this respect, VMD stands for *Visual Mobile Designer* and marks the classes that are used by the VMD. These classes provide a GraphPinScene implementation, as shown in the previous section. In addition to the scene, there are also special classes for nodes, edges, and pins that offer a conform design. So, you do not have to care about any details of implementation, such as the creation of widgets, setting of the layout or of a router; you can just add the necessary elements. A VMDGraphScene already has four layers and actions, such as zoom, pan, and select. Let's pick up the simple example with the three nodes (above) again, and realize it with a VMDGraphScene (see Listing 14-5).

Listing 14-5. Creating a Graph Using the VMD Classes

```
import org.netbeans.api.visual.vmd.VMDGraphScene;
import org.netbeans.api.visual.vmd.VMDNodeWidget;
import org.netbeans.api.visual.vmd.VMDPinWidget;
...
public final class VMDTopComponent extends TopComponent {
    private VMDGraphScene scene = new VMDGraphScene();
    public VMDTopComponent() {
        VMDGraphScene scene = new VMDGraphScene();
        scenePane.setViewportView(scene.createView());
        VMDNodeWidget n1 = (VMDNodeWidget)scene.addNode("Node 1");
        n1.setNodeName("Node 1");
        VMDNodeWidget n2 = (VMDNodeWidget)scene.addNode("Node 2");
        n2.setNodeName("Node 2");
        VMDNodeWidget n3 = (VMDNodeWidget)scene.addNode("Node 3");
        n3.setNodeName("Node 3");
        VMDPinWidget p1 = (VMDPinWidget)scene.addPin("Node 1","Pin 1");
        p1.setPinName("Pin 1");
        VMDPinWidget p2 = (VMDPinWidget)scene.addPin("Node 2","Pin 2");
        p2.setPinName("Pin 2");
        VMDPinWidget p3 = (VMDPinWidget)scene.addPin("Node 2","Pin 3");
        p3.setPinName("Pin 3");
        VMDPinWidget p4 = (VMDPinWidget)scene.addPin("Node 3","Pin 4");
        pin4.setPinName("Pin 4");
        scene.addEdge("Edge 1");
        scene.setEdgeSource("Edge 1", "Pin 1");
        scene.setEdgeTarget("Edge 1", "Pin 2");
        scene.addEdge("Edge 2");
        scene.setEdgeSource("Edge 2", "Pin 3");
        scene.setEdgeTarget("Edge 2", "Pin 4");
    }
}
```

The VMDGraphScene uses the type String for the data models of nodes, edges, and pins. As you already know from the previous section, elements are added by the methods addNode(), addPin(), and addEdge(). In this example, you just give the nodes and pins names. With the setProperties() method and with additional set methods, you can set additional properties, such as icons for nodes or for a pin, for example.

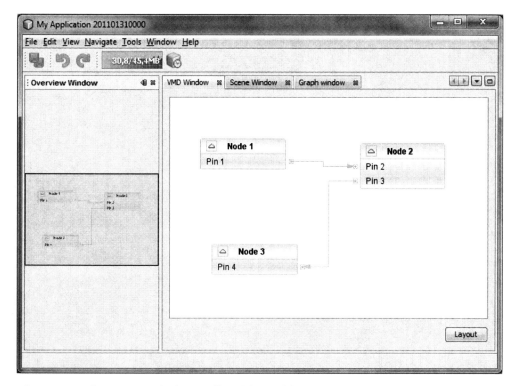

Figure 14-5. The VMD graph classes offer additional features, such as hiding pins or adding icons.

Summary

The Visual Library is a powerful framework for creating graph-oriented user interfaces. This chapter discussed the basic structure of the Visual Library API. You looked at all widget classes in detail. You learned all about events and actions as well as the Scene class, which is the root element. Another important part of this chapter covered the model-view relation. Finally, you saw how you can use the preexisting classes from the Visual Mobile Designer.

CHAPTER 15

Tips and Tricks

In this chapter, you will learn about some helpful features concerning the user interface of the NetBeans Platform. This chapter deals with desktop integration, asynchronous initializing of GUI components, and the implementation of an undo and redo functionality.

Desktop Features

The Desktop class of the Java Platform allows execution of standard applications like an Internet browser or an e-mail client. Pass a File or URI object to the methods provided by the Desktop class. On the basis of these objects, an associated standard application can be launched. For example, if Desktop.open(new File("myfile.pdf")) is executed, Acrobat Reader is launched (if this is the standard application for .pdf files). Table 15-1 shows all methods of the Desktop class.

Table 15-1. Methods in the Desktop Class

Method	Function
isDesktopSupported()	First you should check with this method if the Desktop is supported by the current operating system.
isSupported(Desktop.Action a)	Checks if actions like BROWSE, OPEN, EDIT, PRINT, and MAIL are available.
getDesktop()	Used to get an instance of the Desktop class. This method throws an UnsupportedOperationException if the Desktop class is not supported.
browse(URI uri)	Opens the given URI in the file browser.
open(File file)	Opens the file in the associated program (or in a file browser, if it is a folder).
edit(File file)	Opens the file in the standard editor for this file type.
print(File file)	Sends the file directly to the printer using the standard file application print functionality.

Method	Function
mail()	Opens the e-mail edit window.
mail(URI uri)	Opens the e-mail edit window where the address field is filled with the e-mail address from URI.

System Tray Integration

The Java Platform includes enhanced desktop integration and provides access to the system tray of the underlying operating system. You can add one or more icons which can be equipped with a context menu as well as with a double-click action. A good way to do this for a NetBeans Platform application is with the restored() method of the module installer. First, check whether the operating system has a system tray. If so, you get access to it with the getSystemTray() method. To add a context menu, create a PopupMenu whose actions are defined via an extension point in the layer file (thus, you are able to add actions to the tray icon from different modules). Call this extension point TrayMenu and read out its content by a Lookup. The actions only need to implement the Action corresponding to the ActionListener interface and are registered in the usual way. For example, an action might look like Listing 15-1.

Listing 15-1. Add an Action to the Extension Point of the Tray Menu.

```
@ActionID(
    category = "TrayMenu",
    id = "com.galileo.netbeans.module.FirstTrayAction")
@ActionRegistration(
    displayName = "#CTL_FirstTrayAction")
@ActionReferences({
    @ActionReference(path = "TrayMenu", position = 100)
})
public final class FirstTrayAction implements ActionListener {
    @Override
    public void actionPerformed(ActionEvent e) {
        System.out.println("My First Tray Action");
    }
}
```

You build the context menu out of the registered actions, provided by the Lookup. After creating the context menu, create a TrayIcon object, pass the menu, an icon, and a tooltip to this object and add it to the system tray, as shown in Listing 15-2.

Listing 15-2. Adding a System Tray Icon Whose Content Is Built out of the Data from Layer File

```
import org.openide.modules.ModuleInstall;
import org.openide.util.ImageUtilities;
import org.openide.util.lookup.Lookups;
import java.awt.SystemTray;
import java.awt.TrayIcon;
...
public class Installer extends ModuleInstall {
```

```
@Override
public void restored() {
    if (SystemTray.isSupported()) {
        SystemTray tray = SystemTray.getSystemTray();
        PopupMenu popup = new PopupMenu();
        popup.setFont(new Font("Arial", Font.PLAIN, 11));

        for(Action a : Utilities.actionsForPath("TrayMenu")) {
            MenuItem item = new MenuItem((String)a.getValue(Action.NAME));
            item.addActionListener(a);
            popup.add(item);
        }

        Image image = ImageUtilities.loadImage("com/galileo/netbeans/module/icon.gif");
        TrayIcon trayIcon = new TrayIcon(image, "My Tray Menu", popup);

        trayIcon.addActionListener(new ActionListener() {
            @Override
            public void actionPerformed(ActionEvent e) {
                System.out.println("double click on tray icon");
            }
        });

        try {
            tray.add(trayIcon);
        } catch (AWTException e) {
            System.err.println(e);
        }
    }
}
}
```

Asynchronous Initialization of Graphical Components

When developing graphical user interfaces, it is important to achieve a fast response time. This is especially true for the initialization phase of components, which need to be initialized in a dialog with the user. A good example of this is wizards, discussed in Chapter 13. If the user starts a wizard, the wizard should open and be available immediately. But often data for components (such as a combo box) needs to load from a relatively slow data source or must be calculated and composed from dependent data. In this case, initialize your components in a separate thread asynchronously to the remaining initialization of the user interface. When doing so, take care not to access GUI components from outside the event dispatch thread (EDT).

The NetBeans *Utilities API* provides an easy way to meet this requirement with the service provider interface AsyncGUIJob. This interface specifies two methods to help initialize components asynchronously. The construct() method is executed automatically in a separate thread, so the EDT is not blocked. This lets you load data or perform other long-running initializations without performance being affected. Do not access GUI components in the construct() method, however. As soon as the construct() method has returned, the finished() method is called. As it is called from the Event Dispatch Thread you can add data previously loaded in the construct() method to the GUI components. In the example in Listing 15-3, data is added (loaded in construct()) to a

DefaultComboBoxModel. After loading, you add the created data model to the JComboBox within the finished() method. This asynchronous process is started and connected to the component using the method Utilities.attachInitJob(). This way, independent jobs can be defined and started for various components.

Listing 15-3. Asynchronously Initializing Graphical Components Using the AsyncGUIJob Interface

```
public final class AsynchTopComponent extends TopComponent {
    private JComboBox items = new JComboBox(new String[] { "Loading..." });
    private DefaultComboBoxModel m = new DefaultComboBoxModel();

    private AsynchTopComponent() {
        initComponents();
        Utilities.attachInitJob(items, new AsyncGUIJob(){
            public void construct() {
                // long lasting loading of data
                for(int i = 0; i < 20; i++) {
                    Thread.sleep(200);
                    m.addElement("Item " + i);
                }
            }

            public void finished() {
                items.setModel(m);
            }
        });
    }
}
```

Another possibility for asynchronously initializing GUI components is the SwingWorker class of the Java Platform. It is an abstract class, initializing components in almost the same way as via the AsyncGUIJob interface. Using the SwingWorker class, the previous example with AsyncGUIJob looks like Listing 15-4.

Listing 15-4. Asynchronously Initializing Graphic Components Using the SwingWorker Class

```
SwingWorker<DefaultComboBoxModel, String> worker =
    new SwingWorker<DefaultComboBoxModel, String>() {

    @Override
    protected DefaultComboBoxModel doInBackground() throws Exception {
        // long lasting loading of data
        for(int i = 0; i < 20; i++) {
            Thread.sleep(200);
            m.addElement(new String("Item " + i));
        }
        return m;
    }

    @Override
    protected void done() {
        try {
```

```
      items.setModel(get());
    } catch (Exception ignore) {}
  }
};
```

```
worker.execute();
```

Similar to the `construct()` method, data is created (or loaded) within the method `doInBackground()`. In contrast to the `construct()` method we deliver the created data as the return value of the function (see Listing 15-5). The return type is defined by the first template of the `SwingWorker` class—in this example, `DefaultComboBoxModel`. This method is also executed outside the EDT. The `done()` method is the counterpart to the `finished()` method, which is called from within the EDT as soon as the `doInBackground()` method has finished. Using the `get()` method, you receive data prepared by `doInBackground()`.

Other very useful features of the `SwingWorker` class are the `publish()` and `process()` methods. By using `publish()`, data can be sent from the asynchronously executed `doInBackground()` method to the EDT that is processed by calling `process()`.

Listing 15-5. Adding Data Directly During the Initialization Phase with the SwingWorker Class

```java
items.setModel(m);
SwingWorker<DefaultComboBoxModel, String> worker =
    new SwingWorker<DefaultComboBoxModel, String>() {

    @Override
    protected DefaultComboBoxModel doInBackground() throws Exception {
        for(int i = 0; i < 20; i++) {
            Thread.sleep(200);
            publish("Item " + i);
        }
        return m;
    }

    @Override
    protected void process(List<String> chunks) {
        m.addElement(chunks.iterator().next());
    }
};
```

```
worker.execute();
```

Rather than setting the data model in the `done()` method, the elements are added immediately. In the `doInBackground()` method, single entries are immediately sent to the EDT using `publish()`. Those entries are received with the `process()` method and inserted into the combo box, so they appear right away. The parameter type of `publish()` and `process()` is defined in the second template of the `SwingWorker` class.

Undo/Redo

You can equip any component (and provide the user) with undo/redo support using the context interface `UndoRedo.Provider`. If a component is located in the global proxy Lookup (which implements the UndoRedo.Provider interface), the undo/redo buttons (in the toolbar and in the *Edit* menu) are automatically activated by default.

The undo and the redo functionality is specified by the UndoRedo interface. This interface is implemented by the UndoRedo.Manager class. This manager derives from the UndoManager class of the Java Platform. This class is responsible for managing changes, which can be undone or rebuilt. An instance of this manager returns your component via the getUndoRedo() method specified by the UndoRedo.Provider interface.

The events, which will be added to the manager, are strongly dependent on context. The interface for those events is specified by UndoableEdit. Java already offers some abstract implementations for this interface, such as the AbstractUndoableEdit class. This class provides all methods with a standard implementation. Thus, you just have to overwrite the methods you need. The StateEdit class and the corresponding StateEditable interface are very helpful, too. The StateEditable interface must be implemented by objects, whose data may be changed by users. An example of this would be a DataObject class representing an MP3 file whose ID3 information can be changed by the user.

Listing 15-6 demonstrates this principle on the basis of a very simple class that just has one feature that can be changed by the user via a text field. You keep the undo/redo manager (which you can deliver via the getUndoRedo() method) as a private data element. The TopComponent has two buttons: one to read the attribute of the data object, the other to save the changes made in the text field. If a change is made, first create a StateEdit object that implements the UndoableEdit interface. You have to pass an instance of the StateEditable instances to this object. Of course, this is your data object. Then, pass the UndoableEdit instance, created like this, to the manager (which notifies all listeners) via the undoableEditHappened() method. That way, all Platform undo and redo action buttons are activated or deactivated automatically. Now, you can make all changes in the data object and afterward finish the event via the end() method.

Listing 15-6. Providing an Undo/Redo Manager and Adding an Element When Data Is Changed by the User

```
import javax.swing.event.UndoableEditEvent;
import javax.swing.undo.StateEdit;
import org.openide.awt.UndoRedo;
...
public class MyTopComponent extends TopComponent implements UndoRedo.Provider {
    private UndoRedo.Manager manager = new UndoRedo.Manager();
    private MyObject obj = new MyObject();

    @Override
    public UndoRedo getUndoRedo() {
        return manager;
    }

    private void loadActionPerformed(ActionEvent evt) {
        textField.setText(obj.getProp());
    }

    private void saveActionPerformed(ActionEvent evt) {
        StateEdit edit = new StateEdit(obj);
        manager.undoableEditHappened(new UndoableEditEvent(obj, edit));
        obj.setProp(textField.getText());
        edit.end();
```

```
   }
}
```

The data object (whose changes will be undone or restored) must implement the StateEditable interface. This interface specifies the two methods storeState() and restoreState(). The principle of the StateEdit class is based on storing the features of a data object in a Hashtable. Then, this Hashtable is managed by the StateEdit object; the storeState() method is called when the StateEdit object is created. Features are stored to the hashtable (that is, passed) before changes are applied. In case the user wants to undo some changes again, the StateEdit object calls the restoreState() method. This method delivers a Hashtable which contains the original values. You just need to read these values and apply them. (See Listing 15-7.)

Listing 15-7. Data Object Whose Changed Features Need to Be Restored

```java
public class MyObject implements StateEditable {
   private String prop = new String("init value");

   public void storeState(Hashtable<Object, Object> props) {
      props.put("prop", prop); // save original state
   }

   public void restoreState(Hashtable<?, ?> props) {
      prop = (String)props.get("prop"); // read original state
   }

   public void setProp(String value) {
      prop = value;
   }

   public String getProp() {
      return prop;
   }
}
```

Finally, I will illustrate how easy it is to add undo/redo functionality to a text component; this feature is especially helpful for text. All subclasses of JTextComponent—by default these are JEditorPane, JTextArea, and JTextField—own a Document as data model. You can add an UndoableEditListener to a Document instance via the addUndoableEditListener() method. This listener interface is also implemented by the NetBeans UndoRedo.Manager. You can add this manager, previously stored in the TopComponent and returned by the getUndoRedo() method, to a Document instance as listener. This means, by appending a single line of code, you can add the undo/redo functionality to a text component:

```java
textField.getDocument().addUndoableEditListener(manager);
```

Now the text component itself is able to report its events to the manager, while the undo and redo buttons in turn become activated or deactivated automatically. Of course, this way, you can add undo support to a text component, as well as any component whose data model implements the Document interface or uses an implementation of Document, as the HTMLDocument and PlainDocument classes do, for example.

Summary

In this chapter you got to know helpful interfaces, classes, and concepts of the NetBeans Platform concerning the development of graphic user interfaces. You looked at the Java Platform desktop integration functionality and at how to initialize GUI components asynchronously. Finally you learned how to implement an undo and redo functionality.

PART 3

Ready & Go: Using the NetBeans Platform Standard Modules

CHAPTER 16

Help System

The NetBeans Platform help system is based on *JavaHelp*. The NetBeans Platform provides a module containing the JavaHelp library and provides a class to get access to the help system (see Figure 16-1). To use the help system, you must set a dependency on the *JavaHelp Integration* module in your module via *Properties* ➤ *Libraries*; the menu item *Help* ➤ *Help Contents* will be automatically provided in your application. The user can open the help window via this menu item.

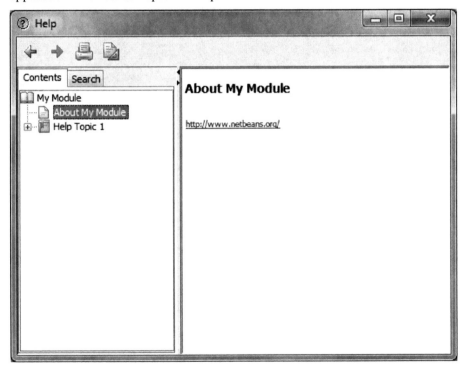

Figure 16-1. Window of the integrated help system

Creating and Integrating a Help Set

The NetBeans IDE provides a wizard to set up a help set. This makes an otherwise tricky process child's play. For this purpose call the menu item *File* ➤ *New File…*, choose the file type *JavaHelp Help Set* in the *Module Development* category, and click *Next.* On the next (and last) page, you will already see a list of files that are created or changed by the wizard. Click *Finish* to constitute the help set.

A help set is added to a module via the HelpSetRegistration annotation. The created help set files are stored in a separate package docs by the wizard. Since a help set does not have a Java file, a Java file is created (*package-info.java*) and the annotation is added, as in Listing 16-1.

Listing 16-1. Registration of a Help Set via an Annotation

```
@HelpSetRegistration(helpSet = "module-hs.xml", position = 3672)
package com.galileo.netbeans.module.docs;
import org.netbeans.api.javahelp.HelpSetRegistration;
```

The HelpSetRegistration annotation with the helpSet attribute refers to the actual help set XML file *module-hs.xml*. This annotation leads to an entry in the layer file in the standard folder Services/JavaHelp. This also means that if you want to consciously avoid annotations, you can register your help set by the following entry in the layer file yourself, as shown in Listing 16-2.

Listing 16-2. Direct Registration of a Help Set in the Layer File

```
<folder name="Services">
    <folder name="JavaHelp">
        <file name="module-helpset.xml" url="module-helpset.xml"/>
    </folder>
</folder>
```

So, you register the *module-helpset.xml* file, which contains a reference on the help set, in the layer file. The layer file then looks like Listing 16-3.

Listing 16-3. Help Set Reference File for the Registration via the Layer File

```
<?xml version="1.0" encoding="UTF-8"?>
<!DOCTYPE helpsetref PUBLIC
    "-//NetBeans//DTD JavaHelp Help Set Reference 1.0//EN"
    "http://www.netbeans.org/dtds/helpsetref-1_0.dtd">
<helpsetref url="nbdocs:/com/galileo/netbeans/module/docs/module-hs.xml"/>
```

In this first step you learned how to create a help set with the NetBeans wizard, and how to register a help set either by a separate annotation or by a layer entry and an additional XML file. In the subsequent sections, we will take a closer look at the separate files.

module-hs.xml

This is the central file which describes and configures the help set. Use the title element to give the help set a name. In the map element, you refer to map files. In these map files are the HTML help pages with your IDs; the content of a help set is defined by these map files. With the view elements, you add the content of our help set to the table of contents and to the index (see Listing 16-4). Additionally, you define the search engine to be used.

Listing 16-4. Help Set Description

```xml
<?xml version="1.0" encoding="UTF-8"?>
<!DOCTYPE helpset PUBLIC
    "-//Sun Microsys Inc.//DTD JavaHelp HelpSet Version 2.0//EN"
    "http://java.sun.com/products/javahelp/helpset_2_0.dtd">
<helpset version="2.0">
    <title>My Module Help</title>
    <maps>
        <homeID>com.galileo.netbeans.module.about</homeID>
        <mapref location="module-map.xml"/>
    </maps>
    <view mergetype="javax.help.AppendMerge">
        <name>TOC</name>
        <label>Table of Contents</label>
        <type>javax.help.TOCView</type>
        <data>module-toc.xml</data>
    </view>
    <view mergetype="javax.help.AppendMerge">
        <name>Index</name>
        <label>Index</label>
        <type>javax.help.IndexView</type>
        <data>module-idx.xml</data>
    </view>
    <view>
        <name>Search</name>
        <label>Search</label>
        <type>javax.help.SearchView</type>
        <data engine="com.sun.java.help.search.DefaultSearchEngine">JavaHelpSearch</data>
    </view>
</helpset>
```

module-map.xml

The actual HTML help pages are registered in the map file and a unique ID is given to them by the target attribute. The unique ID is then used for the table of contents and for the index. Additionally, those exact IDs are also used for a HelpCtx object, namely for realizing context-sensitive help. (See Listing 16-5.)

Listing 16-5. Mapping of Help Topics IDs on HTML Pages

```xml
<?xml version="1.0" encoding="UTF-8"?>
<!DOCTYPE map PUBLIC
    "-//Sun Microsystems Inc.//DTD JavaHelp Map Version 2.0//EN"
    "http://java.sun.com/products/javahelp/map_2_0.dtd">
<map version="2.0">
    <mapID target="com.galileo.netbeans.module.about" url="module-about.html"/>
</map>
```

module-toc.xml

With this file you can determine the content of the table of contents. Here, you register the ID of the corresponding help page (which you want to add to the table of contents) by the tocitem element. Doing so, the tocitem element can be arbitrarily nested so the help pages can be grouped. (See Listing 16-6.)

Listing 16-6. Table of Contents of a Help Set

```
<?xml version="1.0" encoding="UTF-8"?>
<!DOCTYPE toc PUBLIC
   "-//Sun Microsystems Inc.//DTD JavaHelp TOC Version 2.0//EN"
   "http://java.sun.com/products/javahelp/toc_2_0.dtd">
<toc version="2.0">
   <tocitem text="My Module">
      <tocitem text="About My Module" target="com.galileo.netbeans.module.about"/>
   </tocitem>
</toc>
```

module-idx.xml

In this file, you list the IDs of the help pages, which you want to include in the index, with the indexitem element. (See Listing 16-7.)

Listing 16-7. Index of a Help Set

```
<?xml version="1.0" encoding="UTF-8"?>
<!DOCTYPE index PUBLIC
   "-//Sun Microsystems Inc.//DTD JavaHelp Index Version 2.0//EN"
   "http://java.sun.com/products/javahelp/index_2_0.dtd">
<index version="2.0">
   <indexitem text="About My Module" target="com.galileo.netbeans.module.about"/>
</index>
```

Help Pages

The previously presented XML files are only of use for the configuration of the help set and the help system. You can create the help pages themselves as a standard HTML page. The wizard has already created a first example page when creating the help set. This is the *module-about.html* file. It has also already been attached to the help set via the file *module-map.xml*. So, you can add your own help pages exactly the same way.

Inserting Links into Help Pages

Within a help page, you can define links both to external sites and to other help pages, even though they belong to another module.

Links to External Web Sites

Typically, external web sites are called in an external browser, since the help window is inadequate for that purpose. So, the BrowserDisplayer class, which you refer to with the object HTML element, is responsible for this. You define the link itself via the content parameter (see Listing 16-8).

Listing 16-8. Link Embedded in Help Pages

```
<object
    classid="java:org.netbeans.modules.javahelp.BrowserDisplayer">
    <param name="content" value="http://www.netbeans.org">
    <param name="text" value="http://www.netbeans.org">
    <param name="textFontSize" value="medium">
    <param name="textColor" value="blue">
</object>
```

The BrowserDisplayer class passes the link to the URLDisplayer service. The default implementation of this service provided by the NetBeans Platform opens the link in the internal web browser of the NetBeans Platform, though. Since this browser mostly displays web sites insufficiently, it would be the best for us to call the standard browser of the operating system. Since the URLDisplayer class is designed as a service and the Java Platform provides a method for calling the standard browser (via the Desktop class), you can realize this by a specific service provider. To do so, you create the ExternalURLDisplayer class which derives from the service class HtmlBrowser.URLDisplayer. This interface is located in the *UI Utilities* module to which you must consequently define a dependency under *Properties* ➤ *Libraries*. This interface specifies the showURL() method which gets the link to open as URL object. Then, you just have to pass this link to the browse() method of the Java Desktop class in the form of a URI object. Then, the Java Desktop class opens the corresponding web site in its standard browser. (See Listing 16-9.)

Listing 16-9. Service Provider for Opening Links in Help Pages Externally

```
@ServiceProvider (service = HtmlBrowser.URLDisplayer.class, position = 0)
public class ExternalURLDisplayer extends HtmlBrowser.URLDisplayer{
    public void showURL(URL link) {
        try {
            Desktop.getDesktop().browse(link.toURI());
        } catch(Exception ex) {
            Logger.getLogger("global").log(Level.SEVERE, null, ex);
            // show the user a message dialog
        }
    }
}
```

This service provider is registered and thus published via the ServiceProvider annotation (see Chapter 5).

Links to Other Help Pages

You can easily add links to help pages of other modules via the nbdocs protocol with the href element, as shown in Listing 16-10.

Listing 16-10. Links on Help Pages of Other Modules

```
<a href="nbdocs://org.netbeans.modules.usersguide/org/netbeans/
    modules/usersguide/configure/configure_options.html">Using the Options Dialog</a>
```

It is important that you first indicate the code name base of the module. In this example, it is `org.netbeans.modules.usersguide`. Subsequently, you define the path to the help page. In case the module and the help page are not available, the help system is able to display relevant information to the user because of the specification of the code name base. You link on your own module-internal help pages the same way.

Context-Sensitive Help

Context-sensitive help enables the user to directly access help and the corresponding topic relating to the current context, in which the user actually is. Therefore, the user does not have to search for the desired topic, but the respective page is directly displayed. A context-sensitive help is realized by the connection of separate components with the ID of a corresponding help page. The NetBeans Platform defines the `HelpCtx.Provider` interface, so a component can announce the help ID to the help system in a simple manner. This interface specifies the `getHelpCtx()` method which must be implemented by the corresponding component and thus delivers a `HelpCtx` object containing an ID.

Numerous frequently-used classes of the NetBeans Platform API already implement the `HelpCtx.Provider` interface. Among these are, for example, the classes `Node`, `DataObject`, `TopComponent`, `SystemAction`, `WizardDescriptor.Panel`, and `DialogDescriptor`. Then, you only have to overwrite the `getHelpCtx()` method in their subclasses. Typically, the context help is called by the user with (*F1*). An additional key for calling help is displayed on a dialog or a wizard which delivers an ID via the `getHelpCtx()` method.

A shortcut definition must be available, so the help can be called with (*F1*). If it was not already made by the NetBeans Platform—so you cannot open the help window with (*F1*)—you can define this shortcut yourself in the layer file with the following entry, as shown in Listing 16-11.

Listing 16-11. Make the Help System Accessible by F1.

```
<folder name="Shortcuts">
    <file name="F1.shadow">
        <attr name="originalFile"
                stringvalue="Actions/Help/org-netbeans-modules-javahelp-HelpAction.instance"/>
    </file>
</folder>
```

If the user presses (*F1*), the `HelpAction` is executed. The `HelpAction` automatically searches the component that is currently focused. If the focused component implements the `HelpCtx.Provider` interface, the ID of the help page is determined by the `getHelpCtx()` method. Furthermore, you also have the possibility to provide a `JComponent` subclass with a help ID using the **setHelpIDString()** method:

```
JComponent c = ...
HelpCtx.setHelpIDString(c, "com.galileo.netbeans.module.about");
```

Remember, your component must be focusable, so it can be found by `HelpAction`. By default, the `TopComponent` class is not focusable, (you can find that out with the `isFocusable()` method). You can achieve this simply by calling setFocusable(). So, a TopComponent subclass, which delivers its help ID via getHelpCtx(), would then look like Listing 16-12.

Listing 16-12. Context-Sensitive Help for Components

```
public final class MyTopComponent extends TopComponent {
    public MyTopComponent() {
        setFocusable(true);
    }
    public HelpCtx getHelpCtx() {
        return new HelpCtx("com.galileo.netbeans.module.about");
    }
}
```

If MyTopComponent is focused and the user presses (*F1*), the help system and the help page are called. The help page has the ID com.galileo.netbeans.module.about. You can define this ID in connection with the desired page in the map file of the help set (see the section "Creating and Integrating a Helpset"). If you only want the help window without a special page to be called, you can return HelpCtx.DEFAULT_HELP. Beyond that, you can also pass a Class object to the HelpCtx constructor, instead of passing the ID in the form of a String. Then, the HelpCtx object detects the ID by means of the complete class name. So, if you used new HelpCtx(getClass()) in the MyTopComponent example, the help ID would be com.galileo.netbeans.module.MyTopComponent.

Opening the Help System

If you want to call the help system yourself, you can get access via the Lookup. There, an implementation of the Help class is registered (see Listing 16-13).

Listing 16-13. Calling the Help System Concerning a Certain Topic

```
Help h = Lookup.getDefault().lookup(Help.class);
if(h != null)
    h.showHelp(new HelpCtx("com.galileo.netbeans.module.about"));
    // h.showHelp(HelpCtx.DEFAULT_HELP);
```

You pass a HelpCtx instance, which represents a help page, to the showHelp() method. You pass the ID of the desired help page, which you determined in the map file, to the constructor. If you want to open the help window with the default help page, you can use HelpCtx.DEFAULT_HELP.

Summary

In this chapter, you learned how to use the NetBeans Platform help system, which is based on the standard JavaHelp framework. We looked at how to create your own help sets and how to insert links into help pages. One important thing you learned in this chapter was how to create context-sensitive help.

CHAPTER 17

Output Window

The NetBeans Platform provides the *Output Window* module as a comfortable and practical display area for showing messages to the user. Multiple different outputs can be output parallel in different tabs. The output window and the I/O API of the NetBeans Platform are closely connected. So, the standard I/O provider implementation redirects its output to the output window. (See Figure 17-1.)

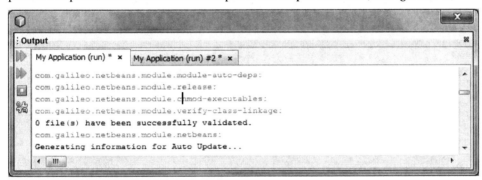

Figure 17-1. Output Window

Producing Output

First, ensure in the properties of your NetBeans Platform application under *Properties* ➤ *Libraries* that the two modules *Output Window* and *I/O APIs* are activated in the cluster *platform*, so this module is available for you since you can only define a dependency on the modules when they are activated here. Now, you must define a dependency on the I/O API module in the module that wants to use the output window. To do so, open the *Properties* of your modules and add the I/O API module as dependency under *Libraries* with the *Add Dependency…* button. Then, your output could look like Listing 17-1.

Listing 17-1. Using the Output Window Module

```
InputOutput io = IOProvider.getDefault().getIO("Task", true);
io.getOut().println("Info message");
io.getErr().println("error message");
io.getOut().close();
io.getErr().close();
```

You get the service provider of the IOProvider service, which is located in the output window, by the IOProvider.getDefault() method over the Lookup. If the output window module, and thus the service provider, does not exist, the getDefault() method would provide a standard implementation which would write the outputs on the standard output. So, the output window is implemented as a global service. (For more information see Chapter 5.) Consequently, the output window could be easily substituted by your own window without having to adapt the source code. The getIO() method delivers an InputOutput object with which you can access the window. You can define a name which is displayed on the tab or in the headline. With the boolean parameter you determine whether a new tab is created or whether an already existing tab with the same name will be reused. With the methods getOut() and getErr() you get an object of the OutputWriter class. This class is a subclass of the Java PrintWriter class. Thus, you can output messages by println(), as usual. The text output by getErr() is displayed red in the output window. It is important that you close the streams again with the close() method when you finish all your output. So, the name of the tab, which is displayed in bold, is displayed as usual again, signaling to the user that the task is completed. If multiple tasks are displayed you can ensure that the corresponding one is active via the InputOutput.select() method.

You can open the output window in your application with the menu item *Window* ➤ *Output* ➤ *Output.* This menu item is added by the output window module. The output window offers you a context menu with which you can search in the output, for example, or delete output in a tab,.

Adding Actions

The output window contains a toolbar on which you can place your own actions. For example, in Figure 17-1 are four Ant-specific actions. For this purpose, there is a variant of the getIO() method, which expects an array of the type Action as second parameter. So, very simple action classes, which just have to implement the Java Action interface, can be passed. It is important that your action class defines an icon, which can be displayed in the toolbar, by the property Action.SMALL_ICON. Subsequently, you will see an example class for such an action which derives from the AbstractAction class that already implements the Action interface. You create an ImageIcon in the constructor and set this for the property SMALL_ICON.

```
public class StopTask extends AbstractAction {
    public StopTask() {
        putValue(SMALL_ICON, ImageUtilities.loadImageIcon("icon.gif", true));
    }
    public void actionPerformed(ActionEvent evt) {
        // stop the task
    }
}
```

Now, you pass an array with an instance of the StopTask class to the getIO() method as second parameter.

```
InputOutput io = IOProvider.getDefault().getIO("Task", new Action[]{new StopTask()});
```

Inserting/Displaying Hyperlinks

You gain access to the output window by the previously described methods getOut() and getErr(). For this purpose, those methods return an OutputWriter instance. This class represents an extension of the PrintWriter class of the Java Platform. It specifies two additional println() methods with which hyperlinks can be displayed in the output window. For this purpose, indicate the text as String object and an OutputListener instance. This listener is responsible for executing the action which will be carried out by clicking on the link.

In Listing 17-2 you gain access to the corresponding OutputWriter instance via the getOut() method. As previously mentioned, the println() method gets the name of the link and it gets a listener.

Listing 17-2. Creating a Hyperlink in the Output Window

```
InputOutput io = IOProvider.getDefault().getIO("Task", true);
OutputWriter ow = io.getOut();
try {
    ow.println("My Link", new MyHyperlinkListener());
} catch (IOException ex) {
    Exceptions.printStackTrace(ex);
}
```

You can implement a corresponding listener with an OutputListener interface, as shown in Listing 17-3.

Listing 17-3. Listener for the Reaction on Hyperlinks in the Output Window

```
import org.openide.windows.OutputEvent;
import org.openide.windows.OutputListener;

public class MyHyperlinkListener implements OutputListener {

    @Override
    public void outputLineSelected(OutputEvent ev) {
        // Action for selection of the link/line
    }

    @Override
    public void outputLineAction(OutputEvent ev) {
        // Action for click on the link
    }

    @Override
    public void outputLineCleared(OutputEvent ev) {
        // Action for deletion of the link/line
    }
}
```

As you see in Listing 17-3, you must implement three methods. You cannot only react on clicks, but must also react on selecting and deleting a link. If you need access to a certain object within the listener, you can just create an according constructor and pass the desired object to it when adding the link or the listener.

Summary

You can use the output window for your own purposes. Thus, you can create output in a simple way when developing, or you can display helpful information to the user, later. In this chapter you learned how to access the output window, how to add your own actions, and how to insert and display hyperlinks.

CHAPTER 18

Navigator

You can display context-dependent panels with the *Navigator* window and the *Navigator API*. Typically, these panels are used by the NetBeans IDE editor for navigation in a document, for example,. Here, the constructors, methods, and additional elements of a Java class are displayed (see Figure 18-1). As a result, the user can navigate within the document. However, this is just one application case; the panels displayed in the navigator can be used for any purpose.

Figure 18-1. Navigator panel for a .java file

The Navigator API specifies the interfaces of a panel, which can be displayed in the navigator, by the interface `NavigatorPanel`. Panels are added declaratively via the layer file of your module. Doing so, a panel is linked to a certain MIME type. If a file with the corresponding MIME type is opened, the accordingly-registered panel is displayed. If no `FileObject`, `DataObject`, or `Node` with a certain MIME type is provided (with which the corresponding navigator panel can be found) the `NavigatorLookupHint` interface can be implemented by the component which displays the context. The interface can then be provided via the local Lookup. This interface just specifies a method with which a MIME type can be returned. Thus, the navigator module is able to find a panel if no file with a MIME type exists.

Creating Panels

I will continue with the example from Chapter 5 (extending it with an additional module), in order to show you the usage of the Navigator API. This example involved a search list that is able to display the entries of the type Mp3FileObject. The currently selected element is provided via a local Lookup. This element provides information about the music title. You want to use this element in your new module, and display all available albums of the current artist in a navigator panel. This process is illustrated in the following steps and in Figure 18-2. This example makes it even clearer how easy and flexible it is to extend an application that is based on the NetBeans Platform with additional modules and components.

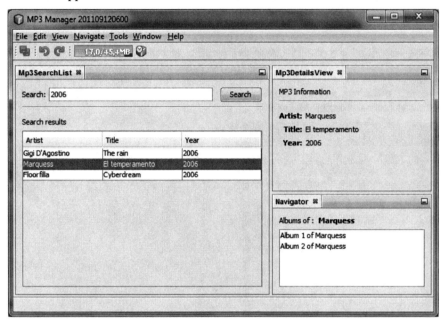

Figure 18-2. Context-dependent navigator panel

First you must activate the *Navigator API* module (located in the *ide* cluster) in your NetBeans Platform application under *Properties ➤ Libraries,* since the Navigator API does not belong to the standard distribution of the Platform, but to the IDE distribution. Then, you apply a new module named *MP3 Navigator* and add this to your application project. Add a dependency to the modules *MP3 Object, Navigator API,* and *Utilities API* under *Properties ➤ Libraries.* Listing 18-1 shows classes out of these modules. Afterward, you create a new *JPanel Form* by the wizard. Then, you change the base class from JPanel to JComponent in the newly created class and implement the two interfaces NavigatorPanel and LookupListener. Then, you can arbitrarily create the content of the panel with the Form Editor. In this example, I only added two labels and a list to the panel for displaying the albums. Subsequently, the most important parts of the class are shown. The complete and runnable example can be downloaded from the Source Code/Download area of the Apress web site at www.apress.com for this book.

Listing 18-1. The Most Important Parts of the Navigator Panel Implementation

```java
public class Mp3AlbumNavigatorPanel extends JComponent
    implements NavigatorPanel, LookupListener {
    private Lookup.Result<Mp3FileObject> result = null;

    public Mp3AlbumNavigatorPanel() {
        initComponents();
    }

    @Override
    public JComponent getComponent() {
        return this;
    }

    @Override
    public void panelActivated(Lookup context) {
        result = Utilities.actionsGlobalContext().lookupResult(Mp3FileObject.class);
        result.addLookupListener(this);
    }

    @Override
    public void panelDeactivated() {
        result.removeLookupListener(this);
        result = null;
    }

    @Override
    public void resultChanged(LookupEvent event) {
        Collection<? extends Mp3FileObject> mp3s = result.allInstances();
        if(!mp3s.isEmpty()) {
            Mp3FileObject mp3 = mp3s.iterator().next();
            //search for albums of selected artist and display it
            albumsOf.setText(mp3.getArtist());
            DefaultListModel model = new DefaultListModel();
            model.addElement("Album 1 of " + mp3.getArtist());
            model.addElement("Album 2 of " + mp3.getArtist());
            albums.setModel(model);
        }
    }
}
```

The navigator module gets the panel to display via the getComponent() method which specifies the NavigatorPanel interface. The methods panelActivated() and panelDeactivated() are called when the panel is displayed or hidden. When activating the panel, you create a Lookup.Result for the class type Mp3FileObject via the global proxy Lookup. The global proxy Lookup delivers the local Lookup of the search list with the activated Mp3FileObject. You register a LookupListener for the Lookup.Result in order to be able to react in case another entry was chosen in the search list. When something changes, the resultChanged() method is called. In this method you can then display the desired content on the navigator panel. For simplicity's sake, this example only presents two entries. Usually, you would search for albums of this artist in a database at that position.

Registering Panels

You must register the panel in the layer file of your module, so the navigator module can find and create the panel. For this purpose the navigator module defines the folder Navigator/Panels. Below this folder, assign your panel to a MIME type for which the panel will be displayed. Select audio/mpeg here. (See Listing 18-2.) However, any other type would be conceivable.

Listing 18-2. Registration of the Navigator Panel in the Layer File

```
<folder name="Navigator">
    <folder name="Panels">
        <folder name="audio">
            <folder name="mpeg">
                <file name="com-galileo-netbeans-module-mp3navigator-
                          Mp3AlbumNavigatorPanel.instance"/>
            </folder>
        </folder>
    </folder>
</folder>
```

Now, you should ask yourself how the navigator module knows when to display which panel. Usually, the navigator module reads the MIME type of the currently active node. In case no nodes exist, as in this example, the Navigator API provides the interface NavigatorLookupHint. This interface specifies the getContentType() method with which the context component—in this case the Mp3SearchList class—delivers the MIME type, to which a navigator panel will be displayed. You implement this interface in the class Mp3SearchList and return the MIME type audio/mpeg exactly as you registered the panel in the layer file; see Listing 18-3.

Listing 18-3. Implementation of the NavigatorLookupHint Interface, Which Determines the Panel to Be Displayed

```
import org.netbeans.spi.navigator.NavigatorLookupHint;
...
public final class Mp3SearchList extends TopComponent implements ListSelectionListener {

    public Mp3SearchList() {
        ...
        associateLookup(new ProxyLookup(new AbstractLookup(content),
            Lookups.singleton(new Mp3AlbumNavigatorLookupHint())));
    }

    private static final class Mp3AlbumNavigatorLookupHint implements NavigatorLookupHint {
        public String getContentType() {
            return "audio/mpeg";
        }
    }
}
```

You create the inner class Mp3AlbumNavigatorLookupHint which implements the NavigatorLookupHint interface. You must now add an instance of this class to your local Lookup. Since you already determined an AbstractLookup as local Lookup, which contains the currently selected entry of the search list, you cannot directly add this instance. So, you must create a `ProxyLookup` to which you can pass the `AbstractLookup` and a Lookup (which you create via the factory `Lookups`). Then, define this proxy Lookup as local Lookup by the method `associateLookup()`. As soon as the top component `Mp3SearchList` is focused, the navigator module is informed by the global Lookup about the existence of a `NavigatorLookupHint` instance. As a result, the navigator can call the `getContentType()` method, and thus open the appropriate navigator panel according to the return value.

Of course, when multiple different panels exist, the navigator component becomes interesting. You can create any number of navigator panels and assign the corresponding MIME type in the `Navigator/Panels` folder. The navigator module then automatically switches the panels, depending on which component is currently active. Finally, the Navigator API also provides the `NavigatorHandler` class. This class contains the static `activatePanel()` method to which you can pass a `NavigatorPanel` instance. This way, you can also programmatically open a panel.

Summary

The navigator module is a universal component for displaying context-dependent data structures. This chapter discussed how to create panels which can be displayed by the navigator module. You also learned both methods by which the navigator module locates panels.

CHAPTER 19

Properties

With the *Properties* window you can display the properties of a node in a simple way. This means you can display the properties of the data or of the action which is represented by this node (for more information see Chapter 12). Thus, you give the user the possibility to change it. A set of properties is managed by the Sheet class of the Nodes API. The AbstractNode class (usually the basis of a node) provides such a Sheet via the method getSheet(). To provide such a Sheet, you just have to overwrite the createSheet() method. Then, you can add your specific properties to this Sheet. I will provide an example to demonstrate how this works. You want to display the ID3 information of the just selected or activated MP3 file. However, you do not read the ID3 information for simplicity's sake, but just use fixed exemplified values; one condition is that you at least have your own node class which derives from AbstractNode. Creating the MP3 file type in Chapter 7, you saw that the DataNode class is used by default. So let's look at the MP3 file type example once again (you can also just create an MP3 file type with the NetBeans wizard) and implement your own node class. The properties, shown in the properties window, will look like those shown in Figure 19-1.

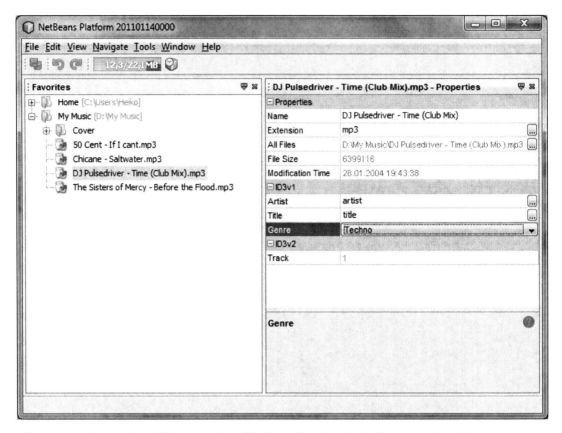

Figure 19-1. *Presentation of the properties of the just selected node in the properties window*

Providing Properties

As already mentioned, you must overwrite the createSheet() method in the corresponding node class; in this example the newly created Mp3DataNode class that represents the files of the type *.mp3*. At the beginning, you need a Sheet instance which you can simply create via the method of the base class and which already adds a Set of basic properties to the instance (this is the first area named *Properties* in Figure 19-1). If you do not want this information you can of course create an instance yourself via the standard constructor of Sheet. So, you already learned that the properties shown can be organized in areas that can be hidden or displayed by the user depending on their needs. The properties of such an area are managed by the Sheet.Set class. You create two Sheet.Set objects via the factory method createPropertiesSet(), in order to apply the two areas *ID3v1* and *ID3v2*. It is important that you give a Sheet.Set a unique name (used for internal management) via the setName() method, otherwise only the last added Sheet.Set will be displayed. With the setDisplayName() method you determine the name which will be used for the area as title.

Listing 19-1. Via the Method createSheet() You Can Create a Sheet Instance Containing the Desired Properties, Which Will Be Displayed in the Properties Window.

```java
public class Mp3DataNode extends DataNode {
    protected Sheet createSheet() {
        Sheet s = super.createSheet();
        Sheet.Set id3v1 = Sheet.createPropertiesSet();
        Sheet.Set id3v2 = Sheet.createPropertiesSet();
        id3v1.setName("ID3v1");
        id3v1.setDisplayName("ID3v1");
        id3v2.setName("ID3v2");
        id3v2.setDisplayName("ID3v2");
        Mp3DataObject mp3 =getLookup().lookup(Mp3DataObject.class);

        try {
            Property artistProp =
                new PropertySupport.Reflection<String>(mp3, String.class, "artist");
            Property titleProp   =
                new PropertySupport.Reflection<String>(mp3, String.class, "title");
            PropertySupport.Reflection<String> genreProp   =
                new PropertySupport.Reflection<String>(mp3, String.class, "genre");
            Property trackProp =
                new PropertySupport.Reflection<Integer>(mp3, Integer.class, "getTrack", null);

            artistProp.setName("Artist");
            titleProp.setName("Title");
            genreProp.setName("Genre");
            trackProp.setName("Track");
            id3v1.put(artistProp);
            id3v1.put(titleProp);
            id3v1.put(genreProp);
            id3v2.put(trackProp);
        } catch (NoSuchMethodException ex) {
            ex.printStackTrace();
        }
        s.put(id3v1);
        s.put(id3v2);
        return s;
    }
}
```

You gain access to the data object, meaning the MP3 file, which provides the features, via the Lookup. Then you create an object for each property, making sure to distinguish between properties that can be changed by the user and read-only properties. For the features that the user will be able to change in the *Properties* window, you create a PropertySupport.Reflection instance with the corresponding type, in this case String. As first parameter you pass the data object; as second parameter, pass the data type of the property; and as third parameter, you pass the name of the get and set method of the corresponding property. For the first property you pass artist, for example. This means that the Mp3DataObject class must provide both the setArtist() method and getArtist(). Otherwise, a NoSuchMethodException occurs. For properties the user must not or will not change, use a variant of the constructor. In fact, you can separately pass the get and set method to the constructor. You only pass null as set method so a property cannot be changed now. Listing 19-3 shows an excerpt of the Mp3DataObject class.

Listing 19-2. *The Data Object Must Provide Its Properties via get Methods. If These Properties Will Be Changable Too You Also Need the Corresponding set Methods.*

```java
public class Mp3DataObject extends MultiDataObject {
    public String getArtist() {
        return this.artist;
    }
    public void setArtist(String artist) {
        this.artist = artist;
    }
    ...
    public int getTrack() {
        return this.track;
    }
}
```

We give a name to the created instances which represent the separate properties via the setName() method and then add the instance to the desired Sheet.Set via the put() method. In turn, you add the put method to the Sheet with put() which you then return.

User-Defined Properties Editor

You can use a self-defined editor for a property value to support the user entering, changing properties, checking (date), or restricting (fixed defined selection of values). In Figure 19-1 you may have noticed that the genre can be selected via a combo box. You can set this via the call

genreProp.**setPropertyEditorClass**(GenrePropertyEditor.class);

for each single property, while GenrePropertyEditor is a user-defined editor with a combo box. Next we will look at how such an editor is buil, referring to the relevant classes and methods. Please find the complete code of the example as a complete project on this book's web page, available in the Source Code/Download area of the Apress web site at www.apress.com.

First, you derive the GenrePropertyEditor class from the Java class PropertyEditorSupport. This is a basis-implementation of the PropertyEditor interface which must be implemented by all user-defined editors. Additionally, you implement the two interfaces ExPropertyEditor and InplaceEditor.Factory, too. Via the attachEnv() method of ExPropertyEditor we get delivered a PropertyEnv object by which we can contact the properties window in a way. You register an InplaceEditor.Factory instance on it (so, your class itself) which is responsible for creating the editor. Actually, the getInplaceEditor() method does that. This method only creates and delivers the editor when requested. You provide the implementation of the graphic editor component as private inner class which derives from InplaceEditor, as you probably guessed because of the return value of getInplaceEditor(). Since you want to use a combo box as editor, you define it as private data element and initialize it with the desired values. (See Listing 19-3.) Then, this component must be delivered before the getComponent() method. The other important methods of the InplaceEditor are setValue() and getValue(). With those, the value of the combo box can be set on the basis of the property and the other way around. Additionally, there is the reset() method with which changes can be taken back (typically when pressing *Esc*).

Listing 19-3. User-Defined Editor with Which the Genre Property Can Be Selected via a Combo Box

```java
public class GenrePropertyEditor extends PropertyEditorSupport
   implements ExPropertyEditor, InplaceEditor.Factory {
   private InplaceEditor ed = null;

   public void attachEnv(PropertyEnv propertyEnv) {
      propertyEnv.registerInplaceEditorFactory(this);
   }

   public InplaceEditor getInplaceEditor() {
      if(ed == null)
         ed = new Inplace();
      return ed;
   }

   private static class Inplace implements InplaceEditor {
      private PropertyEditor editor = null;
      private PropertyModel  model  = null;
      private JComboBox genres = new JComboBox(
         new String[] {"Techno", "Trance", "Rock", "Pop"});

      public JComponent getComponent() {
         return this.genres;
      }

      public Object getValue() {
         return this.genres.getSelectedItem();
      }

      public void setValue(Object object) {
         this.genres.setSelectedItem(object);
      }

      public void reset() {
         String genre = (String) editor.getValue();
         if(genre != null)
            this.genres.setSelectedItem(genre);
      }
   }
}
```

Summary

The properties window is a simple and common way to display and change the properties of arbitrary objects. In this chapter you learned how to provide your properties to be displayed in the properties window. You also learned how you can implement a user-specific property editor.

CHAPTER 20

Options and Settings

With the *Options Dialog API and SPI,* you can easily create option panels with which the user can comfortably manage the settings and options of your application. This module provides the basic structure of an option dialog into which you can integrate your panels, as shown in Figure 20-1. There are two or three possible variants of panels. There are primary and secondary panels. A secondary panel is a subcategory of a primary panel in form of a tab. There are two kinds of primary panels: primary panels that manage options themselves, and primary panels that only function as containers and contain secondary panels. Preferably the settings are saved and loaded using the Preferences API. The NetBeans Platform provides a specific implementation which will be explained in more detail in the "Managing Settings" section.

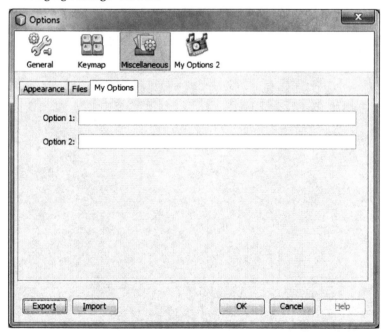

Figure 20-1. Standard options dialog within which you can integrate your panels

Creating Options Panels

The NetBeans IDE provides a wizard for creating an options panel (for all three kinds), shown in Figure 20-2. This wizard can be found under *File ➤ New File…* in the category *Module Development ➤ Options Panel*. Depending on your purpose, choose either a *Primary Panel* (with or without secondary panels) or a *Secondary Panel* and indicate the data the wizard needs. Finally, the wizard creates the panel and registers it via an annotation.

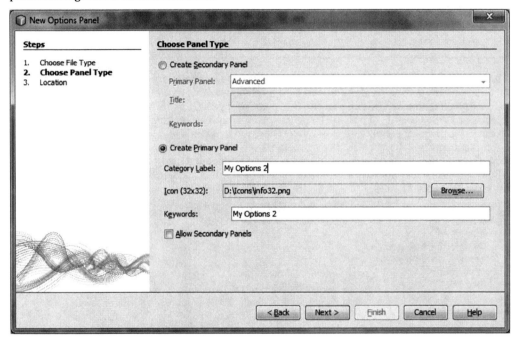

Figure 20-2. NetBeans wizard for creating options panels

A panel consists of a view and a controller. The view is responsible for providing the GUI and for loading and saving the data. The controller creates the view and at the same time is a broker between the options dialog and the view. The panel, meaning the view, is derived from the JPanel class. You can arbitrarily place your components, with which the options are displayed and set, on this panel. Listing 20-1 uses two text fields. You save and load the value of these fields via the Preferences API (see the "Managing Settings" section) in the methods store() and load(), which are called by the controller when opening and closing the panel.

The options dialog can only be closed by the user when the appropriate settings haven been selected. Therefore, a panel must inform the option dialog about its state, either valid or invalid. Implement validation via the valid() method. In this example, for example, you want to make sure the user enters a value in the first field, so you add a DocumentListener to the option1 text field. Now, each time the user makes an entry in the first text field, the controller is informed via Controller.changed(), which in turn calls the valid() method, only returning true when at least one character is entered into the text field.

Listing 20-1. View of the Options Panel, Only Deriving from JPanel

```
public final class ModuleOptions1Panel extends JPanel implements DocumentListener {
    private JTextField option1;
    private JTextField option2;
    private final ModuleOptions1PanelController controller;

    public ModuleOptionsPanel(ModuleOptions1PanelController ctl) {
        this.controller = ctl;
        initComponents();
        option1.getDocument().addDocumentListener(this);
    }

    public void insertUpdate(DocumentEvent event) {
        controller.changed();
    }

    public void removeUpdate(DocumentEvent event) {
        controller.changed();
    }

    public void changedUpdate(DocumentEvent event) {
        controller.changed();
    }

    public void load() {
        option1.setText(
            NbPreferences.forModule(ModuleOptions1Panel.class).
            get("option1", "default"));
    }

    public void store() {
        NbPreferences.forModule(ModuleOptions1Panel.class).
            put("option1", option1.getText());
    }

    public boolean valid() {
        if(option1.getText().length() == 0) {
            return false;
        } else {
            return true;
        }
    }
}
```

Now let us look at the responsibilities of the controller. Since the controller needs to interact with the options dialog, its interfaces are determined by the abstract class OptionsPanelController. The controller's most important task is the creation of the view, using getPanel(), which you provide via the method getComponent(). As you can see, the method getComponent() receives a Lookup. This is a proxy Lookup, containing the Lookups of all controllers available in the options dialog. The controller uses the getLookup() method to make a Lookup available, which is already implemented by the abstract class

243

OptionsPanelController. However, this default implementation just provides an empty Lookup. So, in order to provide certain objects in the Lookup, you have to overwrite the getLookup() method. Consequently, you can communicate with other option panels via this so-called master Lookup, which you get via getComponent(). You already learned in Chapter 5 how communication can be realized using local Lookups and a global proxy Lookup (in this case, the master Lookup).

The update() method is called when the panel is loaded the first time. Here, you call the load() method of the panel in order to load the data, so to initialize the fields. If the user clicks the *OK* button, the applyChanges() method of the options dialog is called. So here you save the data via the store() method. However, if the user cancels the dialog, the cancel() method is called, in which you obviously do not save the data. Should the situation arise, you can roll back the changes you already made. Using the isValid() method, you inform the options dialog whether the data of the panels is okay. If this is not the case, the *OK* button is automatically deactivated. Moreover, you must inform the options dialog whether the data has changed. You do this using the isChanged() method. With getHelpCtx(), you can provide a HelpCtx object that contains a reference to a help page, which will be displayed when the user clicks the options dialog's *Help* button.

To inform the options dialog about changes in data, you must give it the possibility of registering (see Listing 20-2). You achieve this via the methods addPropertyChangeListener() and removePropertyChangeListener(). You already know the changed() method from the view class ModuleOptions1Panel. This method is called by the view when data is changed, and thus informs the options dialog about the changes. The options dialog is registered as a listener. As a result, the options dialog in turn checks whether the data is valid.

Listing 20-2. Options Panel Controller

```
import org.netbeans.spi.options.OptionsPanelController;
...
@OptionsPanelController.SubRegistration(
    location = "Advanced",
    displayName = "#AdvancedOption_DisplayName_ModuleOptions1",
    keywords = "#AdvancedOption_Keywords_ModuleOptions1",
    keywordsCategory = "Advanced/ModuleOptions1")
public final class ModuleOptions1PanelController extends OptionsPanelController {

    private ModuleOptions1Panel panel;
    private final PropertyChangeSupport pcs = new PropertyChangeSupport(this);
    private boolean changed;

    public JComponent getComponent(Lookup masterLookup) {
        return getPanel();
    }

    private ModuleOptionsPanel getPanel() {
        if (panel == null) {
            panel = new ModuleOptions1Panel(this);
        }
        return panel;
    }

    public void update() {
        getPanel().load();
```

```
        changed = false;
    }

    public void applyChanges() {
        getPanel().store();
        changed = false;
    }

    public void cancel() {
    }

    public boolean isValid() {
        return getPanel().valid();
    }

    public boolean isChanged() {
        return changed;
    }

    public HelpCtx getHelpCtx() {
        return null;
    }

    public void addPropertyChangeListener(
        PropertyChangeListener l) {
        pcs.addPropertyChangeListener(l);
    }

    public void removePropertyChangeListener(
        PropertyChangeListener l) {
        pcs.removePropertyChangeListener(l);
    }

    public void changed() {
        if (!changed) {
            changed = true;
            pcs.firePropertyChange(OptionsPanelController.PROP_CHANGED, false, true);
        }
        pcs.firePropertyChange(OptionsPanelController.PROP_VALID, null, null);
    }
}
```

Option panels are registered by annotations and thus added to the option dialog. A primary panel that does not contain secondary panels is provided with the @OptionsPanelController.TopLevelRegistration annotation. A primary panel functioning as container for secondary panels is provided with the @OptionsPanelController.ContainerRegistration annotation. A secondary panel is registered via the @OptionsPanelController.SubRegistration annotation. The annotation is added to the controller, which is itself responsible for creating the corresponding panel.

Primary Panel

Using the annotation for the registration of a primary panel, you must assign a name via the
categoryName attribute and an icon via the iconBase attribute (see Listing 20-3). The icon and the name
are located in the top bar of the option dialog (see Figure 20-1). Optionally, you can add the attributes
keywords and keywordsCategory with the appropriate values, so the option panel can be found by
QuickSearch. Furthermore, you can assign an identifier via the id attribute. With this identifier, a panel
can directly be opened via the OptionsDisplayer.open() method. Ideally, you use a constant string of
your controller class for this purpose. You can influence the order in which the panels in the options
dialog are displayed, via the position attribute. bear in mind that you can also read values from a
Bundle.properties file via the # sign concerning the currently displayed annotations.

Listing 20-3. Registration of a Primary Panel with Your Own Options via Annotations

```
@OptionsPanelController.TopLevelRegistration(
    categoryName = "#OptionsCategory_Name_ModuleOptions2",
    iconBase = "com/galileo/netbeans/module/icon.png",
    keywords = "#OptionsCategory_Keywords_ModuleOptions2",
    keywordsCategory = "ModuleOptions2",
    id = ModuleOptions2PanelController.ID)
```

If you do not want to use annotations, you can alternatively create the layer entry (which is
displayed in Listing 20-4) in the standard folder OptionsDialog. Such an entry is actually created
automatically by the annotation shown in Listing 20-3.

Listing 20-4. Registration of a Primary Panel with Your Own Options via Layer Entry

```
<folder name="OptionsDialog">
    <file name="ModuleOptions2OptionsCategory.instance">
        <attr name="controller" newvalue=
            "com.galileo.netbeans.module.ModuleOptions2PanelController"/>
        <attr name="instanceCreate" methodvalue=
            "org.netbeans.spi.options.OptionsCategory.createCategory"/>
        <attr name="categoryName" bundlevalue=
            "com.galileo.netbeans.module.Bundle#OptionsCategory_Name_ModuleOptions2"/>
        <attr name="iconBase" stringvalue=
            "com/galileo/netbeans/module/icon.png"/>
        <attr name="keywords" bundlevalue=
            "com.galileo.netbeans.module.Bundle#OptionsCategory_Keywords_ModuleOptions2"/>
        <attr name="keywordsCategory"stringvalue="ModuleOptions2"/>
        <attr name="title" bundlevalue=
            "com.galileo.netbeans.module.Bundle#OptionsCategory_Title_ModuleOptions2"/>
    </file>
</folder>
```

Secondary Panel

A secondary panel is registered in a similar way. The annotation
@OptionsPanelController.SubRegistration distinguishes two attributes for this. In contrast to a primary
panel, a secondary panel does not have an icon (see Figure 20-1, again). Instead, you specify the category

(meaning the primary panel container) to which your panel will be added via the location attribute (see Listing 20-5).

Listing 20-5. Registration of a Secondary Panel via Annotation

```
@OptionsPanelController.SubRegistration(
    location = "Advanced",
    displayName = "#AdvancedOption_DisplayName_ModuleOptions1",
    keywords = "#AdvancedOption_Keywords_ModuleOptions1",
    keywordsCategory = "Advanced/ModuleOptions1",
    id = ModuleOptions1PanelController.ID)
```

The corresponding layer entry mainly differs from the entry of a primary panel in one respect: another factory method is assigned via the instanceCreate attribute which is used for creating the secondary panel. Furthermore, it is important that the assignment to the primary panel occurs via a subfolder. In Listing 20-6 this is the folder Advanced in the standard folder OptionsDialog.

Listing 20-6. Registration of a Secondary Panel with Your Own Options via Layer Entry

```
<folder name="OptionsDialog">
  <folder name="Advanced">
    <file name="com-galileo-netbeans-module-ModuleOptions1PanelController.instance">
      <attr name="controller" newvalue=
        "com.galileo.netbeans.module.ModuleOptions1PanelController"/>
      <attr name="instanceCreate" methodvalue=
        "org.netbeans.spi.options.AdvancedOption.createSubCategory"/>
      <attr name="displayName" bundlevalue=
        "com.galileo.netbeans.module.Bundle#AdvancedOption_DisplayName_ModuleOptions1"/>
      <attr name="keywords" bundlevalue=
        "com.galileo.netbeans.module.Bundle#AdvancedOption_Keywords_ModuleOptions1"/>
      <attr name="keywordsCategory"
        stringvalue="Advanced/ModuleOptions1"/>
      <attr name="toolTip" bundlevalue=
        "com.galileo.netbeans.module.Bundle#AdvancedOption_Tooltip_ModuleOptions1"/>
    </file>
  </folder>
</folder>
```

Secondary Panel Container

Previously, you learned how to implement and register primary and secondary panels. A primary panel that will contain the secondary panel (a so-called secondary panel container) only consists of the registration of such a container. For this use the annotation @OptionsPanelController.ContainerRegistration. The attributes used for this correspond to those already discussed in the sections "Primary Panel" and "Secondary Panel." You must indicate categoryName, iconBase, and id. You define a folder via id which the secondary panels can use for its assignment via the location attribute. (See Listing 20-7.)

Listing 20-7. Registration of a Secondary Panel Container via Annotation

```
@OptionsPanelController.ContainerRegistration(
    id = "ModuleOptions3",
    categoryName = "#OptionsCategory_Name_ModuleOptions3",
    iconBase = "com/galileo/netbeans/module/info32.png",
    keywords = "#OptionsCategory_Keywords_ModuleOptions3",
    keywordsCategory = "ModuleOptions3")
```

Remember that the annotation, shown in Listing 20-7, is used in conjunction with a package and not with a class. You can also register a container with a self-created layer entry instead of an annotation, as shown in Listing 20-8.

Listing 20-8. Registration of a Secondary Panel Container via Layer Entry

```
<folder name="OptionsDialog">
    <file name="ModuleOptions3.instance">
        <attr name="instanceCreate" methodvalue=
            "org.netbeans.spi.options.OptionsCategory.createCategory"/>
        <attr name="advancedOptionsFolder" stringvalue="OptionsDialog/ModuleOptions3"/>
        <attr name="categoryName" bundlevalue=
            "com.galileo.netbeans.module.Bundle#OptionsCategory_Name_ModuleOptions3"/>
        <attr name="iconBase" stringvalue=
            "com/galileo/netbeans/module/info32.png"/>
        <attr name="keywords" bundlevalue=
            "com.galileo.netbeans.module.Bundle#OptionsCategory_Keywords_ModuleOptions3" />
        <attr name="keywordsCategory" stringvalue="ModuleOptions3"/>
    </file>
    <folder name="ModuleOptions3">
        <attr intvalue="0" name="position"/>
    </folder>
</folder>
```

In Listing 20-8 you can see that first a file with some attributes is created in the standard folder OptionsDialog. Via the instanceCreate attribute, the factory method is specified which then creates the container. The advancedOptionsFolder attribute indicates the folder to which the secondary panels must be assigned in order to be displayed in this container. If you want to determine the position of the just registered container within the options dialog, you can already create the folder (as in Listing 20-8) and add the position attribute with the wished value.

Via the OptionsDisplayer class you gain access to the options dialog, so you can directly open the dialog from your context with a certain panel:

```
OptionsDisplayer.getDefault().open(ModuleOptions2PanelController.ID);
```

Use the identifier (id attribute) previously defined via the annotations.

Managing Settings

Settings and configuration data inside a NetBeans Platform application is preferably saved and loaded via the Java Preferences API. The Java Platform specifies an interface via the Preferences class. With this interface, settings and configuration data can be saved and loaded independent of their physical location. Different implementations can be provided with which the data, for example, in a file, in a system registry or even in a database can be saved. The data is saved in a hierarchic structure in form of key value pairs. An instance of the Preferences class represents a node in this hierarchy. You can imagine a node like a directory in a file system below which the data can be saved.

With the NbPreferences class the Utilities API makes available an implementation of the Java Preferences specification for the NetBeans Platform. This implementation ensures that the settings are stored in the central configuration directory of the application, which is located in the user directory. The settings are stored as normal *.properties* files. Thus, the settings, which you save via Preferences, like all other settings in a NetBeans Platform application, are managed user-specifically. The NbPreferences class provides two static methods. With the forModule() method a Preferences node is delivered whose data are saved in a separate *.properties* file in the *config/Preferences* directory for each module (see Figure 20-3). With the root() method an application global Preferences node which manages its data in the *config/Preferences.properties* file is delivered.

Figure 20-3. *With the NetBeans Preferences implementation, settings can be saved either module-specifically in the Preferences directory or application-globally in the Preferences.properties file*

Then, you can easily save and read your settings with the methods specified by the Preferences class. If you want to save the name and port of a server, for example, we use the call shown in Listing 20-9.

Listing 20-9. *Saving and Loading of Settings via the Preferences API*

```
Preferences node = NbPreferences.forModule(this.getClass());
String name = node.get("server.name", "localhost");
int    port = node.getInt("server.port", 8080);
node.put("server.name", name);
node.putInt("server.port", port);
```

Besides the methods for accessing data, shown here, further methods are available with which you can easily save arrays or boolean values, too, for example. Furthermore, with the *Java Preferences API* you can register a NodeChangeListener and a PropertyChangeListener on a Preferences instance (meaning a node), in order to add and delete of child nodes as well as to react on changes of data.

Summary

With the Options Dialog API and SPI, the NetBeans Platform provides a precast options dialog. In this options dialog you can quickly and easily integrate your own (private) panels. You already learned how settings can be managed centrally and in a homogenous way by the user. You also learned how the NetBeans Preferences API facilitates simply saving the settings.

CHAPTER 21

Palette

The Form Editor is a very good example for using the palette module. The Form Editor places its AWT and Swing components on the palette (see Figure 21-1). These components can then be moved via drag-and-drop. You can also add components to the palette during runtime. The content of the palette window is managed and provided by a PaletteController. Such a PaletteController can be made available by a top component via the Lookup. This means that as soon as a top component, in whose Lookup is located a PaletteController instance, becomes active, the palette window is opened and its content is displayed. A PaletteController is created via the PaletteFactory class. There are two ways to provide the components. You can either register the components, which will be displayed on the palette, with XML files in the layer file, or you can use a two-stage or three-stage node hierarchy. We will look at both approaches here.

Note that you are not limited to providing a palette to your own top components, but you can also register a palette for a certain file type in the layer file which is just displayed when a file of this type is opened in the NetBeans editor. This is especially helpful if you want to extend the functionality of the NetBeans IDE. This topic will be explored in Chapter 22.

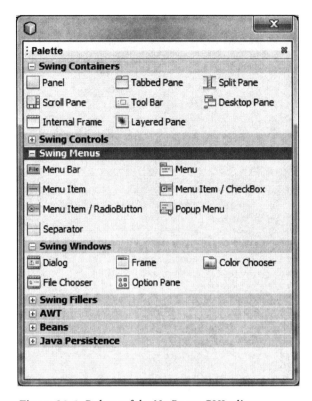

Figure 21-1. *Palette of the NetBeans GUI editor*

Palette Entries via the Layer File

A component, which will be placed on the palette, is defined via the XML file shown in Listing 21-1.

Listing 21-1. XML File That Defines a Palette Entry

```
<!DOCTYPE editor_palette_item PUBLIC
   "-//NetBeans//Editor Palette Item 1.1//EN"
   "http://www.netbeans.org/dtds/editor-palette-item-1_1.dtd">
<editor_palette_item version="1.1">
   <body></body>
   <icon16 urlvalue="file:/E:/icon16.jpg"/>
   <icon32 urlvalue="file:/E:/icon32.jpg"/>
   <inline-description>
      <display-name>My Palette Item</display-name>
      <tooltip>My Palette Item</tooltip>
   </inline-description>
</editor_palette_item>
```

With the elements icon16 and icon32 you define each an icon that will be displayed for this entry, depending on the user's settings. Typically, they are the size 16 and 32 pixels, but they can also be bigger. However, it makes sense to assign a 16 pixels-sized icon even for the icon16 attribute because this attribute is also used for the display in the palette manager which can be called via the context menu of the Palette window, since only 16-pixel icons can be displayed there. Interestingly, you can also use absolute paths, as shown in this section's example. Thus, not only icons of the module can be used, but also icons from a user-defined directory. This can be especially useful if you want the user to have the ability to add entries to the palette during runtime.

With the inline-description element and its both subelements display-name and tooltip you can determine the text with which the entry will be displayed in the palette. Alternatively, you can use the element description instead of inline-description. With its attribute localizing-bundle you can indicate a resource bundle which provides the values for display-name and tooltip. By the attributes display-name-key and tooltip-key you indicate the keys for these values. This way, you can also internationalize palette entries; it can be very helpful to look at the DTD of this XML file (DTDs are found in the Appendix).

You can now define any number of components. Those components must be registered in the layer file of your module in order to add it to a palette. For this purpose you can define an arbitrary folder. Below this folder, create a subfolder for each category which will be displayed on the palette. Then, the XML files are entered into this subfolder. The result is the following entry, for example:

```
<folder name="MyPaletteItems">
    <folder name="My Category">
        <file name="myitem1.xml" url="myitem1.xml"/>
        <file name="myitem2.xml" url="myitem2.xml"/>
    </folder>
</folder>
```

Now, just a PaletteController instance is missing, which you then add to the top component, for which the palette entries will be displayed (see Listing 21-2). As already mentioned at the beginning of this chapter, you use the PaletteFactory class for this purpose. This class provides a factory method, namely createPalette(). To this method you just have to pass the MyPaletteItems folder you defined in the layer file. Then, the classes PaletteFactory and PaletteController do the rest. You must provide an implementation of the PaletteActions class as second parameter. This class provides actions for certain events. In the simplest case, you create an empty implementation of this abstract class and return an empty array in the methods null.

Listing 21-2. Creating a Palette Instance and Connecting It with a Top Component

```
public MyTopComponent() {
    ...
    try {
        associateLookup(Lookups.fixed(
            PaletteFactory.createPalette("MyPaletteItems", new MyActions())));
    } catch(IOException e) {
        // MyPaletteItems cannot be found
    }
}
```

Creating a Palette via Your Own Nodes

Entries of a palette are represented by a node. In the previous section you defined each entry via an XML file. For each of these entries a standard node is provided automatically. You can also provide palette components via your own node implementation instead of an XML definition. These nodes must be present in a three-stage hierarchy. The top layer is only a root node, which you can pass to the createPalette() method in order to create the elements. The nodes on the second level, meaning all child nodes of the root node, are one category. In turn, its child nodes are then used as palette entries. For example, let's say you want to create a palette for managing music albums, which can be added to a playlist via drag-and-drop (as you can see in Figure 21-2).

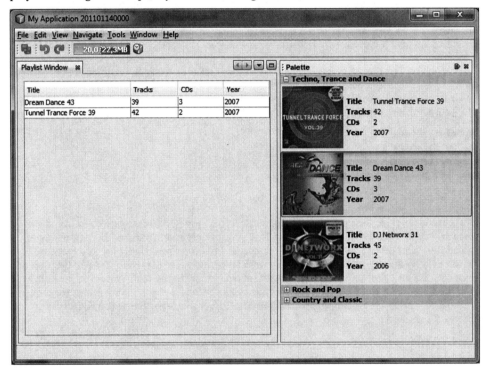

Figure 21-2. Using the palette for managing music albums, which can be added to a playlist via drag-and-drop

Node Classes

As you already learned in Chapter 12, child nodes are created by a ChildFactory class. You create such a class for managing the categories, which will be displayed on the palette, in this case as genre. For this purpose, you derive from the ChildFactory<String> class. The nodes are created by the createNodesForKey() method. For this example (see Listing 21-3), you just create three GenreNode instances directly.

As you might imagine, you read the genres from a database and then create the GenreNode objects for it. (In Chapter 26, which deals with embedding and using the Java DB, we will use and extend this example.) The GenreNode class itself is explicitly easy. The genre is passed to its constructor as parameter which is directly passed to the AlbumNodeFactory class. Thus, you are in the second (respectively third) level of the node hierarchy (see Listing 21-4).

Listing 21-3. All Genres, Which Will Be Displayed on the Palette, Are Created by GenreNodeFactory.

```
import org.openide.nodes.ChildFactory;
import org.openide.nodes.Node;
...
public class GenreNodeFactory extends ChildFactory<String> {

   @Override
   protected boolean createKeys(List<String> toPopulate) {
      toPopulate.add("root");
      return true;
   }

   @Override
   protected Node[] createNodesForKey(String key) {
      return new Node[]{
         new GenreNode("Techno, Trance and Dance"),
         new GenreNode("Rock and Pop"),
         new GenreNode("Country and Classic")};
   }
}
```

Listing 21-4. A Genre Represented by the GenreNode Class

```
import org.openide.nodes.AbstractNode;
import org.openide.nodes.Children;

public class GenreNode extends AbstractNode {
   public GenreNode(String genre) {
      super(Children.create(new AlbumNodeFactory(genre), false));
      this.setDisplayName(genre);
   }
}
```

The AlbumNodeFactory class, which is responsible for creating the albums of a certain genre, is basically built like the GenreNodeFactory class. First you create three node instances of the type AlbumNode in the createNodesForKey() method directly and pass the genre to this method. With this parameter, for example, you were able to search in a database for albums belonging to this genre. The data of an album is managed by the Album class (see Listing 21-5).

Listing 21-5. The AlbumNodeFactory Class Creates the Nodes of the Albums for a Certain Genre.

```
import org.openide.nodes.ChildFactory;
import org.openide.nodes.Node;
...
public class AlbumNodeFactory extends ChildFactory<String> {
   private String genre;
```

```
    public AlbumNodeFactory(String genre) {
       this.genre = genre;
    }

    @Override
    protected boolean createKeys(List<String> toPopulate) {
       toPopulate.add(genre);
       return true;
    }

    @Override
    protected Node[] createNodesForKey(String key) {
       return new Node[] {
          new AlbumNode(
             new Album("Tunnel Trance Force 39", "42", "2","2007",
                "com/galileo/netbeans/module/cover_small.jpg",
                "com/galileo/netbeans/module/cover_big.jpg")),
          new AlbumNode(
             new Album("Dream Dance 43", "39", "3", "2007",
                "com/galileo/netbeans/module/cover2_small.jpg",
                "com/galileo/netbeans/module/cover2_big.jpg")),
          new AlbumNode(
             new Album("DJ Networx 31", "45", "2", "2006",
                "com/galileo/netbeans/module/cover3_small.jpg",
                "com/galileo/netbeans/module/cover3_big.jpg"))
       };
    }
}
```

At last, the AlbumNode class is responsible for displaying the albums on the palette (as you can see in Figure 21-2). Since an AlbumNode does not own additional child nodes, you pass an empty container to the constructor of the base class via Children.LEAF. You determine the name via setDisplayName(), which will be displayed on the palette. You can use HTML here for an attractive presentation (see Listing 21-6). For this purpose, I created the getLabel() method, which puts together an HTML string, which displays the data of the album in a table. The value of the getHtmlDisplayName() is used in the palette manager, which you can open via the context menu of the palette. You provide the icon of the corresponding entry with the getIcon(), method. In this example, the icon is a cover of an album. Thus the user can choose between big and small icons. So you should deliver a small icon (typically 16 pixels) and a bigger icon, depending on the type parameter.

Listing 21-6. The AlbumNode Class Is Responsible for Displaying a Palette Entry.

```
import org.openide.nodes.AbstractNode;
import org.openide.nodes.Children;
...
public class AlbumNode extends AbstractNode {
   private Album album = null;

   public AlbumNode(Album album) {
      super(Children.LEAF);
      this.album = album;
```

```
        this.setDisplayName(getLabel());
    }

    public String getHtmlDisplayName() {
        return "<b>" + album.getTitle() + "</b> (" + album.getTracks() + " Tracks)";
    }

    public Image getIcon(int type) {
        return album.getIcon(type);
    }

    private String getLabel() {
        String label = "<html>" +
            "<table cellspacing=\"0\" cellpadding=\"1\">" +
                "<tr>" +
                    "<td><b>Title </b></td>" +
                    "<td>" + album.getTitle() + "</td>" +
                    ...
    }
}
```

Creating and Adding a Palette

After creating this node hierarchy, which provides the data for the palette, you can now create a palette and add it to the Lookup of the playlist top component. Thus, the palette is always displayed as soon as a playlist is active. So first, create a root node in the constructor of the PlaylistTopComponent class. Your palette data comes from this root node. You pass a children container, which is created by the factory method Children.create(), to this root node. This children container cares about the management of the data. At the same time, you pass a GenreNodeFactory instance which is responsible for creating the data. Then, you just need a PaletteActions instance which has no further significance at the moment. Later you can create a PaletteController instance out of it via createPalette(). You can pack this instance into a Lookup, which you define as a local Lookup of the top component via associateLookup().

```
import org.netbeans.spi.palette.PaletteActions;
import org.netbeans.spi.palette.PaletteController;
import org.netbeans.spi.palette.PaletteFactory;
...
public PlaylistTopComponent() {
    ...
    Node root = new AbstractNode(Children.create(new GenreNodeFactory(), false));
    PaletteActions    a = new MyPaletteActions();
    PaletteController p = PaletteFactory.createPalette(root, a);
    associateLookup(Lookups.fixed(p));
}
```

Drag-and-Drop Functionality

The drag-and-drop functionality is still missing for dragging the albums from the palette to the playlist window. For this purpose, two supplements are necessary. One for the Album and AlbumNode classes and one for the top component or the table, which will receive instances of the Album class.

The data you want to pass is located in the Album class. You implement the Transferable interface on the Album class, in order to be able to directly pass them to the playlist top component via drag-and-drop (see Listing 21-7). A DataFlavor (which you create as a static instance in Album) is needed for identifying the data. With the getTransferDataFlavors() method you return your special DataFlavor. The getTransferData() method is called by the playlist window. Return the album instance to this method via this, if the requested DataFlavor is of the type DATA_FLAVOR. If another DataFlavor is requested, you trigger an exception.

Listing 21-7. The Album Class Contains the Data and Implements the Interface Transferable, So It Can Be Passed Via Drag and Drop.

```java
import java.awt.datatransfer.DataFlavor;
import java.awt.datatransfer.Transferable;
import java.awt.datatransfer.UnsupportedFlavorException;
...
public class Album implements Transferable {
    public static final DataFlavor DATA_FLAVOR = new DataFlavor(Album.class, "album");
    ...

    public DataFlavor[] getTransferDataFlavors() {
        return new DataFlavor[] {DATA_FLAVOR};
    }

    public boolean isDataFlavorSupported(DataFlavor flavor) {
        return flavor == DATA_FLAVOR;
    }

    public Object getTransferData(DataFlavor flavor) throws UnsupportedFlavorException {
        if(flavor == DATA_FLAVOR) {
            return this;
        } else {
            throw new UnsupportedFlavorException(flavor);
        }
    }
}
```

Actually, the user does not move the Album object itself, but an AlbumNode instance. This means the drag event is triggered on the node. Therefore, you overwrite the drag() method which was already specified by the Node class. This method delivers a Transferable instance—in this case the album instance, which is represented by the AlbumNode (see Listing 21-8).

Listing 21-8. Making the AlbumNode Drag-Suitable

```java
import java.awt.datatransfer.Transferable;
...
public class AlbumNode extends AbstractNode {
    private Album album = null;
    ...
    public Transferable drag() throws IOException {
        return album;
```

```
    }
}
```

Finally, you still have to extend the PlaylistTopComponent so it can receive a palette entry. For this you need a TransferHandler, which is registered on the object. This object will be able to receive the data; here, it is the albums table and its scroll area scrollPane. You implement a specific transfer handler named AlbumTransferHandler, in order to determine which data you want to accept and to process the data. To do so you just overwrite two methods. First, the canImport() method, which is always called when an object is dragged on or above the component. In this component, you decide whether that object will be accepted. This check is done by the DataFlavor which was previously determined in Album. If this method returns true, the user receives a (mouse symbol) signal that the component is able to receive the object. The other method to overwrite is the importData() method. This method is called when the drop event is triggered. Via the TransferSupport object (which is passed), you receive exactly that Transferable instance delivered to the AlbumNode class by the previously implemented drag() method. With the getTransferData() method and with your DataFlavor object, you are then able to determine the corresponding Album object. Finally, you add the object's data to the table. (See Listing 21-9.)

Listing 21-9. Receiving an Album Object Passed via Drag and Drop

```
import javax.swing.TransferHandler;
import javax.swing.TransferHandler.TransferSupport;
...
public final class PlaylistTopComponent extends TopComponent {

    private TransferHandler th = new AlbumTransferHandler();

    public PlaylistTopComponent() {
        ...
        albums.setTransferHandler(th);
        scrollPane.setTransferHandler(th);
    }

    private final class AlbumTransferHandler extends TransferHandler {

        public boolean canImport(TransferSupport support) {
            return support.isDataFlavorSupported(Album.DATA_FLAVOR);
        }

        public boolean importData(TransferSupport support) {
            try {
                Album a = (Album)support.getTransferable().getTransferData(Album.DATA_FLAVOR);
                DefaultTableModel model = (DefaultTableModel)albums.getModel();
                model.addRow(new Object[]{a.getTitle(),
                                          a.getTracks(),
                                          a.getCDs(),
                                          a.getYear()});
                return true;
            } catch(Exception e) {
                Exceptions.printStackTrace(e);
                return false;
```

```
            }
          }
        }
      }
```

Summary

The palette module of the NetBeans IDE is concerned with the management and graphic display of components, in order to facilitate quick access. In this chapter you learned how to define palette entries in the layer file. Additionally you implemented an example to create a specific node class that represents palette items. In this example you also saw how easy it is to implement drag-and-drop support for your own palette items.

Use & Extend: Advanced APIs of the NetBeans Platform & ID

CHAPTER 22

Palette API

In Chapter 21, you created a palette. From this palette you could drag music albums on the top component (which you implemented yourself) via drag-and-drop. As indicated, it is also possible to register a palette for a certain file type. This means that when a file of this type is opened in the NetBeans editor, the palette registered for this type is automatically opened. The following example will show how this actually works.

Let's assume you want to provide a palette for manifest files (.*mf*) (see Figure 22-1). First you define the items, which will be provided on the palette, each with an XML file and a class. Then you register this item in the layer file. Afterwards, you implement a class that creates a palette for the already defined and registered items. Finally, you register this class in the layer file for the manifest file type.

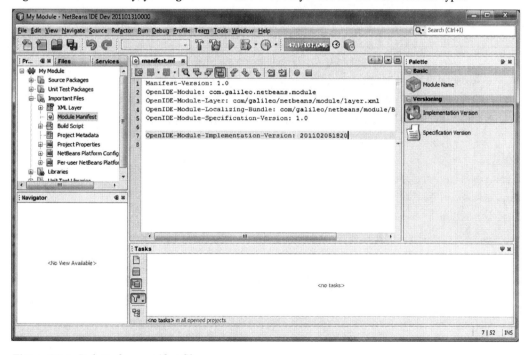

Figure 22-1. Palette for manifest files

Defining and Registering Palette Items

A single palette item is defined by an XML file of the type *editor-palette-item* (see DTD in the Appendix). In such a file you can assign the class called by drag-and-drop which is responsible for inserting. You define two icons in different sizes and assign the text and a tooltip for these items. As a result, the palette item *Module Name* looks like that shown in Listing 22-1.

Listing 22-1. Definition of a Palette Item by an XML File

```
<?xml version="1.0" encoding="UTF-8"?>
<!DOCTYPE editor_palette_item PUBLIC
   "-//NetBeans//Editor Palette Item 1.1//EN"
   "http://www.netbeans.org/dtds/editor-palette-item-1_1.dtd">
<editor_palette_item version="1.1">
  <class name="com.galileo.netbeans.module.items.ModuleName"/>
  <icon16 urlvalue="com/galileo/netbeans/ModuleName16.png"/>
  <icon32 urlvalue="com/galileo/netbeans/ModuleName32.png"/>
  <inline-description>
     <display-name>Module Name</display-name>
     <tooltip>Module Name</tooltip>
  </inline-description>
</editor_palette_item>
```

Note You can also outsource the values of the two text elements `display-name` and `tooltip` into a resource bundle, in order to internationalize palette items. For this purpose, the element `inline-description` is substituted by `description`. Instead of these two values you then assign the keys under which they can be found in the resource bundle. Furthermore, you assign which resource bundle is to be used, of course:

```
<description
  localizing-bundle="com.galileo.netbeans.module.Bundle"
  display-name-key="DISPLAY"
  tooltip-key="TOOLTIP"/>
```

You defined the `ModuleName` class by the `class` element. This class is called when you drag the entry from the palette into a manifest file. For this purpose, the class implements the interface `ActiveEditorDrop`. This interface is part of the Text API, on which you must define a dependency. The `handleTransfer()` method of the `ActiveEditorDrop` interface is automatically called by the drop event. With it, a `JTextComponent` is delivered as a parameter. With this component, you can access the current document, meaning the manifest file, in which you want to insert the palette entry. Since in this case the process repeats for each palette entry and only differs according to the text to insert, you implement an abstract `ManifestItem` class. This class does the inserting of the entry in the manifest document. The corresponding text is delivered by the `getItem()` method. This method must be implemented by the subclasses. (See Listing 22-2.)

Listing 22-2. Abstract Class That Cares About Inserting the Manifest File.

```
import org.openide.text.ActiveEditorDrop;
...
public abstract class ManifestItem implements ActiveEditorDrop {
    public abstract String getItem();

    public boolean handleTransfer(JTextComponent editor) {
        try {
            Document doc = editor.getDocument();
            int pos = editor.getCaretPosition();
            doc.insertString(pos, getItem() + "\n", null);
        } catch (BadLocationException ex) {
            Logger.getLogger(ManifestItem.class.getName()).log(Level.SEVERE, null, ex);
        }
        return(true);
    }
}
```

The structure of the classes of the concrete palette items are trivial.

```
public class ModuleName extends ManifestItem {
    public String getItem() {
        return("OpenIDE-Module-Name: My Module");
    }
}
```

For an additional entry:

```
public class ModuleSpecVersion extends ManifestItem {
    public String getItem() {
        return("OpenIDE-Module-Specification-Version: 1.0");
    }
}
```

Of course, you could still extend these classes, so a dialog is displayed to the user. In such a dialog, the user can directly assign the concrete values, such as the name or the version of the module. You just have to register it in the layer file in a folder (which you create), in order to complete the first step of defining the separate items. In this case, it makes sense to call the folder ManifestPalette. Below this folder you can create additional folders. Each of those folders then represents a category in the palette, into which the entries can be grouped. (See Listing 22-3.)

Listing 22-3. Registration of the Palette Entries in Your Own Folder

```
<folder name="ManifestPalette">
    <folder name="Basic">
        <file name="ModuleName.xml" url="items/ModuleName.xml"/>
    </folder>
    <folder name="Versioning">
        <file name="ModuleSpecVersion.xml" url="items/ModuleSpecVersion.xml"/>
        <file name="ModuleImplVersion.xml" url="items/ModuleImplVersion.xml"/>
    </folder>
</folder>
```

Creating and Registering the Palette Controller

You already implemented and registered the items for the palette in the layer file in the ManifestPalette folder. Now, your task is to create a PaletteController instance for this folder, which manages these entries. To do this create a class named ManifestPalette. Add the method createPalette() to this class. This method assisted by the PaletteFactory class of the Palette API creates a PaletteController instance, as shown in Listing 22-4.

Listing 22-4. Palette Controller Class Responsible for Managing Your Entries

```
import org.netbeans.spi.palette.PaletteActions;
import org.netbeans.spi.palette.PaletteController;
import org.netbeans.spi.palette.PaletteFactory;
...
public class ManifestPalette {
    private static PaletteController palette;

    public static PaletteController createPalette() {
        try {
            if (palette == null) {
                palette = PaletteFactory.createPalette("ManifestPalette", new MyPaletteActions());
            }
            return(palette);
        } catch (Exception ex) {
            Logger.getLogger(ManifestPalette.class.getName()).log(Level.SEVERE, null, ex);
        }
        return null;
    }

    private static final class MyPaletteActions
        extends PaletteActions {
        ...
    }
}
```

We now come to the crucial part, which is the registration of this controller for the manifest file type. First, you have to determine the registered MIME type for the manifest files. You can easily find out this type by means of the layer tree of the *Projects* view under *Important Files* ➤ *XML Layer* ➤ *<this layer in context>*. There, you can find the MIME type text/x-mainfest under Editors. So, you register the controller in the folder Editors/text/x-manifest in your layer file as follows:

```
<folder name="Editors">
    <folder name="text">
        <folder name="x-manifest">
            <file name="ManifestPalette.instance">
                <attr name="instanceOf" stringvalue="org.netbeans.spi.palette.PaletteController"/>
                <attr name="instanceCreate"
                    methodvalue="com.galileo.netbeans.module.ManifestPalette.createPalette"/>
            </file>
```

```
        </folder>
    </folder>
</folder>
```

Thus, the controller for your manifest palette items is automatically created when opening a manifest file in the editor via the createPalette() method. This controller is provided to the palette module via the Lookup. Then, the palette module can display the corresponding entries as shown in Figure 22-1.

Extending an Existing Palette

Besides creating your own palette for a file type, for which there is no palette so far, you can add entries to an already existing palette. To do this you just have to know the name of the folder in the layer file. You can easily search for already existing palette folders in the layer tree (*Important Files* ➤ *XML Layer*). For example, the folder for HTML files is called HTMLPalette. You can also add your entries to the already existing folder HTMLPalette the same way as with your own folder ManifestPalette. For example, this could then look like Listing 22-5.

Listing 22-5. Adding Entries of an Already Existing Palette

```
<folder name="HTMLPalette">
    <folder name="My HTML Items">
        <file name="item1.xml" url="items/item1.xml"/>
        <file name="item2.xml" url="items/item2.xml"/>
    </folder>
</folder>
```

Summary

With the Palette API you can not only extend your NetBeans Platform application but also the NetBeans IDE. You can create file-specific palettes or extend already existing ones. In this chapter you learned how to create and register palette items as well as palette controllers. In the last part of this chapter we looked at how to extend preexisting palettes.

Task List API

The Task List module of the NetBeans IDE enables you to display tasks, notifications, or error messages as shown in Figure 23-1. The entries of the Task List can be arranged in groups, giving the user a better overview; the user can also determine from what sections entries will be shown. By default, three sections, called scopes, are defined within the Task List module. One scope corresponds to the currently opened file, another scope corresponds to the main project and its opened dependent projects, and the third to all opened projects. The entries are supplied by scanners working with the fixed scope.

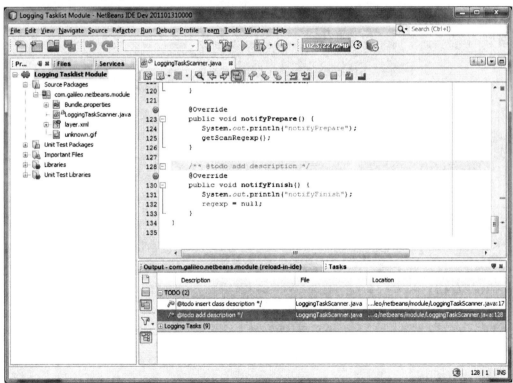

Figure 23-1. Task List module of the NetBeans IDE

For the Task List module there is the *Task List API* with which you can flexibly expand the scope of operation of the module. It is essentially about providing additional scanner. The expansions are integrated via extension points in the layer file. How this works is best shown in an example. Let's say you want to implement a scanner which displays all positions at which a direct output of information is used, such as with System.out.println(). Before delivering a product, for example, you can ensure that all important positions were substituted by logging outputs or just removed.

Implementing Scanner

You derive your own scanner implementation from the abstract FileTaskScanner class. A scanner has a name and a description of what it can achieve. Optionally, you can connect a scanner to an options panel. With this options panel the user can individually configure the scanner. For example, you can use the ToDo scanner of the NetBeans IDE to configure the tokens, which will become identified as a ToDo task within a file. For simplicity's sake, you define these tokens directly in the scanner. Then the three parameters name, description and path to the options panel (null, if no options panel is used) are passed to the base class constructor. Since the scanner is later declaratively registered in the layer file and afterward initialized by the Task List framework, you provide the factory method create(). Via this method, a LoggingTaskScanner instance can be created.

The most important part of the scanner is the scan() method, as you could probably already guess. With this method you get passed the file which is to be searched. You go though this file with a Pattern (for recognizing the tokens) and with a Matcher. Create a Task instance for each position found. Afterward, you add this instance to a list which is returned. The TodoTaskScanner class was used as a template for the implementation in Listing 23-1. A Task instance is created via the static method Task.create(). You pass the searched file, the group to which the entry shall be added, a description (typically the line in which the token was found), and the number of the line to this method.

Listing 23-1. Scanner Implementation

```
import org.netbeans.spi.tasklist.FileTaskScanner;
import org.netbeans.spi.tasklist.Task;
import org.openide.filesystems.FileObject;
...
public class LoggingTaskScanner extends FileTaskScanner {

    private static final String GROUP_NAME = "logging-tasklist";
    private static final String[] TOKENS = {
        "System.out.println",
        "System.err.println",
        "printStackTrace"};
    private Pattern  regexp   = null;
    private Callback callback = null;

    public LoggingTaskScanner(String name, String desc) {
        super(name, desc, null);
    }

    public static LoggingTaskScanner create() {
        String name = NbBundle.getBundle(LoggingTaskScanner.class).
                            getString("LBL_loggingtask");
```

```
        String desc = NbBundle.getBundle(LoggingTaskScanner.class).
                            getString("HINT_loggingtask");
        return new LoggingTaskScanner(name, desc);
    }

    public List<? extends Task> scan(FileObject file) {
        List<Task> tasks = new LinkedList<Task>();
        int lineno = 0;
        try {
            for (String line : file.asLines()) {
                lineno++;
                Matcher matcher = getScanRegexp().matcher(line);
                if (matcher.find()) {
                    String description =
                        line.subSequence(matcher.start()+1, line.length()).toString();
                    Task task = Task.create(file, GROUP_NAME, description, lineno );
                    tasks.add(task);
                }
            }
        } catch (IOException ex) {
            Exceptions.printStackTrace(ex);
        }
        return tasks;
    }

    private Pattern getScanRegexp() {
        if (regexp == null) {
            // create Pattern for the Tokens
        }
        return regexp;
    }

    public void attach(Callback callback) {
        if(callback == null && this.callback != null) {
            regexp = null;
        }
        this.callback = callback;
    }

    @Override
    public void notifyPrepare() {
        getScanRegexp();
    }

    @Override
    public void notifyFinish() {
        regexp = null;
    }
}
```

The user can activate or deactivate scanners via the context menu of the Task List window. You are informed about whether the scanner is active or not by the attach() method. If the callback parameter has the value null, the scanner has been deactivated. You can access the Task List framework via the Callback instance. Finally, there are still the two methods notifyPrepare() and notifyFinish(). The notifyPrepare() method is called before initiation of a scan by the Task List framework in which you can do preparations for the following call of the method scan(). Finally, the notifyFinish() method is called.

Registering Scanner and Group

The Task List framework defines three extension points in the layer file with which extensions can be registered. These are

```
TaskList/Groups
TaskList/Scanners
TaskList/ScanningScopes
```

First, you create a new group in which the logging tasks will be grouped. You already determined an ID in the scanner with logging-tasklist. With it the tasks, created in the scanner, can be assigned to the group. A group can easily be created via the createGroup() method of the Task class; you just need to specify some other attributes with which the group is configured. In addition to the ID, you determine keys for the corresponding values of the resource bundle. For registering the scanner, you assign the base class, and you assign the factory method for creating the scanner (see Listing 23-2).

Listing 23-2. Creating a Task Group and Registering the Scanner via the Extension Points of the Task List Framework

```xml
<filesystem>
  <folder name="TaskList">
    <folder name="Groups">
      <file name="LoggingTaskGroup.instance">
        <attr name="instanceCreate" methodvalue="org.netbeans.spi.tasklist.Task.createGroup"/>
        <attr name="localizingBundle" stringvalue="com.galileo.netbeans.module.Bundle"/>
        <attr name="groupName" stringvalue="logging-tasklist"/>
        <attr name="diplayNameKey" stringvalue="LBL_loggroup"/>
        <attr name="descriptionKey" stringvalue="HINT_loggroup"/>
        <attr name="iconKey" stringvalue="ICON_logging"/>
        <attr name="position" intvalue="400"/>
      </file>
    </folder>
    <folder name="Scanners">
      <file name="LoggingTaskScanner.instance">
        <attr name="instanceOf" stringvalue="org.netbeans.spi.tasklist.FileTaskScanner"/>
        <attr name="instanceCreate" methodvalue=
            "com.galileo.netbeans.module.LoggingTaskScanner.create"/>
      </file>
    </folder>
  </folder>
</filesystem>
```

Summary

The Task List API is part of the NetBeans IDE and you can use it to extend the standard Task List module in any way. In this chapter you learned how to create your own scanner implementation.You also saw how to register the Task List scanner and groups.

CHAPTER 24

Quick Search API

The Quick Search feature of the NetBeans Platform is an infrastructure for easily searching various files in different sources (shown in Figure 24-1). The Quick Search module has a simple API for providing so-called search provider implementations.

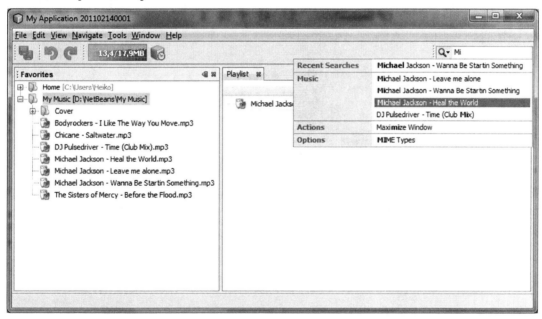

Figure 24-1. Quick Search feature

The search box of the Quick Search module can be added to a toolbar or to the menu bar. Then the user can type in the desired term there. The registered search providers are already asynchronously queried for corresponding results when typing in. An action can be triggered by clicking a result. Listing 24-1 shows how to implement a search provider combined with the Favorites module. You search for MP3 files in its folders. Clicking a found file should add it to the playlist.

Implementing Quick Search Provider

The NetBeans IDE provides a wizard for creating the basic structure and the registration of a search provider. Call this wizard with *File ➤ New File ➤ Module Development ➤ Quick Search Provider*. First, we name the provider class and define the package in which the class shall be created. Additionally, we define the category with which the results are grouped in the Quick Search popup (see Figure 24-1). You are able to influence the order of these categories, too. A small number means that the referring category is listed at the top. Finally, you have to choose a *command prefix*. If this prefix is separated from the search term by a space, it is only searched in the referring category.

Listing 24-1. Quick Search Provider Implementation

```
import org.netbeans.spi.quicksearch.SearchProvider;
import org.netbeans.spi.quicksearch.SearchRequest;
import org.netbeans.spi.quicksearch.SearchResponse;
...
public class MyMusicQSProvider implements SearchProvider {
   private DataFolder f;

   public MyMusicQSProvider() {
      FileObject fo = FileUtil.getConfigFile("Favorites");
      f = DataFolder.findFolder(fo);
   }

   @Override
   public void evaluate(SearchRequest req, SearchResponse resp) {
      for (DataObject data : f.getChildren()) {
         if (data instanceof DataShadow) {
            DataShadow obj = (DataShadow) data;
            for (final FileObject child : obj.getOriginal().getPrimaryFile().getChildren()) {
               if (child.getName().toLowerCase().contains(req.getText().toLowerCase())
                  && child.getExt().toLowerCase().equals("mp3")) {
                  if(!resp.addResult(new AddToPlaylist(child),child.getName())) {
                     return;
                  }
               }
            }
         }
      }
   }

   private static final class AddToPlaylist implements Runnable {
      private FileObject fo;

      public AddToPlaylist(FileObject fo) {
         this.fo = fo;
      }

      @Override
      public void run() {
         try {
```

```
            PlaylistTopComponent.addFile(DataObject.find(fo).getNodeDelegate());
        } catch (DataObjectNotFoundException ex) {
            Exceptions.printStackTrace(ex);
        }
    }
  }
}
```

First, you want to get access to the folders which are shown in the Favorites window. You do so in the constructor of the search provider. The only method you have to overwrite is the evaluate() method. It gets transferred the text that had been typed in in the Quick Search search box in form of a SearchRequest object. Let's look at all folders which had been added to the Favorites window and detect those MP3 files whose file name contains the search string. Add the search results to the SearchResponse object by the addResult() method. Doing so you transfer a Runnable instance and the name to be displayed in the list of results of the search (which can be formatted with HTML). This instance is executed when clicking the referring entry in the list of results. In this example you implement the AddToPlaylist class. You transfer the constructor to the found file. In the run() method (which is executed on the click event) you determine a Node instance which represents the file. Then you add it to the playlist.

Registering Quick Search Provider

A search provider implementation has to be made public to the Quick Search module with an entry in the layer file; the extension point QuickSearch is provided there. The entry is automatically created when you create the provider with the NetBeans IDE wizard. Search providers are assigned to a category. This way, the search results can be shown categorized in the list of results (see Figure 24-1). You decide the position of the category in the list of results with the position attribute. With the command attribute, you can indicate a prefix with which a search can be limited on this category. In this example, that means the search can be limited on the shown search provider by the entry *MP3 <search string>*.

It is possible to add multiple search provider implementations to one category. The name of a search provider is specified by the displayName attribute. (See Listing 24-2.)

Listing 24-2. Registration of a Search Provider

```xml
<folder name="QuickSearch">
    <folder name="Music">
        <attr name="command" stringvalue="MP3"/>
        <attr name="position" intvalue="100"/>
        <file name="com-galileo-netbeans-module-MyMusicQSProvider.instance">
            <attr name="displayName"
                bundlevalue="com.galileo.netbeans.module.Bundle#MyMusicQSProvider.instance"/>
        </file>
    </folder>
</folder>
```

Integrating Quick Search UI

The Quick Search search box is not provided in your application by default. It can be added to a toolbar by the dialog *Customize Toolbars.* By a layer entry you can also permanently assign the Quick Search UI to a toolbar. This way you ensure that it already exists when starting the application. You can determine the name of the Quick Search action with the layer tree and then create a link. As shown in Listing 24-3 you add the action to the newly created toolbar QuickSearch.

Listing 24-3. Adding the Quick Search UI

```
<folder name="Toolbars">
    <folder name="QuickSearch">
        <file name="org-netbeans-modules-quicksearch-QuickSearchAction.shadow">
            <attr name="originalFile" stringvalue="
                Actions/Edit/org-netbeans-modules-quicksearch-QuickSearchAction.instance"/>
            <attr name="position" intvalue="400"/>
        </file>
    </folder>
</folder>
```

Hiding Existing Search Provider Categories

Search providers for actions and operations, among others, belong to the NetBeans Platform, by default. These are each assigned to a category. You can hide categories by means of the standard System Filesystem functionality (i.e., in the same way as you hide menu entries). You can exclude the referring search providers from the search. To do so you only need to add the suffix _hidden to the category's name. Add the following entry in Listing 24-4 to the layer file, for example, in order to delete both first stated search provider categories:

Listing 24-4. Deleting Search Provider Categories

```
<folder name="QuickSearch">
    <folder name="Actions_hidden"/>
    <folder name="Options_hidden"/>
</folder>
```

Summary

It is possible to add providers to the Quick Search function of the NetBeans Platform by means of the Quick Search API. These providers search for any data and objects at any place. In this chapter you learned how to implement and register Quick Search providers. You also looked at how to integrate the Quick Search UI and how to hide existing search provider categories.

Auto Update Services API

With its plugin manager the NetBeans Platform provides a useful tool to the user. With this tool, individual parts of applications (single modules or several related modules) can be installed, uninstalled, activated, deactivated, or updated. It is possible to directly access these functionalities by means of the Auto Update Services A PIand create really different applications.

It is possible to access all existing modules because of the class UpdateManager. One module (unit) is represented by the class UpdateUnit; this class is a kind of wrapper for different elements. Such elements could be

- The installed module itself

- The module which had been installed for the current locale setting

- The predecessor of an installed update (backup)

- A list of available updates (in update centers)

- A list of available localizations (in update centers)

The named elements are each represented by the class UpdateElement. This class provides the name, the category, the author, or the icon of the module, among other things. Actions such as installing or uninstalling are managed by an OperationContainer instance. To create such an instance a factory method is provided for each action.

The following sections demonstrate the usage of the Auto Update Services API by means of typical applications.

Automatic Update in the Background

Business applications often require that updates are automatically installed on the clients without user interaction. This ensures that all users work with the same and the latest version of the application.

Search Updates

The first step is to search the modules that must be installed. The search takes place in all registered update centers. That means in the first delivery of your application, at least one update center should be registered. Via this update center the new modules should be included. You can register an update center quite easily by means of the NetBeans IDE. To do so, just call *File ➤ New File ➤ Module Development ➤ Update Center*. You can find more information on this in Chapter 36.

Search for both the latest and the updated modules by the method shown in Listing 25-1. It is important to make the desired (or all) update provider(s) load information from the update centers

about the provided modules. In this example you determine all providers via the
UpdateUnitProviderFactory and execute its refresh() method. After that, you determine all provided
modules that can be updated or reinstalled via the UpdateManager, which also takes all providers into
account. To do so, filter with !unit.getAvailableUpdates().isEmpty() all modules which are already
installed and which are not updated. Now you just have to distinguish between a new module and an
updated module using the method getInstalled(). If it says null, a version of this module is not yet
installed; that means it is a new module. According to this query you add the modules to the appropriate
list.

Listing 25-1. Searching New and Updated Modules

```
private List<UpdateElement> install = new ArrayList<UpdateElement>();
private List<UpdateElement> update = new ArrayList<UpdateElement>();

public void searchNewAndUpdatedModules() {
    for (UpdateUnitProvider provider : UpdateUnitProviderFactory.
            getDefault().getUpdateUnitProviders(false)) {
        try {
            provider.refresh(null, true);
        } catch (IOException ex) {
            LOG.severe(ex.getMessage());
        }
    }
    for (UpdateUnit unit : UpdateManager.getDefault().getUpdateUnits()) {
        if (!unit.getAvailableUpdates().isEmpty()) {
            if (unit.getInstalled() == null) {
                install.add(unit.getAvailableUpdates().get(0));
            } else {
                update.add(unit.getAvailableUpdates().get(0));
            }
        }
    }
}
```

In the approach shown in Listing 25-1, all update centers are queried by the UpdateManager. You can
also restrict the search to a separate provider to ensure that the modules are automatically installed out
of a dedicated update center, as shown in Listing 25-2. You determine the desired update provider by the
UpdateUnitProviderFactory via name (according to the definition in the layer file). In contrast to the
previous approach, you do not search for the update manager then, but determine it directly on the
provider.

Listing 25-2. Searching Modules in a Special Update Center

```
private static final String UC_NAME = "com_galileo_netbeans_module_update_center";

public void searchNewAndUpdatedModulesInDedicatedUC() {
    for (UpdateUnitProvider provider : UpdateUnitProviderFactory.
            getDefault().getUpdateUnitProviders(false)) {
        try {
            if (provider.getName().equals(UC_NAME)) {
                provider.refresh(null, true);
```

```
            for (UpdateUnit u : provider.getUpdateUnits()) {
                if (!u.getAvailableUpdates().isEmpty()) {
                    if (u.getInstalled() == null) {
                        install.add(u.getAvailableUpdates().get(0));
                    } else {
                        update.add(u.getAvailableUpdates().get(0));
                    }
                }
            }
        }
    } catch (IOException ex) {
        LOG.severe(ex.getMessage());
    }
    }
}
```

Installing and Restarting Updates

Operations on modules are executed via an OperationContainer. It is possible to add any amount of UpdateElement instances to this container. Please note that each operation container is responsible for one certain action. That means in this case that two different containers are needed. These are created via the referring factory methods OperationContainer.createForInstall() and OperationContainer.createForUpdate(). Adding the elements does not depend on the type. This is why you create a helper method for your purposes. (See Listing 25-3.)

***Listing 25-3.** Adding the Update Elements to an Operation Container*

```
public OperationContainer<InstallSupport> addToContainer(
        OperationContainer<InstallSupport> c,
        List<UpdateElement> modules) {
    for (UpdateElement e : modules) {
        if (container.canBeAdded(e.getUpdateUnit (), e)) {
            OperationInfo<InstallSupport> operationInfo = c.add(e);
            if (operationInfo != null) {
                c.add(operationInfo.getRequiredElements());
            }
        }
    }
    return container;
}
```

The helper method shown in Listing 25-3 first checks whether a module is compatible with the container. For each module this is checked by the method canBeAdded(). In that case you add the module; an OperationInfo instance is delivered when the module has not been found in the container yet. This instance helps adding the needed dependencies from the current module by means of the method getRequiredElements(). In this example, this call could be skipped, because all available modules are added anyway. However, with the method getBrokenDependencies() you could check whether a dependency cannot be fulfilled.

In addition to filling the container with elements, downloading and installing modules works the same way; a helper method is useful for this step. An OperationContainer is passed to this method.

Through this operation container the modules can then be installed. After that you download, check, and finally install the modules by the methods doDownload(), doValidate(), and doInstall() of the InstallSupport instance. If the method doInstall() returns an OperationSupport.Restarter, a reboot is necessary to finish the installation. However, you do not want to reboot at this time, and instead leave the decision about when to reboot to the user and so use the method doRestartLater(). (See Listing 25-4.)

Listing 25-4. Downloading and Installing the Module and Afterward Notifying the User

```java
public void installModules(OperationContainer<InstallSupport> container) {
    try {
        InstallSupport support = container.getSupport();

        if (support != null) {
            Validator vali = support.doDownload (null, true);
            Installer inst = support.doValidate(vali, null);
            Restarter restarter = support.doInstall(inst, null);

            if (restarter != null) {
                support.doRestartLater(restarter);
                if (!isRestartRequested) {
                    NotificationDisplayer.getDefault().notify(
                        "Die Anwendung wurde aktualisiert",
                        ImageUtilities.loadImageIcon("com/galileo/netbeans/module/rs.png", false),
                        "Click here to restart",
                        new RestartAction(support, restarter));
                    isRestartRequested = true;
                }
            }
        }
    } catch (OperationException ex) {
        LOG.severe(ex.getMessage());
    }
}
```

The user still needs to be informed about the necessary reboot of the application; for this the notification displayer, which is integrated in the status bar of the NetBeans Platform, works well. The hint is displayed to the user in a balloon. The practical advantage of this is that you can add an action which is displayed as a link. That way the user can directly reboot. You need the InstallSupport and the Restarter instance for the reboot. You give both to the RestartAction which then executes the reboot (as shown in Listing 25-5).

Listing 25-5. Action Class to Execute a Reboot

```java
private static final class RestartAction implements ActionListener {
    private InstallSupport support;
    private OperationSupport.Restarter restarter;

    public RestartAction(
            InstallSupport support,
            OperationSupport.Restarter restarter) {
```

```
        this.support = support;
        this.restarter = restarter;
    }

    @Override
    public void actionPerformed(ActionEvent e) {
        try {
            support.doRestart(restarter, null);
        } catch (OperationException ex) {
            LOG.severe(ex.getMessage());
        }
    }
}
```

Automatically Starting Installation

Finally you have to start the automatic execution of the process in the background. One possibility is to install the updates when starting the application. You can do this in a simple way by a warm-up task. This would look like the methods which were implemented into the whole as shown in Listing 25-6.

Listing 25-6. Executing the Automatic Update Installation by a Warm-Up Task

```
import org.netbeans.api.autoupdate.InstallSupport;
import org.netbeans.api.autoupdate.OperationContainer;
import org.netbeans.api.autoupdate.OperationException;
import org.netbeans.api.autoupdate.OperationSupport;
import org.netbeans.api.autoupdate.UpdateElement;
import org.netbeans.api.autoupdate.UpdateManager;
import org.netbeans.api.autoupdate.UpdateUnit;
import org.netbeans.api.autoupdate.UpdateUnitProvider;
import org.netbeans.api.autoupdate.UpdateUnitProviderFactory;
import org.openide.awt.NotificationDisplayer;
import org.openide.util.RequestProcessor;
...
public class AutoInstaller implements Runnable {
    private static final Logger LOG = Logger.getLogger(AutoInstaller.class.getName());

    @Override
    public void run() {
        RequestProcessor.getDefault().post(
            new AutoInstallerImpl(), 1000);
    }

    private static final class AutoInstallerImpl implements Runnable {
        private List<UpdateElement> install = new ArrayList<UpdateElement>();
        private List<UpdateElement> update = new ArrayList<UpdateElement>();
        private boolean isRestartRequested = false;

        @Override
        public void run() {
            searchNewAndUpdatedModules();
```

```
        OperationContainer<InstallSupport> installContainer =
            addToContainer(OperationContainer.createForInstall(), install);
        installModules(installContainer);

        OperationContainer<InstallSupport> updateContainer =
            addToContainer(OperationContainer.createForUpdate(), update);
        installModules(updateContainer);
    }

    public OperationContainer<InstallSupport> addToContainer(
            OperationContainer<InstallSupport> container,
            List<UpdateElement> modules) { ... }

    public void installModules(
            OperationContainer<InstallSupport> container) { ...}

    public void searchNewAndUpdatedModules() { ... }
    }

    private static final class RestartAction
            implements ActionListener { ... }
}
```

A warm-up task is executed asynchronously when starting the application. Only the Runnable interface has to be implemented. It is also possible to hold back the start for a certain time by the RequestProcessor class. The warm-up task only has to be registered in the layer file as follows:

```
<folder name="WarmUp">
   <file name="com-galileo-netbeans-module-AutoInstaller.instance"/>
</folder>
```

Deactivating Modules Automatically

In the example showing how to automatically update an application in the previous section you got to know the Auto Update Services API for finding, downloading, installing, and updating modules. Furthermore, the API makes it possible to activate or deactivate certain modules. There are very interesting applications for this. For example, you can switch off certain modules or functionalities for certain user groups (by the login information). The method is quite similar to that described in the previous section. First, you determine all available modules (including the already installed modules) via the UpdateManager. By the additional filter UpdateManager.TYPE.MODULE you ensure that only application modules and not localization modules are delivered. Via the getInstalled() method you check whether you are dealing with an installed module. This way new modules are filtered. Search for modules to deactivate in the remaining modules that are activated. Deactivating works via the unique code name base. (See Listing 25-7.)

Listing 25-7. Searching for Certain Active Application Modules

```
List<String> modules = Collections.singletonList("com.galileo.netbeans.module3");
OperationContainer<OperationSupport> cont = OperationContainer.createForDirectDisable();
for (UpdateUnit unit : UpdateManager.getDefault().getUpdateUnits(UpdateManager.TYPE.MODULE)) {
```

```
        if (unit.getInstalled() != null) {
            UpdateElement elem = unit.getInstalled();
            if (elem.isEnabled()) {
                if (modules.contains(elem.getCodeName())) {
                    if (cont.canBeAdded(unit, elem)) {
                        OperationInfo<OperationSupport> operationInfo = cont.add(elem);
                        if (operationInfo != null) {
                            cont.add(operationInfo.getRequiredElements());
                        }
                    }
                }
            }
        }
    }
}
```

For deactivating modules you create a referring container with the factory method `OperationContainer.createForDirectDisable()`. Add the desired modules to it. Before doing so, check again whether the modules are compatible with the container. If the module is successfully added you can add all modules that are dependent of the module to deactivate via the `OperationInfo` instance. Finally, ensure that the container is not empty. Then deactivate the modules via the method `doOperation()` (see Listing 25-8.)

Listing 25-8. *Deactivating Application Modules*

```
if (!cont.listAll().isEmpty()) {
    try {
        Restarter restarter = cont.getSupport().doOperation(null);
    } catch (OperationException ex) {
        LOG.severe(ex.getMessage());
    }
}
```

Summary

You can access all functions, which your plugin manager provides, using the Auto Update Services API, making it possible to realize quite interesting applications. In this chapter you learned how you can execute an application-specific automatic update in the background and how you can disable modules programmatically.

Server & Database: Enterprise Applications and the NetBeans Platform

Java DB

Apache Derby is a relational database management system (RDBMS) hidden behind Java DB. This database system is implemented 100% in Java and can therefore be used as a platform-independent system. The Java DB is very small for a complete database management system; it can be delivered directly with its application because no special installation and no further actions for operating a database are necessary. Java DB is therefore predestined for use in a rich client application. Since Java Platform 6, Oracle delivers the client database Java DB by default; the NetBeans IDE naturally supports the Java DB in terms of management and server action.

Integrating the Java DB

You can get the Java DB with your Java Platform installation or you can download the latest version at http://www.oracle.com/technetwork/java/javadb. You will find the file *derby.jar,* which is the actual database system that also provides the driver, in the subdirectory *lib*. There is also the file *derbyclient.jar,* which is used when the Java DB is executed on a server and when you do not want to deliver the database system with your application. However, this discussion will mainly deal with the client-side use and therefore with embedding the Java DB in its application. Using the terminology of a NetBeans Platform application, you want to add the Java DB as an independent and separate module to your application; that is, you create a library wrapper module. First, call *File ➤ New Project...*and choose *NetBeans Modules ➤ Library Wrapper Module*. The next step is to select the file *derby.jar* and the additional file *derbyLocale_de_DE.jar,* which contains the German versions of all reports of the database system. Alternatively you can of course add a different language package or additional packages. In this example use org.apache.derby as code name base and Java DB Embedded as name. Now you just have to define a dependency on this module which was just created in your application module that wants to access the database. The database system is then automatically booted when the JDBC driver is called for the first time.

Registering Drivers

If you have worked with the JDBC API already you are probably more or less familiar with the call Class.forName(). The referring database driver for the database system you use is indirectly loaded, so the driver manager is able to establish a connection to its database. The DriverManager class has been extended by the JDBC API 4.0, which is part of the Java Platform 6, so it can load the database drivers which were registered over the *META-INF/services* directory. Ideally you or the driver itself can declaratively register the implementation of the java.sql.Driver interface. The advantage of this is that the call Class.forName() can be completely omitted and the driver is only loaded when it is needed the first time. This way, Java DB registers its needed drivers, too. For us that means we are able to directly establish a connection via the DriverManager and we do not have to worry about the driver.

Creating and Using a Database

After packing the Java DB in a wrapper module and adding it to your NetBeans Platform application, and after you defined a dependency to the NetBeans Platform application, you can directly access the database system and create your first database. Each database is managed by Java DB in a separate directory which has the same name as the database, as shown in Figure 26-1. These directories are created in a system directory which you have to define first. An ideal location would be the user directory, for example, in which the NetBeans platform and its application-specific settings are also saved. You can get the path over the system properties so you do not need to think about independent platform paths.

This base directory becomes registered with the name derby.system.home.

```
System.setProperty("derby.system.home",
        System.getProperty("netbeans.user",
        System.getProperty("user.home")) + "/databases");
```

You get to the path of the application-specific directory by the feature netbeans.user. If this feature is not set, use the standard value of the user directory, which you get via user.home. Within the detected directory, the database should be located in the directory *databases*. If you have not set the feature derby.system.home, Java DB uses the current directory of the application.

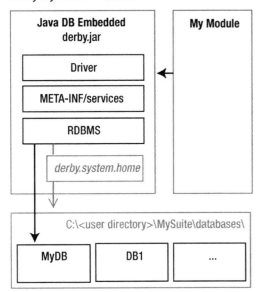

Figure 26-1. *Integrating Java DB as library wrapper module in your own application. The physical location of the databases is set by the feature derby.system.home.*

The feature of the Java DB that the database system must not be started explicitly is very practical. The databases each are started up separately when first accessing the database; you do not have to worry about managing the operation of the local database, which you can use and call in exactly the same way as you may already know from using a server database.

After setting the system directory as described above, you can establish a connection to the database through the driver manager:

```
Connection connection = DriverManager.getConnection(
      "jdbc:derby:MyDB;create=true", "user", "password");
```

So now, how do you create a database? This is done by defining the attribute create=true which is added to the connection URL. If the database MyDB does not exist it is created first. Subsequently a connection to this database is established. If the database exists, only the connection is established. This attribute is very important, especially in the embedded local usage of the Java DB, because the application of the database is automatically created installing or starting the first time. Java DB defines a number of additional attributes which are not very important now, though. You can find information about these attributes in the Java DB reference manual, which is located in the directory of the Java DB distribution, together with additional documents. Instead of attaching the attributes to the URL, you can also save them in a Properties object and transfer it as a second parameter to the getConnection() method:

```
Properties props = new Properties();
props.put("user", "user");
props.put("password", "password");
props.put("create", "true");
Connection connection = DriverManager.getConnection("jdbc:derby:MyDB", props);
```

Shutting Down a Database

A database automatically starts up when a connection to a database is established. Shutting down is different. The database system cannot recognize when an application is finished (and would thus shut down abruptly) so you should explicitly shut down the database system when finishing the application; a consistent condition is then guaranteed. Shutting down the system means all active databases are implicitly shut down. Optionally, you can separately finish databases, too.

The best way to accomplish this task is to do it with a module installer or in a lifecycle manager implementation (see Chapter 8). In a module installer use the close() method as shown in Listing 26-1.

Listing 26-1. Shutting Down the Database System Finishing an Application

```
import java.sql.DriverManager;
import java.sql.SQLException;
import org.openide.modules.ModuleInstall;

public class Installer extends ModuleInstall {
   @Override
   public void close() {
      try {
        DriverManager.getConnection("jdbc:derby:;shutdown=true");
      } catch (SQLException ex) {}
   }
}
```

With that the whole Java DB system is shut down finishing your application. If you want to shut down an individual database you just have to add `jdbc:derby:` behind the referring database name. If, for example, you want to finish the database MyDB, the call would be as follows:

```
DriverManager.getConnection("jdbc:derby:MyDB;shutdown=true");
```

Bear in mind that shutting down, meaning the parameter shutdown=true, always triggers an exception which provides a report about the shutdown.

Developing a Database by Means of the NetBeans IDE

In an effort to simplify the development of database-supported applications a Java DB support is integrated into the NetBeans IDE. By means of the IDE you can start and stop the database system, create databases, and establish a connection to the databases. The graphic support for creating and configuring tables especially simplifies development. This allows you to define and change the individual table colums and data types in a very simple way.

Installing and Starting the Java DB System

To use this support you first have to define the installation path of the Java DB. Call the *Services* window with *Window ➤ Services* and then choose *Properties* from the context menu of the *Java DB* node. The path should already point to the Java DB directory of the Java Platform installation. If you downloaded the Java DB yourself or if you have a separate installation, you can of course set the path on it, too. You also have to set another path in which the database will be created and set.

After you have completed these settings, you can start the database server through the context menu with *Start Server*. This is necessary because now the database system is no longer integrated in an application, but is operated as an independent server. The server usually accepts connections on port 1527, which is displayed in the output window.

Integrating a Java DB Server Driver into Your Application

Since the Java DB database system is not integrated in its applications, but is operated as a server, it is necessary to add another driver to your application. This driver, which is necessary to establish the connection to a Java DB server, is located in the file *derbyclient.jar* (introduced in the section "Integrating the Java DB.") . Add this to your application by means of a library wrapper module and define in your module that a database connection wants to connect with its dependency.

Creating and Configuring a Database

Your application is now ready for accessing a deleted Java DB server. You can create a new database in the NetBeans IDE with *Create Database...* out of the context menu of the node *Databases ➤ Java DB* in the *Services* window, which is shown in Figure 26-2. When doing so, you have to insert a name, a username, and a password for the database. After inserting these data, the database is created and a connection is established. You can establish a connection via the context menu item *Connect...* of the referring connection. If a connection is established successfully, the tables, indices, and the foreign keys of the database are displayed. Using the context menu you can create new entries to each.

For example, you can create a new table over the context menu of *Tables* with *Create Table...*, look at the content of a table with *View Data...*, or give an SQL order with *Execute Command*.

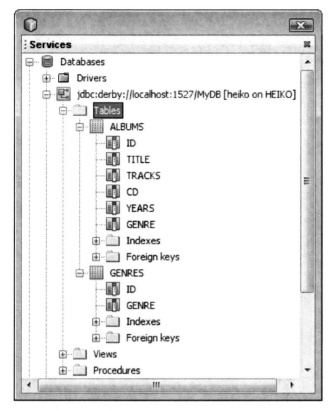

Figure 26-2. *You get access to the Java DB databases in the Services window in which you can also configure it.*

Accessing the Database out of Your Application

Now you will deal with the application that wants to use the database. The definition of the feature `derby.system.home`, which was needed when using the integrated application of the Java DB system, is no longer necessary. To successfully create a connection to the Java DB server out of your application you have to adapt the connection URL, since you need to specify the name (or the IP address) and the port on which the database server accepts connections:

```
Connection connection = DriverManager.getConnection(
    "jdbc:derby://localhost:1527/MyDB;", "user", "password");
```

Since the database server in this case is located on the same computer as the application, use the specification `localhost` or the IP address `127.0.0.1` and define the port as `1527`. You can also get this URL from the already established connection in the services window of the NetBeans IDE.

Retrieving and Importing Structures of Tables

Next I will show you a very helpful feature of the database explorer in the services window. It is possible to display the SQL source code with which your table was created in order to copy it as is into your application for the initial creation of the database tables or in an SQL script file. Call the context menu of the wanted table, where you will find the point *Grab Structure...*; call it to save the structure in a file. Then just choose *Recreate Table...* in the context menu, and choose the just created file. The SQL source code, which is necessary to create the table, will then be displayed in a window. You can also supply this functionality to its original purpose and so import tables out of a foreign database in your database.

Example Application

I want to finish this chapter with a really simple example to explain some idiosyncrasies of the Java DB around creating table structures and show you how to cleverly integrate the Java DB in the lifecycle of your application. In this example, you will manage music albums that can be assigned to a certain genre.

Configuration, Access, and Shutdown

You want to configure the Java DB database system, centrally manage access to it, and, when the time comes, shut down the system again by a module installer. First, you set the path in which the database will be stored in the restored() method, which is called when starting the application, or the module with the feature derby.system.home (see Listing 26-2). The database will be created in the subdirectory *databases* in the user-specific user directory. In addition, you call the method initTables() in which you first want to check by means of a SELECT query whether the needed tables were already created. If the application is started the first time (the tables do not exist yet), this triggers an SQLException which we catch and then create the two tables albums and genres.

Create the table genres first, because the table albums will depend on it. Each entry in the table will get a unique ID which will be assigned by the database in ascending order. You achieve this by assigning GENERATED ALWAYS AS IDENTITY for the column id. So even if you define a value for the column id, adding an entry to the table, the automatically-created value is used. Alternatively, you can use BY DEFAULT instead of ALWAYS; then only a value is created when you do not explicitly assign an ID. With PRIMARY KEY you finally define the column id as the primary key through which the connection to the entries in the albums table will be established. You create this directly afterward and define the key column id in the same way. Additional columns are title, tracks, cds, years, and genre. However, you do not directly write in the genre in the column genre, but the ID of a genre entry out of the table genre. So, the column genre in albums is a foreign key. You define it by FOREIGN KEY (genre) and define the relation to the column id in genres by REFERENCES genres (id). Add three example entries in the table genres, so that when creating an album a genre can be chosen.

Listing 26-2. Installing the Database System and the Database at the Start

```java
import java.sql.Statement;
import java.sql.Connection;
import java.sql.DriverManager;
import java.sql.SQLException;
import org.openide.modules.ModuleInstall;
import org.openide.util.Exceptions;

public class Installer extends ModuleInstall {
    private static Connection conn = null;
    @Override
    public void restored() {
        System.setProperty("derby.system.home",
            System.getProperty("netbeans.user",
            System.getProperty("user.home")) + "/databases");
        initTables();
    }
    private void initTables() {
        try {
            Statement stmt = getConnection().createStatement();
            stmt.executeQuery("SELECT id FROM genres");
            stmt.close();
        } catch(SQLException e) {
            try {
                Statement stmt = getConnection().createStatement();
                stmt.execute("CREATE TABLE genres (" +
                    "id INTEGER GENERATED ALWAYS AS IDENTITY, " +
                    "genre VARCHAR(100), " +
                    "PRIMARY KEY(id))");
                stmt.execute("CREATE TABLE albums (" +
                    "id INTEGER GENERATED ALWAYS AS IDENTITY, " +
                    "title  VARCHAR(100), " +
                    "tracks VARCHAR(10), " +
                    "cds    VARCHAR(10), " +
                    "years  VARCHAR(10), " +
                    "genre  INTEGER, " +
                    "PRIMARY KEY(id), " +
                    "FOREIGN KEY(genre) REFERENCES genres (id))");
                stmt.execute("INSERT INTO genres (genre) " +
                    "VALUES('Techno, Trance & Dance')");
                stmt.execute("INSERT INTO genres (genre) " +
                    "VALUES('Rock & Pop')");
                stmt.execute("INSERT INTO genres (genre) " +
                    "VALUES('Country & Classic')");
                stmt.close();
            } catch(SQLException ex) {
                Exceptions.printStackTrace(ex);
            }
```

```
      }
  }
```

You provide central access to the database with the static method getConnection(). This way, the users in particular do not have to worry about the connection URL. Furthermore, the Connection object (which is to say, the connection to the database) is held centrally and does not have to be established anew and finished each time. The method getConnection() is also a factory method, which establishes a connection if there is not one yet, or brings the Connection object back, if it has been established. You are informed about the application finishing by the method close(). This is where you eventually add the still-established connection to the database and then you shut down the complete Java DB system, (and automatically your database MyDB, too) by jdbc:derby:;shutdown=true. (See Listing 26-3.)

Listing 26-3. Centrally Providing the Connection and Shutting Down the Database

```
public static Connection getConnection() throws SQLException {
    if(conn == null || conn.isClosed()) {
        conn = DriverManager.getConnection(
            "jdbc:derby:MyDB;create=true", "user", "password");
    }
    return conn;
}
@Override
public void close() {
    try {
        conn.close();
        DriverManager.getConnection("jdbc:derby:;shutdown=true");
    } catch (SQLException ex) {}
}
}
```

Data Models and Data Accessing Module

As you already saw when you created the tables, you want to manage data for two different classes: albums, whose information is managed in the table albums, and genres, which are located in the table genres. To do this you create for each a data model, as shown in Listing 26-4. These are the classes Album and Genre which provide certain set and get methods. Please bear in mind that there is no persistence logic in these classes. You want to manage those in a separate class.

Listing 26-4. Data Model for an Album

```
public class Album {
    private Integer id;
    private String  title;
    private String  tracks;
    private String  cds;
    private String  year;
    private Genre   genre;
    public Album(Integer id, String title, String tracks, String cds, String year) {
        this.id     = id;
        this.title  = title;
        this.tracks = tracks;
```

```
      this.cds    = cds;
      this.year   = year;
   }
   public Integer getId() {
      return id;
   }
   public String getTitle() {
      return title;
   }
   ...
}
```

You overwrite both methods `toString()` and `equals()`, which are necessary for a correct representation and choice of a genre or in the dialog for creating an album in the class Genre, as shown in Listing 26-5.

Listing 26-5. Data Model for a Genre

```
public class Genre {
   private Integer id;
   private String  genre;
   public Genre(Integer id, String genre) {
      this.id    = id;
      this.genre = genre;
   }
   public Integer getId() {
      return id;
   }
   public String getGenre() {
      return genre;
   }
   public String toString() {
      return genre;
   }
   public boolean equals(Object obj) {
      if(obj instanceof Genre) {
         if(((Genre)obj).getId() == id) {
            return true;
         }
      }
      return false;
   }
}
```

To implement the data model and the business logic,—meaning the user interface with which the file should be managed, independent of the underlying persistence layer—you encapsulate the term on the database and all SQL instructions in a separate data access class DataModel, which executed the desired changes and queries on the database and which provides the data with the data models Album and Genre.

The methods to implement into the class DataModel are getAlbums() and getGenres(), which provide all available albums and genres in the form of a list (see Listing 26-6). The methods insertAlbum(), updateAlbum(), and deleteAlbum() also enable you to insert, change, or delete the albums in the database.

Listing 26-6. The Class Data Model Encapsulates the Access to the Java DB and Provides Data by Means of the Referring Data Models Album and Genre.

```java
import java.sql.PreparedStatement;
import java.sql.ResultSet;
import java.sql.SQLException;
import java.sql.Statement;
import java.util.ArrayList;
import java.util.List;
import org.openide.util.Exceptions;

public class DataModel {
    public static List<Album> getAlbums() {
        List<Album> albums = new ArrayList<Album>();
        try {
            Statement stmt = Installer.getConnection().createStatement();
            ResultSet rs = stmt.executeQuery(
                "SELECT * FROM albums INNER JOIN genres ON albums.genre = genres.id");
            while(rs.next()) {
                Album album = new Album(rs.getInt(1),
                    rs.getString(2), rs.getString(3),
                    rs.getString(4), rs.getString(5));
                album.setGenre(new Genre(rs.getInt(7), rs.getString(8)));
                albums.add(album);
            }
            rs.close();
            stmt.close();
        } catch(SQLException e) {
            Exceptions.printStackTrace(e);
        }
        return albums;
    }

    public static List<Genre> getGenres() {
        List<Genre> genres = new ArrayList<Genre>();
        try {
            Statement stmt = Installer.getConnection().createStatement();
            ResultSet rs =stmt.executeQuery("SELECT * FROM genres");
            while(rs.next()) {
                genres.add(new Genre(rs.getInt(1), rs.getString(2)));
            }
            rs.close();
            stmt.close();
        } catch(Exception e) {
            Exceptions.printStackTrace(e);
        }
        return genres;
    }
```

```java
public static void updateAlbum(Album a) throws SQLException {
    PreparedStatement stmt =
        Installer.getConnection().prepareStatement(
            "UPDATE albums SET title=?, tracks=?, cds=?, years=?, genre=? WHERE id=?");
    stmt.setString(1, a.getTitle());
    stmt.setString(2, a.getTracks());
    stmt.setString(3, a.getCds());
    stmt.setString(4, a.getYear());
    stmt.setInt(5, a.getGenre().getId());
    stmt.setInt(6, a.getId());
    stmt.execute();
}

public static void insertAlbum(Album a) throws SQLException {
    PreparedStatement stmt = Installer.getConnection().prepareStatement(
            "INSERT INTO albums (title, tracks, cds, years, genre) VALUES(?, ?, ?, ?, ?)",
            Statement.RETURN_GENERATED_KEYS);
    stmt.setString(1, a.getTitle());
    stmt.setString(2, a.getTracks());
    stmt.setString(3, a.getCds());
    stmt.setString(4, a.getYear());
    stmt.setInt(5, a.getGenre().getId());
    stmt.execute();
    // Auto Increment Wert auslesen und setzen
    ResultSet rs = stmt.getGeneratedKeys(); rs.next();
    album.setId(rs.getInt(1));
}
public static void deleteAlbum(Album a) throws SQLException {
    PreparedStatement stmt =
        Installer.getConnection().prepareStatement("DELETE FROM albums WHERE id = ?");
    stmt.setInt(1, a.getId());
    stmt.execute();
}
}
```

Representing and Editing Data

Let us now look at the components that enable the representation of the data and allow the user to manage and edit music albums. You want to list albums in a table within a top component (see Figure 26-3). First you create a class AlbumsTopComponent which contains a table of the type JTable. You need a model for the table, so this table can represent and manage the albums in terms of the already-created data model Album. Since this data model is only necessary at this point you implement it as private inner class AlbumsTableModel. So the data is stored in a List of the type Album. Since you need access to this model later, start it as a private data element. The data model is connected to the table by the method setModel(). Typically, table entries can be edited or looked at closely by double clicking. To realize this functionality, register a MouseListener or MouseAdapter at the JTable-instance albums. The MouseListener or MouseAdapter call the method editAlbumActionPerformed() when double clicking. I will cover the functionality of this method later in this section.

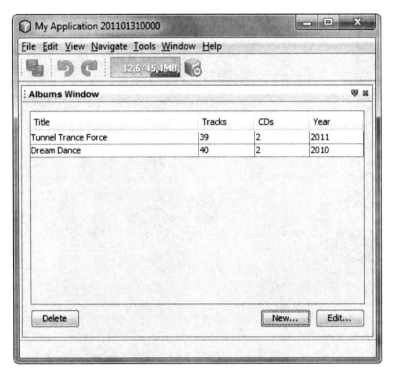

Figure 26-3. Listing the database entries in a table

```java
import java.awt.event.MouseAdapter;
import java.awt.event.MouseEvent;
import javax.swing.table.AbstractTableModel;
import org.openide.util.Exceptions;
...
public final class AlbumsTopComponent extends TopComponent {
    private JTable albums;
    private AlbumTableModel model = new AlbumTableModel();
    public AlbumsTopComponent() {
        initComponents();
        albums.setModel(model);
        albums.addMouseListener(new MouseAdapter() {
            public void mouseClicked(MouseEvent event) {
                if(event.getClickCount() == 2) {
                    editAlbumActionPerformed(null);
                }
            }
        });
    }

    private static final class AlbumTableModel
        extends AbstractTableModel {
```

```
   private String[] columns = {"Title","Tracks","CDs","Year"};
   private List<Album> data = new ArrayList<Album>();
   public Album getRow(int row) {
      return data.get(row);
   }
   @Override
   public int getRowCount() {
      return data.size();
   }
   @Override
   public int getColumnCount() {
      return columns.length;
   }
   @Override
   public String getColumnName(int col) {
      return columns[col];
   }
   @Override
   public Object getValueAt(int row, int col) {
      Album album = data.get(row);
      switch(col) {
         case 0: return album.getTitle();
         case 1: return album.getTracks();
         case 2: return album.getCds();
         case 3: return album.getYear();
      }
      return "";
   }
   public List<Album> getData() {
      return data;
   }
}
```

Of course when you open the top component, all current entries will be read and represented. This is why you overwrite the method componentOpened(), in which we query all entries of the database by means of the method getAlbums() via our DataModel which abstractly manages the access to the database. You add this model to the data model of the table and inform the view, meaning the JTable instance, about the changed data by the method fireTableDataChanged(). Finally, you implement three other action methods with which the user should be able to add, edit, and delete entries. To create a new album this would be the method newAlbumActionPerformed(). In this method you call a dialog in which the user can insert the needed data by means of a static method. You create this dialog in the next and last step. If this method gives back an Album instance, so the dialog was finished successfully, you add the data in the database. If this step could be executed without exception, you add the album to the table.

```
public void componentOpened() {
   model.getData().clear();
   model.getData().addAll(DataModel.getAlbums());
   model.fireTableDataChanged();
}

private void newAlbumActionPerformed(ActionEvent evt) {
   Album album = AlbumEditDialog.newAlbum();
```

```
    if(album != null) {
        try {
            DataModel.insertAlbum(album);
            model.getData().add(album);
            model.fireTableDataChanged();
        } catch(SQLException e) {
            Exceptions.printStackTrace(e);
        }
    }
}
```

The method editAlbumActionPerformed() is executed by a double click or by *Edit*. Similar to creating a new entry, you call a dialog again. However, to do so you use the method editAlbum() to which you can transfer an Album instance. The data of the instance will be edited in the dialog. The just-selected line of the table provides the method getSelectedRow(); with its output you are then able to read the referring data out of the data model of the table. The user has the option of changing data in the dialog that appears. Pressing the button afterwards, the editAlbum() method gives back the changed Album instance. You see the changes in the database by the updateAlbum() method of the data access module. It is still possible to delete an existing entry in a database: the method deleteAlbumActionPerformed() will do this.

First, ask the user if he or she actually wants to delete the data to prevent the deletion of unintentional entries. The query dialog needed for this is realized by means of the NetBeans Dialogs API. You create a NotifyDescriptor.Confirmation instance for it and enable the dialog to display by the notify() method. When the user agrees to delete, you remove the entry from the database by the deleteAlbum() method and, when this operation has finished successfully, finally delete the album from the table and refresh the table. (See Listing 26-7.)

Listing 26-7. Top Component to Display and Edit Existing Albums in the Database

```
private void editAlbumActionPerformed(ActionEvent evt) {
    if (albums.getSelectedRowCount() > 0) {
        Album album = AlbumEditDialog.editAlbum(model.getRow(albums.getSelectedRow()));
        if(album != null) {
            try {
                DataModel.updateAlbum(album);
                model.fireTableDataChanged();
            } catch(SQLException e) {
                Exceptions.printStackTrace(e);
            }
        }
    }
}

private void deleteAlbumActionPerformed(ActionEvent evt) {
    if (albums.getSelectedRowCount() > 0) {
        Album album = model.getRow(albums.getSelectedRow());
        NotifyDescriptor d = new NotifyDescriptor.Confirmation(
            "Are you sure you want delete the album " +
            album.getTitle(),
            "Confirm Album Deletion");
```

```
        if (DialogDisplayer.getDefault().notify(d) == NotifyDescriptor.YES_OPTION) {
            try {
                DataModel.deleteAlbum(album);
                model.getData().remove(album);
                model.fireTableDataChanged();
            } catch(SQLException e) {
                Exceptions.printStackTrace(e);
            }
        }
    }
  }
}
```

The last task is to set the dialog with which the data can be recorded and edited. You want to use the advantages of the Dialogs API again and do not construct a complete dialog yourself, but just the panel with the referring fields to capture the data (see Figure 26-4). Thus you create a simple JPanel class. This is best achieved with *File ➤ New File... ➤ Swing GUI Forms ➤ JPanel Form*.

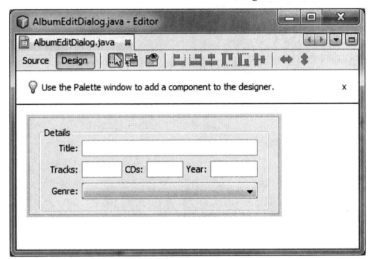

Figure 26-4. Dialog panel for editing and creating entries

You load all genres out of the database in the constructor of this panel and then add it to the combobox; you just need the methods newAlbum() and editAlbum(), which you are familiar with from the previous step. For an easy use of the dialogs you implement them as static methods; these methods are factories which care themselves about creating the dialogs. This is why you first create an instance of our own class AlbumEditDialog. You create a dialog by means of a DialogDescriptor to which pass the just created panel, and the dialog is already done. As usual, we show the dialog with the method notify(). As soon as the user pressed *OK* you create an album object out of the data and return it. If not, you just deliver null and signal that the user cancelled. In the case of the editAlbum() method, you just proceed the same way setting the dialog. You just preset the fields with the values of the transferred albums. After finishing the dialog no new Album object is created,though; you just update the data with the referring set methods and redeliver those updated instances. (See Listing 26-8.)

Listing 26-8. Dialog for Editing and Creating New Albums

```java
import javax.swing.JPanel;
import org.openide.DialogDescriptor;
import org.openide.DialogDisplayer;

public class AlbumEditDialog extends JPanel {
    private AlbumEditDialog() {
        initComponents();
        for(Genre g : DataModel.getGenres()) {
            genre.addItem(g);
        }
    }

    public static Album newAlbum() {
        AlbumEditDialog d = new AlbumEditDialog();
        DialogDescriptor desc = new DialogDescriptor(d, "New...");
        if(DialogDisplayer.getDefault().notify(desc) == DialogDescriptor.OK_OPTION) {
            Album album = new Album(0,
                d.title.getText(), d.tracks.getText(),
                d.cds.getText(), d.year.getText());
            album.setGenre((Genre)d.genre.getModel().getSelectedItem());
            return album;
        } else {
            return null;
        }
    }

    public static Album editAlbum(Album album) {
        AlbumEditDialog d = new AlbumEditDialog();
        d.title.setText(album.getTitle());
        d.tracks.setText(album.getTracks());
        d.cds.setText(album.getCds());
        d.year.setText(album.getYear());
        d.genre.getModel().setSelectedItem(album.getGenre());
        DialogDescriptor desc = new DialogDescriptor(d, "Edit...");

        if(DialogDisplayer.getDefault().notify(desc) == DialogDescriptor.OK_OPTION) {
            album.setTitle(d.title.getText());
            album.setTracks(d.tracks.getText());
            album.setCds(d.cds.getText());
            album.setYear(d.year.getText());
            album.setGenre((Genre)d.genre.getModel().getSelectedItem());
            return album;
        } else {
            return null;
        }
    }
}
```

So now you have created all the necessary classes for accessing the database and for managing and representing the data. This is the end of the example application for Java DB usage.

Summary

Databases are usually located on a server. However, Java DB offers a client database solution. In this chapter we looked at how such a database can be integrated in your NetBeans Platform application.

CHAPTER 27

Hibernate

In Chapter 26 you learned about using the client database solution Java DB within a rich client application. You had to disassemble the files to save them in the relational database system and you also had to extract the data of the database in a conventional way via SQL over the JDBC interface. You then had to assemble your objects—in this example, Album and Genre. You encapsulated this functionality in the class DataModel—you may have noticed that this can become quite complicated and error-prone. This is one of the reasons database creators put such an effort into developing and standardizing object-oriented databases, although they cannnot establish and enforce against the relational systems, yet. This is mainly because of the widespread use of the RDBMS: new applications have to access data that is saved in relations.

This is why so-called object relational bridges have been developed; they take care of saving and loading object data in and out of rational databases and thus form an abstraction layer for the underlying database system. Probably the most popular and widely used implementation of such a bridge is Hibernate. Hibernate does the mapping of the object data on relations, which should be as transparent as possible. Ideally, that means you do not need to worry about where and how your data is saved.

This chapter will show how Hibernate can be usefully integrated in a rich client application on the basis of the NetBeans Platform. I will only cover the basic concepts of using Hibernate here, however; this chapter will not discuss all the details of the wide functionalities of Hibernate.

Integrating the Hibernate Libraries

At first, you should download the current *Hibernate* distribution (here version 3.6.1) from http://hibernate.org. This distribution brings along all the necessary third-party libraries, examples, and comprehensive documentation in addition to the Hibernate library itself. You want to encapsulate these libraries as a separate module again, as you did with the Java DB; this will provide Hibernate functionality to the application. To do so, call in *File ➤ New Project...* and then *NetBeans Modules ➤ Library Wrapper Module*. Add the following libraries to the distribution:

- hibernate3.jarlib/jpa/hibernate-jpa-2.0-api-1.0.0.Final.jar

- lib/required/antlr-2.7.6.jar

- lib/required/commons-collections-3.1.jar

- lib/required/dom4j-1.6.1.jar

- lib/required/javassist-3.12.0.GA.jar

- lib/required/jta-1.1.jar

- lib/required/slf4j-api-1.6.1.jar

Hibernate uses the Simple Logging Facade for Java (SLF4J) API to create the log output. As the name suggests, this API provides a façade for different logging frameworks, including Log4J or the Java Platform Logging Framework. A framework does not need to be "compulsively" present for the façade; it does make sense, however, to provide such a framework, especially for the development of an application, because Hibernate gives out numerous helpful reports. SLF4J provides its own simple logging implementation, too. This implementation is part of the SLF4J package, which you can download at http://slf4j.org. So, now add this JAR file to the Hibernate module, too:

```
slf4j-simple-1.6.1.jar
```

If problems occur using libraries within the NetBeans platform, they will most likely be classloader problems. Hibernate itself uses the system classloader and can thus access the entities without explicitly defined dependencies. The Proxy Factory of the Javassist library—which is responsible for the proxy production of objects to the runtime (necessary for the lazy loading)—uses a different classloader and consequently does not find classes out of the Hibernate libraries or classes out of your application modules. Advantageously, you can provide your own classloader provider implementation to the class javassist.util.proxy.ProxyFactory by the ProxyFactory.ClassLoaderProvider interface and create a module installer for the Hibernate module. Use the restored() method to provide the system classloader to the application of the ProxyFactory at the start (see Listing 27-1).

Listing 27-1. Providing a Classloader Provider Implementation

```
import javassist.util.proxy.ProxyFactory;
import org.openide.modules.ModuleInstall;

public class Installer extends ModuleInstall {
    @Override
    public void restored() {
        ProxyFactory.classLoaderProvider = new ProxyFactory.ClassLoaderProvider() {
            @Override
            public ClassLoader get(ProxyFactory pf) {
                return Thread.currentThread().getContextClassLoader();
            }
        };
    }
}
```

Usually, the context classloader of the current thread is the system classloader (if no other was used). Transfer this to the ProxyFactory object via the get() method.

Structure of the Exemplified Application

Now I will show you how to use Hibernate with the albums example from Chapter 26, so you can appreciate the advantages of an object relational bridge. In addition, you can use the already integrated database system Java DB again now. Add the library wrapper module with the Hibernate libraries to the already created Platform application. Each module that wants to use the Hibernate functionality is able to define a dependency to the application. In this example, it is only the application module (*My Module*). Open the *Properties* window over the context menu and add the *Hibernate* module under *Libraries.* You have to add a dependency on the *Java DB* module to the *Hibernate* module in the same way so Hibernate can access the Java DB database driver.

So far you have managed the classes for your entities, genre and album, in the application module. Since Hibernate needs access to these classes, you should define another dependency from Hibernate to the application module. That would lead to a cyclic dependency; the module system of the NetBeans Platform would quickly report an error and the application would not even start. This is why you outsource your entity classes in a separate module, so the cyclic dependency is solved. This constellation with the additional module is graphically illustrated in Figure 27-1.

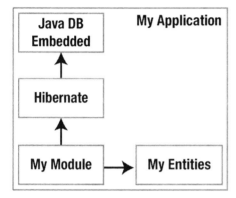

Figure 27-1. The application components and their dependencies

---

■ **Tip** When developing your application,using the embedded version of the Java DB (in this case, the module *Java DB Embedded*) is not recommended; instead, use the server variant that is already integrated in the NetBeans IDE. Integrate the Java DB driver as module in your application as described in Chapter 27, adjust it in the *hibernate.cfg.xml* file to the connection URL, and start the database server in the NetBeans IDE with *Start Server* in the context menu of the node *Databases* ➤ *Java DB* in the service window. This way it is possible to look at the database schema produced by Hibernate.

Configuring Hibernate

After integrating Hibernate you now have to provide some configuration information. You define this information by an XML file which is called *hibernate.cfg.xml* by default. You definitely need to specify the database driver, the URL to connect with the database, the necessary authentication data, and the SQL dialect which should be used. This configuration file then looks as follows in Listing 27-2.

Listing 27-2. Hibernate Configuration File

```
<?xml version="1.0" encoding="utf-8"?>
<!DOCTYPE hibernate-configuration PUBLIC
   "-//Hibernate/Hibernate Configuration DTD 3.0//EN"
   "http://hibernate.sourceforge.net/hibernate-configuration-3.0.dtd">
<hibernate-configuration>
   <session-factory>
      <property name="connection.driver_class">org.apache.derby.jdbc.EmbeddedDriver</property>
      <property name="connection.url">jdbc:derby:hibernate-db;create=true</property>
      <property name="connection.username">user</property>
      <property name="connection.password">password</property>
      <property name="dialect">org.hibernate.dialect.DerbyDialect</property>
   </session-factory>
</hibernate-configuration>
```

First, you define the database class, which in this case is org.apache.derby.jdbc.EmbeddedDriver for the Java DB database system. Add the URL so Hibernate can establish a connection to your database; you already know that this is composed for the Java DB. Along with the username and the password, which will eventually be necessary, you have to define the SQL dialect. Hibernate provides corresponding classes for all major database systems in the package org.hibernate.dialect. You can find more information about additional configuration options from the Hibernate reference documentation.

All this begs the question, where to put this file. Because the data is in a separate file, you have the option of using several Hibernate modules with different configurations. You can then either save the file in the *src* directory of an application module or directly save it in the Hibernate module. It is important that it is on the referring class path, because this is where it is searched for. Optionally,as you will see later, you can define an alternative URL to the configuration file when producing an Configuration object.

Mapping Objects on Relations

Now that Hibernate is ready, the question arises as to how Hibernate saves your objects in the database. How is the referring object structure mapped on a relation? You create a so-called *mapping file* for each object which persists precisely this mapping information. This involves, among other things, information with which name and with which type object attributes in a relation are saved, but more important, how associations between different objects are handled. Much detailed information is possible and needed, depending on the complexity of the object structure and the purpose of the application. In this setting you cannot go into detail, so restrict the application on the mapping information which is necessary for your exemplified classes.

Let's look at such a mapping first for our example class Genre. You remember that in it you managed a number as a unique ID and a string for the genre name itself. (See Listing 27-3.)

Listing 27-3. Object Relational Mapping for the Class Genre: Genre.hbm.xml

```
<!DOCTYPE hibernate-mapping PUBLIC
   "-//Hibernate/Hibernate Mapping DTD 3.0//EN"
   "http://hibernate.sourceforge.net/hibernate-mapping-3.0.dtd">
<hibernate-mapping package="com.galileo.netbeans.myentities">
   <class name="Genre" table="Genre" lazy="true">
```

```
        <id name="id">
            <generator class="increment"/>
        </id>
        <property name="genre"
                    not-null="true"
                    length="30"
                    column="genre"/>
    </class>
</hibernate-mapping>
```

By the class element you define the class name and the name of the table in which the files of an object of the type Genre are saved. With the element id you define your object attribute with the same name as primary key for the table which will be assigned in ascending order. At last, you only need to define the second and last attribute genre with the property element. If you look at an excerpt of the mapping for the class Album, it gets a little more interesting, because a genre can be assigned to an album; there can be multiple albums of the same genre, however. Therefore you have a many-to-one relation. You define this with the element which has the same name and set its lazy attribute to false, as shown in Listing 27-4. This way the Genre object is loaded together with the Album and not just when it is needed. By determining fetch="join" you induce Hibernate to detect the genre at the same time as querying the album data by a JOIN query. This is a query optimization: only one instead of two queries is needed to load a class completely out of a database.

Listing 27-4. Define the Association on the Genre with Many-to-One

```
<!DOCTYPE hibernate-mapping PUBLIC
    "-//Hibernate/Hibernate Mapping DTD 3.0//EN"
    "http://hibernate.sourceforge.net/hibernate-mapping-3.0.dtd">
<hibernate-mapping package="com.galileo.netbeans.myentities">
    <class name="Album" table="Album" lazy="true">
        <id name="id">
            <generator class="increment"/>
        </id>
        <many-to-one name="genre" lazy="false" fetch="join"/>
        <property name="title"
                    not-null="true"
                    length="30"
                    column="title"/>
```

Now you have to make these mappings, which typically end with *hbm.xml* and which are in the same package as the classes, known in Hibernate. This is done by an entry in the configuration file *hibernate.cfg.xml* in which you already did the database settings. You list all files by the element mapping. Furthermore, you define the feature hbm2ddl with the value update. So, if it is not there yet, Hibernate automatically creates the database schema for us out of the information of the mapping files when the application starts, as shown in Listing 27-5.

Listing 27-5. Making the Mapping Files Public in the Configuration File

```
<hibernate-configuration>
    <session-factory>
        ...
        <property name="hbm2ddl.auto">update</property>
        <mapping resource="com/galileo/netbeans/myentities/Genre.hbm.xml"/>
```

```
    <mapping resource="com/galileo/netbeans/myentities/Album.hbm.xml"/>
  </session-factory>
</hibernate-configuration>
```

SessionFactory and Sessions

Now the configuration work is completed and you can get in touch with Hibernate for the first time. To do this, first create an object of the class Configuration which manages the configuration you created before in the file *hibernate.cfg.xml*. This class wants to get its information from the *hibernate.properties* file by default. However, you organized your information in an XML document, which is why you induce the Configuration instance to search for this file with the configure() method. This method is also available in some parameterized variants, which you can transfer a File or a URL in the configuration file to. We use the parameter-less version which directly expects the configuration with the name *hibernate.cfg.xml* on the class path. Usually, such a Configuration is only created once. Based on this configuration we create a SessionFactory with the method buildSessionFactory(). A SessionFactory is also held throughout the duration of the complete runtime of the application.

In other words, you manage the Configuration and the SessionFactory instance in your module at a central place. A module installer class would be good for that purpose; you would create a static instance of a SessionFactory there (see Listing 27-6).

Listing 27-6. Central Management and Providing the SessionFactory

```java
import org.hibernate.Session;
import org.hibernate.SessionFactory;
import org.hibernate.cfg.Configuration;
import org.openide.modules.ModuleInstall;

public class Installer extends ModuleInstall {
    private static final SessionFactory sessionFactory;
    static {
        try {
            sessionFactory = new Configuration().configure().buildSessionFactory();
        } catch (Throwable ex) {
            throw new ExceptionInInitializerError(ex);
        }
    }
    public static Session createSession() {
        return sessionFactory.openSession();
    }
    public static Session currentSession() {
        return sessionFactory.getCurrentSession();
    }
    @Override
    public void close() {
        sessionFactory.close();
    }
}
```

The database is accessed through sessions. A Session is a relative short-lived object which is responsible for the interaction between application and database. So there is a JDBC connection hidden behind a Session. A session is thus also responsible for the creation of a transaction and contains a cache. You create each a new Session with the method openSession(). An even more current session is delivered with the method getCurrentSession(). If there is none, a new one is created and bound to the current thread. If a transaction is finished (by commit() or rollback()), which was created by this Session, it is automatically closed. This way of using sessions is the easiest and the most comfortable and is therefore preferred.

Saving and Loading Objects

With the Installer class you created a helper for easy saving and loading of objects. You want to use it directly. You remember that we created the class DataModel. This class was responsible for the interaction with the database and so was a mapper between SQL and your objects. Hibernate now does all these tasks for us. You still want to use the class, however, because then you do not have to change your remaining application and at the same time you encapsulate the Hibernate interaction. This is probably the most interesting part of this chapter, because this is where the greatest simplification arises (see Listing 27-7).

Listing 27-7. The Class DataModel Interacts with the Database over Hibernate

```
import com.galileo.netbeans.myentities.Genre;
import com.galileo.netbeans.myentities.Album;
import java.util.List;
import org.hibernate.Session;
import org.hibernate.Transaction;

public class DataModel {
    public static List<Album> getAlbums() {
        Session s = Installer.currentSession();
        Transaction t = s.beginTransaction();
        List<Album> list = (List<Album>)s.createCriteria(Album.class).list();
        t.commit();
        return list;
    }
    public static List<Genre> getGenres() {
        Session s = Installer.currentSession();
        Transaction t = s.beginTransaction();
        List<Genre> list = (List<Genre>)s.createCriteria(Genre.class).list();
        t.commit();
        return list;
    }
    public static void updateAlbum(Album album) {
        Session s = Installer.currentSession();
        Transaction t = s.beginTransaction();
        s.update(album);
        t.commit();
    }
    public static void insertAlbum(Album album) {
        Session s = Installer.currentSession();
        Transaction t = s.beginTransaction();
        s.save(album);
```

```
        t.commit();
    }
    public static void deleteAlbum(Album album) {
        Session s = Installer.currentSession();
        Transaction t = s.beginTransaction();
        s.delete(album);
        t.commit();
    }
}
```

For each action we use a current—or possibly new—Session for each action, with which you create a transaction. Then you are able to save, update, and execute the wanted action on the Session and you can successfully close the transaction with commit(). As already mentioned, it is not necessary to explicitly close the Session, because it is automatically closed finishing the transaction.

This example naturally deals with very simple application cases. For this reason you have one transaction for each action during a session which has the same lifetime. (You can get information about the granularity of sessions and transactions that should be used from the Hibernate documentation.) So now you have completely migrated our example, which first transferred its data via SQL over the JDBC interface quasi "rough draft" between application and database. Thus the application runs entirely abstracted from the underlying persistence system and you can save and query objects comfortably and transparently.

Summary

Hibernate is an object relational bridge. This allows you to create a transparent interface between application and database. In this chapter you learned how to integrate Hibernate in a NetBeans Platform application. You saw how to configure Hibernate and how the mapping between objects and relations is done. The chapter dealt with sessions and session factories as well as with the saving and loading of objects.

Java Persistence API

The target of the Java Persistence API (JPA) is to specify a standardized, simple to use persistence model that can be used with both Java SE and Java EE.The best features and ideas flowed in, mainly from Hibernate, TopLink, and JDO. Consequently, an application that uses the interfaces of the JPA is completely independent of a special framework such as Hibernate. Its application keeps the same independence as it had before it was used with the Java Database Connectivity (JDBC) interface.

The JPA is mainly characterized by its lightness and its slimness. One of the main features of the JPA is the specification of the object relational mapping by the Java annotations directly in the persistence object. A separate mapping file as used with Hibernate in Chapter 27 is not necessary anymore (it should be mentioned that no explicit mapping of the object structures on relations is necessary). It is possible, though, to influence the standard mapping strategy by annotations. This makes the specification of entities much easier. Still, the JPA specifies the SQL-related query language *Java Persistence Query Language* (JPQL) for both static and dynamic queries, which makes it independent of a proprietary query language as HQL. The persistence layer can be classified in three areas: the API itself in the package javax.persistence, the query language, JPQL and the annotations to define the mapping information.

Meanwhile, a set of projects and frameworks provides a JPA implementation, to which Hibernate and EclipseLink or OpenJPA belong. We take a look at the JPA interface now, because you already got to know the native interface of Hibernate. By the way, the JPA interface of Hibernate does not look very different from the native interface. You will see quite clearly that Hibernate was a model when JPA was specified.

Hibernate and the Java Persistence API

Since Hibernate 3.5, the Hibernate implementation of the JPA is a built-in feature and is located in the *hibernate3.jar*. Together with the used libraries and the JPA itself you create a module called Hibernate, exactly as described in Chapter 27. Pay attention to the hints on the classloader and to the logging.

Java Persistence Configuration

The configuration of the persistence layer occurs in a very similar way to the native Hibernate interface (see Listing 28-1). The configuration is provided in the file *persistence.xml* in the directory *META-INF*. The files are bundled in *persistence units*.

Listing 28-1. Configuration of the Persistence Layer: META-INF/persistence.xml

```xml
<persistence xmlns="http://java.sun.com/xml/ns/persistence"
    xmlns:xsi="http://www.w3.org/2001/XMLSchema-instance"
    version="1.0">
    <persistence-unit name="HibernateJPA" transaction-type="RESOURCE_LOCAL">
        <provider>org.hibernate.ejb.HibernatePersistence</provider>
        <class>com.galileo.netbeans.myentities.Genre</class>
        <class>com.galileo.netbeans.myentities.Album</class>
        <properties>
            <property name="hibernate.connection.driver_class"
                value="org.apache.derby.jdbc.EmbeddedDriver"/>
            <property name="hibernate.connection.url"
                value="jdbc:derby:hibernatejpa-db;create=true"/>
            <property name="hibernate.connection.username"
                value="user"/>
            <property name="hibernate.connection.password"
                value="password"/>
            <property name="hibernate.dialect"
                value="org.hibernate.dialect.DerbyDialect"/>
            <property name="hibernate.hbm2ddl.auto"
                value="update"/>
        </properties>
    </persistence-unit>
</persistence>
```

We open a persistence-unit called HibernateJPA, which you will use later when producing an EntityManagerFactory. There you will list all classes which should be managed by the EntityManager of this factory. You have to define the same features again as in *hibernate.cfg.xml*, whereas the prefix hibernate has to be prefixed to the features. You discard the created file *persistence.xml* in the module *My Entities* in the directory *src/META-INF*.

The advantage of implementing the entities in JPA is that, due to the attribute accessor methods (not for each attribute), which should be kept persistent, access methods have to be provided (that is, get and set methods) or attributes have to be made publicly, since JPA can also read and write private attributes. In addition, a special interface does not need to be implemented or derived from a given class. Entities that are to be administered persistently by the JPA are ordinary Java objects. Only a few annotations are necessary within the class. These are essentially the identification of the class as entity with the annotation @Entity, the definition of an identity with @Id, and the declaration of the attributes. So the classes' possibilities for expression are not limited in any way. A hierarchy of objects is managed by default by JPA as in a relation. This mapping strategy can be adjusted via annotations in order to adapt newly implemented objects to an existing database schema, for example. (See Listing 28-2.)

Taking the entity's definition into consideration, let's look at the classes Genre and Album again. You only need to insert the annotation @Entity in front of the class definition. Additionally, set the class attribute id as identity of the class by the annotation @Id. At the same time, instruct the persistence layer (in this case, Hibernate) to create a value for this attribute. The attribute genre is an ordinary attribute, so it does not need to be labeled separately. It is automatically included if it is not marked as transient. Optionally, common attributes can be marked with the annotation @Basic. Bear in mind that it is not mandatory to provide get and set methods for your attributes. In the class Genre, for example, you can omit the methods getId() and setId() if you do not need them.

Listing 28-2. You Define Your Class As an Entity That Can Be Saved in a Relational Databank System with Only a Few Annotations. The Previous Mapping Files Can Be Dropped Completely.

```
import javax.persistence.Entity;
import javax.persistence.GeneratedValue;
import javax.persistence.Id;
@Entity
public class Genre {
    @Id
    @GeneratedValue
    private Integer id;
    private String genre;
    public Genre() {
    }
    ...
}
```

There is only thing more to do in the class Album. You need to explicitly define a column name for the attribute year, since by default the column is named as the attribute itself. However, this results in an error in the case of year at the first query, because year is part of SQL. This is why you define a user-specific name with the annotation @Column. Finally, you just have to define the association of the Genre class as @ManyToOne and both your entities are ready. (See Listing 28-3.)

Listing 28-3. Definition of the Entity Albums with the Association on the Class Genre

```
import javax.persistence.Column;
import javax.persistence.Entity;
import javax.persistence.GeneratedValue;
import javax.persistence.Id;
import javax.persistence.ManyToOne;

@Entity
public class Album {
    @Id
    @GeneratedValue
    private Integer id;
    private String title;
    private String tracks;
    private String cds;
    @Column(name = "years")
    private String year;
    @ManyToOne
    private Genre genre;

    public Album() {
    }
    ...
}
```

To get your entities access to the annotations you have to add a dependency on the module *Hibernate* to the module *My Entities*. The Hibernate EntityManager uses the system classloader, so you do not need to add dependencies on your entities to the Hibernate module which would have led to a cyclical dependency. If that was the case, you would have had to pack the annotation in a separate module and you would get a more complicated constellation. This way, you end up with the layout and dependencies shown in Figure 28-1.

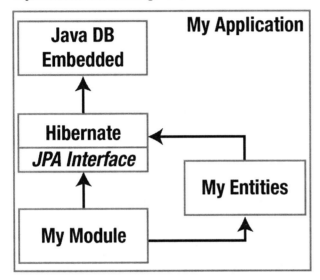

Figure 28-1. *Dependencies between the modules using the JPA interface of Hibernate*

EntityManagerFactory and EntityManager

Similar to the SessionFactory in the native Hibernate interface, an EntityManagerFactory is available with the Java Persistence API. This factory is created for a certain persistence unit. So EntityManagers, which were produced by this factory, are able to save and manage the objects in the defined database which are defined in the referring persistence unit. Normally, an EntityManagerFactory is created only once and held during the whole application runtime like the SessionFactory. You get an instance of such a factory over the bootstrap class Persistence by calling the following:

```
EntityManagerFactory emf = Persistence.createEntityManagerFactory("HibernateJPA");
```

The transferred parameter HibernateJPA defines the name of one persistence unit defined in the file *persistence.xml*. The factory is produced for the persistence unit.

The equivalent of a session—which to some extent represents a wrapper of a JDBC link—is up to the JPA in the class EntityManager. Through this manager you can access the database and save, delete, find, and query objects there. Usually, one EntityManager is used for a certain process. However, it is a bad practice if you create a new EntityManager for each query or action. Hence it is important to choose an adequate runtime of an EntityManager depending on the application context. Since there are only a few trivial database actions in this example, for simplicity's sake let's only use one EntityManager for the whole runtime. In practice it does not make sense to use an EntityManager for each and every action.

As with the SessionFactory, it makes sense to manage the EntityManagerFactory in one module installer class (see Listing 28-4). This way you can also easily and properly finish having the factory shut down the application.

Listing 28-4. Central Management of and Providing the Entity Manager Factory

```java
import javax.persistence.EntityManager;
import javax.persistence.EntityManagerFactory;
import javax.persistence.Persistence;
public class Installer extends ModuleInstall {
   public static final EntityManagerFactory EMF;
   public static final EntityManager       EM;
   static {
      try {
         EMF = Persistence.createEntityManagerFactory("HibernateJPA");
         EM = EMF.createEntityManager();
      } catch (Throwable ex) {
         throw new ExceptionInInitializerError(ex);
      }
   }
   @Override
   public void close() {
      EM.close();
      EMF.close();
   }
}
```

Saving and Loading Objects

Finally, it remains to be clarified how to access your objects over an EntityManager. Take the class
DataModel, in which you implemented the interaction with the native Hibernate interface, again. You
want to substitute it now with the JPA. Let's take a look at the methods getAlbums() and getGenres(), for
example. As usual, you first create a transaction in which you want to execute your query or action. With
the method getTransaction() you get an instance of an EntityTransaction by the EntityManager. Start
the transaction with begin() and then create a Query instance for the *JPQL* query SELECT a FROM Album a.
This query provides all objects of the table Album. You get this result in the form of a List by the
getResultList() method. Finish the transaction successfully with commit(). (See Listing 28-5.)

Listing 28-5. Interaction with the Database with the EntityManager

```java
import javax.persistence.Query;

public class DataModel {

   public static List<Album> getAlbums() {
     Installer.EM.getTransaction().begin();
     Query q = Installer.EM.createQuery("SELECT a FROM Album a");
     List<Album> list = q.getResultList();
     Installer.EM.getTransaction().commit();
     return list;
   }

   public static List<Genre> getGenres() {
```

```
    Installer.EM.getTransaction().begin();
    Query q = Installer.EM.createQuery("SELECT g FROM Genre g");
    List<Genre> list = q.getResultList();
    Installer.EM.getTransaction().commit();
    return list;
}

public static void updateAlbum(Album album) {
    Installer.EM.getTransaction().begin();
    Installer.EM.persist(album);
    Installer.EM.getTransaction().commit();
}

public static void insertAlbum(Album album) {
    updateAlbum(album);
}

public static void deleteAlbum(Album album) {
    Installer.EM.getTransaction().begin();
    Installer.EM.remove(album);
    Installer.EM.getTransaction().commit();
}
}
```

Summary

The Java Persistence API (JPA) is a uniform interface for object-relational bridges such as Hibernate. JPA enables transparent usage and easy compatibility between persistence systems. In this chapter you used the JPA compliant interface of Hibernate.

CHAPTER 29

MySQL and EclipseLink

In Chapter 26, you created an application with which you saved music albums in a Java DB database. In this first step, you split the objects to be saved in SQL statements and assembled them from SQL results again. An object-relational mapping (ORM) framework like Hibernate does this work for you. Chapter 27 dealt with how to integrate Hibernate into a NetBeans Platform application and how to use the native interface of Hibernate. In Chapter 28 you got to know the Java Persistence API (JPA) that specify the interface of an ORM framework. Using the JPA, you could make the application independent of a special implementation, in this case Hibernate.

In the following sections, EclipseLink will be substituted for Hibernate and you will use a MySQL server instead of the Java DB database system (see Figure 29-1). Beyond the integration of these two components you will also learn how to let create entities out of relations with the NetBeans IDE. The application logic which is in *My Module* remains unchanged.

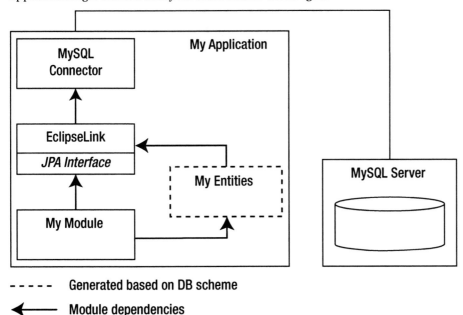

Figure 29-1. Structure of the application for the integration of EclipseLink and MySQL

Installing MySQL Database

First, create a MySQL database. This chapter assumes you have already installed a MySQL server or have access to one. You can download the free-to-use community edition at http://dev.mysql.com/downloads. Then open the *Services* window in the NetBeans IDE. There you will find the node *Databases*. Choose *Register MySQL Server...* out of its context menu (see Figure 29-2).

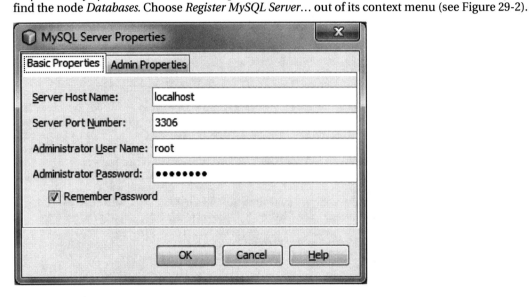

Figure 29-2. *Registering MySQL Server in the NetBeans IDE*

Type in the name of the server, the port, the username and the password (in this example *localhost*) into the dialog that appears. You get a *MySQL Server* node as shown in Figure 29-3. Now you can create a database out of this node with *Create Database...* in the context menu. Name it *eclipselink-db*.

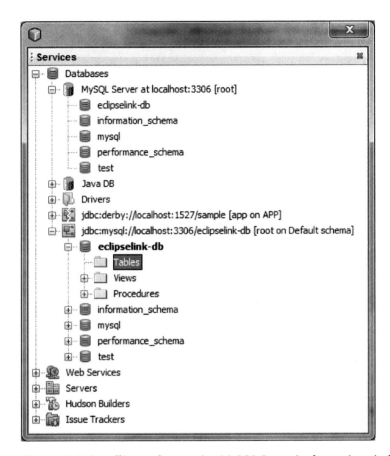

Figure 29-3. *Installing and managing MySQL Server in the service window*

The approach in this chapter is different from that of previous chapters: the entity classes are created out of the relations of the database. Hence, in the next step you create the necessary tables. Both tables *album* and *genre* should have the structure shown in Listing 29-1. Open the connection which you created before in the Services window and select the action *Execute Command...* in the context menu of the node *eclipselink-db* ➤ *Tables* to create the table (see Figure 29-3). You can directly type in the schema as an SQL statement (see Listing 29-1). Alternatively, you can also select the action *Create Table...* and create both tables manually.

Listing 29-1. *Schema of Both Tables album and genre*

```
CREATE TABLE genre (
    id INT NOT NULL,
    genre VARCHAR(30) NOT NULL,
    PRIMARY KEY(id)
)
CREATE TABLE album (
```

```
    id INT NOT NULL AUTO_INCREMENT,
    title VARCHAR(30) NOT NULL,
    tracks VARCHAR(30) NOT NULL,
    cds VARCHAR(30) NOT NULL,
    year VARCHAR(30) NOT NULL,
    genre INT NOT NULL,
    PRIMARY KEY(id),
    FOREIGN KEY(genre) REFERENCES genre(id)
)
```

Finally, register the MySQL server within the NetBeans IDE. You have now created a database and the necessary tables.

Integrating MySQL Driver

Integrate the MySQL JDBC driver (Connector/J) so the NetBeans Platform application can connect itself to the MySQL server and the NetBeans Platform gets access to the database. Do this with a new library wrapper module with *File ➤ New Project… ➤ NetBeans Modules ➤ Library Wrapper Module.* You can download the driver directly from http://dev.mysql.com/downloads or get it from the NetBeans IDE in the *ide/modules/ext* directory.

The module is called *MySQL Connector* here and you add it to the NetBeans Platform application (see Figure 29-4).

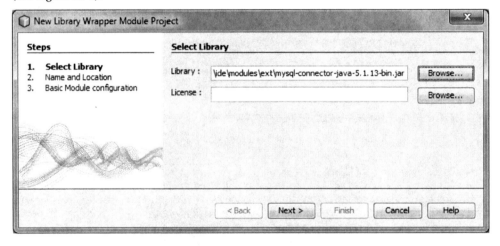

Figure 29-4. Integrate the MySQL JDBC driver in your application.

Integrate EclipseLink

You do not want to get access directly to the database through the JDBC interface, but through the ORM framework EclipseLink (JPA 2.0). Hence you have to make sure that the necessary libraries are available. Create a library wrapper module and add the Java Persistence API as well as the EclipseLink library as a special implementation of the JPA. You can get both libraries out of the NetBeans IDE from the directory *java/modules/ext/eclipselink*:

eclipselink-2.2.0.jar

eclipselink-javax.persistence-2.0.jar

Name this wrapper module *EclipseLink* and add it to your NetBeans Platform application.

Creating Entities out of Database Schema

In the preceding chapters you created the entity classes yourself. Based on its structures, the tables were automatically created by the ORM framework. Now you want to reverse the process. You already created the necessary tables for your application at the beginning of the chapter. The NetBeans IDE can now create the referring entity classes automatically. This process becomes interesting when you have to implement an application on an existing database.

Unfortunately, the NetBeans IDE wizard to create the entity classes on the base of tables is only provided for Java projects, not for module projects. Therefore you have to take a small detour. First, create a Java project with *File* ➤ *New Project…* ➤ *Java* ➤ *Java Class Library*. Then you can start the actual wizard with *File* ➤ *New File…* ➤ *Persistence* ➤ *Entity Classes From Database*. Choose the referring database connection (*eclipselink-db*) first and then add the tables *album* and *genre* with *Add >*. On the subsequent page, the classes to create are listed. Define the package (*com.galileo.netbeans.myentities*) and choose the option *Create Persistence Unit*. Meanwhile, the necessary JPA configuration (*persistence.xml)* is created as shown in Figure 29-5 (see also Chapter 28).

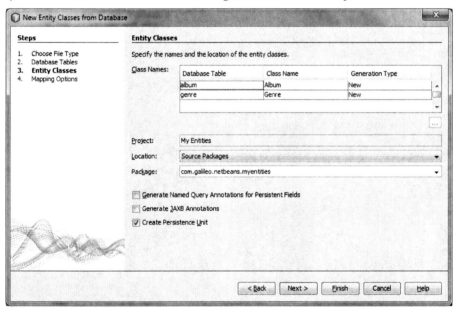

Figure 29-5. Creating the entity classes on the base of existing databank tables

On the last page of the wizard use *java.util.List* as *Collection Type* and deactivate all options. After the entity classes have been created, you can create a library. To do so, call *Build* from the project's context menu. Add the JAR file to a library wrapper module of your NetBeans Platform application in the next step. Call it *My Entities* and use *com.galileo.netbeans.myentities* as the code name base.

Build Up and Test Application

Now you have created a module for the MySQL driver and the EclipseLink implementation of the Java Persistence API. You did not create the entity classes Album and Genre yourself but let the NetBeans IDE create and annotate them. Out of that you created a NetBeans module. You can take the application module My Module as it is, because the advantage of using JPA is that you can change the underlying ORM framework. You only have to designate the new persistence unit name when creating the Entity Manager Factory in the Installer class. If you define the dependencies as in Figure 29-1 you can start and test the application.

Summary

In this chapter you used the widespread database MySQL to store your objects using the JPA implementation EclipseLink. You learned how to create classes out of relations and you also saw the great advantage of using the Java Persistence API, when you changed the persistence provider without impacting applications code and logic.

CHAPTER 30

Web Services

The *Amazon Product Advertising API* allows you to search for products or information about several products, and even execute operations in the shopping cart. This chapter will show you how to create the necessary classes with the NetBeans IDE and how to use those classes within a NetBeans Platform application.

Creating a Web Service Client

In the first step, you do not open a NetBeans module, but a Java class library that can be created by a wizard. Call *File ➤ New Project*, in the category *Java* choose the project type *Java Class Library*. Call the project *Amazon Web Services* and close the wizard with *Finish*. Then choose *File ➤ New File ➤ Web Services ➤ Web Service Client*. You directly specify the file to use by the URL *http://webservices.amazon.com/AWSECommerceService/DE/AWSECommerceService.wsdl.* (this only works when you are online). If you want to work offline, you can download the WSDL file and specify it as a local file in the wizard (see Figure 30-1). Call the package in which the web service classes are produced com.amazon.advertising.api.

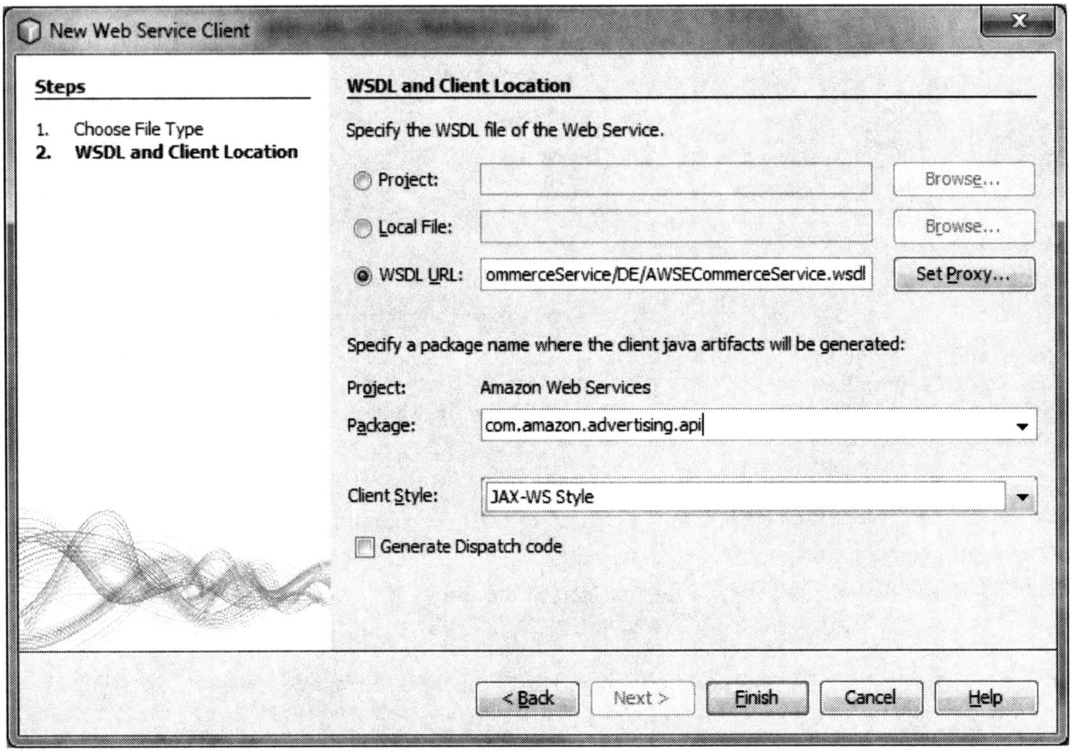

Figure 30-1. Creating a web service client for the Amazon Product Advertising API

Keep *JAX-WS Style* as the client style. Press *Finish* so all classes, which are necessary to use the web service, can be created by means of the description in the WSDL file. You deactivate the default set *Wrapper Style* for a better arranged usage of the web service operations, as you will see later. Open the newly added *Web Services References* folder in the project's view; there should be an entry *AWSECommerceService* in it. Open the context menu of this entry and choose *Edit Web Service Attributes.* Expand the node *AWSECommerceServicePortType* beneath *Port Types* on the WSDL Customization tab and deactivate the option *Enable Wrapper Style* (see Figure 30-2). This setting is then applied to all operations of this port type.

Figure 30-2. Deactivating wrapper style for the Amazon Web service

If you apply the settings with *OK* the web service client classes should become updated. Now you can execute a *Build* and get the web service client as a JAR file *dist/Amazon_Web_Services.jar* in the project folder. In the next step you can use this file within a NetBeans module as *Amazon Web Services API*.

Using the Web Service

In the last paragraph, a Java interface for the usage of the Amazon Web service has been created. You can proceed in the exact same way with other web services. To call a web service out of a NetBeans Platform application you first create a NetBeans Platform application with *File ➤ New Project... ➤ NetBeans Modules ➤ NetBeans Platform Application*. You can give the application any name. In the next step you add the web service client to the application. To do so, you create a library wrapper module with *File ➤ New Project… ➤ NetBeans Modules ➤ Library Wrapper Module*. Add the JAR file *Amazon_Web_Services.jar* to the library wrapper module and call it *Amazon Web Services*, too.

The web service client is now available within your NetBeans Platform application. Now you can create an application module in which to use the web service. With *File ➤ New Project… ➤ NetBeans Modules ➤ Module* you add a further module to the Platform application. Add a dependency to the Amazon Web service module that the module can also use the web service client. To demonstrate a call of a web service operation, create a top component. With that you want to search the available pictures of a product by means of the *ASIN* (Amazon Standard Identification Number). Thinking about the MP3 Manager (developed in Chapter 44) the following usage is imaginable: save the ASIN in the ID3 tag of an MP3 file and then you can display the available cover of the currently playing MP3 file—or you can search for and display albums of the currently played artist.

In the exemplified application, as shown in Figure 30-3, you want to search for a product by means of the typed-in ASIN and display its preview as used on the Amazon web site. To do so, take a closer look at the necessary query with which you can call the Amazon web service. This query should be executed asynchronously to avoid an obstruction of the complete application. Keep in mind that accessing the GUI components only works from the Event Dispatch Thread. You have to be informed as soon as the query is executed and you can display the picture. The easiest way to achieve this is with a `SwingWorker` class. Create your own class that derives from `SwingWorker<String, Object>`.

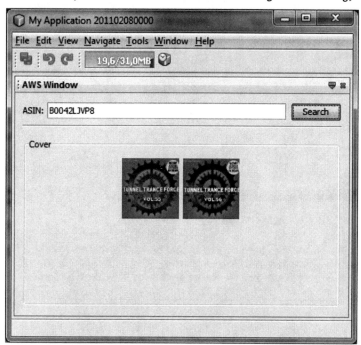

Figure 30-3. Query product information over the Amazon Product Advertising API

The method `doInBackgroud()`, which you have to overwrite, is automatically executed asynchronously. This is where you place your web service query. If that is executed the method is queried by the `SwingWorker` class (see Listing 30-1). You can detect the value of the method `doInBackground()` by the method `get()` quite easily—in this example, the URL of the product picture.

Listing 30-1. Executing a Web Service Query and Displaying the Results by Means of a SwingWorker Class

```java
import com.amazon.advertising.api.AWSECommerceService;
import com.amazon.advertising.api.AWSECommerceServicePortType;
import com.amazon.advertising.api.ImageSet;
import com.amazon.advertising.api.Item;
import com.amazon.advertising.api.ItemLookup;
import com.amazon.advertising.api.ItemLookupRequest;
import com.amazon.advertising.api.ItemLookupResponse;
...
final class AWSTopComponent extends TopComponent {
    private static final String AWS_KEY = <your access key>;
    private static final String SEC_KEY = <your secret key>;

    private final class ImageLookupByASIN extends SwingWorker<String, Object> {
        private String asin = "";

        public ImageLookupByASIN(String asin) {
            this.asin = asin;
        }

        @Override
        public String doInBackground() {
            String url = "";
            try {
                AWSECommerceService service = new AWSECommerceService();
                service.setHandlerResolver(new AWSHandlerResolver(SEC_KEY));
                AWSECommerceServicePortType port = service.getAWSECommerceServicePort();

                ItemLookupRequest request = new ItemLookupRequest();
                request.setIdType("ASIN");
                request.getItemId().add(asin);
                request.getResponseGroup().add("Images");

                ItemLookup il = new ItemLookup();
                il.setAWSAccessKeyId(AWS_KEY);
                il.getRequest().add(request);

                ItemLookupResponse response = port.itemLookup(il);
                Item i = response.getItems().get(0).getItem().get(0);

                ImageSet is = i.getImageSets().get(0).getImageSet().get(0);
                url = is.getThumbnailImage().getURL();
            } catch (Exception e) {
                Exceptions.printStackTrace(e);
            }
            return url;
        }

        @Override
        protected void done() {
```

```
        try {
            cover.add(new JLabel(new ImageIcon(new URL(get()))));
            cover.updateUI();
        } catch (Exception e) {
            Exceptions.printStackTrace(e);
        }
    }
}

    private void searchActionPerformed(ActionEvent evt) {
        new ImageLookupByASIN(asin.getText()).execute();
    }
}
```

First, you determine the port of the Amazon web service in the asynchronously executed doInBackground() method. You want to execute the *ItemLookup* operation which you configure by an ItemLookup and an ItemLookupRequest object. With the request object you determine that you want to search for a product by means of the *ASIN*. You add the ASIN, which was passed to the ImageLookupByASIN object as parameter, to the item ID list. You can determine and narrow the information delivered by the web service by the *Reponse Group*. As you are only interested in the URLs of the pictures and the other product information is not important, you use the group type *Images*.

For the usage of the Amazon Web Service (AWS) you need a so-called *AWS Access Key* and an *AWS Secret Key*. Both are assigned to you by a free login at *http://aws.amazon.com*. Queries to the Amazon web services have to be signed. The signature is produced and determined by a secret key of the class AWSHandlerResolver. (You can find this class in the example project which is available from the Source Code/Download Page for this book at www.apress.com.) You transfer the access key to the ItemLookup object by the setAWSAccessKeyId() method. You also add the ItemLookupRequest object. By doing so you compose the parameters necessary for the query. Now you can execute the operation itemLookup() on the web service port you determined before. You get the result of the query in an ItemLookupResponse object which contains a list of found products in terms of Item objects. As there is only one product for an ASIN you can take the first item from the list directly. One item contains an ImageSet out of which you extract and to which you return the preview.

Now the whole query is completed and the SwingWorker class calls the method done(). In this method you can get the URL by means of the get() method. Finally, you can directly create an ImageIcon object out of it which you are able to display afterwards (see Figure 30-3).

Summary

This chapter dealt with the topic of web services. You created a Web Service API (a web service client) for AWS from the corresponding WSDL file. To this end, you made use of the related NetBeans IDE tooling support. Next, you learned how to integrate the web service client into your own NetBeans Platform application. All in all, the example showed how easy it is to use a web service in your own application.

CHAPTER 31

Java Enterprise Edition and the NetBeans Platform

Java Enterprise Edition (Java EE) provides the basis for developing distributed multilayered business applications out of modular components. Particularly with business applications, the NetBeans Platform is used in connection with large quantities of data which often must be edited in a complex way. The question of how to usefully merge these two worlds, Java Enterprise Edition and the NetBeans Platform, naturally arises.

By default in Java EE, an application client is provided for the client-side usage of Java EE applications. This application client is executed in an Application Client Container (ACC). Unfortunately, such a container is not qualified for integration in a NetBeans Platform application. Another possibility is to forego the advantages of an ACC and directly address Java EE applications—specifically, Enterprise Java Beans (EJBs). But the ACC creates wrapper classes automatically at runtime. These wrapper classes, together with a special classloading strategy, forbid integration into the NetBeans Platform; an unmanageable number of libraries is another problem. The origin of this problem is the communication of the components spread through RMI-IIOP (Java Remote Method Invocation over the Internet Inter-Orb Protocol), among others.

Now, a Java EE application can contain web services besides Enterprise Java Beans. These web services are even treated as EJBs. The communication works with the simple SOAP protocol over the HTTP protocol (see Figure 31-1). You already learned in Chapter 30 how easy it is to call web services out of a NetBeans Platform application. The reason for this is that the protocol needs little implementation effort; from this it follows that there is only a small number of libraries needed. Besides, just two necessary APIs—JAX-WS and JAXB— have been part of the Java Platform since Java 6. No external libraries are necessary.

From this point of view, I suggest you use web services as a sort of façade or rather as middleware for Enterprise Java Beans. This way, it is possible to easily call EJBs from a NetBeans Platform application. An already existing structure of EJBs can remain unchanged because the web service layer is only put in front of it, so to speak. Moreover, such a façade facilitates aggregation and orchestration of different beans.

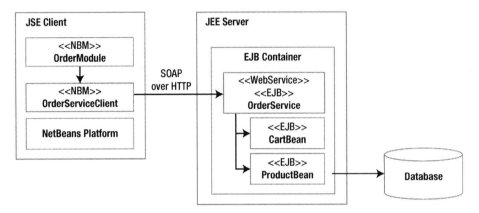

Figure 31-1. *Architecture of a Java EE application with web services as communication interface with EJBs*

The following sections will illustrate the implementation of such an architecture by means of a simple example. In that example, the user of the NetBeans Platform should be able to query products from the server and put several products in a shopping cart which is managed on server side.

Persistent Entities

The first step is to implement a persistent entity class that represents a product. Since you implement the class as a persistent entity, you are able to directly manage the products in a database via the entity manager; instances can just be put in or removed from a database. You must implement the persistent entity and later on the EJBs and the web service interface in an EJB module. For simplicity's sake this example uses only one module. You create this project in the NetBeans IDE with *File ➤ New Project... ➤ Java EE ➤ EJB Module* and call the project *OrderSystem*. Please use the *GlassFish Server 3.1* and *Java EE 6*.

Before starting the implementation it is advisable to first create a database; next it is possible to create a persistence unit for it. In the simplest case, use the integrated Java DB as database. Find this database under *Databases* in the *Services* window. Click *Create Database...* in the context menu and you can create a new database. Call it *ProductDatabase*. (See Figure 31-2.)

Next you can add a new persistent entity class to the EJB module project with *File ➤ New File... ➤ Persistence ➤ Entity Class*. Call it *Product* and add it to the package com.galileo.netbeans.entities. For the primary key use the datatype Long. If no persistence unit has been created yet, you can create one at the end. Call the persistence unit *OrderSystemPU*. Use the preset *EclipseLink* implementation of the JPA 2.0 as persistence provider. With *Data Source* you define the JNDI title jdbc/ProductDatabase for the database you just created. As *Table Generation Strategy* you choose *Create*. Tables necessary for the persistent entities will be created automatically if they do not exist yet.

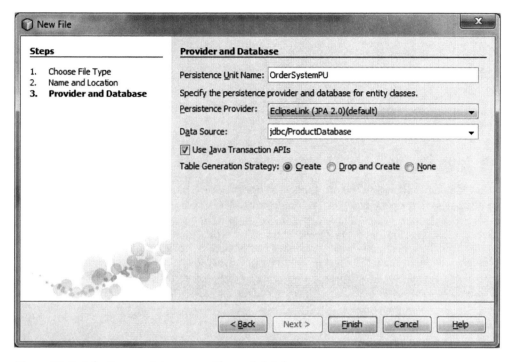

Figure 31-2. *Selecting persistence provider and database*

After creating the entity class you can add the desired attributes. This works very well with the NetBeans IDE if you choose *Insert Code...* in the editor's context menu or use the key combination *Alt+Insert*. In the context menu that opens up you can choose the option *Add Property*. By doing so the getter and setter methods are automatically created for the appropriate features. Add the features outlined in Listing 31-1 to the Product class.

Listing 31-1. *Persistent Entity for the Management of Products*

```
import javax.persistence.Entity;
import javax.persistence.GeneratedValue;
import javax.persistence.GenerationType;
import javax.persistence.Id;

@Entity
public class Product implements Serializable {
    @Id
    @GeneratedValue(strategy = GenerationType.AUTO)
    private Long id;
    protected String orderId;
    protected String name;
    protected Double price;
```

```
    public Long getId() {
        return id;
    }

    public void setId(Long id) {
        this.id = id;
    }
    ...
}
```

Enterprise Java Beans

To manage the available products and the products in a shopping cart, implement an EJB in each case. You can add a bean class to the project which is already created by clicking *File* ➤ *New File...* ➤ *Enterprise JavaBeans* ➤ *Session Bean.* Call the EJB class for the product management *ProductBean* and add it to the package com.galileo.netbeans.beans. The session type should be *Stateless.* (See Figure 31-3.) You have to use this class locally (the web service will be located in the same module, which is why it is possible to access it locally); since EJB 3.1 it is no longer necessary to specify an interface.

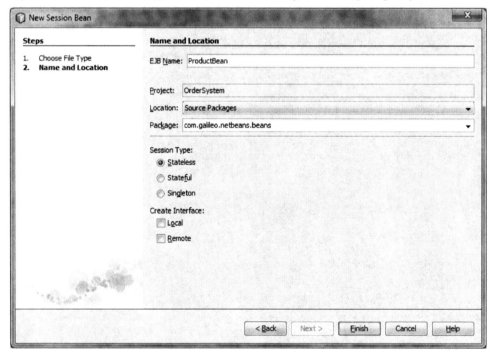

Figure 31-3. Creating the ProductBean class to manage the products

Now, equip the bean class ProductBean with two methods; one to add products and one to get a complete list of all saved products. You get access to the products on the database by means of an entity manager of the Java Persistence API (JPA). For this purpose you can use the code wizard of the NetBeans

IDE again. Press *Alt+Insert* inside your class and choose the option *Use Entity Manager....* in the context menu. The entity manager will be created as a private data element. Annotate the entity manager with the annotation @PersistenceContext, and define with it the name of the persistence unit (according to the configuration in the *persistence.xml* file). The instance of the entity manager is injected by the EJB container at runtime. (See Listing 31-2.)

Listing 31-2. Stateless Session Bean to Manage the Products

```
@Stateless
@LocalBean
public class ProductBean {

    @PersistenceContext(unitName = "OrderSystemPU")
    private EntityManager em;

    public void addProduct(Product product) {
        em.persist(product);
    }
    public List<Product> getProducts() {
        return em.createQuery(
            em.getCriteriaBuilder().createQuery(Product.class)).getResultList();
    }
}
```

You need a bean class for the implementation of the shopping cart next. For this purpose select *File* ➤ *New File...* ➤ *Enterprise JavaBeans* ➤ *Session Bean* again and create an EJB named CartBean with the wizard. Add the EJB to the package com.galileo.netbeans.beans. The session type should be *Stateful* and an interface is again not needed in this case because it can only be accessed locally by the web service. (See Listing 31-3.)

Listing 31-3. CartBean Class to Manage the Shopping Cart

```
import com.galileo.netbeans.entities.Product;
import java.util.ArrayList;
import java.util.List;
import javax.ejb.LocalBean;
import javax.ejb.Stateful;

@Stateful
@LocalBean
public class CartBean {
    private List<Product> products = new ArrayList<Product>();

    public void addProduct(Product product) {
        products.add(product);
    }

    public List<Product> getProducts() {
        return products;
    }
}
```

```
    public Double getSum() {
        Double sum = 0.0;
        for (Product p : products) {
            sum += p.getPrice();
        }
        return sum;
    }

    public Integer getAmount() {
        return products.size();
    }
}
```

Now you have implemented two simple session beans and one persistent entity. Surely, the application could be extended with many more Java EE features, but this chapter is mainly about calling EJBs via a web service interface.

Web Service

This section will deal with creating a web service interface that functions to some extent as a communication layer to call the EJBs. There are two ways to create a web service. It can either be implemented in a EJB module so it represents a session bean or, if implemented in a web application, you can implement the web service as a session bean with a web service interface or as a plain web service.

In this example the web service will be integrated into the already existing EJB module. Surely, you could also create a new EJB module for this purpose. However, in that case it is necessary to create a local interface for both ProductBean and CartBean. That way, the web service can refer to the EJBs. Add a web service to the EJB module with *File ➤ New File... ➤ Web Services ➤ Web Service*. Call it *OrderService* and add it to the package com.galileo.netbeans.service. As you can see, the web service must be created as a stateless session bean in this kind of container, which is just an additional annotation in the implementation. (See Figure 31-4.)

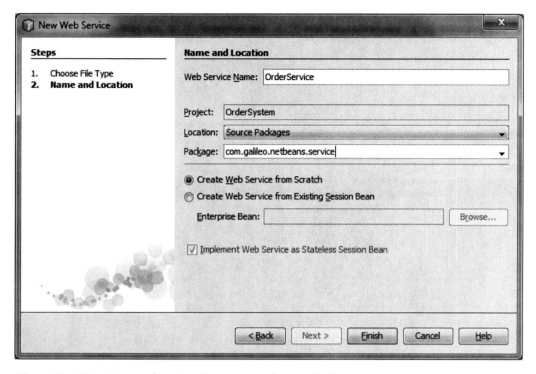

Figure 31-4. *Creating a web service class as a stateless session bean*

Now add references of both beans to the basic structure of the web service. Because of *Dependency Injection* this is quite simple, but you can use the advantages of the code wizard. Thus, press *Alt+Insert* and choose *Call Enterprise Bean*. Then you can choose the desired EJB in the selection dialog. This way you create references to a ProductBean as well as to a CartBean object, as depicted in Listing 31-4. In the same easy way, with the code wizard (with *Add Web Service Operation...*) you add the desired web service methods, which will finally be available in your NetBeans Platform application. (See Figure 31-5.)

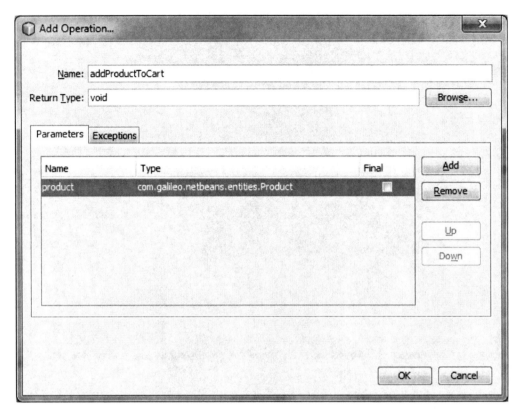

Figure 31-5. Adding web service methods with the code wizard

Add the annotation @WebService to the web service and give the annotation a name. Both EJB references will automatically be initialized by the EJB container at runtime.

Listing 31-4. Implementation of Web Services As Façade for EJBs

```
import com.galileo.netbeans.beans.CartBean;
import com.galileo.netbeans.beans.ProductBean;
import com.galileo.netbeans.entities.Product;
import java.util.List;
import javax.ejb.EJB;
import javax.jws.Oneway;
import javax.jws.WebService;
import javax.jws.WebMethod;
import javax.jws.WebParam;
import javax.ejb.Stateless;

@WebService(serviceName = "OrderService")
@Stateless
public class OrderService {
```

```
@EJB
private ProductBean productBean;
@EJB
private CartBean cartBean;

@WebMethod(operationName = "addProductToCart")
@Oneway
public void addProductToCart(
    @WebParam(name = "product") Product product) {
    cartBean.addProduct(product);
}

@WebMethod(operationName = "getSumOfCart")
public Double getSumOfCart() {
    return cartBean.getSum();
}

@WebMethod(operationName = "getAmountOfCart")
public Integer getAmountOfCart() {
    return cartBean.getAmount();
}

@WebMethod(operationName = "getProducts")
public List<Product> getProducts() {
    return productBean.getProducts();
}

@WebMethod(operationName = "addProduct")
@Oneway
public void addProduct(
    @WebParam(name = "product") Product product) {
    productBean.addProduct(product);
}
}
```

Now you have equipped two enterprise beans with a web service interface. A web service is described by a WSDL file, and on the basis of a WSDL file a web service client is created. However, you do not have to create the WSDL file, because the GlassFish server creates it on demand. So you just have to deploy the EJB module with the web service on the server. Choose *Deploy* in the context menu of the referring project. Make sure the database server is started besides the GlassFish server so that the web service calls can be executed successfully.

Web Service Client

You cannot create a web service client directly in a NetBeans Platform application if you want to use it instead of a Java EE application client. For this a normal Java project is needed. In the simplest case, just create a Java class library project with *File ➤ New Project... ➤ Java ➤ Java Class Library*. Add a web service client to it with *File ➤ New File... ➤ Web Services ➤ Web Service Client* as shown in Figure 31-6.

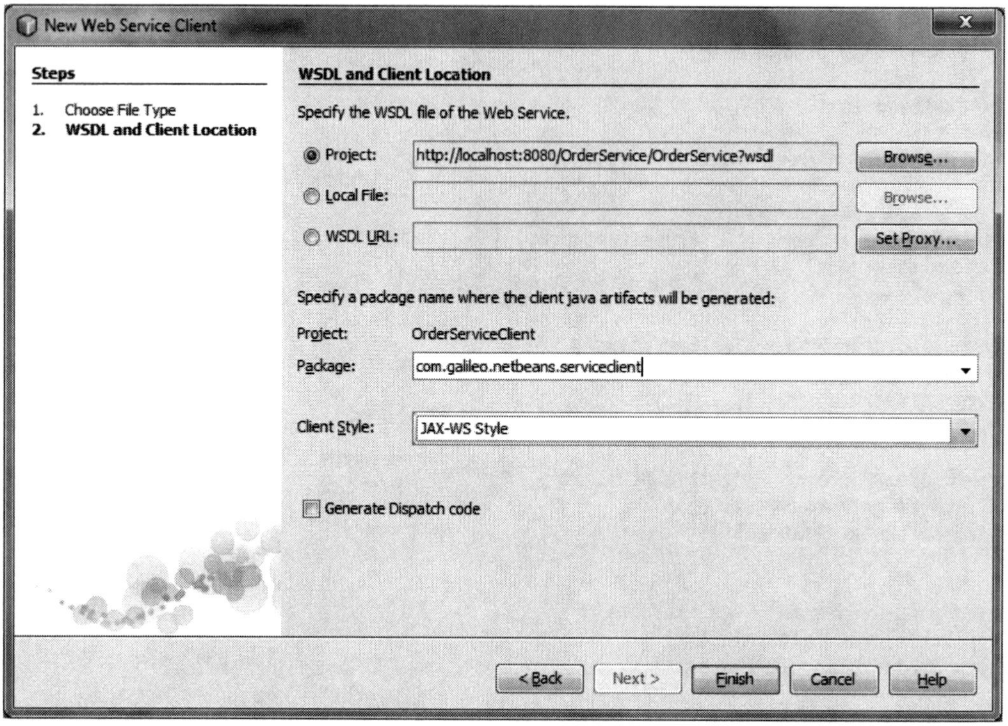

Figure 31-6. Creating a web service client

Pass the URL of the WSDL file to the wizard (see Figure 31-6). You can do that by simply choosing *Browse...* in the web service projects menu. Specify a package name and finish the wizard so the web service client classes are automatically created out of the information of the WSDL file. Create a JAR file out of this client with *Build*. In the next section, you will see that the JAR file will be integrated in the NetBeans Platform application.

NetBeans Platform Application

Assuming you have already created a NetBeans Platform application, add a library wrapper module to which you add the already created JAR file with the web service client. In addition, create an application module with a dependency on the integrated web service client module. First, add an action, which adds products to the database as test, to the application module (see Listing 31-5).

Listing 31-5. Adding Test Products

```
import com.galileo.netbeans.client.OrderService;
import com.galileo.netbeans.client.OrderService_Service;
import com.galileo.netbeans.client.Product;
...
public final class CreateProducts implements ActionListener {
    @Override
```

```
public void actionPerformed(ActionEvent e) {
    OrderService_Service service = new OrderService_Service();
    OrderService port = service.getOrderServicePort();
    Product p1 = new Product();
    p1.setName("Product 1");
    p1.setOrderId("P1");
    p1.setPrice(2.99);
    Product p2 = new Product();
    p2.setName("Product 2");
    p2.setOrderId("P2");
    p2.setPrice(3.99);
    ...
    port.addProduct(p1);
    port.addProduct(p2);
    }
}
```

Now you need a top component that contains a table in which all available products can be listed (see Figure 31-7).

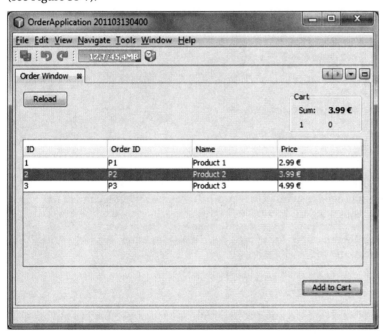

Figure 31-7. NetBeans Platform application for the demonstration of accessing the EJBs by web services

You do not have to create the OrderService object yourself. Instead the already created OrderService_Service class gives you an instance with the method getOrderServicePort() (see Listing 31-6). Then you can execute the server side–implemented methods as completely transparent on this instance. By clicking the *Reload* button all products should be selected and added to the table. With *Add to Cart* all selected products will be transferred to the CartBean. Simultaneously, the current sum and the quantity of products will be requested from the CartBean.

Listing 31-6. *Read Data with the Web Service from the Server and Restore It*

```
import com.galileo.netbeans.client.OrderService;
import com.galileo.netbeans.client.OrderService_Service;
import com.galileo.netbeans.client.Product;
...
public final class OrderTopComponent extends TopComponent {
    private OrderService_Service service = new OrderService_Service();
    private OrderService port;

    public OrderTopComponent() {
        ...
        port = service.getOrderServicePort();
    }

    private void addToCartActionPerformed(ActionEvent evt) {
        if (tableView.getSelectedRowCount() > 0) {
            port.addProductToCart(tableModel.getRow(tableView.getSelectedRow()));
            cartSum.setText(port.getSumOfCart() + "  ");
            cartAmount.setText("" + port.getAmountOfCart());
        }
    }

    private void reloadProductsActionPerformed(ActionEvent evt) {
        tableModel.getList().clear();
        tableModel.getList().addAll(port.getProducts());
        tableModel.fireTableDataChanged();
    }
}
```

So now an application example has been created with which EJBs can be addressed out of the context of a NetBeans Platform application. In this approach no typical application client (with RMI-IIOP) went into action, but rather a much easier web service interface (with SOAP over HTTP). Renouncing consciously one or the other functionality of the application container, you have a huge advantage in terms of "simple integration" and flexibility.

Summary

The NetBeans Platform is often used when the Java Enterprise Edition is used, too. What has not been taken into account so far is the interaction of these two "worlds." In this chapter you learned how you can easily access EJBs out of your NetBeans Platform application. To demonstrate this you created a simple server-side shopping system which you deployed to a GlassFish application server and accessed this Java EE application from a NetBeans Platform–based application.

RESTful Web Services

This chapter is about providing and consuming server-side data by RESTful web services. Similar to web services over SOAP, it is possible to access a Java EE server application by a NetBeans Platform application. This chapter will show you which steps are necessary to create and integrate a RESTful web service client. You will create a simple product database with a persistent entity class and a RESTful web service class that gives access to the data. The server picks the data directly over the entity manager. But it is also possible to access Enterprise Java Beans (EJBs) which provide the needed data.

Creating a Web Application

Whereas it is possible to provide a SOAP-based web service within an EJB module, a *Web Application* project (WAR file) is necessary for a RESTful web service. Then, this application will be executed within a web container of the Java EE server. Use the NetBeans IDE wizard and create a web application project with *File ➤ New Project... ➤ Java Web ➤ Web Application.* Call the project *OrderSystem* and assign it to a Java EE server. Finally, complete the wizard with *Finish.* (See Figure 32-1.)

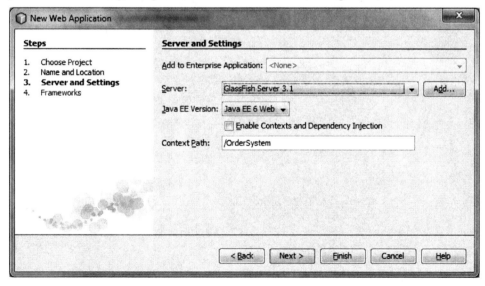

Figure 32-1. Creating a web application project and assigning it to a server

Creating Persistent Entity

First, you create a persistent entity class that will represent the data to be managed. This way, you are able to read, change, save, and delete products in a database. The NetBeans IDE provides a wizard as well. It is possible to directly create a persistence unit, too; however, you should configure a database in advance. You can use the integrated Java DB, which you can configure in the *Services* window under *Databases,* over the context menu (see Chapter 26).

Call *File ➤ New File... ➤ Persistence ➤ Entity Class* to create a persistent entity class. Call it *Product* and assign it to the package com.galileo.netbeans.order.entities. Activate the option *Create Persistence Unit* to let the wizard create it (you will need to enter more information on the following wizard page). Name the persistence unit *OrderSystemPU* and choose *EclipseLink* as persistence provider. To use the previously created database, use *jdbc/ProductDatabase* as data source. Choose *Create* as table generation strategy so the necessary tables in the database are automatically generated when the first product is added. (See Figure 32-2.)

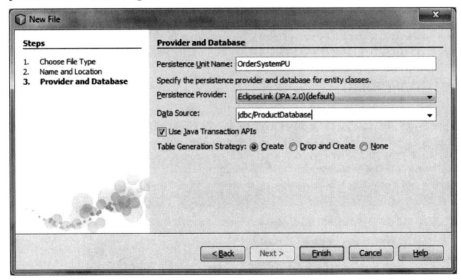

***Figure 32-2.** Creating a persistence entity class and a persistence unit*

The class is created with the attribute id which uniquely identifies an entry in a database. The value of this ID is automatically given by the database. You add further attributes as an example (orderId, name, price) with referring getter and setter methods. (See Listing 32-1.)

***Listing 32-1.** Persistent Entity Class Product with JPA Annotation for Saving the Object in the Database*

```
import java.io.Serializable;
import javax.persistence.Entity;
import javax.persistence.GeneratedValue;
import javax.persistence.GenerationType;
import javax.persistence.Id;
```

```
@Entity
public class Product implements Serializable {
    @Id
    @GeneratedValue(strategy = GenerationType.AUTO)
    private Long    id;
    private String orderId;
    private String name;
    private Double price;

    public Long getId() {
        return id;
    }
    public void setId(Long id) {
        this.id = id;
    }
    public String getName() {
        return name;
    }
    public void setName(String name) {
        this.name = name;
    }
    ...
}
```

Creating a RESTful Web Service

There are several wizards available for creating a RESTful web service. Besides creating a simple service you can directly create a web service for your use case, too. Meanwhile, the referring methods to manipulate and query the data are automatically created. Call *File ➤ New File... ➤ Web Services ➤ RESTful Web Services from Entity Classes* and add the class Product which you have created before. Add the service class to the package com.galileo.netbeans.order.service.

The created service is split in two classes: AbstractFacade and ProductFacadeREST. The AbstractFacade class is an abstract implementation of methods for getting access to databases over the entity manager. Those methods that should be provided as services are implemented in ProductFacadeREST; the entity manager is managed in this class. (See Listing 32-2.)

Listing 32-2. RESTful Web Service Class to Manipulate and Get Data of the Type Product

```
import com.galileo.netbeans.order.entities.Product;
import javax.ws.rs.Consumes;
import javax.ws.rs.DELETE;
import javax.ws.rs.GET;
import javax.ws.rs.POST;
import javax.ws.rs.PUT;
import javax.ws.rs.Path;
import javax.ws.rs.PathParam;
import javax.ws.rs.Produces;

@Stateless
@Path("com.galileo.netbeans.order.entities.product")
public class ProductFacadeREST extends AbstractFacade<Product> {
```

```
@PersistenceContext(unitName = "OrderServicePU")
private EntityManager em;

public ProductFacadeREST() {
    super(Product.class);
}

@POST
@Override
@Consumes({"application/xml"})
public void create(Product entity) {
    super.create(entity);
}

@PUT
@Override
@Consumes({"application/xml"})
public void edit(Product entity) {
    super.edit(entity);
}

@DELETE
@Path("{id}")
public void remove(@PathParam("id") Long id) {
    super.remove(super.find(id));
}

@Override
protected EntityManager getEntityManager() {
    return em;
}
...
}
```

The methods have annotations to identify which HTTP operations are used. Besides, the format in which the data is transferred is defined with @Consumes and @Produces. In addition to the type application/xml you can also choose application/json.

So, you have created a simple RESTful web service you can now provide on the server with *Deploy*. The interface of the service is defined by a WADL file which is also published by the Java EE server. You can test the service with a web interface: *Test RESTful Web Services* in the context menu of the application project.

Install NetBeans Platform Application

After creating a web service you now come back to the NetBeans Platform. First, create a NetBeans Platform application project which you will call *OrderApplication*. Before creating an application module, you have to add accessory modules from the extended NetBeans IDE to the application. To do so, go into the *Properties* of the project on the category *Libraries*. There you add the following modules:

- enterprise/RESTful Web Service Libraries

- ide/JAXB 2.2 Library

- ide/JAXB API

The *Jersey* libraries, which represent the reference implementation of the Java API for RESTful web services (JAX-RS), are hidden behind the module RESTful Web Service Libraries.

RESTful Web Service Client

Now you will create a service client class for the web services. To do so, you first create an application module which you name *OrderModule*. Call *File ➤ New File... ➤ Web Services ➤ RESTful Java Client* on this new module. Call the service class *OrderServiceClient*, add it to the package com.galileo.netbeans.order.module, and then choose the web service for which a client class will be created with the option *From Project* over the *Browse...* button. (See Figure 32-3.)

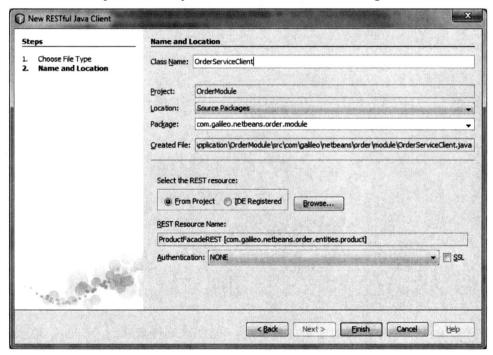

Figure 32-3. Creating a service client for a RESTful web service

Now let's take a look at the created class. All methods provided by the service are implemented with the JAX-RS implementation; signatures that allow a completely transparent calling-in of the service are used. (See Listing 32-3.)

Listing 32-3. RESTful Web Service Client with the Completely Transparent Object Which Can Be Transferred to and from the Java EE Server

```java
import com.sun.jersey.api.client.Client;
import com.sun.jersey.api.client.UniformInterfaceException;
import com.sun.jersey.api.client.WebResource;
...
public class OrderServiceClient {
    private WebResource webResource;
    private Client client;
    private static final String BASE_URI = "http://localhost:8080/OrderSystem/resources";

    public OrderServiceClient() {
        ClientConfig config = new DefaultClientConfig();
        client = Client.create(config);
        webResource = client.resource(BASE_URI).
            path("com.galileo.netbeans.order.entities.product");
    }

    public void create(Object requestEntity) throws UniformInterfaceException {
        webResource.type(MediaType.APPLICATION_XML).post(requestEntity);
    }

    public <T> T findAll(Class<T> responseType) throws UniformInterfaceException {
        WebResource resource = webResource;
        return resource.accept(MediaType.APPLICATION_XML).get(responseType);
    }
    ...
}
```

If you look at the created class in Listing 32-3, you see that the type of data a method returns is defined by the type of the passed class object. To get the raw data in XML format you could just use the type String. However, you want to create an entity class (similar to the server-side class) for the data. Out of the XML data the desired entity class instance is automatically created by JAXB along with the referring annotations. If the getter and setter methods match the names of the referring XML elements (and so the attributes of the server-side class), you do not need to do anything beyond annotating the class with @XmlRootElement. (See Listing 32-4.)

Listing 32-4. Entity Class Which Is Created Automatically by the JAXB Framework and Which Staffs the Attributes with the XML Data

```java
import javax.xml.bind.annotation.XmlRootElement;

@XmlRootElement
public class Product {
    private Long    id;
    private String orderId;
    private String name;
    private Double price;
```

```
    ...
}
```

Now, you can use this class in all cases in which you transfer objects or get a single object. In case a list of objects is delivered to you by a service method (see the method in Listing 32-3), you have to create a helper class. A list of objects is embraced in XML by an additional tag (<Products>). So that this tag and the subordinate objects can be created correctly, the helper class shown in Listing 32-5 is necessary.

Listing 32-5. Helper Class for Automatically Creating a Product List

```java
import java.util.ArrayList;
import java.util.List;
import javax.xml.bind.annotation.XmlRootElement;

@XmlRootElement
public class Products {
    private List<Product> product = new ArrayList<Product>();

    public List<Product> getProduct() {
        return product;
    }

    public void setProduct(List<Product> product) {
        this.product = product;
    }
}
```

The usage of the web service client is really simple. As a test, you can add several products to the database and then query certain or all objects and deliver their data, as shown in Listing 32-6.

Listing 32-6. Testing the Service Client of the RESTful Web Service

```java
public final class TestRESTAction implements ActionListener {

    @Override
    public void actionPerformed(ActionEvent e) {
        OrderServiceClient client = new OrderServiceClient();

        Product p = new Product();
        p.setName("Test Product");
        p.setOrderId("P1");
        p.setPrice(3.99);
        client.create(p);

        Product p1 = client.find(Product.class, "1");
        System.out.println("P1: " + p1);

        Products pro = client.findAll(Products.class);
        System.out.println("Products: " + pro.getProduct().size());
    }
}
```

Summary

RESTful web services provide a very simple possibility to access server-side resources out of a NetBeans Platform application. In this chapter, you learned how to create a RESTful web service and the corresponding client module. You used the client module to access a simple product database from a NetBeans Platform application.

Authentication and Multi-User Login

To begin this discussion of authentication and logging in multiple users, let's go back to the login dialog you created in Chapter 13. With this dialog you can retrieve the user's login data. Here we will check this data on the server side. There are numerous possibilities for checking login data. In this context, two Java built-in functions are focused on doing so. As soon as a user registered successfully, it is important to adapt the application referring to his or her rights or group membership.

Login Dialog

In Chapter 13, which was about creating application-specific dialogs, you created a login dialog. The focus in that case was on the UI component, not on the login process. You directly implemented the handler's logic within an installer, which was used to show the start of the dialog, even before the application is started. Now that the authentication process and the subsequent adaptation will be added, you want to externalize the logic in a separate LoginHandler class. (See Listing 33-1.)

Listing 33-1. First Part of the Login Handler for Managing the Login Dialog

```
import org.openide.DialogDescriptor;
import org.openide.DialogDisplayer;
import org.openide.LifecycleManager;
...
public class LoginHandler implements ActionListener {
   private static final LoginHandler instance = new LoginHandler();
   private LoginPanel panel = new LoginPanel();
   private DialogDescriptor dialog = null;

   private LoginHandler() {
   }

   public static LoginHandler getDefault() {
      return instance;
   }

   public void showLoginDialog() {
      panel.reset();
      dialog = new DialogDescriptor(panel, "Login", true, this);
```

```
        dialog.setClosingOptions(new Object[]{});
        dialog.addPropertyChangeListener(new PropertyChangeListener() {
            @Override
            public void propertyChange(PropertyChangeEvent evt) {
                if(evt.getPropertyName().equals(DialogDescriptor.PROP_VALUE)
                    && evt.getNewValue().equals(DialogDescriptor.CLOSED_OPTION)) {
                    LifecycleManager.getDefault().exit();
                }
            }
        });

        DialogDisplayer.getDefault().notifyLater(dialog);
    }

    @Override
    public void actionPerformed(ActionEvent evt) {
        if(evt.getSource() == DialogDescriptor.CANCEL_OPTION) {
            LifecycleManager.getDefault().exit();
        } else {
            login();
        }
    }

    private void login() { ... }
}
```

It makes sense to implement the class which should create and display the dialog as a singleton class. First, the method showLoginDialog() creates a DialogDescriptor instance which both the UI panel (with the text field) and a reference to the LoginHandler instance are transferred to. You implement the ActionListener interface with its method actionPerformed() by using the LoginHandler class. The method becomes activated as soon as a button is pressed. We cover two cases in this context: if the user presses *Cancel* or the *Esc* key, or closes the dialog, the application finishes. If the user presses *OK*, the login process starts with the input data. Furthermore, you have to install a PropertyChangeListener to be able to react in case the integrated close button in the upper-right corner is pressed.

You are now able to use this LoginHandler class within an installer in the restored() method to display the dialog (see Listing 33-2). You may also want to register an action in the menu with which a change of the user is realized, as shown in Listing 33-3.

Listing 33-2. Executing the Login Handler at Application Start

```
import org.openide.modules.ModuleInstall;
public class Installer extends ModuleInstall {
    @Override
    public void restored() {
        LoginHandler.getDefault().showLoginDialog();
    }
}
```

Listing 33-3. Executing the Login Handler with an Action Which Can Be Assigned to a Menu

```
public final class SwitchUser implements ActionListener {
   @Override
   public void actionPerformed(ActionEvent e) {
      LoginHandler.getDefault().showLoginDialog();
   }
}
```

Directory Server

The data necessary for the authentication of a user are usually managed by a directory server. With the directory server you can swap the necessary information by the Lightweight Directory Access Protocol (LDAP). To implement the example and for the sake of demonstration you want to install a local directory server. You can create and change the necessary structure of the data for its usage.

Installing the Test Environment

The *Apache Directory* project will be used as server. One part of it is *ApacheDS*, which is an LDAP conform directory server written in Java. The other part of the project is the *Apache Directory Studio*, which is a tooling platform you will use as GUI for the directory server ApacheDS. You just need to download and install the directory studio in which ApacheDS is embedded. After installing the software, you can start the studio and install the server. But before installing the server you have to add it. Open the assistant with *File ➤ New...* and choose the entry *Apache DS Server* in the category *Apache DS*. On the following page you just need to give it a name before you finish the assistant with *Finish*. After that you can provide the server. (See Figure 33-1.)

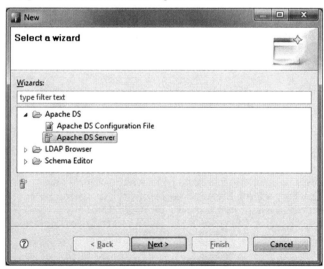

Figure 33-1. Installing the Apache Directory server instance

The created instance is added to the window *Server* with the standard settings. In this window, first start the server. After, you will be able to create a connection with *LDAP Browser* ➤ *Create a Connection* in the context menu. This connection will be added to the *Connections* window. Switch to this window and establish a connection to the server with *Open Connection* in the context menu. If this connection is established, a Directory Information Tree (DIT) is displayed in the *LDAP Browser* window. (See Figure 33-2.) Next you will add the necessary user data to the LDAP browser window.

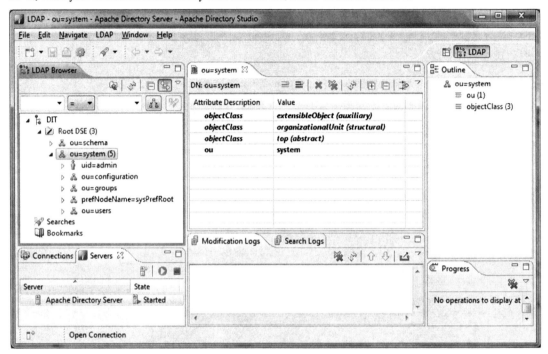

Figure 33-2. *Apache Directory Studio*

Setting Up User Data

After starting up the directory server, now that you have access, you want to set up the user data with which you should be able to log in later. In Figure 33-2 you already see the entry *users* beneath *system* in the DIT. Add two user entries to this entry now. To do so, open *New* ➤ *New Entry* from the context menu of the entry. You want to set up the entry from scratch. On the following page add the object class *inetOrgPerson*. Linked with that, further elements are added. Press *Next* to set the relative distinguished name (RDN) with *uid=<username>* on the next page (where *username* is your username). The next step is setting the common name (cn) and the surname (sn). (See Figure 33-3.) There you can use random values.

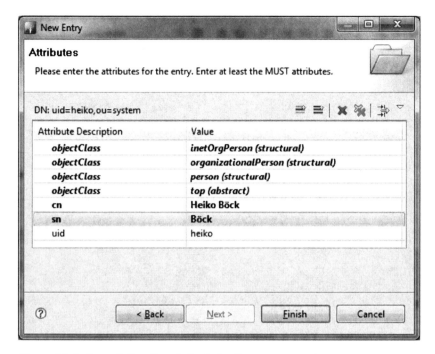

Figure 33-3. *Completing the attribute for the new user entry*

Now, you can set up the new user with *Finish*. What is missing is a password which you can add by an extra attribute. For this purpose activate *New Attribute...* in the list of attributes of the directory studio in the context menu. The type of attribute is *userPassword*. Close the assistant directly with *Finish*. As a result, the password editor will automatically be displayed. You can define the actual password and choose a hash algorithm with it.

Now you can already authenticate the application users. However, in this chapter we want to go one step further and activate or deactivate certain functions within the NetBeans Platform application in dependency of a certain group membership of the user. How such a group membership is displayed in the directory depends on the use case (whether a user belongs to one or more groups). In this example, add the group membership directly to the user entry. Using a multi-value attribute it is possible to assign one user to multiple groups. The main process of this action is the same as adding the password. Use *employeeType* as attribute type. Finish the wizard and directly define the value in the attribute list (for example, *User*). To assign the user to multiple groups just add multiple *employeeType* attributes.

Go on the same way to assign a second user whom you will assign to the *Admin* group. In the following chapters different application configurations for both user groups will be realized.

Authentication

In the preceding paragraphs you made the first steps to query the user's login data when starting the application and let these data checks be performed by a server. What is still missing is the link to the application (client) and the directory (server). As mentioned at the beginning of the chapter, you want to use the LDAP protocol for this. The Java platform even provides multiple ways out-of-the-box for a simple LDAP communication. Obviously, it is best to use the Java Naming and Directory Interface

(JNDI); however, the Java Authentication and Authorization Service (JAAS) can be very helpful, too. You will use JNDI in this example, as it provides more flexibility.

Java Naming and Directory Interface (JNDI)

You often find JNDI connected with Java EE. JNDI is flexible because of factories that can be configured differently. There is also a factory for the directory server and for the LDAP protocol, so those can be used flexibly as well. The login process, meaning the usage of JNDI, is separated in the `SecurityManager` class. In this singleton class you manage the groups of the users which are currently logged in. Now you turn your attention to the `login()` method. At first, you have to combine the following features in a `Properties` instance:

- INITIAL_CONTEXT_FACTORY: This feature defines the factory which you should use. For this application use `com.sun.jndi.ldap.LdapCtxFactory`.

- *PROVIDER_URL*: Defines the URL for the directory server. You have to define the ldap protocol before server name, port, and DN, e.g. `ldap://localhost:10389/ou=system`.

- *SECURITY_AUTHENTICATION*: Indicates the authentication mechanism of the Simple Authentication and the Security Layer (SASL) frameworks. SIMPLE, DIGEST-MD5, GSSAPI, NTLM, GSS-SPNEGO, and CRAM-MD5 are provided.

- *SECURITY_PRINCIPAL*: Indicates the username as complete path in the directory. The path is already given. You insert the username dynamically out of the login dialog.

- *SECURITY_CREDENTIALS*: Transfers the password which belongs to the authenticated user.

Transfer the `Properties` object which was created with these features to the `InitialDirContext` class which tries to establish the connection with the details given. If this trial fails because of typing in a wrong password, for example, a `NamingException` is thrown. You can also use the subclass `InitialLdapContext` instead of `InitialDirContext` dealing with LDAP queries for an advanced control. (See Listing 33-4.)

Listing 33-4. Implementation of Accessing the Directory Server with the JNDI

```
import javax.naming.NamingException;
import javax.naming.directory.Attribute;
import javax.naming.directory.Attributes;
import javax.naming.directory.DirContext;
import javax.naming.directory.InitialDirContext;
...
public class SecurityManager {
    private static final SecurityManager inst = new SecurityManager();
    private String user;
    private List<UserGroup> groups = new ArrayList<UserGroup>();

    private SecurityManager() {
    }
```

```java
public static SecurityManager getDefault() {
    return inst;
}

public boolean login(String user, String password) {
    this.user = "";
    this.groups.clear();
    Properties props = new Properties();

    props.put(DirContext.INITIAL_CONTEXT_FACTORY, "com.sun.jndi.ldap.LdapCtxFactory");
    props.put(DirContext.PROVIDER_URL, "ldap://localhost:10389/ou=system");
    props.put(DirContext.SECURITY_AUTHENTICATION, "simple");
    props.put(DirContext.SECURITY_PRINCIPAL, "uid=" + user + ", ou=users, ou=system");
    props.put(DirContext.SECURITY_CREDENTIALS, password);

    try {
        InitialDirContext ctx = new InitialDirContext(props);
        this.user = user;
        Attributes attr = ctx.getAttributes("uid=" + user + ", ou=users");
        Attribute a = attr.get("employeeType");

        if (a != null) {
            for (String groupName : Collections.list((Enumeration<String>) a.getAll())) {
                UserGroup group = UserGroup.get(groupName);
                if (group != null) {
                    groups.add(group);
                }
            }
        }
        return true;
    } catch (NamingException ex) {
        return false;
    }
}

public List<UserGroup> getUserGroups() {
    return this.groups;
}
}
```

If the connection is successfully established, no exception was thrown. You can query the user's attributes of the InitialDirContext instance this way. Get the attribute *employeeType,* which assigned users to groups. Since it is a multi-value attribute, you can get all values of this attribute with the getAll() method. Create an object for each attribute value. (See *Adapting the Application* later in this chapter.) Add all identified groups to a list and provide it with the getUserGroups() method.

Java Authentication and Authorization (JAAS)

The Java Authentication and Authorization (JAAS) API is an alternative to the JNDI. As you can surmise from the name, the focus is on authentication rather than querying attributes in the directory. As a result, it is not as easy to create the example in Listing 33-4. However, this section will show you how to use and integrate the JAAS API and its configuration in your NetBeans Platform application.

Similar to the JNDI concept, you first need a configuration. JAAS provides such a configuration in a certain file structure. This file is typically defined by a command-line parameter. It makes sense to pack this file in the module in a NetBeans Platform application. Use a variation of the LoginContext constructors, to which a ConfigFile instance can be passed; the configuration file is passed to this instance. You can get that URI or URL with the getResource() method.

The JAAS API provides different login modules for different authentication mechanisms, as it does for the LDAP protocol with which you can communicate with your directory server. In the configuration file shown in Listing 33-5 which login module is used in which configuration is assigned.

Listing 33-5. JAAS Configuration File

```
LoginJaas {
    com.sun.security.auth.module.LdapLoginModule REQUIRED
    userProvider="ldap://localhost:10389"
    authIdentity="uid={USERNAME},ou=users,ou=system"
    useSSL=false
    debug=true;
};
```

Different configurations can be managed in one file. Each is given one name. You indicate the URL to the directory server as with JNDI and specify the path to the user's entry. The user name and the password are queried or set separately, as you can see in Listing 33-6.

Listing 33-6. Authentication with the JAAS API

```
import com.sun.security.auth.login.ConfigFile;
import java.security.Principal;
import javax.security.auth.callback.Callback;
import javax.security.auth.callback.CallbackHandler;
import javax.security.auth.callback.NameCallback;
import javax.security.auth.callback.PasswordCallback;
import javax.security.auth.callback.UnsupportedCallbackException;
import javax.security.auth.login.LoginContext;
...
public class SecurityManager implements CallbackHandler {
    private static SecurityManager inst = new SecurityManager();
    private String user;
    private String password;

    private SecurityManager() {
    }

    public static SecurityManager getDefault() {
        return inst;
    }

    public boolean login(String user, String password) {
        this.user = user;
        this.password = password;
        LoginContext loginContext = null;
```

```
    try {
        URL url = SecurityManager.class. getResource("config.jaas");
        loginContext = new LoginContext("LoginJaas",
                null, this, new ConfigFile(url.toURI()));
        loginContext.login();
        for (Principal p : loginContext.getSubject().getPrincipals()) {
            System.out.println("Principal: <" + p.getClass() + "> " + p.getName());
        }
        return true;
    } catch (LoginException e) {
        return false;
    }
}

@Override
public void handle(Callback[] callbacks) throws IOException, UnsupportedCallbackException {
    for (Callback cb : callbacks) {
        if (cb instanceof NameCallback) {
            NameCallback nc = (NameCallback) cb;
            nc.setName(this.user);
        } else if (cb instanceof PasswordCallback) {
            PasswordCallback pc = (PasswordCallback) cb;
            pc.setPassword(this.password.toCharArray());
        }
    }
}
}
```

Transfer a CallbackHandler object to the LoginContext constructor. Implement the CallbackHandler interface directly in the SecurityManager class. The method handle() is provided an array with Callback instances. Check the type of instances and referring actions. This is mainly setting the user name and the password which can be queried during the login process by the login() method. If the authentication is carried out completely, you can query the user's features by different Principal instances.

Adapting the Application

This section will deal with the functionalities of the NetBeans Platform for adapting the application to a specific user. On the one hand, it is about how to dynamically adapt the System Filesystem, which contains the configuration of the menu. On the other hand, it is about how to switch on and off certain functions on the module layer.

You need the login() method of the LoginHandler class from the beginning of this chapter which was withheld until now. This method transfers the data typed in by the user to the security manager (see the previous section *Authentication*). The security manager is concerned with the authentication on the server. If the user is logged in successfully, get the referring user groups with the method getUserGroups(). If the list is empty, the user is not assigned to any group, so the user has no authority. Otherwise, give the list to the UserGroupFileSystem class (discussed in the following section *System Filesystem*) certain modules become activated or deactivated. Implement this functionality in the class UserGroupModuleSystem (discussed later in this chapter in the section *Module System*). See Listing 33-7.

Listing 33-7. Adaptation of the Application After Successful Login

```java
public class LoginHandler implements ActionListener {
    ...
    private void login() {
        if(!SecurityManager.getDefault().login(panel.getUsername(), panel.getPassword())) {
            panel.setInfo("Wrong password or username");
        } else {
            List<UserGroup> groups = SecurityManager.getDefault().getUserGroups();
            if (groups.isEmpty()) {
                panel.setInfo("You have no access rights");
            } else {
                try {
                    UserGroupFileSystem.getDefault().setUserGroups(groups);
                    UserGroupModuleSystem.handleModules(MOD2DISABLE, false);
                    UserGroupModuleSystem.handleModules(MOD2ENABLE, true);
                    dialog.setClosingOptions(null);
                } catch (Exception ex) {
                    Exceptions.printStackTrace(ex);
                }
            }
        }
    }
}
```

The following sections explain how both the UserGroupFileSystem and UserGroupModuleSystem classes are implemented and which configurations are necessary for the adaptation.

System Filesystem

System Filesystem has been more or less important in nearly every chapter of this book. It is important in the dynamic adaptation of certain user groups as the central registry of, for eaxmple, actions, menu entries, windows, or option panels. Anyway, System Filesystem is the concept which makes a dynamic adaptation possible in general. There are two features which you want to take advantage of. One is the possibility of hiding certain entries by the suffix _hidden. The other is the possibility of adding additional configurations at runtime.

You will implement the class UserGroupFileSystem. However, first you need to think about how to manage a user group (see Listing 33-8). The enum type UserGroup will help with this.

Listing 33-8. Management of the Information of a User Group

```java
public enum UserGroup {
    ADMIN("Admin", "configs/admin.xml"),
    USER("User", "configs/user.xml");
    private String groupName;
    private String configPath;

    UserGroup(String groupName, String configPath) {
        this.groupName = groupName;
```

```java
        this.configPath = configPath;
    }

    public URL getConfig() {
        return UserGroup.class.getResource(configPath);
    }

    public String getGroup() {
        return this.groupName;
    }

    public boolean equals(String groupName) {
        return this.groupName.equals(groupName);
    }

    @Override
    public String toString() {
        return this.groupName;
    }

    public static UserGroup get(String groupName) {
        for (UserGroup group : UserGroup.values()) {
            if (group.groupName.equals(groupName)) {
                return group;
            }
        }
        return null;
    }
}
```

Define the name of the group and the path of the referring configuration in this enum type with the elements USER and ADMIN. Doing so, the method getConfig() directly delivers a URL on the XML file.

Earlier, you defined the two user groups Admin and User. Now you want to create a small test configuration for each with which certain menus can be displayed or hidden. So, a menu will be provided to the user group User which is not provided to the group Admin, and the other way around. (See Listing 33-9.)

Listing 33-9. Configuration of the User Group User

```xml
<filesystem>
    <folder name="Menu">
        <folder name="Tools_hidden"/>
        <folder name="Admin_hidden"/>
    </folder>
</filesystem>
```

With the configuration shown in Listing 33-9, the menu *Tools* and *Admin* of users of the group User will be hidden.

Listing 33-10. Configuration of the User Group Admin

```
<filesystem>
   <folder name="Menu">
      <folder name="Edit_hidden"/>
      <folder name="User_hidden"/>
   </folder>
</filesystem>
```

In contrast with the configuration shown in Listing 33-10, the menu *Edit* and *User* are hidden for Admin group members.

One or more such configurations which exist as XML files can be managed by an XMLFileSystem together in a MultiFileSystem which acts as proxy. A MultiFileSystem implementation can be registered as a service provider while adding it to the System Filesystem during the startup. Since the System Filesystem is able to react on changes, it is possible to set the actual configuration subsequently, in other words, after the login. To do so, create a UserGroupFileSystem class which deduces from MultiFileSystem (see Listing 33-11). Register the class with the @ServiceProvider annotation in order to find and load it.

Listing 33-11. MultiFileSystem Implementation with Which Dynamic Configurations Can Be Set

```
import org.openide.filesystems.FileSystem;
import org.openide.filesystems.MultiFileSystem;
import org.openide.filesystems.XMLFileSystem;
import org.openide.util.Lookup;
import org.openide.util.lookup.ServiceProvider;

@ServiceProvider(service = FileSystem.class)
@ServiceProvider(service = UserGroupFileSystem.class)
public class UserGroupFileSystem extends MultiFileSystem {

    public UserGroupFileSystem() {
        setPropagateMasks(true);
    }

    public static UserGroupFileSystem getDefault() {
        return Lookup.getDefault().lookup(UserGroupFileSystem.class);
    }

    public void setUserGroups(List<UserGroup> groups) throws Exception {
        FileSystem[] fileSystems = new FileSystem[groups.size()];
        for (int idx = 0; idx < fileSystems.length; idx++) {
            fileSystems[idx] = new XMLFileSystem(groups.get(idx).getConfig());
        }
        setDelegates(fileSystems);
    }
}
```

The registered class becomes automatically initialized during the startup. However, there is no configuration set so far. so it is a virtually empty file system. It is necessary to call in the method setPropagateMasks(true) in the constructor, so the entries with suffix _hidden have an effect. The global lookup provides the instance which has been added to the System Filesystem already. So this instance makes it possible for you to inject dynamic entries into the System Filesystem afterward.

The setUserGroups() method, to which you transfer a list with UserGroup objects out of the login handler, sets the configuration in the end. For this purpose create an XMLFileSystem instance and create an array out of it for the XML file of each group. Then, transfer this array to the setDelegates() method so the changes become propagated.

Module System

First, you want to define declaratively which modules should become explicitly activated or deactivated for which user group. To do this, just extend both XML files which already exist. In the newly defined folders any number of modules can be listed, but only those modules that are attributed with codeNameBase. This way, you can indicate a unique identification of the module (see Listing 33-12).

Listing 33-12. Configuration of the Modules for the User Group User

```
<filesystem>
    <folder name="Modules2Disable">
        <file name="AdminModule">
            <attr name="codeNameBase" stringvalue="com.galileo.netbeans.module.admin"/>
        </file>
    </folder>
    <folder name="Modules2Enable">
        <file name="UserModule">
            <attr name="codeNameBase" stringvalue="com.galileo.netbeans.module.user"/>
        </file>
    </folder>
</filesystem>
```

For users of the group *User* the module AdminModule should be deactivated and the module UserModule should be activated. For the user group *Admin* it is set the other way around, as shown in Listing 33-13.

Listing 33-13. Configuration of the Modules for the User Group Admin

```
<filesystem>
    <folder name="Modules2Disable">
        <file name="UserModule">
            <attr name="codeNameBase" stringvalue="com.galileo.netbeans.module.user"/>
        </file>
    </folder>
    <folder name="Modules2Enable">
        <file name="AdminModule">
            <attr name="codeNameBase" stringvalue="com.galileo.netbeans.module.admin"/>
        </file>
    </folder>
</filesystem>
```

These configurations will be read and interpreted by the class UserGroupModuleSystem. Implement the method handleModules() which is parameterized. Like this the method can be used for the activation as well as for the deactivation. You can pass the folder in the configuration file to the method.

In this folder you search for all file elements and read its attribute codeNameBase so you can add the unique identification of the module to the list. Detect the module instances for all modules of this list with the update manager, which can access all modules. Then add those to the referring operation container. Finally, with this container activation or deactivation can take place (see Listing 33-14).

Listing 33-14. Activation and Deactivation of Modules Depending on the Configuration Provided

```java
import org.netbeans.api.autoupdate.OperationContainer;
import org.netbeans.api.autoupdate.OperationSupport;
import org.netbeans.api.autoupdate.UpdateManager;
import org.netbeans.api.autoupdate.UpdateUnit;
import org.openide.filesystems.FileObject;
import org.openide.filesystems.FileUtil;
import org.openide.util.Exceptions;

public class UserGroupModuleSystem {

    public static void handleModules(String folder, boolean en) {
        FileObject fo = FileUtil.getConfigFile(folder);
        List<String> modules = new ArrayList<String>();
        for (FileObject fi : fo.getChildren()) {
            modules.add((String)fi.getAttribute("codeNameBase"));
        }
        try {
            OperationContainer<OperationSupport> cont;
            if (en) {
                cont = OperationContainer.createForEnable();
            } else {
                cont = OperationContainer.createForDirectDisable();
            }
            for (UpdateUnit uu : UpdateManager.getDefault().getUpdateUnits()) {
                if (uu.getInstalled() != null
                    && modules.contains(uu.getInstalled().getCodeName())
                    && uu.getInstalled().isEnabled() == !en) {
                    cont.add(uu.getInstalled());
                }
            }
            if (!cont.listAll().isEmpty()) {
                cont.getSupport().doOperation(null);
            }
        } catch (Exception ex) {
            Exceptions.printStackTrace(ex);
        }
    }
}
```

Once more, the advantage of the module-based NetBeans Platform becomes clear with the activation or deactivation of modules. Deactivating a module, all components, such as menu entries or windows, are automatically deleted at runtime. Activating the module, all components are simply added again.

Summary

Enterprise applications must often be adapted dynamically to different groups of users. This chapter showed you the possibilities available with the NetBeans Platform. You used JNDI and JAAS in combination with an Apache directory server to manage user data. You learned how you can adapt the user interface for a specific user group and how to load and disable predefined modules.

Pack & Ship: Adapting, Delivering, and Actualizing Applications

Internationalization and Localization

Professional applications—especially flexible ones—should be designed to adapt as easily as possible to other countries and languages. For this reason, the Java and NetBeans Platform and the NetBeans IDE provide a great deal of support for internationalization, making it easy to internationalize and localize your application. It is worth preparing even very small applications and applications that were initially designed for only one language for localization.

String Literals in Source Code

String literals in source code are outsourced in *.properties* files. Therefore, the language-dependent literals can be separated and easily changed into other languages. This is possible even after the release of an application. The constants are saved as key-value pairs in a simple *.properties* file:

```
CTL_MyTopComponent = My Window
HINT_MyTopComponent = This is My Window
```

Such a resource file is managed by the Java class ResourceBundle. A ResourceBundle is responsible for the resources of a particular Locale setting that specifies both the country and the language. For easy handling of *.properties* files and for access to a ResourceBundle instance, the NetBeans Platform provides the class NbBundle. The resource file must be named *Bundle.properties*; however, such a file is typically created for each package. The easiest way to create ResourceBundle objects is with the following call:

```
ResourceBundle bundle = NbBundle.getBundle(MyTopComponent.class);
```

Thus, the class NbBundle creates a ResourceBundle object for the *Bundle.properties* file, provided in the package of the class MyTopComponent. The required string literal is easily read via the ResourceBundle method getString():

```
String msg = bundle.getString("CTL_MyTopComponent");
```

If you just want to read few literals inside your class, you can use the method getMessage() to read a literal directly without creating a ResourceBundle instance before the following:

```
String msg = NbBundle.getMessage(MyTopComponent.class, "CTL_MyTopComponent");
```

Furthermore, it is possible to add a placeholder to your string literals. This is most often required if numbers or a file name/path will be inserted. A pair of braces is used as a placeholder, which includes the number of the parameter:

```
Result = {0} MP3-Files found for {1}
```

You can directly pass these parameters to the getMessage() method, which then replaces the placeholder with the parameter. Alternatively, you can pass up to three parameters or an array with an unlimited number of parameters:

```
String label = NbBundle.getMessage(MyTopComponent.class, "Result",
                            new Integer(results.size()), search.getText());
```

Within a *.properties* file, literals are just saved in one language. To add another language to your application, provide the literals—with the same keys—in a file named Bundle_<language>_<country>.properties in the same folder. The class NbBundle returns the ResourceBundle for this file using the method getBundle(). This file is equivalent to the Locale setting, which returns Locale.getDefault(). The *Bundle.properties* file that does not contain a language and country identifier is the default bundle. This bundle is always used if there is no special bundle for the Locale setting available. A specific bundle can also be requested by passing a Locale object to the getBundle() method. To know in which order the bundles are searched, the method NbBundle.getLocalizingSuffixes() lists all suffixes in the order used.

The method Locale.getDefault() returns the Locale setting of the virtual machine by default. To run and execute the whole application with a specific Locale setting, set the command-line parameter locale. With this parameter you can pass a language and country identifier to the application. You can find more information on this in Chapter 35.

The NetBeans IDE provides a wizard for the internationalization of string literals for your source files. With this wizard you can scan your files for strings which can then be moved to a *.properties* file. You can edit the key, the value, and the code that will be pasted instead of the literal. You can find the wizard in the menu under *Tools ➤ Internationalization ➤ Internationalization Wizard*, as shown in Figure 34-1.

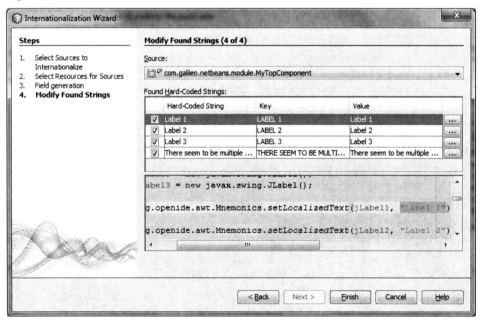

Figure 34-1. You can automatically move string literals to a bundle and paste the necessary source code with the internationalization wizard.

String Literals in the Manifest File

In addition to the string literals of the source files, you can also internationalize the textual information of the manifest file. There are two options for doing so. The first option is to append a language identifier to the manifest attributes and thus use the same attribute several times:

```
Manifest-Version: 1.0
OpenIDE-Module: com.galileo.netbeans.module
OpenIDE-Module-Name: My Module
OpenIDE-Module-Name_de: Mein Modul
```

The second (preferred) option is to outsource the attributes you intend to internationalize into a *.properties* file. Then, the attribute names are used as keys and are provided in bundles for each language. Define the bundle with the OpenIDE-Module-Localizing-Bundle attribute as shown in Listing 34-1 (see also Chapter 3), so the attributes are read out of the bundle (see Listings 34-2 and 34-3).

Listing 34-1. Manifest.mf

```
Manifest-Version: 1.0
OpenIDE-Module: com.galileo.netbeans.module
OpenIDE-Module-Localizing-Bundle: com/galileo/netbeans/module/Bundle.properties
```

Listing 34-2. Bundle.Properties

```
OpenIDE-Module-Name = My Module
```

Listing 34-3. Bundle_de.Properties

```
OpenIDE-Module-Name = Mein Modul
```

Internationalization of Help Pages

Generally, help pages, including the help set configuration files, are internationalized like *.properties* files by appending country and/or language identifiers. Since a help set typically consists of a large number of files, this would result in a very confusing structure. Therefore, it is also possible to store the files intended for internationalization in a subfolder, as shown in Figure 34-2. Language and country identification is no longer necessary, because that information is already represented by the subfolder.

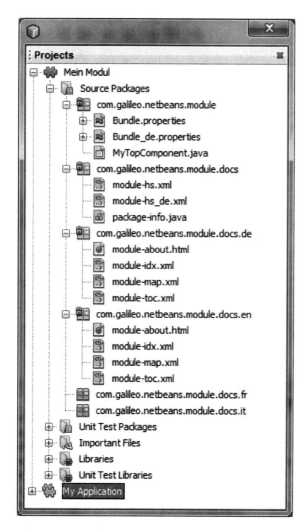

Figure 34-2. Help sets for specific languages are stored in a separate directory.

Only the help set file `module-hs.xml` remains in the root directory, and has not attached an identifier. In this file, you delegate to the corresponding folders. The help set file without an identifier is always used when the current `Locale` setting does not match the existing files. The help set file points to the English version of the help pages (see Listing 34-4).

Listing 34-4. Help Set File Which Refers to a Language-Specific Package

```
<maps>
    <homeID>com.galileo.netbeans.module.about</homeID>
    <mapref location="en/module-map.xml"/>
</maps>
```

```
<view mergetype="javax.help.AppendMerge">
    <name>TOC</name>
    <label>Contents</label>
    <type>javax.help.TOCView</type>
    <data>en/module-toc.xml</data>
</view>
<view mergetype="javax.help.AppendMerge">
    <name>Index</name>
    <label>Index</label>
    <type>javax.help.IndexView</type>
    <data>en/module-idx.xml</data>
</view>
```

You should also consider that the registration of the help set only occurs once for the module-hs.xml file by the HelpSetRegistration annotation in the *package-info.java* file. Then the help sets containing a country/language identification are automatically found.

Internationalizing Other Resources

The NetBeans Platform provides additional possibilities for internationalizing other application components besides the areas of internationalization already described.

Graphics

Not only texts can be adapted by language and country; graphics, such as icons, can also be adapted. The ImageUtilities class provides a variant of the loadImage() method that is usually used for loading graphics, in order to simplify it. You can set a boolean parameter whether an available language/country-specific version of the graphic will be loaded depending on the current Locale setting. The method NbBundle.getLocalizingSuffixes() lists possible identifications which are searched for.

```
Image img = ImageUtilities.loadImage("resources/icon.gif", true);
```

If the current Locale setting, for example, is *de_DE*, it is first searched for *icon_de_DE.gif* and *icon_de.gif*.

Arbitrary Files

The NetBeans Platform defines a special protocol for loading other arbitrary internationalized resources. This is the *nbresloc* protocol, an extension of the *nbres* protocol, with which you can load resources from all available modules. You can easily create a URL object for a resource addressed by this protocol:

```
URL u = new URL("nbresloc:/com/galileo/netbeans/icon.png");
ImageIcon icon = new ImageIcon(u);
```

If the Locale setting is de_DE and a file named icon_de_DE.png or icon_de.png exists, this icon is loaded instead of icon.png.

Folders, Files, and Attributes in the Layer File

The System Filesystem provides two special attributes to internationalize names and icons of folders and files. This is very helpful, for example, for menus whose names are only declared in the layer file and thus cannot be read via the NbBundle class (as is the case for actions). These two attributes are SystemFileSystem.localizingBundle and SystemFileSystem.icon. With the first attribute, you can refer to your resource bundle, leaving out the *.properties* extension. In this resource bundle, a key is automatically searched that matches the complete path of the folder or of the file which contains the SystemFileSystem.localizingBundle attribute. For this example, this is Menu/MyMenu and Menu/MyMenu/MySubMenu. With the SystemFileSystem.icon attribute, you can additionally set an icon for the folder or for the file. Use the nbresloc protocol so it can also be loaded as an internationalized version. (See Listings 34-5, 34-6, and 34-7.)

Listing 34-5. Layer.xml

```
<folder name="Menu">
    <folder name="MyMenu">
        <attr name="SystemFileSystem.localizingBundle"
                stringvalue="com.galileo.netbeans.module.Bundle"/>
        <folder name="MySubMenu">
            <attr name="SystemFileSystem.localizingBundle"
                    stringvalue="com.galileo.netbeans.module.Bundle"/>
            <attr name="SystemFileSystem.icon"
                    urlvalue="nbresloc:/com/galileo/netbeans/module/icon.png"/>
        </folder>
    </folder>
</folder>
```

Listing 34-6. Bundle.properties

```
Menu/MyMenu=Extras
Menu/MyMenu/MySubMenu=My Tools
```

Listing 34-7. Bundle_de.properties

```
Menu/MyMenu=Extras
Menu/MyMenu/MySubMenu=Meine Tools
```

The System Filesystem provides the bundlevalue attribute type in order to internationalize attributes within the layer file. Thus, you can outsource, for example, the name of an action, which is determined by an attribute in the layer file, in a properties bundle.

```
<file name="com-galileo-netbeans-MyFirstAction.instance">
    <attr name="displayName" bundlevalue="com.galileo.netbeans.module.Bundle#CTL_MyAction"/>
</file>
```

Thus, the name of the action is determined by the CTL_MyAction key. For this purpose, indicate the name of the package and of the bundle. Which bundle is finally used depends on the locale settings and is automatically determined.

Administration and Preparation of Localized Resources

Up to this point, this discussion has assumed that the localized resources have been stored in the same folder as the module, whether the *Bundle.properties* files or graphics. However, how do you ensure that the resources for each language are separately managed, and how can you later extend an already-provided module with an additional translation? For this purpose the NetBeans Platform makes it possible to separate the resources to localize from the remaining parts (which are mainly the classes) of a module. Figure 34-3 shows the *locale* directory which is located below the directory in which the module is stored. The resources for a language in a JAR archive in this folder are extended with a language/country identifier. The archive has the same name as the module JAR archive. In this *Locale Extension Archive*, all language/country-specific resources are managed. They have the same package structure as the module. This way, the resources are separated and can be updated individually. For example, translations of the NetBeans Platform modules are provided in the same manner.

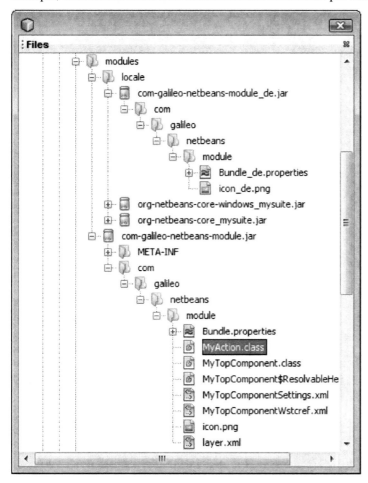

Figure 34-3. *Preparation of language-specific resources in a separate JAR archive in the directory locale*

Note that the individual localized resources still need the language/country identifier. The *Locale Extension Archive* needs no manifest file, because the archive is exclusively identified by the name of the localized package and is added to the class path of the module classloader.

In this example, the resources for German are in the *locale* folder as a locale extension archive. The English resources that have no identifier are the default resources and are located in the JAR archive of the module. Now, it is interesting that you can put the default resources into a locale extension archive, because it has no identifier and can be made available in the *locale* directory; the resources you plan to localize are completely separated from the module itself. This is particularly the case when adding another language is done by a third person because it is obvious which resources must be localized.

Summary

This chapter showed how to internationalize an application, adapting it to several languages. You learned the specifics of internationalizing source code and the manifest file, as well as adapting help pages and other resources, such as graphics.

Branding and Packaging Application

As described in Chapter 3, there are two different types of containers used by the NetBeans Platform: a *Module Suite* and a *NetBeans Platform Application*. While a module suite represents a pure collection of connected related modules, a NetBeans Platform application provides the basic structure for an independent application. This means you can user-specifically adapt a NetBeans Platform application and then create an installable package out of it. The following sections will explain how this works.

Branding

A Platform application provides a separate dialog for the so-called branding, or product-specific adaptation, of your application. There are numerous settings in this dialog, including the adaptation of the name and the different icons as well as for determining a splash screen and the window system's behavior. Interestingly, you can arbitrarily change all texts defined by the Platform, such as the names of certain windows. In the following sections we will take a closer look at this; to get started, click on *Branding…* in the context menu of your Platform application. An example of branding in a NetBeans Platform application is shown in Figure 35-1.

Name, Icons, and Splash Screen

You can determine the name of your application and assign icons for the sizes 16 × 16, 32 × 32, and 48 × 48 on the first tab (*Basics*) of the branding dialog. Those icons are used for different purposes. For example, the icon sized 16 × 16 is used for the title bar of your application. The icon sized 32 × 32 is used for the taskbar. However, you can also indicate a different icon for each.

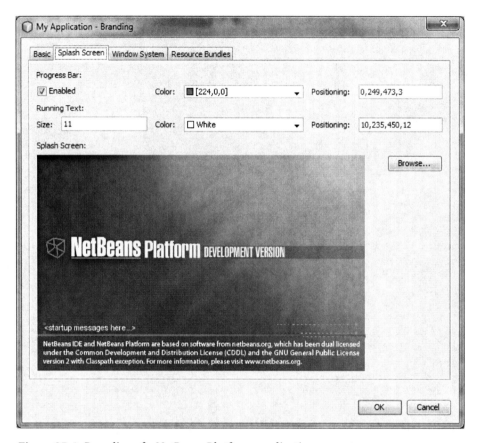

Figure 35-1. Branding of a NetBeans Platform application

On the *Splash Screen* tab you can select a splash screen which is displayed when starting your application. This splash screen is also used for the About dialog. Furthermore, a progress bar can be displayed on the splash screen. You can display or hide the progress bar and determine its color. You can easily determine the position of the progress bar on the splash screen via drag-and-drop. There, you can also determine the position of the text field in which status information is displayed when loading the application. You can also determine the text's color yourself.

Window System Behavior

In Chapter 10 you already learned how to individually determine the window's behaviour within the NetBeans window system. On the *Window System* tab, you can apply these settings globally for the whole window system, meaning for all windows. (See Figure 35-2.)

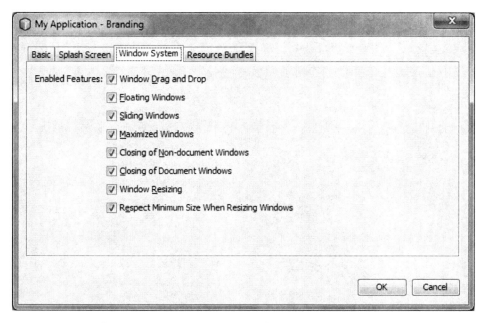

Figure 35-2. *Configuring the window system's behavior*

In addition to the already known parameters, you can also determine whether the size of the windows within the window system can or cannot be changed. Moreover, you can determine whether a window can be closed or not in an editor mode (document) or in a view mode (non-document).

Resource Bundles

You can change all text constants of the NetBeans Platform and comfortably adapt them to your needs on the *Resource Bundles* tab (see Figure 35-3). In the upper-right corner, a search field is provided to filter text constants for keys and values. This way you keep track of these numerous bundles.

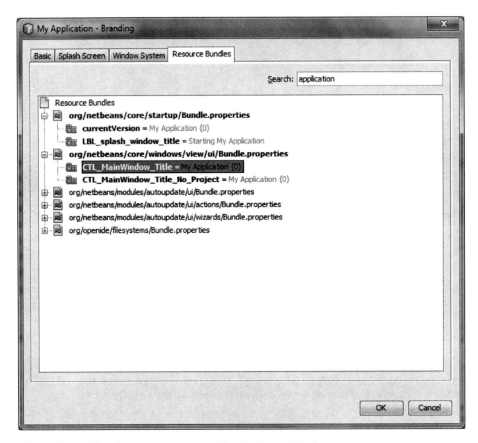

Figure 35-3. *Adapting text constants of the NetBeans Platform*

If you want to delete the version number, for example (which is displayed behind the title of your application by default), first search for `application` to get a range of key value pairs. This way, you also find the text constant with the key `CTL_MainWindow` which determines the name of your application. Double-clicking this entry, you can change the value. You delete the part {0} after the title. Thus, you make it so that the version number is no longer displayed. All altered texts are displayed in bold in order to keep the overview of all changes.

If you change something concerning the text constants, they are not changed in the original files. Instead, the NetBeans IDE creates new *.properties* files with the changed texts in the *branding* directory of your Platform application in the original folder hierarchy of the corresponding module. (See Figure 35-4.) When creating the application a so-called branding module with the *Branding Name* as suffix in its name is created. Define the branding name in the *Properties* of your Platform application under *Application*. This way, you can deliver your application with different brandings parallel. You can define which branding is chosen when starting the application by a command-line parameter; this is covered in the "Command Line Parameters" section.

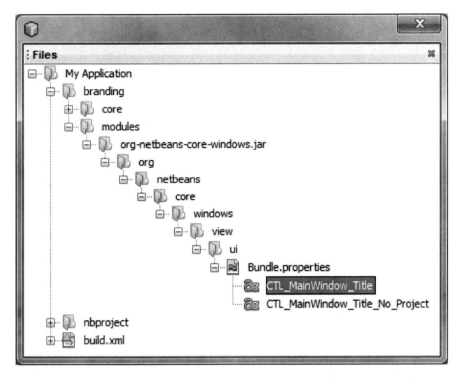

Figure 35-4. *Administration of the changed text constants in branding modules*

You can switch to the original values any time, because the changed text constants are managed separately. Open the *Files* view if you want to reset single or multiple changed values when developing. In the *Files* view you find the *branding* folder in the directory of your Platform application. In this folder you find the corresponding properties files (see Figure 35-4). There, you can either delete separate values or whole files.

Command-Line Parameters

Start your finished application by a operating system-specific launcher which is provided by the NetBeans Platform. This launcher is an *.exe* file for the Windows operating system, for example. You can influence this launcher and thus the start and the execution of the application by a series of parameters. Note that you either use a double back slash or a single slash for all paths. Command-line parameters are listed in Table 35-1.

Overview of Parameters

Table 35-1. Command-Line Parameter and Its Meaning

Parameter	Description
`--clusters <path>`	Paths to the clusters in which the modules are located. The path separator ";" is used for Windows and ":" is used for UNIX.
`--branding <name>`	Determining the branding name.
`--jdkhome <path>`	Path to a Java Platform base directory.
`-J<JVM Option>`	With this, parameters can be passed to the virtual machine. It is often used for defining properties, for example: `-J-Dorg.netbeans.core.level=100`
`--cp:p <classpath>`	With this parameter, you can prepend resources to the class path of the application. Those resources are also accessible via the Java System Classloader `ClassLoader.getSystemResource()`.
`--cp:a <classpath>`	With it you can add resources to the class path of the application. These resources can then be accessed by the Java System Classloader `ClassLoader.getSystemResource()`.
`--laf <L&F classname>`	Definition of a specific look and feel class. Add the following line, in order to use the L&F which is integrated in the Java Platform, for example: `--laf com.sun.java.swing.plaf.nimbus.NimbusLookAndFeel`
`--fontsize <size>`	With this parameter you can determine the font size of the whole application.
`--locale <language[:country]>`	Current locale setting, for example, `de:DE`. Note that the language and country identifier are separated by a colon instead of an underscore.
`--userdir <path>`	With it you can determine an alternative path in which the user-defined application settings are saved. This way, for example, even multiple instances of the application (which read their data from a separate directory) can be executed.

You can define and pass those parameters either directly to the launcher or via the *etc/<branding name>.conf* file which is located in the distribution of the application. There you can determine any options via the `default_options` attribute. Furthermore, you can separately assign the path of the Java Platform, the user directory, and additional clusters in this file.

Determining Parameters While Developing

With the `run.args.extra` attribute you can determine parameters in the *project.properties* file of your Platform application or module (if the module does not belong to another application). You can use this attribute to define command-line parameters while developing the application within the NetBeans IDE. For example, if you test another locale setting and you want to switch on the output of a logger, you enter the following into the *project.properties* file:

```
run.args.extra = --locale fr:FR \
                -J-Dcom.galileo.netbeans.module.level=100
```

Creating Distribution

The NetBeans IDE provides different types for creating a distribution of your application. For the end user, an installer package is the most interesting form of distribution because the user only has to click the installer to automatically install the complete software.

Installer Package

The NetBeans IDE is able to create a operating system-specific installer package from your application, as shown in Figure 35-5. To do so, just define which package you want to create in the *Properties* of your Platform application under *Installer*. Optionally, you can add a software license and choose whether the installer package will be compressed.

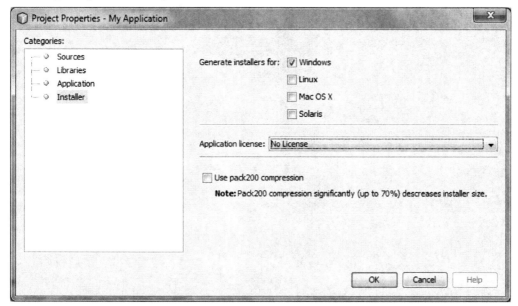

Figure 35-5. Creating Platform-specific installer packages

You can create installer packages for Windows, Linux, Max OS X, and Solaris. If you now select *Package as...* ➤ *Installers* from the application context menu, the NetBeans IDE creates the desired installer packages in the *dist* directory.

ZIP Distribution

Packing the application as a ZIP distribution is a very common form of delivery. All parts necessary for executing the application are packed up, as for an installer package. This includes the modules of the NetBeans Platform, your own application modules, a launcher for starting the application, and some configuration files. (See Figure 35-6.) You start the creation of this complete package with *Package as...* ➤ *ZIP Distribution* in the context menu of your application project. The finished distribution is saved in the *dist* directory in the corresponding project folder.

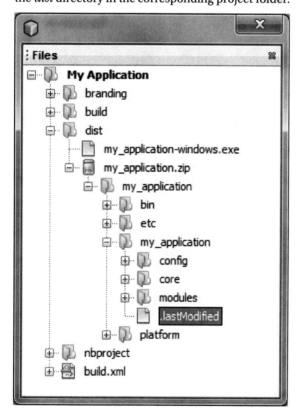

Figure 35-6. *Parts of a ZIP distribution*

- The Platform-specific launchers are located in the *bin* directory. Among these, there is also an *.exe* file.

- The *etc* directory contains configuration files which are used by the launcher. This includes the *<branding id>.conf* file in which you can define command-line parameters or a path to a JDK (see the "Creating Distribution" section).

- The directories *my_application* and *platform* are clusters. In the *my_application* cluster your application modules are located with your configuration files and the adapted Platform modules. Consequently, all modules of the NetBeans Platform, including the modules of the NetBeans Runtime Container (see Chapter 2), are in the *platform* cluster.

Java Web Start Package

With Java Web Start, your application can be started directly and executed from the Internet. For this purpose, call the menu item *JNLP* ➤ *Build* from the context menu of your Platform application. As a result of this call, you will receive a *.war* file in the *dist* distribution. This file can then be directly copied to the deploy directory of a servlet container. The *WEB-INF/web.xml* file is the deployment descriptor which defines the JNLP servlet that is located in the *WEB-INF/lib* directory.

Mac OS X Application

A fourth and last possibility for a distribution, the creation of a Mac OS X application, is also available. For this purpose call the context menu *Package as…* ➤ *Mac OS X Application* of the corresponding Platform application. Bear in mind that you cannot execute this on the Windows Platform, because the *ln* command, among others, is accessed but not provided in Windows.

Summary

In this chapter, you learned how to create and configure your stand-alone NetBeans Platform application. You also looked at the customization of NetBeans Platform modules, where you adapted out-of-the-box modules to your application-specific needs.

The launcher of your created application can be influenced in various ways. Therefore, you had a look at each of the command-line parameters and how they are used. Finally, this chapter dealt with the creation of deployment-ready application distributions.

Updating a NetBeans Platform Application

During software lifecycles, it nearly always happens that you want to provide updates for your application because of fixed errors, new functionalities, or to implement new requirements. It would be very cumbersome if you needed to redistribute the entire application when you just needed to provide a patch or a new feature. This is one of the advantages of a modular architecture of the application: you can offer updates on the module layer. For the user, installing updates must be as simple and intuitive as possible. To that end, the NetBeans Platform in conjunction with the Plugin Manager provides an Auto Update service. This module is able to automatically search for updated or new modules in a set of predefined update centers, and to dynamically load them at runtime. Beyond that, users are able to manually install downloaded updates or new modules via the Plugin Manager.

The Auto Update Service

Updates are made available as NBM files. These update packages must be offered via an update center. Within a NetBeans Platform application, update centers can be defined in which the Auto Update service searches for updates. Update center definitions can be made manually or they can be delivered with an application module. The user can configure the application so that updates are automatically searched at a certain time. Of course updates can also be initiated manually. Figure 36-1 shows the components of the Auto Update service.

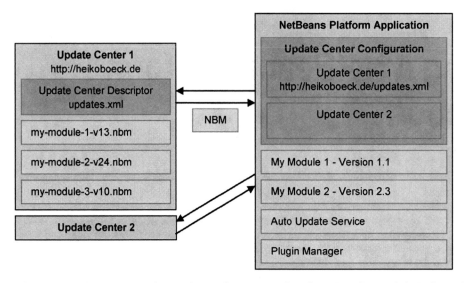

Figure 36-1. Components that make up the Auto Update functionality and their dependencies

The NBM File

Modules that you want to make available as an update are distributed in the form of NBM files. These consist of a JAR archive containing the actual module together with its configuration data and update information required by the Plugin Manager (see Figure 36-2). An NBM file may also contain the libraries required by the module. The content of the module JAR file and its related configuration files have already been described in Chapter 3.

One file I have not yet discussed is the info.xml file. This file contains information displayed to the user when choosing existing modules or modules to be installed in the Plugin Manager (see Listing 36-1). The manifest element contains information from the module's manifest file. For example, the defined dependencies are very important. If the user chooses a module in the Plugin Manager that is dependent on another module, the latter is automatically activated so it can be downloaded simultaneously with the selected module. If dependencies cannot be satisfied, the user can install the module without being able to activate it, though. Finally, you can also add license information via the license element, which was displayed to the user before installation of the module began. This forces the user to confirm that licensing requirements have been satisfied so the module can be installed.

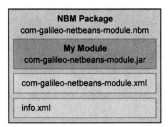

Figure 36-2. Parts of an NBM file

Listing 36-1. Information File of an NBM File

```
<?xml version="1.0" encoding="UTF-8"?>
<!DOCTYPE module PUBLIC
    "-//NetBeans//DTD Autoupdate Module Info 2.5//EN"
    "http://www.netbeans.org/dtds/autoupdate-info-2_5.dtd">
<module codenamebase="com.galileo.netbeans.module"
        distribution="./com-galileo-netbeans-module.nbm"
        downloadsize="7123"
        homepage="http://heikoboeck.de"
        license="AD9FBBC9"
        moduleauthor="Heiko Boeck"
        needsrestart="false"
        releasedate="2007/10/16">
    <manifest AutoUpdate-Show-In-Client="true"
              OpenIDE-Module="com.galileo.netbeans.module"
              OpenIDE-Module-Name="My Module"
              OpenIDE-Module-Implementation-Version="071016"
              ...
              OpenIDE-Module-Specification-Version="1.0"/>
    <license name="AD9FBBC9">Place your license information here</license>
</module>
```

An NBM file is created automatically by the NetBeans IDE by just calling *Create NBM* in the context menu of the desired module. When you choose *Create NBM*, the IDE attempts to sign the NBM file. To make this possible, a so-called keystore must be prepared and generated (see Figure 36-3). Use the *Keystores Manager* of the NetBeans IDE, which is only available after installation of the *Mobility* plugin. This mobility plugin is part of the complete NetBeans IDE installation package. However, you can also install this plugin via the Plugin Manager (*Tools ➤ Plugins ➤ Available Plugins*), later. Open the Keystores Manager via *Tools ➤ Keystores*. Next, create a keystore file via *Add Keystore...*, including a file name and a directory where the keystore will be located. A recommended location is the *nbproject* folder of your module. After entering a password of at least six characters, click OK to create the keystore.

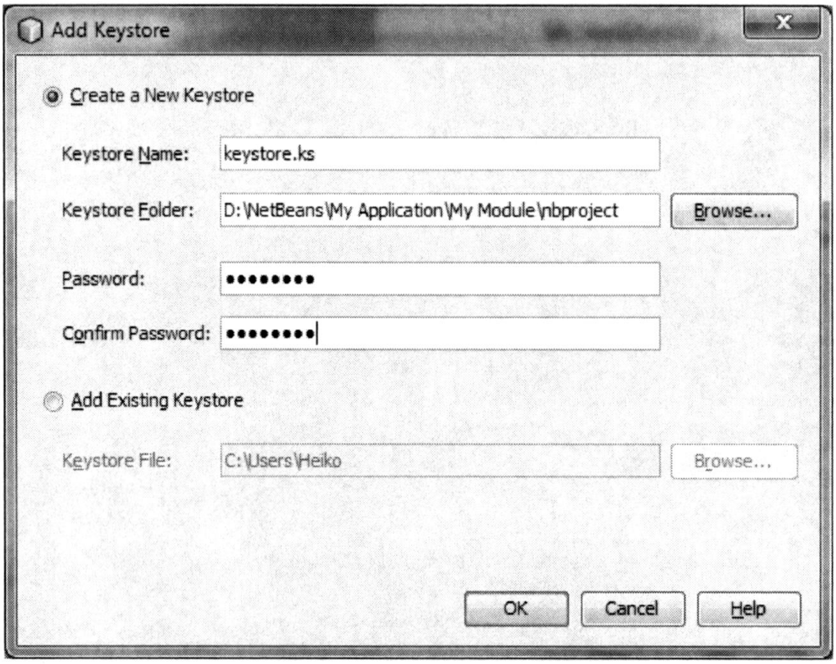

Figure 36-3. Creating a keystore

Now, a key pair has to be added. With this key pair the NBM file can then be signed. Choose the keystore (on the left) in the Keystores Manager for this purpose, and then click the *New...* button (on the right). In the following dialog (shown in Figure 36-4) you must assign an alias and you provide personal information. Make sure to provide the same password as when creating the keystore. Next, click *OK* to close the dialog and create the key pair in the keystore.

Figure 36-4. Creating a key pair

Alternatively, you can create a keystore and a key pair even without the NetBeans IDE. Instead, you can use the *keytool* tool which is part of the JDK. The call would than look like this:

```
<JDK path>/bin/keytool -genkey
    -storepass mypassword
    -alias mymodule
    -keystore <module path>/nbproject/keystore.ks
```

To enable the IDE to find the keystore and key pair, define the following two properties in the nbproject/project.properties file (found within the *Projects* window, under *Important Files ➤ Project Properties*). If this file does not exist, you can create it yourself. Use keystore to define the path to your keystore relative to the module project folder. Use the nbm_alias key to set the alias for the key pair to be used, since one keystore may contain multiple key pairs.

keystore=nbproject/keystore.ks
nbm_alias=mymodule

Now invoke the *Create NBM* order again, which lets the IDE sign the NBM file. Doing so, a dialog is shown for entering the password assigned to the keystore. Enter the correct password in order to enable the successful signature. If you do not want to enter this password each time, you can add the storepass feature to the properties file:

storepass=mypassword

Then, in the Plugin Manager, the user can see the module certificate, after downloading the selected module is completed, but before the final installation process begins. Be aware that a warning will be shown that the module is not to be trusted. To prevent this, provide a certificate from an official certificate vendor such as VeriSign.

Update Centers

NBM files—that is, updates for a distributed application—are put into an update center, from which they can be downloaded. Such an update center is nothing other than a storage place where the modules are placed, generally on a server accessible via the Internet. Use an *Update Center Descriptor*, in the form of an XML file, to describe the module location and other details (see Listing 36-2). This way, the Auto Update service finds the module, while determining whether the module is updated or new. The update center descriptor lists the content of the info.xml file (explained in the previous section) for each of the NBM files in the update center. As a result, the Auto Update service of the application is able to determine which updated or which new modules are provided in which version, without having to open or download the NBM files. The license element is just defined outside the module element, not inside. Therefore, you are able to use one license for multiple modules at the same time. Thus, only one license is displayed to the user. Multiple usage of the license element is possible, too, in order to provide a separate license for each module.

Listing 36-2. Update Center Descriptor: updates.xml

```
<?xml version="1.0" encoding="UTF-8" ?>
<!DOCTYPE module_updates PUBLIC
    "-//NetBeans//DTD Autoupdate Catalog 2.5//EN"
    "http://www.netbeans.org/dtds/autoupdate-catalog-2_5.dtd">
<module_updates timestamp="08/54/21/17/04/2007">
    <module codenamebase="com.galileo.netbeans.module"
            distribution="./com-galileo-netbeans-module.nbm"
            ...
    </module>
    <module codenamebase="com.galileo.netbeans.module2"
            distribution="./com-galileo-netbeans-module2.nbm"
            ...
    </module>
    <license name="AD9FBBC9">Place your license information here</license>
</module_updates>
```

The root element of the update center descriptor is the module_updates element. The module_updates element just contains the timestamp attribute, whose timestamp is compared to the previous timestamp by the Auto Update service. This means that the Auto Update service reads an update center only when the timestamp date is more recent than the date of the last connection. Optionally, modules can be grouped in the update center descriptor, via the module_group element. This allows modules to be displayed as a group (semantically or context-orientated) in the Plugin Manager; you can encapsulate the element in any way. In the module element, the distribution attribute is very important, because it defines the location from which the module will be downloaded. Rather than a relative location, as shown in this example,an absolute URL can be provided, pointing to the location of the module.

The address of such an update center descriptor is used as a server URL in the update center configuration. You do not have to create the update center descriptor yourself, though. If you right-click the context menu of a NetBeans Platform application, you will find the menu item *Package as ➤ NBMs* there. Click it and the update center descriptor with the file name *updates.xml* is created along with the separate NBM files of all modules belonging to this Platform application. You will find these files in the *build/updates* directory.

Providing a Language Pack

In Chapter 34, you already learned how to provide the language-specific content of your module in another language. You got to know two variants: on the one one hand, directly placing the localized resources in the module; on the other, providing it by a separate JAR file in the *locale* directory. So far, this example has assumed that you can access the module or respectively the application. But how can you provide an additional language pack for users of your already-provided application?

You can easily provide additional language packs for an already delivered module just as you would provide an updated or new module via an update center. The only difference is that the manifest element is substituted by the l10n element in the update descriptor (*info.xml*) and in the update center descriptor (*updates.xml*). This has the following structure:

```
<l10n langcode="de"
      module_major_version="1"
      module_spec_version="1.0"
      OpenIDE-Module-Name="Mein Modul"
      OpenIDE-Module-Long-Description="German localization of My Module."
/>
```

First, indicate the language with the langcode attribute which contains this pack. With the version attributes you can determine for which version this language pack is meant. The language pack is activated only if this matches the version of the installed module.

Configuring and Installing on the Client-Side

The desired update centers must be installed in the *Plugin Manager*, which you can open via *Tools ➤ Plugins*. Your rich client application is then able to get new or updated modules from an update center. In the *Settings* tab you can install any update center (see Figure 36-5). The URL of an update center must refer to the update center descriptor (see the "Update Centers" section). In this view you can also deactivate certain update centers and thus exclude them from the update process.

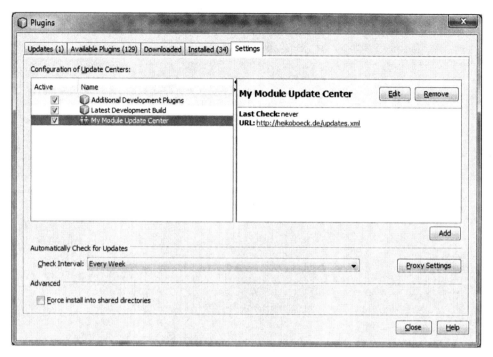

Figure 36-5. *Configuration of the update centers to be searched for new modules*

When switching to the *Updates* tab, use the *Reload Catalog* button to allow the Auto Update service to look for updates in the defined update centers. Updated versions of modules are searched for those modules that are already installed in the application. For searching new modules, use the same approach in the *Available Plugins* tab. The found modules are displayed immediately in a list, from which you can select those you need. Use the *Update* or *Install* button to add selected modules to the application. Modules that are also locally available—that is, those that are personally downloaded—can be installed as well. To do so, switch to the *Downloaded* tab, and then click *Add Plugins...* to add the desired NBM files. Finally, click *Install* to install the selected plugins.

The last tab to be discussed is the *Installed* tab (see Figure 36-6). All currently installed modules are listed there, organized by categories. You can deactivate modules in this view, as well as completely uninstall them.

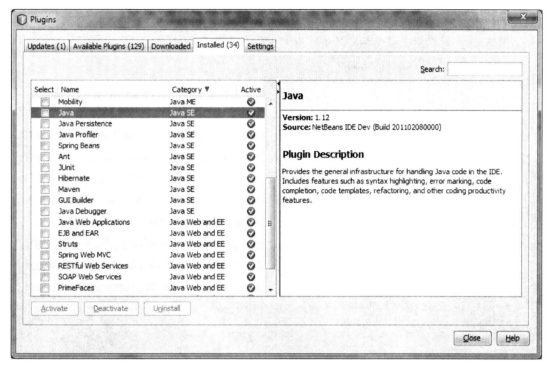

Figure 36-6. *The Installed tab lists all installed modules. Here, you can deactivate and uninstall modules.*

New Update Center

As already mentioned, users of your application may register additional update centers in the Plugin Manager. However, you can also add update center information to one of your modules. Once this module is loaded in an application, the registered update center is also automatically provided there. So, you are able to add an additional update center to an already delivered application. For adding such update center information to your module, a wizard is provided under *File ➤ New File... ➤ Module Development ➤ Update Center*. The wizard registers the entered update center information, consisting of the name and URL in the standard folder Services/AutoupdateType in the layer file. Such an entry then looks like that shown in Listing 36-3.

Listing 36-3. *Update Center Definition in the Layer File*

```
<folder name="Services">
    <folder name="AutoupdateType">
        <file name="my_module_update_center.instance">
            <attr name="displayName"
                    bundlevalue="com.galileo.netbeans.module.Bundle
                    #Services/AutoupdateType/my_module_update_center.instance"/>
            <attr name="enabled" boolvalue="true"/>
```

```
                <attr name="instanceCreate" methodvalue=
                    "org.netbeans.modules.autoupdate.updateprovider.
                    AutoupdateCatalogFactory.createUpdateProvider"/>
                <attr name="instanceOf" stringvalue="org.netbeans.spi.autoupdate.UpdateProvider"/>
                <attr name="url" bundlevalue=
                    "com.galileo.netbeans.module.Bundle#my_module_update_center"/>
            </file>
        </folder>
</folder>
```

The actual files have been outsourced in a resource bundle:

```
my_module_update_center=http://heikoboeck.de/updates.xml
Services/AutoupdateType/my_module_update_center.instance=My Update Center
```

This example assumed that the update center is publicly accessible via the Internet address per *http*. However, you can also use the *file* protocol to install an update center with it, for example, on a company-internal server.

```
file:/D:/NetBeans/MyUpdateCenter/updates/updates.xml
```

Automatically Installing Updates

An NBM file can also be installed without user interaction. To do this, just put the NBM file in the *update/download* directory of a cluster. The update is then automatically installed when the application is next started. After, the NBM file is removed and the application is started anew. Backups of original versions of the actualized modules are found in the *update/backup/netbeans* directory. Bear in mind that the update is always installed in this cluster where the update is stored, even if the module that should be updated is installed in a different cluster.

The *Auto Update Services API* offers further possibilities for management, automatic installation, uninstallation, or deactivation of modules. Chapter 25 will cover the functionalities of the Auto Update Services API.

Summary

This chapter introduced you to the update facilities of the NetBeans Platform. First, you saw how the Auto Update service works. An NBM file is an update package and can be created from your module by the NetBeans IDE. Next, you learned how to provide and configure update centers. You also saw how a module is configured to provide a localized version of an existing module. Finally, this chapter dealt with the configuration of update centers on the client-side and how updates can be installed automatically.

Test & Tooling: Developing and Testing NetBeans Platform Applications

CHAPTER 37

Maven and the NetBeans Platform

The NetBeans Platform uses the build tool Ant by default. Maven,an alternative to Ant, has until now only been provided as an additional plugin, with limited support from the IDE. But this has changed; Maven is now an integral part of the NetBeans IDE. The NetBeans IDE involves the Maven distribution and numerous wizards to create different project types. This chapter will focus on Maven support when developing NetBeans Platform applications.

The configuration for a Maven project is hierarchical and modular, so it is quite suitable as a build system for NetBeans Platform applications. In Maven projects the complete build process is carried out by Maven, which means it is easy to work even without the NetBeans IDE. The functionality of Maven itself is organized into separate plugins; due to Maven's widespread use, plugins are available for numerous tasks. The necessary configuration files remain small and clearly organized.

Basics and Structure of a Maven Project

In Maven, all the necessary information for a software project is defined in a so-called *POM* (project object model) file. Each module (such as a JAR file) contains its own file. A project can consist of several modules. A parent POM file which aggregates these modules can be created so these modules can be collectively created. At the same time, subordinate modules can inherit features of the parent POM file. In this way a hierarchic structure arise, and this structure can be extended further down. (See Figure 37-1.)

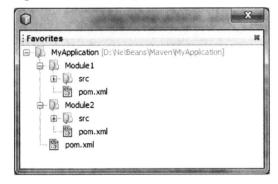

Figure 37-1. File structure of a multi-module project with parent POM file to inherit features and aggregation of several modules

Parent POM File

One of the most important features of Maven is the possibility of inheritance. This means that a parent POM can be referenced from a POM file. Elements which are defined there can be inherited or overridden. At the same time, it is possible to aggregate modules. All modules that will belong to this project are defined in a parent POM file. This way, a software project, which consists of several modules, can be created as a unit.

The basic structure of a parent POM file is shown in Listing 37-1. There the file, or rather the project, is identified in principle by the elements groupId, artifactId, and version. As it is no module (e.g., JAR file), but a parent POM file, the packaging type *pom* is used. Below the element dependencies you can define dependencies on other modules. This is especially important for single modules which use classes out of other modules. At that place you can define the version of a dependency in advance in the parent POM file to ensure that all modules, which define the referring dependency, use the same version. You can already preconfigure plugins, which are used in the build process, with the element build. The actual aggregation of several modules belonging together occurs by the element modules. So if a build process is started with this parent POM file, the modules *Module1* and *Module2* are built. If the build process fails at one module, the whole process is cancelled.

Listing 37-1. Example of a Parent POM file with Which Several Modules Are Summarized

```xml
<?xml version="1.0" encoding="UTF-8"?>
<project xmlns="http://maven.apache.org/POM/4.0.0"
xmlns:xsi="http://www.w3.org/2001/XMLSchema-instance"
xsi:schemaLocation="http://maven.apache.org/xsd/maven-4.0.0.xsd">
    <modelVersion>4.0.0</modelVersion>
    <groupId>com.galileo.netbeans</groupId>
    <artifactId>MyApplication</artifactId>
    <version>1.0-SNAPSHOT</version>
    <packaging>pom</packaging>
    <name>MyApplication</name>
    <repositories>...</repositories>
    <build>...</build>
    <modules>
        <module>Module1</module>
        <module>Module2</module>
    </modules>
    <properties>...</properties>
</project>
```

Module POM File

The POM file for a module consists of exactly the same basic structure. Obviously, the element parent is used instead of the element modules at this point. So you refer to the POM file to use, whose settings will be inherited. The name, which was given by artifactId, must be the same as the name indicated in the parent POM file under modules. Now you define that you are dealing with a module. You do this with the packaging element; this can be *jar* or *nbm* for a NetBeans Platform, module, for example. (See Listing 37-2.)

Listing 37-2. Example of a Module POM File Which Inherits from a Parent POM File

```
<?xml version="1.0" encoding="UTF-8"?>
<project xmlns="http://maven.apache.org/POM/4.0.0"
xmlns:xsi="http://www.w3.org/2001/XMLSchema-instance"
xsi:schemaLocation="http://maven.apache.org/xsd/maven-4.0.0.xsd">
    <modelVersion>4.0.0</modelVersion>
    <parent>
        <artifactId>MyApplication</artifactId>
        <groupId>com.galileo.netbeans</groupId>
        <version>1.0-SNAPSHOT</version>
    </parent>
    <artifactId>Module1</artifactId>
    <packaging>nbm</packaging>
    <name>MyModule</name>
    <properties>...</properties>
    <dependencies>
        <dependency>
            <groupId>com.galileo.netbeans</groupId>
            <artifactId>Module5</artifactId>
            <version>1.3</version>
        </dependency>
    </dependencies>
    <build>...</build>
</project>
```

One of the most important features of Maven is dependency management, especially compared to Ant. There, dependencies on other modules (JAR files) or projects are declared for each project or module in the referring POM file. However, the actual and main advantage is the resolution of transitive dependencies by Maven, since Maven even resolves and integrates dependencies of the dependencies. Hence, you do not have to care about the whole class path, which ensures a simple reproducibility of a build any time.

Maven Repositories

Embedding and managing repositories is an integral part of Maven. A repository, in this context, is the location for artifacts (mostly JAR files). Besides the actual artifact, the POM file is also located there. Thus, the POM file allows the resolution of transitive dependencies. The storage structure goes along with a certain convention. For example, the module with the group ID com.galileo.netbeans, artifact ID MyModule, and version 1.0 would be located at
<Repository>/com/galileo/netbeans/MyModule/1.0/MyModule-1.0.jar if needed in another project.

You can define any number of other specific repositories for your project, besides the central Maven repository (http://repo1.maven.org/maven2), which is integrated by default. Add the entry in Listing 37-3 to your POM file to be able to use artifacts out of the repository with the NetBeans modules, for example.

Listing 37-3. Definition of a Maven Repository

```
<repositories>
    <repository>
        <id>netbeans</id>
```

```
    <name>NetBeans</name>
    <url>http://bits.netbeans.org/maven2/</url>
  </repository>
</repositories>
```

Of course, this definition can be added to the parent POM file, so that not every corresponding module has to be configured separately.

Maven manages a local repository; you do not have to download the necessary artifacts from the online repository for each and every build. All downloaded artifacts are located in this local repository, which is searched first to accelerate the build process. Then the process can also be executed offline. You define where your local repository is located in the *settings.xml* file, which usually is located in the user directory at *<user directory>/.m2/settings.xml*. The definition looks like Listing 37-4.

Listing 37-4. Definition of the Local Maven Repository

```
<settings>
  <localRepository>D:\MyLocalRepository</localRepository>
  ...
</settings>
```

Maven Projects in the NetBeans IDE

The NetBeans IDE provides different wizards for creating a NetBeans Platform application and its modules for Maven and Ant, by default. Additionally, useful features are provided as the Maven repository browser, for example.

Creating a NetBeans Platform Application

First of all, you can create a NetBeans Platform application with *File ➤New Project… ➤ Maven ➤ NetBeans Application*. Please note that the project name must not contain spaces, because it is used as artifactId in the POM file. Spaces are not allowed for the artifactId, because of the located artifacts in a repository, but you can give an alternate display name in <name>. Furthermore, you assign a groupId (reverse DNS format like Java packages) and a version. The final step of the wizard is to choose the NetBeans version which your application will be based on. A dependency is automatically set in the POM file on the referring cluster so that the Platform modules are included. Furthermore, it is possible to set whether OSGi bundles will be added as dependencies and whether a first module project will be set directly with the Platform application. Finish the following wizard and you will get the application structure shown in Figure 37-2.

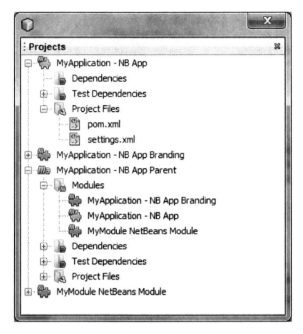

Figure 37-2. *Maven-based NetBeans Platform application project in the NetBeans IDE project's view*

What is striking at first sight is that the actual NetBeans Platform application project does not just consist of one, but three (or four, if you select the option to add a sample module) parts. These are named *NB App, NB App Branding,* and *NB App Branding.* These parts have the following tasks:

- *NB App:* This project determines which components belong to the application, which means dependencies on the NetBeans Platform cluster, on the branding module, and on the application module *MyModule* are defined in the file *pom.xml.* Start your application with *Run* in the context menu of this project.

- *NB App Branding:* With this part of the project, branding resources, meaning the adapted texts and icons, are managed and created as branding modules. You can open the branding dialog with the context menu of this project.

- *NB App Parent:* This is the actual container project for the whole application. That means the POM file of this project is the parent POM file for both the two modules which were described before, and for all further application modules. This is where the aggregation of all modules occurs by the modules attribute. Call *Build* in the context menu of this project for creating the whole application. This way, all affiliated modules are created.

Creating NetBeans Platform Modules

You can create a new Maven application module analogous with *File* ➤ *New Project...* ➤ *Maven* ➤ *NetBeans Module.* To add a new module from an existing Platform application, just choose the basic directory of the desired application creating the module. This is the level on which the parent POM file is located. The module is automatically added to the parent POM file. A referring parent entry is added to the module POM file, too. This way, it also inherits the configuration of the Platform application.

Adding Dependencies

Finally, I will show you how to add a dependency to a module. To do this, call the entry *Add Dependency* in the context menu of the *Dependencies* node. You can add the dependency in the referring dialog either directly by defining the artifact ID, group ID, and version, or by choosing an open project (see Figure 37-3). The search function includes the defined Maven repositories. This way you can add a dependency on a module of the NetBeans Platform, for example. However, that also means that you can only search for modules that are already installed in a repository. So, if you want to define a dependency on a module that is part of your application but not yet created, you have to take the way over *Open Projects*.

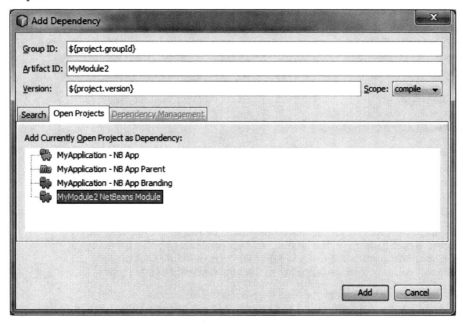

Figure 37-3. *Adding a dependency to a Maven-based NetBeans Platform module*

It is even easier to find modules over the Maven repository browser (see Figure 37-4). Open it with *Window ➤ Other ➤ Maven Repository Browser*. This is where you can add repositories. In those repositories you can search and browse. You can add a module as a dependency (in a special version) with *Add as Dependency* in the context menu of a module.

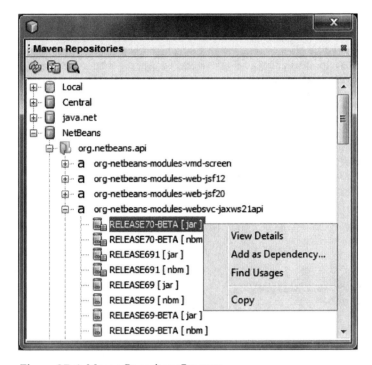

Figure 37-4. *Maven Repository Browser*

Maven Projects Without NetBeans IDE

In the previous section you used the NetBeans IDE to create NetBeans Platform Maven projects. Since the NetBeans IDE actually just transfers parameters of the GUI to Maven you can also use Maven directly. Next, I will show you in detail how to use the NetBeans Maven plugins creating a NetBeans Platform application.

Some preconditions have to be fulfilled before starting with setting a first Maven project:

1. In case you have not yet installed Maven, you can download the latest version from *http://maven.apache.org*. You just have to unpack the downloaded package and store it in a suitable directory.

2. Then create the environment variable M2_HOME, which should point to the basic directory of the Maven distribution. *(C:\Program Files\apache-maven-3.0.3*, for example).

3. Furthermore, the environment variable JAVA_HOME should be set, which points to the JRE directory *(C:\Program Files\Java\jdk1.6.0_24*, for example).

4. Finally, add the directory to the path variable.This way, Maven can be called in without indicating a path in the command line.

Now you are ready to start and create a Maven-based NetBeans Platform application, as described next.

Creating a NetBeans Platform Application

The NetBeans Maven plugin is complemented by the archetype netbeans-platform-app. This archetype creates the complete structure of a NetBeans Platform application project. To find the archetype you need the artifact ID, group ID, and a referring version.

Next, you define the data for the project to create by groupId, artifactId, and version. Use netbeansVersion to define which NetBeans Platform version you want to use. You can see all available versions in the NetBeans Maven repository at http://bits.netbeans.org/maven2/org/netbeans/cluster/platform/maven-metadata.xml.

You can define the package used for the branding module optionally by the parameter package. If you do not define the parameter, the group ID is used as valid value. To make Maven go into the non-interactive mode use the parameter --batch-mode. So, Maven creates the project without manual intervention. You trigger the creation of the project structure with the archetype:generate as goal (see Listing 37-5).

Listing 37-5. Maven Parameters for Creating a NetBeans Platform Application Project with the Command Line

```
>mvn
-DarchetypeArtifactId=netbeans-platform-app-archetype
-DarchetypeGroupId=org.codehaus.mojo.archetypes
-DarchetypeVersion=1.10
-DgroupId=com.galileo.netbeans
-DartifactId=MyApplication
-Dversion=1.0-SNAPSHOT
-DnetbeansVersion=RELEASE70
-Dpackage=com.galileo.netbeans.myapplication
--batch-mode
archetype:generate
```

If you execute the command-line call shown in Listing 37-5 in the desired directory in which the project will be created you will get the structure depicted in Figure 37-5.

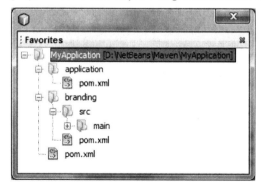

Figure 37-5. Structure of a Maven-based NetBeans Platform application project

The meaning of the parts of the project described in Figure 37-5 is explained in the section *Maven Projects in the NetBeans IDE*. At this point you want to look behind the scenes of the configuration again.

To get an overview of the created POM files and the structure of the project, first look at the parent POM file, meaning the *pom.xml* file on the top level (see Listing 37-6).

Listing 37-6. Parent POM File of a NetBeans Platform Application Project

```xml
<project xmlns="http://maven.apache.org/POM/4.0.0" ... >
    <modelVersion>4.0.0</modelVersion>
    <groupId>com.galileo.netbeans</groupId>
    <artifactId>MyApplication</artifactId>
    <version>1.0-SNAPSHOT</version>
    <packaging>pom</packaging>
    <name>MyApplication - NB App Parent</name>
    <repositories>
        <repository>
            <id>netbeans</id>
            <name>NetBeans</name>
            <url>http://bits.netbeans.org/maven2/</url>
        </repository>
    </repositories>
    <dependencies>
        <dependency>
            <groupId>junit</groupId>
            <artifactId>junit</artifactId>
            <version>4.8.2</version>
            <scope>test</scope>
        </dependency>
    </dependencies>
    <build>
        <pluginManagement>
            <plugins>
                <plugin>
                    <groupId>org.codehaus.mojo</groupId>
                    <artifactId>nbm-maven-plugin</artifactId>
                    <version>3.5</version>
                    <extensions>true</extensions>
                    <configuration>
                        <brandingToken>${brandingToken}</brandingToken>
                        <cluster>${brandingToken}</cluster>
                    </configuration>
                </plugin>
                <plugin>
                    <groupId>org.apache.maven.plugins</groupId>
                    <artifactId>maven-compiler-plugin</artifactId>
                    <version>2.3.2</version>
                    <configuration>
                        <source>1.6</source>
                        <target>1.6</target>
                    </configuration>
                </plugin>
            </plugins>
        </pluginManagement>
    </build>
```

```
<modules>
    <module>branding</module>
    <module>application</module>
</modules>
<properties>
    <netbeans.version>RELEASE70</netbeans.version>
    <brandingToken>myapplication</brandingToken>
</properties>
</project>
```

Next the repository is defined. The NetBeans Platform or the NetBeans IDE modules can be loaded from this repository, so it is provided globally to the project. The dependencies defined in this file under dependencies are provided to all modules (which inherit from the parent POM file). Consequently, you do not have to add dependencies on JUnit any more. Maven plugins, which are later used for the build process, can be preconfigured below the element pluginManagement. So at this point, you define the cluster to use and the branding token for the NetBeans Maven plugin, for example. Furthermore, you can give the information to the compiler plugin that the project is created on a Java base. At the beginning, only the two modules of the project (the branding and the application module) are added below the modules element. All modules you create that will belong to this application will be executed there by your artifact ID. Finally, the properties, which will be provided globally and centrally, are defined. You can access their values with ${...}.

Both POM files of the branding and the application module have the structure of a normal NetBeans Platform module POM file. Let's take a closer look at this next.

Creating NetBeans Platform Modules

After creating a Maven-based NetBeans Platform application project with the command line without any development environment in the section *Creating a NetBeans Platform Application*, you now want to add an application module to it. An archetype is provided for creating a module; the good thing about this is that the relationship is made automatically. That means the module is automatically added to the NetBeans Platform application project when creating it in its basic directory (see Listing 37-7).

Listing 37-7. Maven Parameter for Creating a NetBeans Platform Module Project with the Command Line

```
>mvn
-DarchetypeArtifactId=nbm-archetype
-DarchetypeGroupId=org.codehaus.mojo.archetypes
-DarchetypeVersion=1.7-DartifactId=MyModule
-DgroupId=com.galileo.netbeans
-Dversion=1.0-SNAPSHOT
-DnetbeansVersion=RELEASE70
-Dpackage=com.galileo.netbeans.mymodule
--batch-mode
archetype:generate
```

In contrast to creating a Platform application project, in this case you use the nbm archetype. The parameters match the parameters already described in Listing 37-5. Just indicate the artifact ID, the group ID, and the version for the module to create. You can optionally define the NetBeans version to use and the package to be set as base for this module.

Now let's take a look at the POM file that was produced for this module. At the beginning, the link to the parent POM file is established by the parent element. Consequently, this file inherits the settings of the parent POM file, so it is no longer necessary to define the NetBeans Maven repository or a special Java version, for example. Thus, the configuration file remains small and is easy to maintain. *nbm* is used as packaging type, so when the module is created, a NetBeans module is created. In this module POM file, the JAR plugin is furthermore instructed by the useDefaultManifestFile element to use the already existing manifest.

```
<project xmlns="http://maven.apache.org/POM/4.0.0" ... >
    <modelVersion>4.0.0</modelVersion>
    <parent>
        <artifactId>MyApplication</artifactId>
        <groupId>com.galileo.netbeans</groupId>
        <version>1.0-SNAPSHOT</version>
    </parent>
    <groupId>com.galileo.netbeans</groupId>
    <artifactId>MyModule</artifactId>
    <version>1.0-SNAPSHOT</version>
    <packaging>nbm</packaging>
    <name>MyModule NetBeans Module</name>
    <properties> ... </properties>
    <dependencies>
        <dependency>
            <groupId>org.netbeans.api</groupId>
            <artifactId>org-netbeans-api-annotations-common</artifactId>
            <version>${netbeans.version}</version>
        </dependency>
    </dependencies>
    <build>
        <plugins>
            <plugin>
                <groupId>org.apache.maven.plugins</groupId>
                <artifactId>maven-jar-plugin</artifactId>
                <version>2.3.1</version>
                <configuration>
                    <useDefaultManifestFile>true</useDefaultManifestFile>
                </configuration>
            </plugin>
            ...
        </plugins>
    </build>
</project>
```

The module was automatically added to the parent POM file, so the module belongs to the whole NetBeans Platform application project. For this purpose, the parent POM file was adapted as follows:

```
<modules>
    <module>branding</module>
    <module>application</module>
    <module>MyModule</module>
</modules>
```

Make Packages Public

As already mentioned, a NetBeans module must explicitly define packages as public whose classes are to be made available to other modules. You have to configure the NetBeans Maven Plugin to make packages of a Maven-based NetBeans module public. For this purpose the plugin provides the element publicPackages.

In Listing 37-8 the package com.galileo.netbeans.api is made public for other modules. Consequently, another module can now define a dependency and use classes out of this public package. Further packages can be defined with any number of publicPackage elements.

Listing 37-8. Definining the Public Packages of a NetBeans Module

```
<plugin>
   <groupId>org.codehaus.mojo</groupId>
   <artifactId>nbm-maven-plugin</artifactId>
   <version>3.5</version>
   <extensions>true</extensions>
   <configuration>
      <publicPackages>
         <publicPackage>com.galileo.netbeans.api</publicPackage>
      </publicPackages>
   </configuration>
</plugin>
```

Adding Dependencies

Dependencies between different modules are defined in Maven in the POM file under dependencies. If you want to define a dependency on a certain version of a module, define the artifact ID, the group ID, and a version (optionally). If no version is indicated, the most recently used version is found by meta data in the Maven repository. To add a dependency on the module *MyModule2* to the NetBeans module *MyModule* extend the entry shown in Listing 37-9 in the POM file.

Listing 37-9. Definition of a Dependency Between MyModule and MyModule2

```
<dependencies>
   <dependency>
      <groupId>com.galileo.netbeans</groupId>
      <artifactId>MyModule2</artifactId>
      <version>2.0</version>
   </dependency>
</dependencies>
```

Creating and Executing the Application

Finally, the question remains how to create the application as a whole and how to execute it as a NetBeans Platform application. For creating the whole application, use the standard Maven build phase *install*. All sources are compiled, tests are executed (if existing), the modules are packed and, finally, the whole application is copied in the local repository. Execute this build phase on the parent POM file:

```
D:\NetBeans\Maven\MyApplication>mvn install
```

The goals of the NetBeans Maven plugin, which are listed in Table 37-1, are automatically connected by this build phase (or with the build phase *package*). To this end, a look on the web site of the plugin will be very helpful: `http://mojo.codehaus.org/nbm-maven-plugin/plugin-info.html`. There, you find the parameters of the separate goals that are provided. This way you can adapt the build process to your special needs.

Table 37-1. *Goals of the NetBeans Maven Plugin That Are Automatically Executed When Creating an Application*

Goal	Description
nbm:autoupdate	Creates the auto update information.
nbm:branding	Creates the branding module. Branding contents are stored under *src/main/nbm-branding* in the usual structure.
nbm:cluster-app	Creates the module cluster of a NetBeans Platform application.
nbm:manifest	Produces the manifest file of a module.
nbm:nbm	Creates a module distribution file (NBM).
nbm:standalone-zip	Creates a running distribution with executable as zip file.

After creating the application with `mvn install` you can now start the application with `mvn nbm:run-platform`. Please note that this goal can only be used on POM files with the packaging type *nbm-application*. That means you have to change into the directory of the standard application modules to execute the application:

`D:\NetBeans\Maven\MyApplication\application>`**mvn nbm:run-platform**

Additionally, the goals listed in Table 37-2 are provided. They can be called in explicitly.

Table 37-2. *Goals of the NetBeans Maven Plugin That Can Be Explicitly Executed*

Goal	Description
nbm:run-platform	Starts a NetBeans Platform application. This goal is executed on the standard application module.
nbm:standalone-zip	Creates a running distribution with executable as zip file.
nbm:cluster	Creates a cluster out of all modules which belong to the parent POM.
nbm:populate-repository	Creates Maven meta data from the modules and loads all resources (JAR file, NBM file, Javadoc, etc.) in a local or remote Maven repository.

`nbm:webstart-app`	Creates a webstart (JNLP) application in the form of a WAR file.
	This goal is executed on the standard application module.

With all this you have now installed, created, and executed a NetBeans Platform application without the NetBeans IDE. This mainly shows that the NetBeans IDE is not necessary for developing a NetBeans Platform-based application. Using alternative development environments is enormously simplified by Maven. Chapters 38 and 40 will look at developing a NetBeans Platform application within the Eclipse and IntelJ IDEA IDE.

Summary

Maven is now an integral part of the NetBeans Platform. So besides Ant, not only an alternative build system is provided, but also a perfect opportunity to work independently of the NetBeans IDE. In this chapter you learned how to work with Maven projects within the NetBeans IDE. You also learned how you can you use Maven to create and build NetBeans Platform applications from the command line without the NetBeans IDE.

Eclipse IDE and the NetBeans Platform

In Chapter 37 you learned how easy it is to create applications based on the NetBeans Platform even without the NetBeans IDE. This is possible now because NetBeans Platform applications can be developed with Maven (with the NetBeans Maven plugins). A Maven Repository with all NetBeans modules as Maven modules is available at http://bits.netbeans.org/maven2, so dependencies on NetBeans Platform modules can easily be defined by an XML entry.

Besides Maven, numerous annotations contribute to the independence of a given IDE, since by now, many declarative configuration entries have been created by corresponding wizards. But to compile them manually is complex and error-prone. The corresponding configuration entries and configuration files are created automatically.

Because of the Maven support available for the Eclipse IDE, the way has been cleared for using the NetBeans Platform.

Installing Eclipse IDE

This chapter assumes you have a current version of Eclipse installed. You can get a distribution at http://www.eclipse.org/downloads, though this does not contain support for Maven projects yet. You can install the support for Maven projects with the *M2Eclipse* feature.

The easiest way to receive the M2Eclipse feature is through the *Eclipse Marketplace*. In order to do this just activate *Help ➤ Eclipse Marketplace*. Choose the *Eclipse Marketplace* catalog. All available features will be displayed on the following page. After that you can install *Maven Integration for Eclipse* on the *Install* button. Now that the necessary plugins are determined (see Figure 38-1) close the wizard with *Finish*.

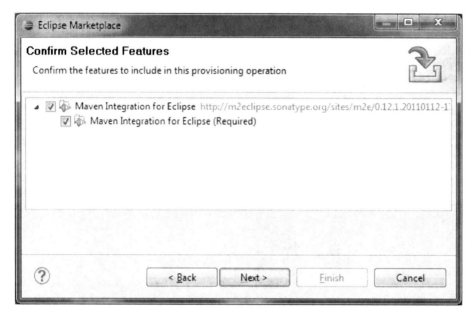

Figure 38-1. Installation of the M2Eclipse feature

After you have installed the Maven feature the next step is to take care that the Eclipse IDE gets started with the Virtual Machine of the JDK, because the Maven plugin uses libraries out of the JDK. You can adapt the *eclipse.ini* file which you can find in the root directory of the Eclipse distribution. In this file you can indicate the Virtual Machine you want to use with the vm parameter as follows:

```
-vm
C:\Program Files\Java\jdk1.6.0_23\bin\javaw.exe
```

This parameter must be indicated in front of the vmargs parameter.

Creating a NetBeans Platform Application

Now that your Eclipse IDE can deal with Maven projects, you can create your NetBeans Platform-based application in Eclipse. To do this call up *File ➤ New ➤ Other...* then choose *Maven* in the category *Maven Project* wizard. Leave the option *Create a simple project* deactivated as you want to choose a special Maven archetype on the subsequent page. This archetype creates the basic structure for a NetBeans Platform application. You get the required *netbeans-platform-app* archetype by filtering in the *Nexus Indexer* catalog for platform, as shown in Figure 38-2.

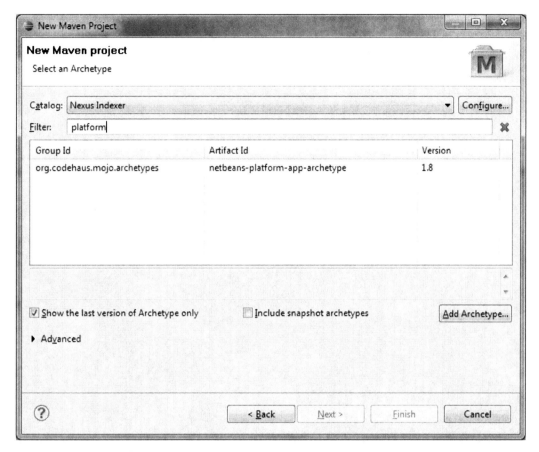

Figure 38-2. Choice of the NetBeans Platform application archetype

Choose this archetype. On the subsequent page you have to choose the group ID, artifact ID, and the version for the application to apply. This package is only used for the branding module. Finally, you determine the NetBeans Platform version to use with the feature `netbeansVersion`. Under `http://bits.netbeans.org/maven2/org/netbeans/cluster/platform` you can check which versions are available through the standard repository. Press *Finish* to create the NetBeans Platform Maven project. (See Figure 38-3.)

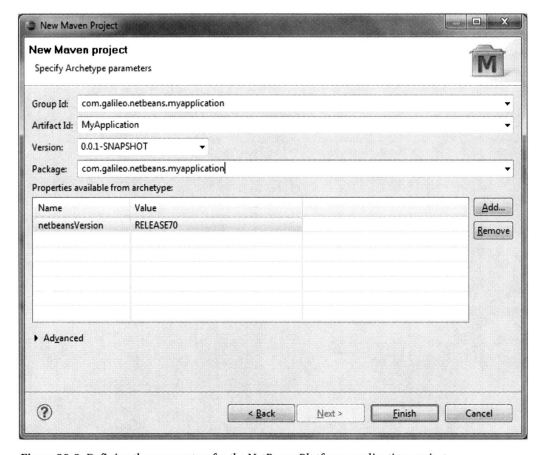

Figure 38-3. Defining the parameters for the NetBeans Platform application project

As described in Chapter 37, three projects will be created by Maven. One project (in the example here named *MyApplication*) represents the parent POM file. Additionally, two Maven module projects which refer to the parent project will be created. One represents the NetBeans Platform with its modules (*application*), the other represents the branding modules (*branding*).

Creating NetBeans Platform Modules

Now you can add a first application module to the base for the NetBeans Platform application that was created above. In order to do so, you can again draw on a wizard. Call the context menu of the parent project in the package explorer (e.g., *MyApplication*) and choose *Maven ➤ New Maven Module Project* (note: if you use the menu instead of the context menu the parent POM file can get overwritten).

On the first page you define a name for the module you want to create. It should be automatically referred to the parent project. Leave the option *Create a simple project* deactivated, because you want to choose a specific NetBeans module archetype on the following wizard page.

You can find the *nbm-archetype* in the *Nexus Indexer* catalog—you can filter the listed items for *nbm*. Choose the *nbm-archetype* now (see Figure 38-4).

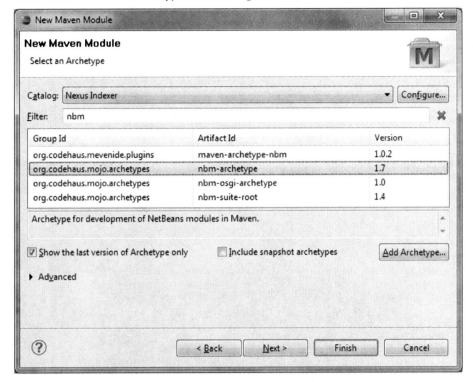

Figure 38-4. Choose the nbm-archetype to create a NetBeans module

On the last wizard page, the group ID should already be preoccupied by the parent project's value. Please define the version of the currently valid module and the base package used. There are no properties listed for this project type, though you must define the property netbeansVersion. This way you specify an existing NetBeans version (see Figure 38-5).

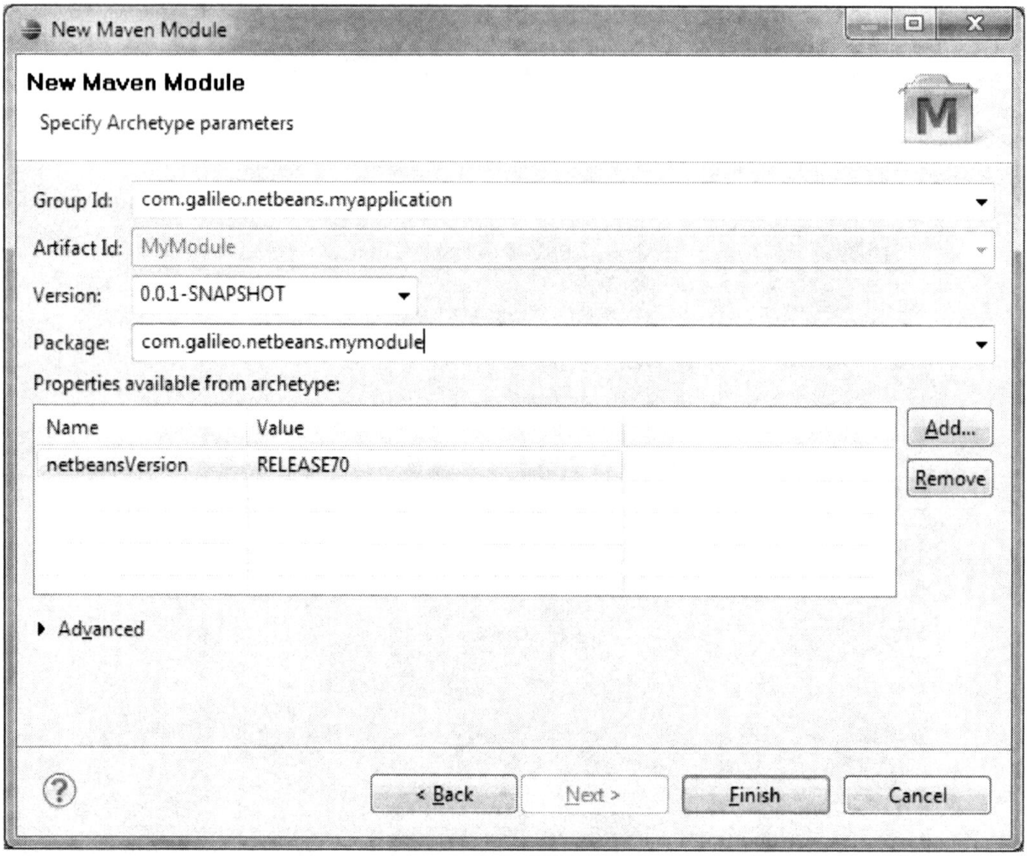

Figure 38-5. Defining the parameters for the NetBeans Platform module project

Finally, the application module is created and automatically added to the parent POM file when you press the *Finish* button. So the whole application can later be automatically created as a unit. The parent POM file refers to the module POM file; the parent POM file inherits the settings and features of the module POM file.

Add Dependencies

In order to be able to get access to classes of other modules, you must define a dependency in the POM file. This is also valid for the usage of classes of the NetBeans Platform modules. If you indicate group ID, artifact ID, and version it is possible to define the dependency in the POM file manually. Alternatively, you can click *Maven ➤ Add Dependency* from the context menu of the module concerned. There you can search for modules and, by pressing *OK*, you can add the chosen dependency. (See Figure 38-6.)

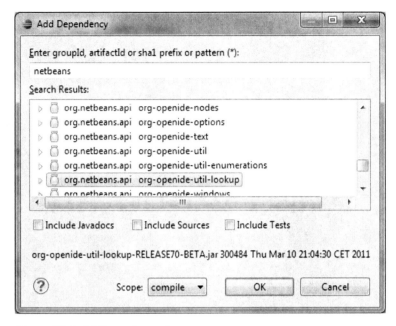

Figure 38-6. Adding a dependency

Starting and Executing an Application

Next I will show you how you can create and start the application as a whole. You can use the standard Maven build phase *install* to create the application. To execute it, choose *Run As* ➤ *Maven install* on the parent project.

To start the application out of the Eclipse IDE, you can use the goal *nbm:run-platform* of the NetBeans Maven plugin. You establish a *Run Configuration* by pressing *Run* ➤ *Run Configurations*. Double-click *Maven Build* and a new configuration will be created. Give it a name (such as *Start Platform*) and define the root directory. The root directory is the *application* project which is automatically created and which represents the NetBeans Platform itself. You can choose the project by pressing the *Browse Workspace...* button. Enter *nbm:run-platform* at *Goals*, accept the settings with *Apply*. Click *Run* to start the application. (See Figure 38-7.)

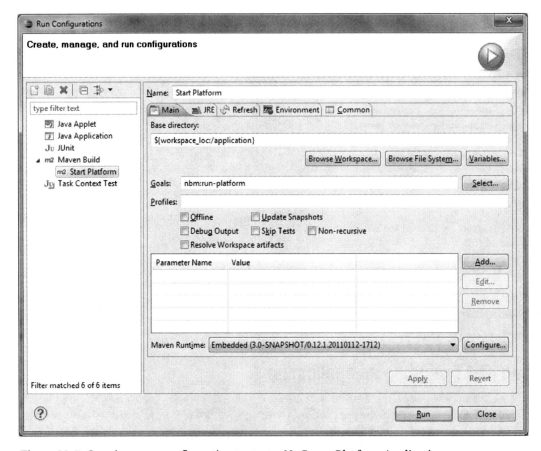

Figure 38-7. Creating a run configuration to start a NetBeans Platform Application

The NetBeans Maven plugin achieves many other goals. Among them, it enables you to create a ZIP distribution. In the section *Creating and Executing the Application* in Chapter 37 you can read which goals are provided. Analogous to these goals you can install a run configuration which you can comfortably use out of the Eclipse IDE.

Summary

Developing NetBeans Platform applications is not just reserved for NetBeans IDE users anymore. Maven support makes the use of NetBeans Platform in the Eclipse IDE very simple. You saw in this chapter how to set up your Eclipse IDE to create, develop and start Maven-based NetBeans Platform applications.

From Eclipse to NetBeans

This chapter describes the basic properties and functions of the NetBeans IDE. The chapter should help facilitate the migration from the Eclipse IDE to the Net Beans IDE, and make it easier to start working with the NetBeans Platform.

The NetBeans IDE

This section introduces techniques, fundamental characteristics, and functions of the NetBeans IDE. It helps smooth the transition from the Eclipse IDE to the NetBeans IDE, and provides an introduction to the NetBeans Platform.

Where Can I find What?

Table 39-1 provides a basic overview of where you can find the windows and functions you know from the Eclipse IDE, within the NetBeans IDE.

Table 39-1. The NetBeans IDE Equivalents for Eclipse Components

Eclipse Component	NetBeans Menu Item
Project Explorer/ Package Explorer	*Window ➤ Projects*
Projects/ Navigator	*Window ➤ Files*
Outline	*Window ➤ Navigating ➤ Navigator*
Properties	*Window ➤ Properties*
Console	*Window ➤ Output ➤ Output*
Problems/ Task List	*Window ➤ Tasks*
Javadoc	*Window ➤ Other ➤ Javadoc*
Error Log	*View ➤ IDE Log*

Plug-in Registry	*Tools* ➤ *Plugins*
Preferences	*Tools* ➤ *Options*

Handling Projects

In the NetBeans IDE, mapping keyboard shortcuts to provided functionalities is done via a *keymap*. This keymap is viewed and edited under *Tools* ➤ *Options* ➤ *Keymap*. That means you can adapt the actions to your own needs. Better yet, is that several keymaps can be managed in parallel. The NetBeans IDE provides an Eclipse keymap out of the box, making it possible to switch to Eclipse profile (also under *Tools* ➤ *Options* ➤ *Keymap*) and use the well-known shortcuts further on. Surely, this makes it much easier, especially for advanced Eclipse users.

Something often missed by Eclipse users in the NetBeans IDE is the *Perspectives* feature. However, a module providing the perspective feature is available at *http://plugins.netbeans.org*. Thus, you can use perspectives in the NetBeans IDE. This module can be downloaded and installed through the *Plugin Manager* (*Tools* ➤ *Plugins*).

From Eclipse Plugin to NetBeans Module

The concept of a plugin in the Eclipse world is equivalent to a NetBeans module. As in the Eclipse IDE, the NetBeans IDE offers a wizard providing the basic structure for a module in a few clicks. Perform this via *File* ➤ *New Project…* ➤ *NetBeans Modules* ➤ *Module*.

While creating a plugin with the Eclipse IDE, several parameters must be declared from the beginning. Among them is the activator, the GUI, and if you want to create a rich client application with the new plugin. The NetBeans IDE Module wizard takes a more general approach. In all three points specified before, decisions can be made later on whether the functionality is needed. An activator - called a NetBeans module installer (more on this later on) - can be added anytime via a separate wizard. This wizard is found under *File* ➤ *New File…* ➤ *Module Development* ➤ *Installer / Activator*. Also, there is no need to bother about whether the module will come with a graphic interface. On this point, separate wizards are available, and you can use them later as needed. One of the most important wizards is the *Window* wizard, for the construction of windows, which are docked and administered in the NetBeans window system. Start this wizard via *File* ➤ *New File…* ➤ *Module Development* ➤ *Window*. You can decide whether to provide a rich client application that the module will be a part of, or whether this module is to become an extension of an already existing application. Although the module wizard asks whether a standalone module or an application module is needed, this is easily changed in the *Properties* dialog of a module, or simply through adding and removing the module from a NetBeans Platform application.

For modules to become self-contained rich client applications, a NetBeans Platform Application project is needed. This project is a container for your modules, and is responsible for branding your application. To create a NetBeans Platform application, a wizard is also provided. Find it under *File* ➤ *New Project…* ➤ *NetBeans Modules* ➤ *NetBeans Platform Application*. Both new and existing modules can be added to the new application. The range of NetBeans modules used by your application, and hence used by your modules, is determined under *Properties* ➤ *Libraries*. Your application (or your modules) is by no means limited to NetBeans Platform modules. Arbitrary NetBeans IDE modules can be added to your application.

Plugin Lifecycle and Events

An Eclipse plugin may contain an *activator*. This class extends the abstract class Plugin or AbstractUIPlugin, depending on whether the plugin contains graphic elements or not. This optional class serves as the conceptual representation of the plugin. Containing no application logic, it mainly reacts to distinguished events; for instance, the methods start() and stop() specified by the interface BundleActivator and implemented by the classes Plugin and AbstractUIPlugin. The methods are called by the Eclipse Platform when the plugin is loaded or closed. By overwriting these methods, special platform-specific tasks can be executed at these times. An Activator in its simplest form looks like that shown in Listing 39-1.

Listing 39-1. Activator Class of an Eclipse Plugin

```
import org.eclipse.core.runtime.Plugin;
import org.osgi.framework.BundleContext;

public class Activator extends Plugin {
    private static Activator plugin;

    public void start(BundleContext context) throws Exception {
        super.start(context);
        plugin = this;
    }

    public void stop(BundleContext context) throws Exception {
        plugin = null;
        super.stop(context);
    }

    public static Activator getDefault() {
        return plugin;
    }
}
```

The counterpart to the Eclipse plugin activator is the module installer of a NetBeans module. This module installer is optional. The NetBeans platform instantiates an installer during module startup. The installer extends the class ModuleInstall (see Listing 39-2).

This class specifies the methods restored() and close(), which are equivalent to methods in the BundleActivator interface. Also available are validate(), for the examination of the starting conditions; closing(), for the examination of stop conditions; and uninstalled(), for uninstallation of the module. As with an activator, these methods can be overwritten and used as required.

Listing 39-2. The Counterpart to the Activator Is a NetBeans Module Installer.

```
import org.openide.modules.ModuleInstall;

public class Installer extends ModuleInstall {

    @Override
    public void restored() {
        // module started
    }

    @Override
    public void close() {
        // module stopped
    }

    public static Installer getDefault() {
        return findObject(Installer.class, true);
    }
}
```

While the activator of an Eclipse plugin is automatically created by a new plugin project, the installer can be created anytime with the Module Installer wizard, found under *File ➤ New File... ➤ Module Development ➤ Installer / Activator*. Thus, the installer is also registered in the manifest file. You can find more detailed information on this in Chapter 3.

Plugin Information

In addition to to starting and stopping plugins, the activator class has other functionalities. It can, for example, provide plugin and manifest information via a Bundle object. Information on NetBeans modules is offered by the NetBeans Platform with a ModuleInfo object. Instances for all modules within the application are available on the Lookup. Out of this set you can retrieve the ModuleInfo instance of your own module. You can provide this instance to the module users over the installer class with the help of the getModule() method, as shown in Listing 39-3.

Listing 39-3. Providing the ModuleInfo Instance, Which Contains Information on the Module

```
import org.openide.modules.ModuleInfo;
import org.openide.modules.ModuleInstall;
import org.openide.util.Lookup;

public class Installer extends ModuleInstall {
    public static final String MODULE_ID = "com.galileo.netbeans.module";
    private ModuleInfo info = null;
    ...
    public ModuleInfo getModuleInfo() {
        if (info == null) {
            Collection<? extends ModuleInfo> all =
                Lookup.getDefault().lookupAll(ModuleInfo.class);
            for (ModuleInfo mi : all) {
```

```
            if (mi.getCodeNameBase().equals(MODULE_ID)) {
                info = mi; break;
            }
        }
    }
    return info;
    }
}
```

Alternatively, you can use the Auto Update Services API (see Chapter 25), which has access to all installed modules and their properties.

The class UpdateElement provides all module information such as name, version, category, or author. (See Listing 39-4.)

Listing 39-4, *Determine Module Information via the Update Manager.*

```
import org.netbeans.api.autoupdate.UpdateElement;
import org.netbeans.api.autoupdate.UpdateManager;
import org.netbeans.api.autoupdate.UpdateUnit;
...
public class Installer extends ModuleInstall {
    public static final String MODULE_ID = "com.galileo.netbeans.module";
    private static UpdateElement moduleInfo;
    ...
    public static UpdateElement getModuleInfo() {
        if (moduleInfo == null) {
            for (UpdateUnit unit : UpdateManager.getDefault().getUpdateUnits(
                UpdateManager.TYPE.MODULE)) {
                if (unit.getInstalled() != null
                    && unit.getInstalled().getCodeName().equals(MODULE_ID)) {
                    moduleInfo = unit.getInstalled();
                    break;
                }
            }
        }
        return moduleInfo;
    }
}
```

Images

Pictures and icons used within an application are not loaded over the installer, but over a central ImageUtilities class in the NetBeans Platform. This class provides the methods loadImage() and loadImageIcon() which should (preferably) be used. Behind them is an icon manager which manages the loaded images and icons and prevents a repeated loading of resources. Use it to load icons from all available modules. It is also possible to load localized resources, as in the following example. If the second parameter is set to true and there is an icon named *icon_de_DE.png* available, then it is loaded (if the locale setting of application is de_DE):

```
Image img = ImageUtilities.loadImage("resources/icon.png", true);
```

Resources

Any plugin resource can be accessed by using the FileLocator class in Eclipse. To simply load resources from a NetBeans module, you extend the Installer class by the method getModuleResource() (see Listing 39-5). Use the module classloader that has access to all module resources. This returns a URL which, using the URLMapper class, maps to the FileObject instance.

Listing 39-5. *The getModuleResource() Method Helps Load Arbitrary Module Resources.*

```
import java.net.URL;
import org.openide.filesystems.FileObject;
import org.openide.filesystems.URLMapper;
import org.openide.modules.ModuleInstall;

public class Installer extends ModuleInstall {
    ...
    public FileObject getModuleResource(String path) {
        URL url = getClass().getClassLoader().getResource(path);
        FileObject resource = URLMapper.findFileObject(url);
        return resource;
    }
}
```

The FileObject class provides extensive methods for working with the resource. The following example demonstrates this by loading content of the *myprops.properties* file out of the *resources* directory of the module into the Properties object.

```
public final class TestAction implements ActionListener {
    public void actionPerformed(ActionEvent e) {
        FileObject res = Installer.getDefault().getModuleResource(
                                "resources/myprops.properties");
        Properties props = new Properties();
        try {
            props.load(res.getInputStream());
            System.out.println("Value:" + props.getProperty("key"));
        } catch(Exception ex) {}
    }
}
```

Settings

Plugin-specific settings, used internally as well as by the user, are managed via a Preferences object or a IPreferenceStore object in Eclipse RCP, which is provided by the Activator class. The NetBeans Platform takes a slightly different approach. For managing settings it contains an implementation of the Java Preferences API. Access to a Preferences instance is obtained via the NbPreferences class. An advantage of this implementation is that data is stored in the NetBeans Platform user directory. A distinction is made between module-specific data and application-specific data. The root() method gives access to settings saved in the *config/Preferences.properties* file. The forModule() method, on the other hand, handles access to data found in a module-specific properties file. For example, if the code name base is com.galileo.netbeans.module, settings will be stored in the *config/Preferences/com/galileo/netbeans/module.properties* file.

```
NbPreferences.forModule(MyClass.class).put("key", "value");
NbPreferences.root().put("key", "value");
```

You can find more detailed information on this topic in Chapter 20.

Application Lifecycle

The lifecycle of Eclipse RCP applications is handled by an `IApplication` instance. It implements the `start()` and `stop()` methods. The first is responsible for starting the application, typically used for creating and opening the main window. The `stop()` method handles the shutting down of the application, where the workbench is closed and other application-specific tasks are carried out. NetBeans Platform applications unfortunately do not have such a comfortable lifecycle management—although, on the other hand, that considerably simplifies development. For example, the main window opens and closes on its own, without coding. Most aspects relating to the lifecycle of an application are handled within individual modules and dealt with via a module installer. Another possibility is to react to the closing of the whole application, rather than the shutdown of individual modules; this is done via the abstract class `LifecycleManager`. The default implementation of the `LifecycleManager` class, provided by the NetBeans Platform, is responsible for the proper shutdown of the application. You can insert your own implementation of this class before the default implementation, so application-specific tasks are handled as the application shuts down. It is important not to forget to call the default implementation from your own implementation. What such a class can look like and how you explicitly shut down your application with the `LifecycleManager` is described in Chapter 8.

Views and Editors

While the Eclipse workbench displays and docks windows of two types—*views* and *editors*—the NetBeans Platform handles these types with one window type. A window displayed within the NetBeans window system is a *Top Component*; the implementation of a window is derived from the `TopComponent` class. This superclass integrates itself as a window into the NetBeans window system and makes a great deal of information available, giving access to its current state as well as its lifecycle. Similar to how views and editors in an Eclipse application are organized, via the relevant extension points, top components are declaratively made available, via the layer file, within the `Mode` folder. A mode is a container for top components. Here, let's return to the view and editor distinction, since modes can be one of these types. Top components are created within one of these modes (see Figure 9-5). A mode's size, position, and type are described in an XML file. In this way you also have the opportunity to register your own modes in the layer file with the corresponding extension point (see Chapter 10 for further information). However, top components are not required to be registered within a mode, where they are displayed in default mode. As with the Eclipse workbench, the user places top components in various positions while the application is running.

For the easy creation and registration of top components, the NetBeans IDE once again provides a very useful wizard. Choose *File* ➤ *New File...* ➤ *Module Development* ➤ *Window* and start using it. The wizard offers you the possibility of configuring a top component and assigning it to a mode. Detailed information about this and other topics relating to the design of the user interface can be found in Part 2.

Summary

This chapter assumed you were an Eclipse user and introduced you to the NetBeans IDE as a tool, and to the NetBeans Platform as a desktop framework. The chapter started by looking at the most commonly used functions and windows in Eclipse and showing where they can be used in the NetBeans IDE. You learned how to adapt the keymap to Eclipse settings. Next, we compared Eclipse plugins to NetBeans modules and compared the terminology of the two platforms, describing the major similarities and differences between them.

IntelliJ IDEA and the NetBeans Platform

The Java development environment IntelliJ IDEA of JetBrains (http://jetbrains.com/idea) is now freely available with the community edition. It provides another alternative for developing NetBeans Platform applications thanks to the integrated Maven project support. In this chapter, I will give both beginners and professionals some tips for using IntelliJ IDEA to successfully set up of a NetBeans Platform-based application.

Presettings

Maven is not part of IntelliJ IDEA. So before you can create a Maven project you have to provide a Maven distribution. You can download the current version at http://maven.apache.org as a zip file. Just unpack it at the desired location. This directory with the Maven distribution has to be made available to IntelliJ IDEA. You can do this either directly in the settings of the IDE under *Settings ➤ Maven* or through the environment variable *M2_HOME* which is usually in Maven. By default, IntelliJ IDEA uses the path that has been defined with this variable. Expect to find the Maven settings file (*settings.xml*) in the user directory by default under *.m2/settings.xml*. Additionally, *.m2/repository* is used in the user directory as local repository.

Creating a NetBeans Platform Application

If Maven is installed and the installation is made known to IntelliJ IDEA you can directly start and set up a NetBeans Platform application project. To do so, call *File ➤ New Project...* and choose the option *Create project from scratch*. On the following page you can give a name to the project to be created and you can define the storage location. Activate the option *Create module* and choose the type *Maven Module*. (See Figure 40-1.)

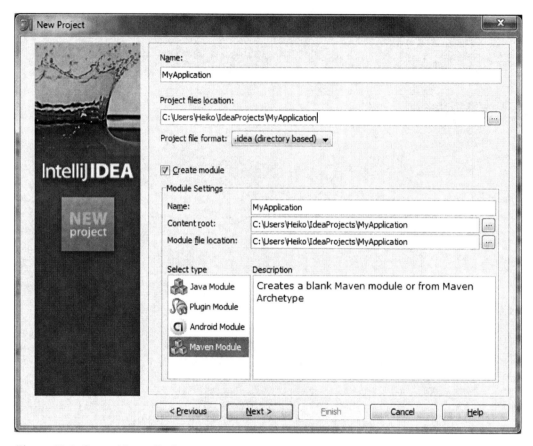

Figure 40-1. Create Maven Project

Go to the next page by clicking *Next*. There you can assign the group ID, artifact ID, and the version for the new project. Because you do not just want to create an empty standard Maven project, but a NetBeans Platform application project, activate the option *Create from archetype*. Choose the latest version of the archetype *netbeans-platform-app-archetype* which belongs to the group *org.codehaus.mojo.archetypes* from the list. (See Figure 40-2.)If it is not listed you can manually add this archetype with the button *Add archetype...*, the named artifact, and group ID. You can see which versions are provided in the official Maven repository under
`http://search.maven.org/#search|ga|1|netbeans-platform-app-archetype`.

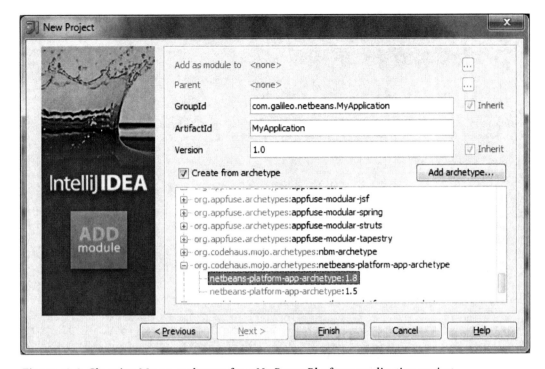

Figure 40-2. Choosing Maven archetype for a NetBeans Platform application project

Complete the wizard with *Finish* and Maven creates the basic structure of a NetBeans Platform application. Initially, that can take quite some time, because several Maven plugins have to be downloaded into the local repository. As already mentioned in Chapter 37, three Maven projects are created in practice: a superordinate parent project which is supposed to bundle the whole NetBeans Platform application, a project for the NetBeans Platform module, and another one for the branding module. These are subordinate to the parent project and thus inherit the features of the POM file. This results in the project structure shown in Figure 40-3.

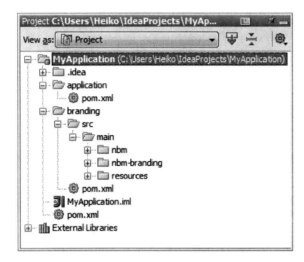

Figure 40-3. *Project structure of a Maven NetBeans Platform application*

In another step, you can now add one or more Maven NetBeans modules to this Maven project. Do this with *File ➤ New Module...* in the menu or with *New ➤ Module* out of the context menu of the already created NetBeans Platform application project. Choose the option *Create project from scratch* and on the following page choose the type *Maven Module*. Give a name to the module and ensure that the module is created in the directory of the parent project. In the next step you will see that the module is added to the parent project and that the module itself inherits from the parent project. You will also see that the group ID and the version are already taken from the parent POM file. You can also define other values optionally; to do so, deactivate the option *Inherit*. There is also a special Maven archetype for creating a NetBeans module. This is the *nbm-archetype* archetype out of the group *org.codehaus.mojo.archetypes*. Choose it from the list or add it manually with *Add archetype*. (See Figure 40-4.)

Figure 40-4. *Choosing Maven archetype for a NetBeans module project*

Complete the wizard with *Finish*. The module is automatically created by Maven and added as a module to the NetBeans Platform project. Within this and other modules you can implement your application logic. There are several classes and APIs available that are described this book; you just need to add the referring NetBeans Platform module as dependency to your application module. In the following section you will learn how to easily search for Platform modules and how to add them as dependencies.

Defining Dependencies

As you already know from the preceding chapters, you can use classes of a NetBeans module only after setting a dependency on the referring module. Do this for a Maven project by adding a Maven dependency to the POM file. IntelliJ IDEA provides a searching assistant for adding a dependency entry.

To get there, open the referring POM file and call *Code ➤ Generate*. Then choose *Dependency* out of the popup menu to open the assistant. You can search for netbeans, for example, choose a special NetBeans module, and add it as dependency. (See Figure 40-5.)

Figure 40-5. Searching for NetBeans modules and adding them as a dependency

You can directly add a dependency entry into the POM file. Besides you can also implement a dependency when implementing your classes out of the editor. Use a class of a module on which no dependency was defined before. This way, an error is displayed in the editor. Then using *Alt+Enter* choose out of the popup menu and add the necessary dependency with the artifact searching assistant.

Building and Executing an Application

Now that you know how to create the basic structure of a NetBeans Platform application, add application modules to it, and add dependencies for using the APIs of the NetBeans Platform modules, you just need to be able to build and execute the NetBeans Platform application and create a distribution.

The *Maven Projects* explorer (*Window ➤ Tool Windows ➤ Maven Projects*) is quite helpful here. First, the whole application with the Maven build phase *install* has to be installed and copied into the local repository. To do this, open the folder *Lifecycle* of the parent project (in the example *MyApplication - NB App Parent*) and start the process with the context menu or by a double-click.

A NetBeans Platform application is executed by means of the Maven plugin *nbm-maven-plugin*. For this the plugin provides the goal *nbm:run-platform*. Please note that you cannot start the application with the parent project; you must do so over the automatically created *NB App* module, which represents the NetBeans Platform itself. You find all the goals provided by the plugin in the *Maven Projects* explorer (see Figure 40-6). You will also find the goal *nbm:standalone-zip*, with which you can finally create your application as a ZIP distribution.

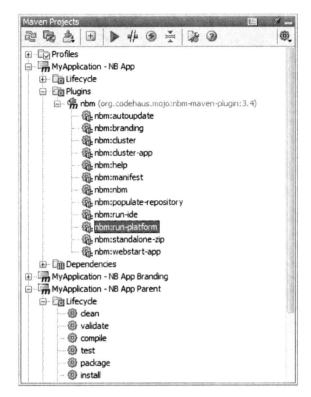

Figure 40-6. Creating and executing the application by means of the Maven project explorer

Alternatively, you can set a run configuration with *Run ➤ Edit Configurations* and directly start a build from the toolbar. With a run configuration, you can also automatically execute the build phase *install* before the goal *nbm:run-platform*. This way you can create and execute your application with one button.

Summary

The IntelliJ IDEA Java development environment of JetBrains is now available freely as a community edition. In this chapter you learned how to use this IDE for developing NetBeans Platform applications.

NetBeans Swing GUI Builder

Probably the most obvious feature of a rich client application is the user interface, which determines the quality of an application based on an intuitive and user-friendly structure of functions and data. It can be a challenge to create a user interface with only a source code editor, however. Not only do you constantly have to imagine the structure of the components, but the result often looks completely different than expected.

In this respect the NetBeans IDE, which contains a powerful Swing GUI Builder, proves to be very innovative. You can create a whole user interface with drag-and-drop and a choice of given parameters. In other words, you do not need to write even a single line of code.

For example, the GUI Builder is automatically used for creating a top component, an options panel, or a wizard for a NetBeans Platform application; you can also create completely generic components. Add them to the palette and you can use them in any other components again. This chapter will first explain a few details about the structure of the GUI Builder; later we will take a more detailed look at the most important features.

Structure of the GUI Builder

When editing GUI components, the GUI Builder supports you with a lot of information and functions in different windows. The next section will give you an overview of those windows and their use.

Editor

The *Editor* (*Window* ➤ *Editor*) is a central part of the GUI Builder. It provides two different views. You can alternate between the *Design* view and the *Source* view. In the Design view, the actual creation of GUI components takes place. You can drag components from the Palette into your Design view on your component where you can individually edit it. In the Source view, you can implement the action of buttons, for example. (See Figure 41-1.)

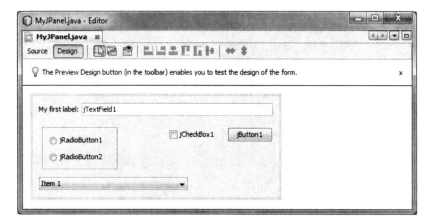

Figure 41-1. Editor of the GUI Builder with Design and Source view

Changing to the Source view you will see areas with code that is automatically produced by the GUI Builder. These so-called *Guarded Blocks* are marked grey and cannot be edited; changes can only be made on the user interface of the GUI Builder. At some places it is possible to insert custom code.

Palette

As soon as you are in the Design view implementing a GUI component in the Editor, the *Palette* window (*Window ➤ Palette*) provides all available Swing and AWT components structured in categories (see Figure 41-2). You can drag-and-drop it into the editor on your own component.

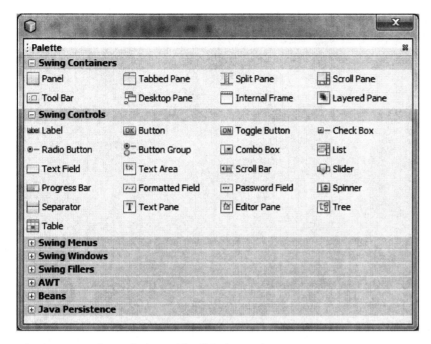

Figure 41-2. Palette window with all Swing and AWT components

---

■ **Note** With the Palette you can not only use the components that are available by default, but you can add your own components and drag-and-drop them in your own application. Right-clicking in the Palette window calls the *Palette Manager*, in which you can import new components from JAR files, registered libraries, or a project. You can also create new categories, structure them differently, or delete categories with the Palette Manager. That way you always keep track.

Inspector

All visible and even invisible components are shown in the *Inspector* window (*Window* ➤ *Navigating* ➤ *Inspector*) in a hierarchic tree structure (see Figure 41-3). When choosing an entry, the referring component in the Editor is selected as well. The Inspector helps you keep track even in complex GUI components. The Inspector is especially helpful when editing a JPanel component which is used as an invisible container.

Figure 41-3. Inspector window for navigating and accessing single components

Properties

Each and every Swing or AWT component offers a multiplicity of possible settings which are all displayed in the *Properties* window (*Window ➤ Properties*). A great advantage of this is that for a lot of features with set values, the desired value can be chosen from a list. Special editors are provided for a lot more features, such as the configuration of the border of a container. Furthermore, the Properties window provides additional views about bindings of features (*Binding*), their actions (*Events*), and user-specific code (*Code*). You do not just get an extensive overview, but a very easy edit functionality at the same time. (See Figure 41-4.) We will come back to the separate views later.

Figure 41-4. *Overview of the features of a selected AWT or Swing component with a lot of possibilities for editing*

Components and Layout

This section will describe how a GUI Builder component is structured and how you can place and structure additional components on it.

Forms

Components created with the GUI Builder are called Forms. There are certain wizards provided for creating a Form under *File ➤ New File ➤ Swing GUI Forms* and *AWT GUI Forms*. Surely, for you as a NetBeans Platform application developer, the *JPanel Form* wizard is the most common for implementing sub-components. For developing top-level components, a special Form wizard is provided under *File ➤ New File ➤ Module Development ➤ Window* (see Chapter 10).

A Form is marked by a *.form* file besides a *.java* file with reserved code blocks. It has the same name and the same directory as the *.java* file. The GUI Builder saves all information about layout and components used and the Java source code that is generated out of it or changes in this XML file.

Design Strategy

The GUI Builder follows a so-called *Free Design* strategy. Whereas you are used to placing the components in a certain set area of a layout manager, in the Design view of the NetBeans GUI Builder you can place your components anywhere. Then it automatically detects the necessary layout attributes and automatically creates the code. The GroupLayout manager is the basis for that. You can arrange your components as they will be displayed in the application. Furthermore, you have the ability to preview them with the *Preview Design* button in the toolbar of the Design view. This way you can test how your component reacts to a change of size.

After a short time working with the enormously intuitive Free Design of the GUI Builder you will hardly miss other layout managers, although you can set alternative layout managers for special purposes. You can choose from the following popular layout managers with a right-click in the Form on *Set Layout*:

- Free Design
- Absolute Layout
- Border Layout
- Box Layout
- Card Layout
- Flow Layout
- Grid Bag Layout
- Grid Layout
- Null Layout

Alignment and Anchoring

One great advantage of the GUI Builder is the support for placing components.Reference lines are displayed (depending on the components already added to the form) to enable the arrangement of new components. A component is automatically arranged according to the reference lines when brought closer to them; you can quickly create an exactly arranged and structured user interface. (See Figure 41-5.)

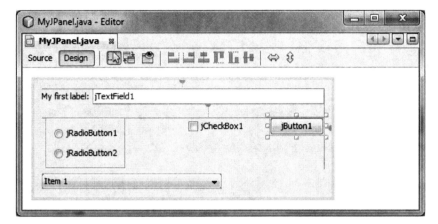

Figure 41-5. Automatic alignment and anchoring of components

So-called *anchoring points* are defined for determining the layout manager behavior when changing the size of a window. Components are either anchored to components next to them or to margins of the form. In Figure 41-5 you see how the button *jButton1* is anchored to the margin of the form and to the text field *jTextField1*. The text field itself is anchored to the upper margin of the form; that is, the size of the form is changed below and thus the button's position is not changed. If the Form is made bigger on the right side, the button "sticks" to the right border. The GUI Builder suggests anchoring points depending on the location (marked visibly in a half-round shape). You can change them with *Anchor* in the context menu, though.

Adapting Components

You have learned how to place and change the place of different components within a Form. Now you also want to adapt these components.

Text and Variable Name

The components which you drag from the Palette to its Form get a default caption referring to the types' name. The variables are named the same way. You can adapt the caption either with *F2* or with *Edit Text* out of the context menu. You can also adapt the variable name in the context menu with *Change Variable Name*.

Application-Specific Code

In the section *Palette* I wrote that there is at first no possibility of editing the code produced by the GUI Builder. However, the *Code Customize,* shown in Figure 41-6, makes this possible. You can call the Code Customizer for each component out of the context menu with *Customize Code*. Doing this, you can add your user-specific code at different locations of the initializing and of the declaration code. Furthermore, it is possible to let the component create either locally or as a field. In that last case you can define additional attributes referring to the access or the storage.

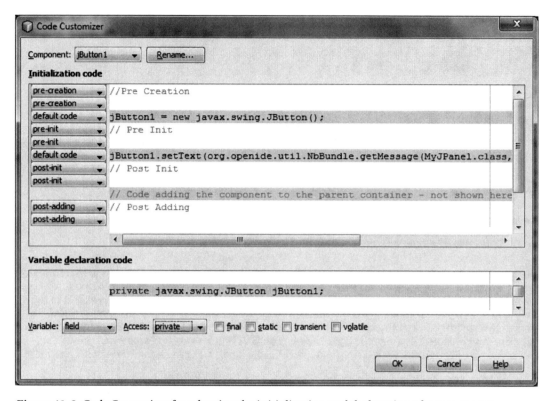

Figure 41-6. Code Customizer for adapting the initialization and declaration of a component

Earlier I mentioned that the Properties window provides a special Code view (*Code*). This offers additional opportunities to intervene besides those options shown in Figure 41-6. Doing this, you can not only easily edit the code, but at the same time you also get a complete overview of all user-specific extensions of the code.

Actions

Actions are an elementary part of a user interface. Actions shall be executed in reaction to an event triggered by the user. Such an event can be a mouse click or pressing a key, for example. You can define an individual action for each event of a component. The GUI Builder connects event and action for you. You can choose from all available events in the context menu (*Events*). Clicking a certain event, a listener is automatically registered for it. This listener calls the method. Then you can implement its body in the Source view.

An example will illustrate this. An action will be implemented for the *actionPerformed* event (so clicking on the button) for the button shown in Figure 41-5. This is why you call the following entry out of the context menu of the button *jButton1*: *Events* ➤ *Action* ➤ *actionPerformed*. The editor automatically changes into the Source view and jumps into the referring method which is called with this event. In Listing 41-1 it is the method jButton1ActionPerformed().

Listing 41-1. Implementation of an Action. Only the Methods Body Can Be Edited.

```
private void jButton1ActionPerformed(java.awt.event.ActionEvent evt) {
    jTextField1.setText("Hello World");
}
```

If you look at the automatically generated code block in the Source view, you will find the registration of a listener (as shown in Listing 41-2) which calls the method with the actual action.

Listing 41-2. Automatic Registration of an Event Listener by the GUI Builder

```
jButton1.addActionListener(new java.awt.event.ActionListener() {
    public void actionPerformed(java.awt.event.ActionEvent evt) {
        jButton1ActionPerformed(evt);
    }
});
```

You can easily get an overview about which events are registered and which other events are provided. Get this overview in the event view (*Events*) of the Properties window. Furthermore, you can also register, delete, or rename multiple *handlers* or jump to their position in the source code. (See Figure 41-7.)

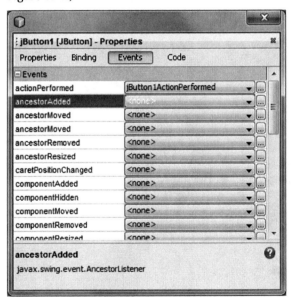

Figure 41-7. Events view for managing the actions handler of a certain component

Beans Binding

On the one hand, you can bind GUI components to a data source with the Beans Binding Framework (JSR 295). On the other hand, you can keep features of different GUI components synchronous with each other. These are tasks which have to be implemented in nearly every rich-client application. The Beans

Binding Framework together with the NetBeans IDE or the GUI Builder ensure that you only have to write a few lines of code.

I will demonstrate the advantages of the Beans Binding Framework and of the support by the GUI Builder with a typical example (shown in Figure 41-8) in which you take an already existing database and create entity classes for its tables. Then you bind the data from the database to a table in a NetBeans Platform application. Furthermore, you bind a detail view to a table. Doing so, some changes both in the table and in the detail view should be possible.

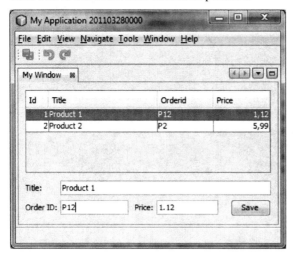

Figure 41-8. Beans Binding example application

Binding Table and Data Source

The first step is to create (or use an already existing) Java DB database. In the Service window you can easily create a new database over the context menu of the *Databases ➤ Java DB* node with *Create Database.* This is called *ProductDatabase* in this example. You add a table with the structure shown in Listing 41-3 to the database and then you create two more test data sets—you can add any number of entries later.

Listing 41-3. Table Structure and Test Data Sets

```
CREATE TABLE product (
    id INT NOT NULL PRIMARY KEY GENERATED ALWAYS AS IDENTITY,
    title   VARCHAR(50) NOT NULL,
    orderId VARCHAR(10) NOT NULL,
    price   DOUBLE      NOT NULL
);

INSERT INTO product (title, orderId, price) VALUES ('Product 1', 'P1', 1.49);
INSERT INTO product (title, orderId, price) VALUES ('Product 2', 'P2', 5.99);
```

Now you need an entity class for this table. However, you do not need to implement this entity class yourself, but can let it be created automatically by a wizard of the NetBeans IDE. For this, a Java class library project is necessary, though. Create it with *File ➤ New Project... ➤ Java ➤ Java Class Library.* You can then use the wizard in this project with *File ➤ New File... ➤ Persistence ➤ Entity Classes From Database* for implementing the necessary entity class. In the first step, select the database connection and after that the table *PRODUCT.* In the following step you deactivate the option for creating named queries and JAXB annotations. However, a persistence unit should be created. On the last page of the wizard, select java.util.List as *Collection Type* and deactivate the option *Attributes for Regenerating Tables,* because you build on an already existing table. Then, you create the class Product with *Finish.* This has getter and setter methods in addition to attributes which have JPA annotations. It will later be necessary to implement a listener logic for propagating a change of a Product instance to the table. The listeners have to be informed at all set methods with the firePropertyChange() method. (See Listing 41-4.)

Listing 41-4. Entity Class for the Table PRODUCT with Change Listener Logic with Which Changes in the Table Can Be Directly Shown

```
import java.beans.PropertyChangeListener;
import java.beans.PropertyChangeSupport;
import javax.persistence.Basic;
import javax.persistence.Column;
...
@Entity
@Table(name = "PRODUCT")
public class Product implements Serializable {
    private static final long serialVersionUID = 1L;

    @Id
    @GeneratedValue(strategy = GenerationType.IDENTITY)
    @Basic(optional = false)
    @Column(name = "ID")
    private Integer id;

    @Basic(optional = false)
    @Column(name = "TITLE")
    private String title;

    @Basic(optional = false)
    @Column(name = "ORDERID")
    private String orderid;

    @Basic(optional = false)
    @Column(name = "PRICE")
    private double price;

    private transient PropertyChangeSupport changeSupport = new PropertyChangeSupport(this);

    public Product() {
    }

    public Product(Integer id) {
        this.id = id;
    }
```

```java
public Product(
    Integer id, String title, String orderid, double price) {
    this.id = id;
    this.title = title;
    this.orderid = orderid;
    this.price = price;
}

public Integer getId() {
    return id;
}

public void setId(Integer id) {
    Integer oldId = this.id;
    this.id = id;
    changeSupport.firePropertyChange("id", oldId, id);
}

public String getTitle() {
    return title;
}

public void setTitle(String title) {
    String oldTitle = this.title;
    this.title = title;
    changeSupport.firePropertyChange("title", oldTitle, title);
}

public String getOrderid() {
    return orderid;
}

public void setOrderid(String orderid) {
    String oldOrderid = this.orderid;
    this.orderid = orderid;
    changeSupport.firePropertyChange("orderid", oldOrderid, orderid);
}

public double getPrice() {
    return price;
}

public void setPrice(double price) {
    double oldPrice = this.price;
    this.price = price;
    changeSupport.firePropertyChange("price", oldPrice, price);
}

public void addPropertyChangeListener(PropertyChangeListener listener) {
    changeSupport.addPropertyChangeListener(listener);
}
```

```
    public void removePropertyChangeListener(
        PropertyChangeListener listener) {
        changeSupport.removePropertyChangeListener(listener);
    }
}
```

The file *persistence.xml* was generated along with the entity class. The persistence unit is configured by this file. So this is where you can edit the connection parameters of the database when necessary. The name of the persistence unit is important; you will need it later to access the data. (See Listing 41-5.)

Listing 41-5. Configuration of the Persistence Unit in persistence.xml

```xml
<persistence ...>
  <persistence-unit name="MyEntitiesLibraryPU" transaction-type="RESOURCE_LOCAL">
    <provider>org.eclipse.persistence.jpa.PersistenceProvider</provider>
    <class>com.galileo.netbeans.myentities.Product</class>
    <properties>
      <property name="javax.persistence.jdbc.url"
          value="jdbc:derby://localhost:1527/ProductDatabase"/>
      <property name="javax.persistence.jdbc.password"
          value="password"/>
      <property name="javax.persistence.jdbc.driver"
          value="org.apache.derby.jdbc.ClientDriver"/>
      <property name="javax.persistence.jdbc.user"
          value="admin"/>
    </properties>
  </persistence-unit>
</persistence>
```

You can create the library project with *Build*. Then you come back to the NetBeans Platform. Create an application with *File* ➤ *New Project* ➤ *NetBeans Modules* ➤ *NetBeans Platform Application*. For this Platform application you have to include two additional modules. To do this, open the cluster *java* in *Properties* ➤ *Libraries* and add the two modules *Beans Binding integration* and *TopLink Essentials*. After that you can add a library wrapper module with the JAR file of the entity class which had been created before. This module will be called *My Entities*.

You need two more library wrapper modules for the connection to the database and for saving the objects. Add one for the database driver; this is the file *derbyclient.jar* which you find in the directory of the Java DB installation. Call this module *Java DB Driver*. You need another library wrapper module for *EclipseLink* as persistence provider. Add the two files *eclipselink-2.2.0.jar* and *eclipselink-javax.persistence-2.0.jar* out of the directory *java/modules/ext/eclipselink* of the NetBeans IDE installation to this module.

Now, there is just one more module missing: the actual application module. Call this *My Module*. You have to define the following dependencies first, so the interaction between those different modules can work:

- The module *My Entities* contains a dependency on the modules *EclipseLink* and *Java DB Driver*.

- The module *My Module* contains a dependency on the module *EclipseLink, My Entities,* and *Beans Binding integration*.

So far, you have installed the application so you can now add a top component to the module *My Module* with *File ➤ New File ➤ Module Development ➤ Window*. This top component should finally look like Figure 41-8. However, before adding the table and the text fields, you need a data source to which you can later bind the table.

To do this, open the context menu of the node *Other Components* in the Inspector window and then select *Add From Palette ➤ Java Persistence ➤ Entity Manager*. Then add a *Query* and a *Query Result* object out of the same category.

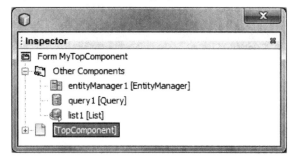

Figure 41-9. Adding and configuring data sources

Please keep the given order (it can be changed after adding over the context menu), because these objects are based on each other. Consequently, the objects have to be created in this order. These objects still have to be configured in the Properties window. Then select the referring object in the Inspector window to be able to adapt the following features:

- You have to define the value for the *persistenceUnit* for the *EntityManager* object. The name of the persistence unit had been determined by the wizard in the *persistence.xml* file before (see Listing 41-5). Use this name.

- You define the JPA query for the parameter *query* for the *Query* object with which the data is detected out of the database. For this example it is SELECT p FROM Product p. Select the name of the already created entity manager, entityManager1, for the parameter *entityManager*.

- For the List object (Query Result) select for the parameter *query* the query1 object which had been created before. Then in the Properties window change to the *Code* view; you can parameterize the list <Product> by indicating the *Type Parameters*.

Now, you can add a table, three labels, and text fields, as well as a button to the Form from the Palette as shown in Figure 41-8. You now come to the part accomplished by the Beans Binding Framework: filling the table (usually, you had to implement a data model first) and synchronously changing data between tables and text fields.

Call the context menu of the table and select *Bind ➤ elements*. Choose the list object list1 which had been created and parameterized before as *Binding Source*. Since you want to display all attributes you can finish the dialog (unchanged) with *OK*. This way, a data model for the table is automatically created, which you can adapt to your needs. To do so, call *Table Contents* in the context menu. In this dialog you can set numerous things individually under *Columns*. Among others, you can change the title or the order of separate columns. (See Figure 41-10.)

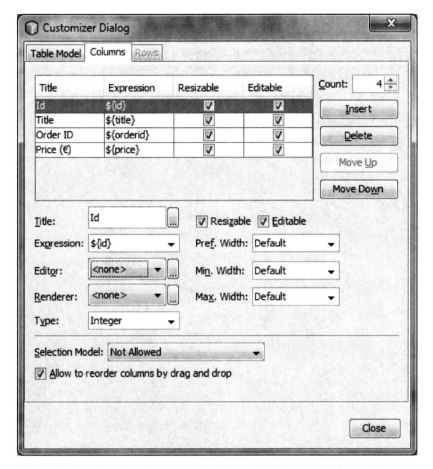

Figure 41-10. Adapting the automatically created data model for a table

Thus, the data source and the table which will create the data are connected. You can already start the application now and you will see that all the entries from the referring table are listed. Plus, you did not have to write a single line of code yourself. The Beans Binding Framework does a lot of work for you, including routine implementation tasks.

Bind Detail View to Table

You want to keep the data between the table and the text fields synchronous. If the entry is selected in the table, its data will be displayed in the text fields. If you now edit a value in the text fields, the value should also change in the table and in the data model. The other way around, if the table is changed, it should be shown in the text fields, too.

Starting from the single fields of the detail view you bind the referring value of the selected entry out of the table. To do this, call the context menu of the first text field, which will contain the title of the product, and choose *Bind ➤ text*. You now use the table which is named in the example as jTable1 as

Binding Source. Choose the desired attribute in the folder *selectedElement* as *Binding Expression.* (See Figure 41-11.)

Figure 41-11. Binding text field to source

You can define the update features in the tab *Advanced.* This means with *Always sync* you can determine that the changes are accepted in both directions. You can also determine at which event (such as typing in text) the updating will take place.

You can now analogously repeat this step of binding text fields to a data source for all remaining text fields. Then you can start the application. At the same time you can select table entries and edit them in the detail view. Looking into the database or restarting the application, you will quickly recognize that the changes have not been made persistent; you have to determine when the changes will be restored in the database. You now add the first line of code to the application.

You need a transaction to put the changes into the database. You directly create such a transaction in the constructor with the entity manager. To do this, change to the Source view and add the line in Listing 41-6 to the constructor:

Listing 41-6. Starting a Transaction

```
public MyTopComponent() {
    ...
    entityManager1.getTransaction().begin();
}
```

Finally, you want to restore the changes in the database with the already added button, *Save.* This means you close the transaction and then start a new transaction for the upcoming changes. An action method for the *actionPerformed* event is directly registered by double-clicking the button. So now you only need to implement the two lines shown in Listing 41-7 as the body of the method.

Listing 41-7. Saving the Changes in the Database

```
private void jButton1ActionPerformed(ActionEvent evt) {
    entityManager1.getTransaction().commit();
    entityManager1.getTransaction().begin();
}
```

Binding Listener

You can register a listener on it to react on changes of the source or of the target of a binding. All bindings that you applied with the GUI Builder are added to a BindingGroup. This binding group is applied as a field in the top component, so you can register a listener on this BindingGroup instance. Then the Binding that triggered the change as argument will be delivered. (See Listing 41-8.)

Listing 41-8. Registering a Listener for Changes of Bindings

```
private org.jdesktop.beansbinding.BindingGroup bindingGroup;
...
bindingGroup.addBindingListener(new AbstractBindingListener() {

    @Override
    public void targetChanged(Binding b, PropertyStateEvent evt) {
        binding.getName();
    }

    @Override
    public void sourceChanged(Binding b, PropertyStateEvent evt) {
    }
});
```

To be able to differentiate between different bindings you can give a name to a binding in the bind dialog (see Figure 41-11) in the tab *Advanced*.

Validator

A validator can be used for checking the data inserted by the user. The desired limits for a value can be checked, for example. You can create a validator class for the example application which was created before. Then you can limit the order ID on 10 characters. Name the class OrderIDValidator and derive it from the class Validator. Use String as type parameter. Then you have to implement the validate() method so you can check the desired range of the value after. If the value is invalid you create a Result instance with which you can deliver an error message. If the value is okay, you just send back null. (See Listing 41-9.)

Listing 41-9. Implementation of a kalidator Class to Ensure Valid Values

```
import org.jdesktop.beansbinding.Validator;
import org.jdesktop.beansbinding.Validator.Result;

public class OrderIDValidator extends Validator<String> {
```

```
    @Override
    public Result validate(String value) {
        if (value.length() > 10) {
            return new Result(null, "Max length of Order ID is 10");
        }
        return null;
    }
}
```

Now, you assign these validator classes to the binding. In order to do this, you first have to compile the class. The easiest way to do this is via *Compile* in the context menu of the class in the project view. After that, open the context menu of the node *Other Components* in the inspector window (the editor must be in the Design view) and call *Add From Palette* ➤ *Beans* ➤ *Choose Bean*. Type in the complete class name including the code name base in the dialog that appears. In this example, use com.galileo.netbeans.module.OrderIDValidator. Thus, the validator is provided in the desired form and you can assign it to the binding. For this purpose, open the bind dialog of the according text field via *Bind* ➤ *text*. Switch to the *Advanced* tab. There, you can select the added instance (orderIDValidator1).

However, we did not think about what will happen if the entered value is invalid, yet. The Beans Binding Framework cares about the fact that the invalid value is not applied. However, typically, you want to respond to the user about it. You already generated a corresponding message in the validator class. You register a BindingListener and implement the method syncFailed(), in order to omit an invalid input and return the message (see the section *Binding Listener*). Check whether you are dealing with a validator error and return the corresponding message. (See Listing 41-10.)

Listing 41-10. Reacting on an Invalid Change of Value

```
bindingGroup.addBindingListener(new AbstractBindingListener() {
    @Override
    public void syncFailed(Binding binding, SyncFailure fail) {
        if ((fail != null) && (fail.getType() == Binding.SyncFailureType.VALIDATION_FAILED)) {
            statusLabel.setText(fail.getValidationResult().getDescription());
        }
    }
});
```

Converter

It is possible to convert between types of data with a converter class. For example, it is possible to show values as text in the GUI while they are saved as number in the database. This conversion occurs in both directions. One converter class derives from the class Converter and doing so, decides the source and target type of data by means of the type parameter. In Listing 41-11, you want to convert between a number and a string.

Listing 41-11. Converter Class for Changing Different Types of Data

```
import org.jdesktop.beansbinding.Converter;

public class ProductCategoryConverter extends Converter<Integer, String> {

    @Override
    public String convertForward(Integer arg) {
```

```
    String value = null;
    switch (arg) {
        case 1:
            value = "Category 1";
            break;
        case 2:
            value = "Category 2";
            break;
    }
    return value;
}

@Override
public Integer convertReverse(String arg) {
    int value = 0;
    if ("Category 1".equals(arg)) {
        value = 1;
    } else if ("Category 2".equals(arg)) {
        value = 2;
    }
    return value;
}
}
```

Adding a converter to a binding takes place the same way as with a validator (see the section *Validator*).

Summary

With the Swing GUI Builder the NetBeans IDE provides the user with a powerful tool for implementing user interfaces. You can also take advantage of the Swing GUI Builder when developing NetBeans Platform applications. In this chapter, you learned about the basic functions of the GUI Builder, its components, and the Layout Manager. Furthermore, you used the Beans Binding Framework and got to know the support that the GUI Builder provides.

Testing NetBeans Platform Applications

Two different kinds of tests can be identified for implementing and running tests with NetBeans Platform applications: unit tests and functional tests. This chapter will address both kinds of tests and the support NetBeans provides for them.

Unit Tests

Unit tests for NetBeans Platform applications are implemented based on the popular test framework *JUnit*. NetBeans provides an extension of JUnit with the library *NB JUnit*. This library provides numerous helper classes, which make testing classes and methods within the NetBeans Platform a lot easier.

■ **Caution** JUnit is no longer part of the NetBeans IDE. Now, at installation you will be asked whether you want to install JUnit or not. The following description presumes that you have agreed to the installation. The JUnit module is installed when starting the IDE the first time. Watch out: for this installation you need writing permission which usually is not available in the standard program directory of Windows 7. It is the same for the Cobertura module, which you will use in the section *Checking Test Coverage*. You can solve this problem by installing the IDE in another directory (with writing permission).

First, I will describe the general process of creating and running tests by means of a simple class. The subsequent sections will address how to successfully test special resources of a NetBeans Platform application, such as services out of the Lookup or files out of the System Filesystem.

General Tests

Let's assume the class Math, shown in Listing 42-1, is the first simple JUnit test class. You want to check its methods for correctness by a unit test. You create this in a module of a NetBeans Platform application.

Listing 42-1. Simple Class with Methods to Be Checked by a Unit Test

```java
public class Math {
   public int add(int a, int b) {
      return a + b;
   }
   public int subtract(int a, int b) {
      return a - b;
   }
}
```

The NetBeans IDE provides various wizards for creating the basic structure of a unit test. In addition to creating an empty test class, you can create a test for assigned classes, so tests can be created for all methods. This saves a lot of time and work. You create a test class for the class to check Math the same way. Call *File ➤ New File ➤ JUnit ➤ Test for Existing Class*. Select the desired class with *Browse*. (See Figure 42-1.)

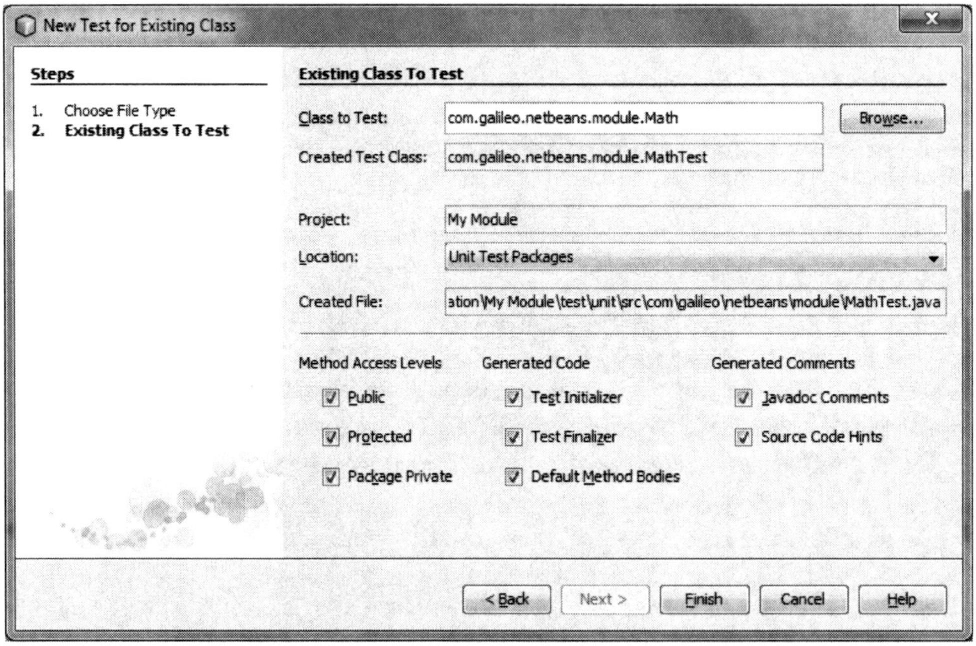

Figure 42-1. Creating test cases for an existing class automatically

As depicted in Figure 42-1 you can choose the methods for which a test will be created. There is a distinction between *Public, Protected,* and *Package Private* methods. You can also determine whether a *Test Initializer* and/or a *Finalizer* method will be created. By the option *Default Method Bodies*, the tests are already implemented based on the signature of the method. You barely need to adapt these implementations, depending on the complexity of the methods which are tested. So this option can save a lot of work. After, press *Finish* to create the test class MathTest, which will be created in a new directory *test/unit/src*. Furthermore, a dependency on the JUnit library is added to the application under *Unit Test Libraries*. Thus you get the project structure shown in Figure 42-2.

Figure 42-2. *Project structure with separate folders for test cases and with the necessary libraries*

■ **Note** If you want to add additional methods with the NetBeans wizard to your class after creating the test class, you can create tests for those methods automatically. To do so, just execute the wizard of the referring class again. Then the existing test class is extended with the test cases for the new methods.

Now let's take a look at the created test class MathTest. You see at the beginning that in this simple case no support by the *NB JUnit* module is necessary; only JUnit classes are used. Furthermore, you recognize that since JUnit 4 the test class no longer has to derive from a special base class. Despite this, the test cases (and some helper methods) are now marked with annotations. Using annotations you are free to give names to the methods. (See Listing 42-2.)

Listing 42-2. *Test Class MathTest for Checking the Methods of the Class Math*

```
import org.junit.After;
import org.junit.AfterClass;
import org.junit.Before;
import org.junit.BeforeClass;
import org.junit.Test;
import static org.junit.Assert.*;

public class MathTest {
```

```
public MathTest() {
}
@BeforeClass
public static void setUpClass() throws Exception {
}
@AfterClass
public static void tearDownClass() throws Exception {
}
@Before
public void setUp() {
}
@After
public void tearDown() {
}

@Test
public void testAdd() {
    System.out.println("add");
    int a = 0;
    int b = 0;
    Math instance = new Math();
    int expResult = 0;
    int result = instance.add(a, b);
    assertEquals(expResult, result);
    // TODO review the generated test code.
    fail("The test case is a prototype.");
}

@Test
public void testSubtract() {
    System.out.println("subtract");
    int a = 0;
    int b = 0;
    Math instance = new Math();
    int expResult = 0;
    int result = instance.subtract(a, b);
    assertEquals(expResult, result);
    // TODO review the generated test code.
    fail("The test case is a prototype.");
}
}
```

Both methods marked with the annotations @Before and @After are automatically executed before running each test of this class. So certain preconditions and resources can be determined and allocated before running the tests. Afterward, they can eventually be released again. A new instance of the class is created for running each single test of a class. This means the constructor is suitable to allocate resources which are for all test cases of a class.

If you need a connection to a database for multiple tests, for example, it makes sense (for performance reasons) to create the connection only once and then close it after finishing all referring tests. For this purpose you can mark two methods with the annotations @BeforeClass and @AfterClass, with which you can do the necessary preparatory work and rework. These methods have to be declared as static, because they are called in before creating the class. Furthermore, this enforces the fact that the resources (such as database connections) that are globally provided by those methods are static as well. This way they are provided to all instances. An example is shown in Listing 42-3.

Listing 42-3. Providing and Opening Resources Before or After Doing All Tests

```
public class DatabaseTest {
    private static Connection conn;

    @BeforeClass
    public static void setUpClass() throws Exception {
        conn = DriverManager.getConnection("url");
    }

    @AfterClass
    public static void tearDownClass() throws Exception {
        conn.close();
    }

    @Test
    public void testAdd() throws Exception {
        Statement stmt = conn.createStatement();
        //...
    }

    @Test
    public void testRemove() throws Exception {
        Statement stmt = conn.createStatement();
        //...
    }
}
```

Let's come back to the test class MathTest. Now you want to complete and then execute both tests which so far are just an automatically created basic structure. First, you can delete the setUp and the tearDown methods, because you do not need them in this case. After that you define useful parameters with the referring expected return values for both tests. The class looks about like it does in Listing 42-4.

Listing 42-4. MathTest with Test Values and with Expected Result Values

```
import org.junit.Test;
import static junit.framework.Assert.*;
public class MathTest {

    @Test
    public void testAdd() {
        System.out.println("testAdd");
        int a = 3;
        int b = 4;
        Math instance = new Math();
        int expResult = 7;
        int result = instance.add(a, b);
        assertEquals(expResult, result);
    }
```

```
@Test
public void testSubtract() {
    System.out.println("testSubtract");
    int a = 5;
    int b = 3;
    Math instance = new Math();
    int expResult = 2;
    int result = instance.subtract(a, b);
    assertEquals(expResult, result);
    }
}
```

After filling both tests with reasonable values, you can now execute them. Choose *Test All* out of the context menu of the Platform application project or choose *Test* out of the context menu of the desired modules to execute the tests of all modules. Alternatively, you can also press *Alt+F6* or call *Run ➤ Test Project*. Then the tests of the projects that are selected in the project view are executed.

The NetBeans IDE provides the special *Test Results* window (*Window ➤ Output ➤ Test Results*) for a good representation (see Figure 42-3). It is automatically opened when running the test. Outputs, which are made within the tests on the standard output are displayed on the right side of the window. You can set different filters with the toolbar on the left side. This way, you can, for example, display the tests with errors only. Furthermore, you have the option to repeat the test either for all or only for the failed tests.

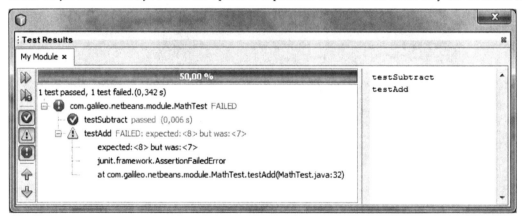

Figure 42-3. Overview of the results of the test

So far, no special support by the NB JUnit module is necessary for general tests. Using the JUnit annotations makes the implementation especially easy and clear. Although you will test NetBeans Platform–specific implementations next, you use the advantages of the NB JUnit module. But before you can use it, you have to activate it. To do this, open the context menu of the *Properties* window of your NetBeans Platform application project. Activate the module *NB JUnit* in the category *Libraries* in the cluster *harness*. It is then possible to automatically add modules needed by this module with the eventually displayed *Resolve* button. After that, you can add the *NB JUnit* module over the context menu of the *Unit Test Libraries* node of your module project with *Add Unit Test Dependency*. Call the newly added module *Edit* out of the context menu and activate the *Include Dependencies Recursively* option to get the provided dependencies of these modules when testing (see Figure 42-4.).

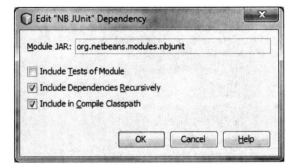

Figure 42-4. The dependencies of the NB JUnit module have to be included recursively.

Testing in the NetBeans Runtime Container Environment

The NB JUnit module enables you to run your tests in the NetBeans Runtime Container environment. Functionalities such as the global Lookup are provided during the test, too, although this requires that you run the tests for the whole NetBeans Platform application project (*Test All*).

Use the class NbModuleSuite for this. You can create a wrapper test which you deliver with the static method suite(), based on a NbModuleSuite.Configuration object.

You see in Listing 42-5 that the test class derives from the class NbTestCase. This is necessary to be able to add it to the Configuration object. You do not need the annotations anymore, which are no longer taken into account. Instead, all tests must have the prefix test.

Listing 42-5. Run Tests in the NetBeans Runtime Container Environment.

```
import junit.framework.Test;
import org.netbeans.junit.NbTestCase;
import org.netbeans.junit.NbModuleSuite;

public class MathTest extends NbTestCase {

    public MathTest() {
        super("MathTest");
    }

    public static Test suite() {
        NbModuleSuite.Configuration config = NbModuleSuite.createConfiguration(MathTest.class);
        return NbModuleSuite.create(config);
    }

    public void testAdd() {
        ...
    }
}
```

Take care in case you have addtional test classes that contain annotations and which you did not add to the suite() method in the wrapper test object. These tests are executed too, but they cannot actually be executed successfully, because they are cancelled by the NetBeans Runtime Container shutdown. Thus, it is recommended to add all tests to run to the wrapper to ensure that all tests are run in the same environment. You can easily mark tests that will not be run with the annotation @Ignore.

You can add any number of test classes or just single tests through the Configuration object with addTest(). Furthermore, you can define which modules (enableModules()) or which clusters (clusters()) will be active. The *platform* cluster is active by default, though. Usually it makes sense for module tests to avoid starting the user interface (this would only waste time) with gui(false) when running a test. Calling these methods, make sure that you call the next method on the return value of the preceding method since the methods of the NbModuleSuite.Configuration class each return a copy of the instance with referringly changed values. So a call would look like this, for example:

```
NbModuleSuite.Configuration config = NbModuleSuite
    .createConfiguration(CalculatorTest.class)
    .addTest(MathTest.class)
    .enableModules(".*")
    .clusters(".*");
```

Lookup and Service Tests

Basically, you can realize tests for modules, which query the services through the global Lookup, as described in the previous paragraph. However, then you must run the tests for the whole application. If you want to test a single module, you can implement the so-called *mock* objects (placeholder objects) to successfully run the module tests. You can do the same thing if a loosely coupled service provider is not provided when developing or testing. The classes for mock objects are implemented as part of the test classes and can then be added to the global Lookup. To do so, you have two options which will be explored in the following scenario (see Listing 42-6, Listing 42-7, and Listing 42-8.).

The following assumes you have the module *My Module* which uses the service CalculatorService (also defined in this example).

Listing 42-6. Class to Check Which Uses a Global Service

```
import org.openide.util.Lookup;
public class Calculator {
    public int add(int a, int b) {
        CalculatorService calc = Lookup.getDefault().lookup(CalculatorService.class);
        return calc.add(a, b);
    }
}
```

Listing 42-7. Service Interface

```
public interface CalculatorService {
    public int add(int a, int b);
}
```

The module *My Module 2* provides a service provider for the CalculatorService.

Listing 42-8. Service Provider in a Separate Module

```
import com.galileo.netbeans.module.CalculatorService;
import org.openide.util.lookup.ServiceProvider;

@ServiceProvider(service=CalculatorService.class)
public class CalculatorImpl implements CalculatorService {
   @Override
   public int add(int a, int b) {
      return a + b;
   }
}
```

Now, you create the test class CalculatorTest for the class Calculator. If you run a test on the module or on the whole application, later you will receive a NullPointerException, because the lookup() call cannot deliver a service implementation. To solve this problem, you can now directly provide a mock service in the test class. You can add this to the global Lookup by means of the class MockServices out of the NB JUnit modle. Do this before running the test in a method that is marked with the annotation @BeforeClass. In the example in Listing 42-9 this is the method setUpClass().

Listing 42-9. Test Class with Mock Service Implementation

```
import org.junit.BeforeClass;
import org.junit.Test;
import static org.junit.Assert.*;

public class CalculatorTest {

   @BeforeClass
   public static void setUpClass() throws Exception {
      MockServices.setServices(CalculatorMockInt.class);
   }

   @Test
   public void testAdd() {
      System.out.println("add");
      Calculator calc = new Calculator();
      assertEquals(calc.add(3, 5), 8);
   }

   public static final class CalculatorMockInt implements CalculatorService {
      @Override
      public int add(int a, int b) {
         return a + b;
      }
   }
}
```

You implement a mock class (it must be public) which you can publish in the global Lookup with MockServices.setServices(). You implement it with the inner class CalculatorMockInt. This way, you can now test independently of the other modules.

An alternative to using the `MockServices` class is implementing a mock class in a separate class or file into the Unit Test package. You can then publish this as usual with the `@ServiceProvider` annotation. A referring entry is applied in the directory *build/test/unit/classes/META-INF/services* before the test execution. (See Listing 42-10.)

Listing 42-10. Implementation and Registration of a Mock System in a Separate File

```
import org.openide.util.lookup.ServiceProvider;

@ServiceProvider(service = CalculatorService.class)
public class CalculatorMockExt implements CalculatorService {
    @Override
    public int add(int a, int b) {
        return a + b;
    }
}
```

■ **Note** When deleting the mock class or its `@ServiceProvider` annotation, the registration still exists in the *META-INF/services* directory. Do a 'clean' before running a new test.

System Filesystem Tests

When running a test, modules can directly access the content of your layer file over the System Filesystem (without further configuration of the tests). However, it is not possible to access the contents of other modules. Anyway, the concerned components should preferably be tested isolated from their environment when running unit tests. Now, the question arises as to how to provide the needed content to a software module in the System Filesystem without having to change to *layer.xml* file itself?

The answer to this question is that your own Filesystem can be added to the System Filesystem during runtime. You thus create the configuration (which is necessary for the software module to test) in an XML file. You save it together with the test classes. You implement a Filesystem implementation there that derives from `MultiFileSystem`. In the constructor you can then create an `XMLFileSystem` instance for each XML file. You can then pass it to the `MultiFileSystem` that acts as proxy for all `XMLFileSystem` instances. This Filesystem implementation is then made public via a `@ServiceProvider` annotation in the global Lookup. Thus, the content of this Filesystem is added to the System Filesystem.

Listing 42-11 demonstrates the method described above with a simple example. You extend the already known class `Math` with another method `multiply()`. This method reads its values out of the System Filesystem.

Listing 42-11. The Method to Test Which Reads Its Values out of the System Filesystem

```
import org.openide.filesystems.FileObject;
import org.openide.filesystems.FileUtil;

public class Math {
    public int multiply(String aName, String bName) {
```

```
        FileObject file = FileUtil.getConfigFile("MyFolder/MyFile");

        int aVal = (int)file.getAttribute(aName);
        int bVal = (int)file.getAttribute(bName);
        return aVal * bVal;
    }
}
```

You create the configuration needed for this in an XML file (in the directory of the unit tests). (See Listing 42-12.) The file is then called *test.xml* here.

Listing 42-12. Configuration That Will Be Available in the System Filesystem

```
<filesystem>
   <folder name="MyFolder">
      <file name="MyFile">
         <attr name="a" intvalue="2"/>
         <attr name="b" intvalue="3"/>
      </file>
   </folder>
</filesystem>
```

Depending on your needs, multiple XML files can be provided. You have to create an XMLFileSystem instance for each file and add them all to a MultiFileSystem instance via the setDelegates() method. For this purpose, you create the class TestFileSystem in the directory of the unit tests (see Listing 42-13).

Listing 42-13. Filesystem Implementation That Adds Different XML Configurations to the System

Filesystem

```
import org.openide.filesystems.FileSystem;
import org.openide.filesystems.MultiFileSystem;
import org.openide.filesystems.XMLFileSystem;
import org.openide.util.Exceptions;
import org.openide.util.lookup.ServiceProvider;

@ServiceProvider(service=FileSystem.class)
public class TestFileSystem extends MultiFileSystem {
   public TestFileSystem() throws Exception {
      setDelegates(new XMLFileSystem(TestFileSystem.class.getResource("test.xml")));

   }
}
```

Via the @ServiceProvider annotation you ensure that the TestFileSystem class is instantiated and added to the System Filesystem when starting. Thus, you can now successfully check the method Math.multiply() for correctness via the test shown in Listing 42-14.

Listing 42-14. Testing the Method multiply() Which Gets Data from the System Filesystem

```java
public class MathTest {
    @Test
    public void testMultiply() {
        System.out.println("testMultiply");
        Math instance = new Math();
        int expResult = 6;
        int result = instance.multiply("a", "b");
        assertEquals(expResult, result);
    }
}
```

You are now able to separately test software modules that read data from other modules via the System Filesystem during runtime.

Checking Test Coverage

For software quality, it is important that (at best) every line of code is run through in a test. This is called test coverage. For checking the test coverage, you can use the *Cobertura* project. Cobertura detects the coverage and creates clear reports when running the test. In these reports, you can see the results in the context of the source code for each class. First, you have to install the plugin *Cobertura Module Test Coverage* via the Plugin Manager.

Creating this report is easy via an Ant target which is integrated into the module build script. Open the folder *Important Files* in the project view and then extend the file *Build Script* so all available Ant targets are displayed. For creating the reports, call *Run Target* in the context menu of the target *coverage-report*.

The created report can be displayed in your browser via the Ant target *display-coverage-report* or you can directly open the report in the directory *build\test\unit\cobertura-report*. (See Figure 42-5.)

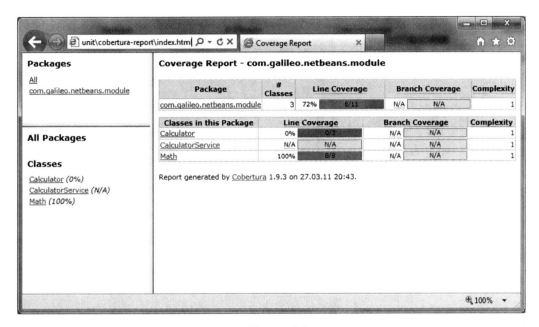

Figure 42-5. *Report about the test coverage of the module tests*

Functional GUI Tests

For creating functional tests, NetBeans provides the module Jelly Tools Platform (based on Jemmy) besides the already mentioned NB JUnit module. Jemmy itself is a library with which automated tests for GUI applications can be created. It contains methods that enable actions, which a user can execute via Swing or AWT components (such as insert text or press button), to be automated. Jemmy provides numerous operator classes with which all Swing components can be accessed. Based on this, the Jelly Tools Platform module implements operator classes for accessing special NetBeans Platform GUI components such as the main application window, the Favorites, the Output window, or different option panels.

Installing the Test Environment

Before creating a first test class, you have to install the test environment in a few simple steps. The following assumes that you have already created and opened a NetBeans Platform application project with at least one module within the NetBeans IDE.

First, create a folder in which the test classes are stored. The easiest way to do this is in the Files window (*Window* ➤ *Files*). You just create the directory *test/qa-functional/src* in the corresponding module directory via *File* ➤ *New File* ➤ *Other* ➤ *Folder*. (See Figure 42-6.)

Figure 42-6. *Structure of the directory for functional test classes*

Thus, the two new folders *Functional Test Packages* and *Functional Test Libraries* are displayed in the Project View (after restarting the IDE). Before you can add the libraries necessary for implementing and executing the functional tests to the folder *Functional Test Libraries*, you have to add the libraries to the application itself. Thus, activate the whole cluster *harness* via *Properties* ➤ *Libraries* in the Platform application project. The (eventually) missing modules can be automatically added with the button *Resolve*.

Then you can add the following libraries from the context menu of the *Functional Test Libraries* folder with *Add Functional Test Depedency*:

- JUnit

- Jelly Tools Platform

- Jemmy

- NB JUnit

You just have to ensure that the dependencies are included recursively for the NB JUnit module. You can activate this option with *Edit...* in the context menu (see Figure 42-4). Now you have created the necessary prerequesites and can implement a first test case in the next section.

Implementing a Test Case

This section will explain the basic approach of implementing functional GUI tests with a simple example. A feature will be saved persistently in a window by pressing a button. Opening the application or the window, the value will automatically be loaded into the appropriate text field. (See Figure 42-7.)

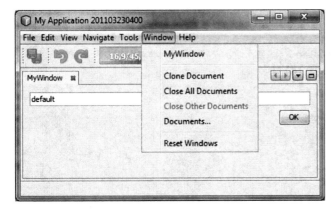

Figure 42-7. *The functionality of the TopComponent MyWindow will be tested.*

So, the window in the form of a top component class could be implemented as shown in Listing 42-15.

Listing 42-15. *The GUI Component to Be Tested and with Which a feature Will Be Saved or Loaded*

```java
import org.openide.windows.TopComponent;
import org.openide.awt.ActionID;
import org.openide.awt.ActionReference;
import org.openide.util.NbBundle;
import org.openide.util.NbBundle.Messages;
import org.openide.util.NbPreferences;

@TopComponent.Description( preferredID = "MyTopComponent",
    persistenceType = TopComponent.PERSISTENCE_ALWAYS)
@TopComponent.Registration( mode = "editor",
    openAtStartup = true)
@ActionID( category = "Window",
    id = "com.galileo.netbeans.module.MyTopComponent")
@ActionReference(path = "Menu/Window")
@TopComponent.OpenActionRegistration(
    displayName = "#CTL_MyAction",
    preferredID = "MyTopComponent")
@Messages( {"CTL_MyTopComponent=MyWindow",
    "CTL_MyAction=MyWindow"})
public final class MyTopComponent extends TopComponent {

    private javax.swing.JButton okButton;
    private javax.swing.JTextField propValue;

    public MyTopComponent() {
        initComponents();
        setName(Bundle.CTL_MyTopComponent());
    }
```

```
    ...
    private void okButtonActionPerformed(ActionEvent evt) {
        NbPreferences.forModule(MyTopComponent.class).put("propKey", propValue.getText());
    }

    @Override
    public void componentOpened() {
        propValue.setText(NbPreferences.forModule(
            MyTopComponent.class).get("propKey", "default"));
    }
}
```

Now, you want to create a test case for this functionality. Create the class MyTopComponentTest with *File* ➤ *New File* ➤ *Java* ➤ *Java Class* under *Functional Test Packages*. You derive functional tests from the class JellyTestCase. As in the section *Testing in the NetBeans Runtime Container Environment* you provide a wrapper test instance that ensures that all tests run within the NetBeans Runtime Container environment. You provide it by the method suite() so you can determine which clusters and modules will be active. You can determine this via a Configuration object. You can also influence which tests are run. (See Listing 42-16.)

Listing 42-16. Test Class to Test the Functionality of MyTopComponent

```
import junit.framework.Test;
import org.netbeans.jellytools.JellyTestCase;
import org.netbeans.jellytools.MainWindowOperator;
import org.netbeans.jellytools.TopComponentOperator;
import org.netbeans.jemmy.operators.JButtonOperator;
import org.netbeans.jemmy.operators.JTextFieldOperator;
import org.netbeans.junit.NbModuleSuite;

public class MyTopComponentTest extends JellyTestCase {

    private static final String EXPECTED_RESULT = "testValue";

    public MyTopComponentTest(String name) {
        super(name);
    }

    public static Test suite() {
        return NbModuleSuite.allModules(MyTopComponentTest.class,
            "testSetValue", "testGetValue");
    }

    public void testSetValue() {
        TopComponentOperator op = new TopComponentOperator("MyWindow");
        JTextFieldOperator text = new JTextFieldOperator(op, 0);
        text.setText(EXPECTED_RESULT);
        JButtonOperator button = new JButtonOperator(op, "OK");
        button.press();
```

```
        op.close();
    }

    public void testGetValue() {
        MainWindowOperator main = MainWindowOperator.getDefault();
        main.menuBar().pushMenu("Window|MyWindow");
        TopComponentOperator op = new TopComponentOperator("MyWindow");
        JTextFieldOperator text = new JTextFieldOperator(op, 0);
        String result = text.getText();
        assertEquals(EXPECTED_RESULT, result);
    }
}
```

In the test class MyTopComponentTest depicted in Listing 42-16 you use the method
NbModuleSuite.allModules() to create a wrapper test instance. A configuration is automatically used, in
which all clusters and modules of the application are active. Additionally, you implement two tests by
testSetValue() and testGetValue() (all methods with the prefix test are executed as test). By the
method allModules() you indicated the two test cases to ensure the order of the execution.

Over an instance of the type TopComponentOperator from the Jelly Tools Platform module you get
access on a TopComponent by name (see also Listing 42-16). You create a JTextFieldOperator instance in
order to be able to input something into the text field. As a container you transfer the
TopComponentOperator. You can set a test value and save the settings via the *OK* button. The settings can
be made via the class JButtonOperator. Finally, you close the window by the close() method.

In a second test, you must first open the window in the main menu of the application. You can
access it with the MainWindowOperator. The MainWindowOperator is able to call a menu entry by an
indicated path. Bear in mind that, analogous to the previous test, you get access to the text field. This
time you read the text and compare it with the previously set value.

A selection of the available operator classes of the Jelly Tools Platform module is listed in Table 42-1.
The Jemmy library provides an operator class for all standard Swing and AWT components. Developing
individual functional test cases, it is surely helpful to take a look at the corresponding API
documentation.

Table 42-1. Selection of Some Important Operator Classes for Implementing Functional GUI Tests

Operator Class	Selection of Methods
FavoritesOperator	invoke()
	tree()
HelpOperator	invoke()
	back()
	next()
MainWindowOperator	getDefault()
	get- / setStatusText()
	getToolbar()
	menuBar()

NbDialogOperator	ok() / yes()
	cancel() / no()
OptionsOperator	invoke()
	selectMiscellaneous()
	selectOption
	treeTable()
OutputOperator	invoke()
	getText()
	getOutputTab()
PluginsOperator	invoke()
	install()
	addPlugin()
	update()
TopComponentOperator	attachTo()
	close()
WizardOperator	back()
	next()
	finish()

Checking Test Coverage

A report about the test coverage can be created by Cobertura, even for the functional tests (see also the section *Checking Test Coverage*). For this purpose, use the Ant target *coverage-report-qa-functional*. After executing the tests and creating the reports, you can call the Ant target from the directory *build\test\qa-functional\cobertura-report*.

Configuration in Case of Maven Projects

Implementing tests for Maven-based NetBeans Platform applications takes place the same way as described in the sections *Unit Tests* and *Functional GUI Tests*, the only differences concern the configuration, which we'll look at next.

Module Tests

Running software tests is an integral part of the build lifecycle in Maven. So, the build phase *test* is executed after *compile* before the actual artifact is created by *package*. These tests are run by the *Maven*

Surefire Plugin. This plugin automatically runs the test cases located under *src/test/java*. By a dependency entry it can be defined which JUnit version is used. Thus, applying a Maven-based NetBeans Platform application project the entry (depicted in Listing 42-17) is already added in the parent POM file.

Listing 42-17. Determining the JUnit Version

```
<dependencies>
    <dependency>
        <groupId>junit</groupId>
        <artifactId>junit</artifactId>
        <version>4.8.2</version>
        <scope>test</scope>
    </dependency>
</dependencies>
```

Writing this entry into the parent POM file, it is automatically provided to all modules. This means no further configuration is necessary.

Module tests can be created by a wizard within the NetBeans IDE, as described in the section *General Tests*, too. If you want to use the JUnit extension implementing your test cases, add the entry shown in Listing 42-18 to the POM file of the corresponding module or to the parent POM file, if the remaining modules also use this module.

Listing 42-18. Adding a Dependency to the NB JUnit Module

```
<dependency>
    <groupId>org.netbeans.api</groupId>
    <artifactId>org-netbeans-modules-nbjunit</artifactId>
    <version>${netbeans.version}</version>
    <scope>test</scope>
</dependency>
```

Functional Tests

Functional GUI tests can also be implemented and run in conjunction with the Jelly Tools Platform module in Maven-based NetBeans Platform applications. For this purpose, add a dependency on the Jelly Tools Platform module as shown in Listing 42-19 to the application module (the module with the *nbm-application* packaging type; see Chapter 37). Add a dependency on the NB JUnit module. Modules needed by these two modules (that is, the transitive dependencies) are automatically added to the class path by Maven.

Listing 42-19. Adding Dependencies for Functional Tests

```
<dependencies>
    <dependency>
        <groupId>org.netbeans.api</groupId>
        <artifactId>org-netbeans-modules-nbjunit</artifactId>
        <version>${netbeans.version}</version>
        <scope>test</scope>
    </dependency>
```

```
    <dependency>
        <groupId>org.netbeans.api</groupId>
        <artifactId>org-netbeans-modules-jellytools-platform</artifactId>
        <version>${netbeans.version}</version>
        <scope>test</scope>
    </dependency>
</dependencies>
```

Furthermore, you must configure the Maven Surefire plugin by the property `cluster.path.final`. Thus, you define your own and the NetBeans Platform cluster. You also do this in the POM file of the application project as depicted in Listing 42-20.

Listing 42-20. Configuration of the Surefire Plugin for Running Functional Tests

```
<build>
    <plugins>
        <plugin>
            <groupId>org.apache.maven.plugins</groupId>
            <artifactId>maven-surefire-plugin</artifactId>
            <version>2.7.1</version>
            <configuration>
                <systemProperties>
                    <property>
                        <name>cluster.path.final</name>
                        <value>${project.build.directory}/
                            ${brandingToken}/${brandingToken}:
                            ${project.build.directory}/
                            ${brandingToken}/platform</value>
                    </property>
                </systemProperties>
            </configuration>
        </plugin>
    </plugins>
</build>
```

Thus, you can now implement functional GUI tests even in Maven-based projects, as already described in the section *Implementing a Test Case*. Just store it in the directory of the module tests under *src/test/java*.

Test Coverage

Cobertura also creates a report about the test coverage for Maven-based NetBeans Platform projects. Adding the following entry to the POM file, you use the *Maven Cobertura Plugin*, as shown in Listing 42-21.

Listing 42-21. Adding the Coburtera Plugin to the POM file

```
<reporting>
   <plugins>
      <plugin>
         <groupId>org.codehaus.mojo</groupId>
         <artifactId>cobertura-maven-plugin</artifactId>
         <version>2.4</version>
      </plugin>
   </plugins>
</reporting>
```

You can start the report generation from the command line (or another IDE) by the following call:

```
mvn cobertura:cobertura
```

Then, the report is stored in the directory *target\site\cobertura* in HTML format. Moreover, a helpful plugin is provided for the NetBeans IDE. You can install the *Maven Test Coverage* plugin with the Plugin Manager and thus, the report can be displayed with the context menu of a module via *Code Coverage ➤ Show Report*. (See Figure 42-8.)

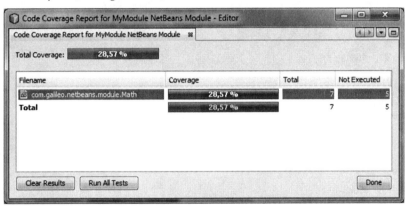

Figure 42-8. Integrated report about the test cover within the NetBeans IDE

You can run the tests and execute the following report generation with *Run All Tests*. You can directly see which lines of the corrresponding class are run through a test and which are not, and open single files in the overview (depicted in Figure 42-9).

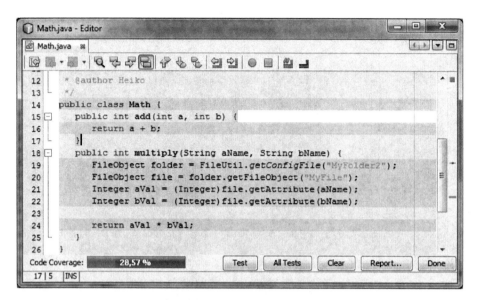

Figure 42-9. Detailed result of the analysis of the test cover

Summary

Doing software testing is an integral part of software development models. In this chapter you learned more about how to easily and efficiently test NetBeans Platform applications. In the first part of this chapter we did module tests with the support of JUnit. In the second part you learned how to test the GUI of a NetBeans Platform application. This is done with the support of the Jelly Tools Platform.

Debugging with the NetBeans IDE

This chapter is about the functionality of the NetBeans debugging environment. In this environment you can debug your NetBeans Platform application using numerous supporting info windows and other useful features.

Debugging Window

The NetBeans debugger uses a series of helpful windows to make debugging as efficient and transparent as possible. In the following sections you will learn more about those windows in detail. The *Debugging* window itself is a combination of different functions. Dedicated windows are provided for each function. Thus, you have an overview of all threads and, when reaching a breakpoint, you have an overview of the complete call stack, too. A symbol (on the right side) shows you which threads are currently paused. You can stop or resume certain threads by means of this symbol. You can also influence all threads at once with the context menu. By double-clicking an entry of the call stack you can directly jump in the source file to the position of the corresponding method. (See Figure 43-1.)

Figure 43-1. Debugging window with all current threads and with the current call hierarchy

Breakpoints

The so-called *Breakpoints* are the base for debugging an application. With these breakpoints you define certain positions in the source code where the execution of the application should be stopped. The support of the IDE offers certain possibilities. For example, you can take a closer look at the current values of variables or you can look at the return value of a method in closer detail at the place where the application was stopped. This way you can get information about erratic behavior of the software.

Different types of breakpoints can be distinguished depending on the position in the source code or on the event. The types of breakpoints provided in the NetBeans IDE are listed in Table 43-1.

Table 43-1. Types of Breakpoints and Their Triggering Events

Type of Breakpoint	Stops on...
Class	Class Load
	Class Unload
	Class Load or Unload
Exception	Caught
	Uncaught
	Caught or Uncaught
Field	Field Access
	Field Modification
	Field Access or Modification
Line	Reaching the line
Method	Method Entry
	Method Exit
	Method Entry or Exit
Thread	Thread Start
	Thread Death
	Thread Start or Death

Apply breakpoints either by clicking the line number (left margin of the source code editor), via the menu with *Debug ➤ New Breakpoint* or with the button ▨ in the toolbar of the Breakpoints window (see Figure 43-2).

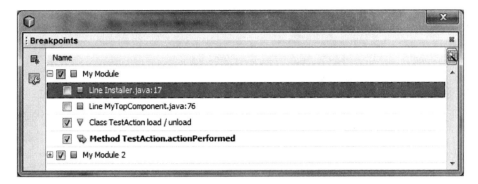

Figure 43-2. Overview of all breakpoints in the breakpoint window

All set breakpoints are displayed in the *Breakpoints* window. For the purpose of clarity, you can also arrange them in groups. You can classify the breakpoints as either user-specific (*Custom Groups*) or you can group them by default using the button ![button] (left margin of the Breakpoints window). The following standard groups are available:

- Programming language: *Language*

- Type of the breakpoint: *Type*

- Project: *Project*

- Files: *Files*

- Debug sessions: *Debug Session*

- Subgroups: *Nested*

Call the context menu of the breakpoint to assign a user-specific group or to assign a breakpoint to an existing group. With *Move Into Group…* you can either directly assign the breakpoint to a group or you can create a new group with *New*. As shown in Figure 43-2, you can specifically activate or deactivate separate breakpoints or groups of breakpoints. The additionally displayed green arrow shows you at which breakpoint your application is paused at the moment. Breakpoints can also be configured so that the application is only paused under certain conditions. Thus, for all types of breakpoints, you can determine that the application is just paused after a certain amount of runs. So you can pause the application, for example, when the breakpoint on one variable is run for the tenth time.

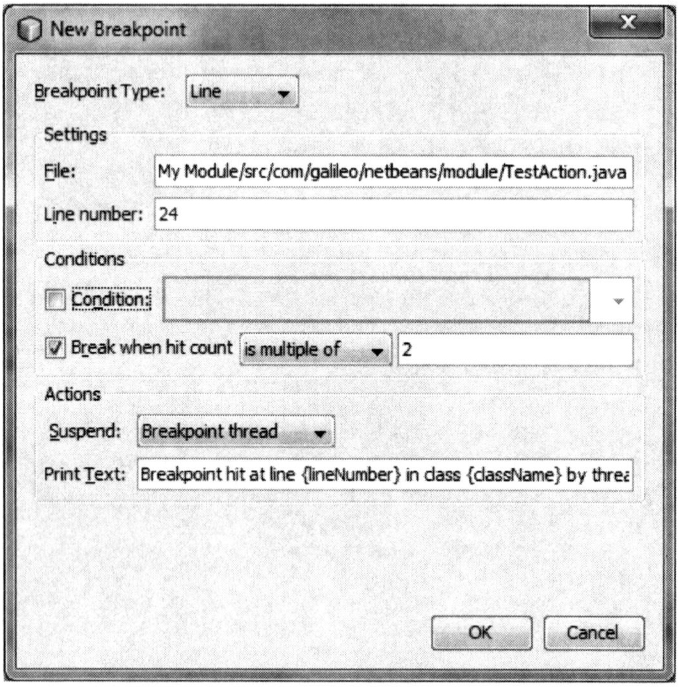

Figure 43-3. Configuring breakpoints individually

Additionally, you can define which classes should be excluded for the breakpoint types *Class* and *Exception*. For the remaining types, you can define any conditions when the breakpoint will be valid by a Boolean expression. By default when reaching a breakpoint, the currently executing thread is paused. However, you can also configure a breakpoint so that either all threads or none is paused. In the latter case, the application just resumes.

Variables

The NetBeans IDE provides different windows and tools in order to check the variables when reaching a breakpoint. In the variables window (*Window ➤ Debugging ➤ Variables*) all variables of the current context are displayed (see Figure 43-4). This way, you can observe the values of the instance variables, the local variables, and the eventually transferred parameters. You can also look at the values of separate variables directly in the editor by pointing to the variable with your mouse.

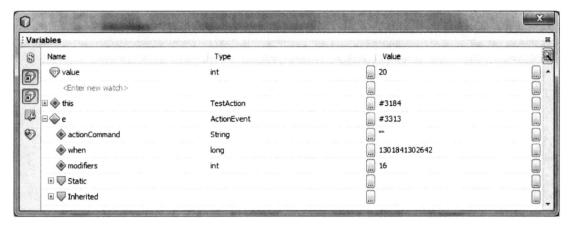

Figure 43-4. *Overview of variables*

By so-called *watches* you can also observe variables outside the context of the current breakpoint. You can add a new watch entry by means of the toolbar on the left side of the Variables window. Additionally, you can just select variables in the source code editor and then add them via drag-and-drop so you can concretely and clearly track the values of certain variables. As an alternative to representing the watches in the Variables window you can use the separate Watches window which you find under *Window ➤ Debugging ➤ Watches*.

Remote Debugging

The easiest way is to start your application directly from the NetBeans IDE in the debug mode. However, the NetBeans IDE also supports debugging applications that had been started outside the NetBeans IDE. For this purpose, it is necessary that you start the application in the debug mode. In connection with this, some parameters must be specified so the NetBeans IDE can successfully connect to the application via the *Java Debug Wire Protocol* (JDWP). Remote debugging parameters are listed in Table 43-2.

Table 43-2. *Remote Debugging Parameters*

Parameter	Description
-Xdebug	Activates the debug mode of the application.
-Xrunjdwp	Loads the reference implementation of the JDWP that facilitates the remote debugging.
transport	Defines the transport channel for JDWP. A connection is established via sockets by *dt_socket*. Alternatively you can use a shared memory. You indicate this by *dt_shmem*.
server	*y*: Application obeys to a connection at defined address.

	n: Application tries to connect a debugger via the indicated connection.
address	Indicates a port which enables the communication between debugger and application.
suspend	*n*: Application starts immediately
	y: Application starts only when a debugger has been connected.

Start your application, for example, by the following parameters, to debug them by means of the NetBeans IDE:

```
-Xdebug -Xrunjdwp: transport=dt_socket,server=y,address=65535,suspend=n
```

To debug an externally started application call *Debug ➤ Attach Debugger*. Select the *Java Debugger (JPDA)* and use *SocketAttach* as connector. Additionally, you indicate the host's name on which the application runs, the port number on which the application accepts requests, as well as a timeout.

Press *OK* after doing the settings as shown in Figure 43-5 to directly establish a connection.

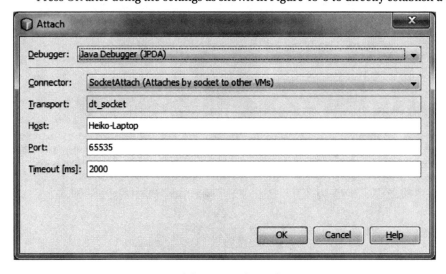

Figure 43-5. Connecting remote debugger with application

Controlling Debugging

The NetBeans IDE provides different actions with which you can quickly detect the concerning points of code for debugging most efficiently. The following list provides a good overview of those actions:

- ▨ *Debug Main Project* (*Ctrl + F5*): Starts the main project (in the debug mode) that is currently opened in the IDE. Only when the debugging is started are the following actions available.

- *Step Over* (*F8*): With it, the complete current code line is executed without descending in eventually existing calls.

- *Step Over Expression* (*Shift + F8*): With this command you can evaluate expressions, which consist of multiple method calls, in detail. In the Variables window, the passed values and the return value are displayed as history for each single method call (see Figure 43-4). If an expression does not contain a further method call, the action behaves like *Step Over*.

- *Step Into* (*F7*): With this command a code line is executed. If this code line contains method calls for which the source code exists, you can descend into the separate calls by this action. If multiple calls exist, you can directly descend into the corresponding method call by one click.

- *Step Into Next Method* (*Shift + F7*): Similar to the *Step* Into action. However, with this one descends directly into the next method of the current line.

- *Step Out* (*Ctrl + F7*): Executes a line. If it is part of a method, all remaining lines are executed and the debugger jumps to the called position.

- *Run to Cursor* (*F4*): Executes all lines up to that line in which the cursor currently is.

- *Continue* (*F5*): With this action you can resume a paused thread by a breakpoint. The application is executed up to the eventually existing next breakpoint.

- *Pause:* With this action you can pause all threads at once.

- *Finish Debugger Session* (*Shift + F5*): This action finishes the current debugger session and thus the application, too, if it had been started out of the IDE.

Call Stack

If your application has been stopped at a breakpoint you can look at the complete call hierarchy up to the current line via the *Call Stack* window (*Window ➤ Debugging ➤ Call Stack*), as shown in Figure 43-6. Double-clicking an entry, it jumps directly to the called position in the editor. That way you can check the variables concerning the called methods.

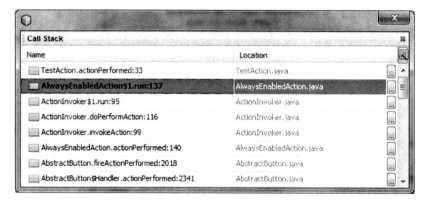

Figure 43-6. Call Stack window for tracking the call hierarchy

To jump into the methods of Java and the NetBeans Platform, the source code must be present. You can see which source directories are available to the debugger in the *Sources* window (*Window* ➤ *Debugging* ➤ *Sources*), as shown in Figure 43-7. This is where you can also add further directories via the context menu by *Add Source Root*. Get the source code of the NetBeans Platform as a separate ZIP file on the download page at http://netbeans.org.

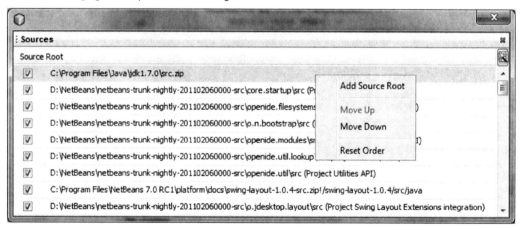

Figure 43-7. Sources window with all source directories that are available when debugging

Heap Walking

With the heap walking functionality the NetBeans IDE provides a substantial tool for tracking memory leaks. It is possible to display an overview of all current instances of your application in the Loaded Classes window, as shown in Figure 43-8. To find the desired instance out of the many instances, you can filter for names or subclasses. If needed, you can also filter instances using a regular expression.

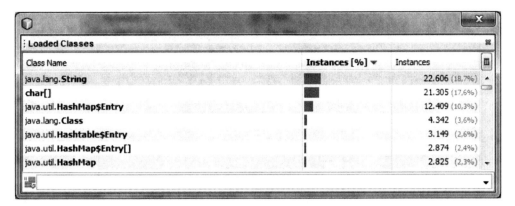

Figure 43-8. Loaded Classes window for displaying the amount of all current instances grouped in classes

You can take an individual look at the instances of a certain class by the context menu of an entry with *Show in Instances View* (see Figure 43-9). Doing so, you can look at the respective values of a chosen instance. You can select an instance on the left. Corresponding references are displayed, as well.

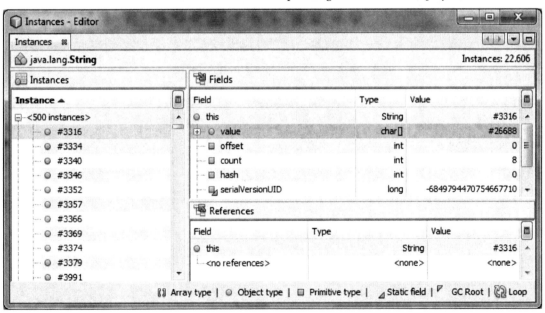

Figure 43-9. Instances window for displaying all current instances of a certain class

Summary

Errors and potential problems within an application can be quickly tracked with an efficiently designed debugging environment. You have such an environment at hand: the NetBeans IDE. In this chapter you got to know the NetBeans Debugging features and how you can use them for NetBeans Platform application debugging.

Play & More: Developing an MP3-Manager—An Example of a NetBeans Platform Application

Sample Project: MP3 Manager

The purpose of this chapter is to demonstrate the design and the implementation of a completely executable application, playing MP3 files on the NetBeans Platform. Of course, this application will be as flexible and modular as possible. Therefore, it will reuse many of the previously implemented and discussed advantages and features of the NetBeans Platform.

This chapter is useful even if you have not read all the previous chapters, as well as if you are trying to dive directly into the NetBeans Platform world. Where more detailed knowledge is required , I will refer you to chapters that deal with the subject in greater detail. The following pages will cover only the most important parts of the implementation. Like all the other examples in this book, this example can be downloaded as a complete NetBeans project from the Source Code/Download area for this book on the Apress web site (www.apress.com).

Design

Essentially, your application should be able to play MP3 files, manage those files in playlists, and display the relevant ID3 information. Furthermore, you want to enable simple editing and addition of ID3 information via the application. Use the Favorites module of the NetBeans Platform as an MP3 library. Using the Palette module, you could manage entire MP3 albums, for example. You could also use the Output module to give feedback to the user while processing ID3 jobs. The great advantage of the application is its easy extensibility, due to the module-based architecture of the NetBeans Platform. However, a well-designed architecture and application structure is also required, so you must think about the functionalities you want to provide as well as the granularity, meaning you must think about how many modules are required to do the job in advance. To provide proper interfaces and extension points, you also have to think about where and how the application needs to be most extensible. You then create the necessary interfaces using the appropriate interfaces and extension points.

In Figure 44-1 you see the structure of the application containing the NetBeans Platform and also the underlying Java Platform. The actual application part, which is marked in Figure 44-1 with *MP3 Manager*, can be roughly divided into three layers:

- The lowest layer contains modules which will be integral parts of the application, containing graphical user-interfaces such as a navigator list, an implementation of the Java Sound SPI for MP3 files, and the database system Java DB. You want to use Java DB for different purposes within the application.

- In a middleware layer you encapsulate service interfaces. This layer facilitates decoupling of the application components, because these components no longer directly depend on each other's implementation, but in most cases only on the provided interfaces.

- The third layer, based on the second, implements the application's components, providing actual functionality using the independent modules.

All modules and their respective responsibilities are listed in the following (later, you will create and implement some of them, step by step):

- *Core*: In this module, important and integral components of the application (which are mandatory for using the application) could be provided.

- *Core UI*: You encapsulate additional user interfaces in this module.

- *JMF-Plugin*: In this module, you encapsulate the Java Media Framework and the MP3 implementation of the Java Sound SPI, which is provided by Sun in the form of a JAR archive. The Java Sound SPI is required for playing MP3-coded audio data.

- *Java DB*: With this module, you integrate the database system Java DB.

- *Services*: You define service interfaces in this module, so the services provided by the application can be expanded dynamically.

- *Player* : This module provides an MP3 player with GUI.

- *Playlist*: With this module, MP3 files can be managed in different lists and thus be provided to the player.

- *ID3 API* : Contains an API for reading and writing the ID3 information of MP3 files.

- *Favorites Branding* : Adapts the menu entries of the Favorites module.

- *Properties Branding:* Adapts the menu entries of the Properties module.

- *Database Searcher*: This is a service provider with which you can search for MP3 files in a database.

- *Filesystem Searcher*: This is a service provider with which you can search for MP3 files on the hard disk drive.

- *Searcher UI*: This module provides a user interface for using the service provider searching MP3s.

- *Indexer*: This module automatically indicates MP3 files that are located on the hard disk drive. With it MP3 files can be found quickly using different criteria.

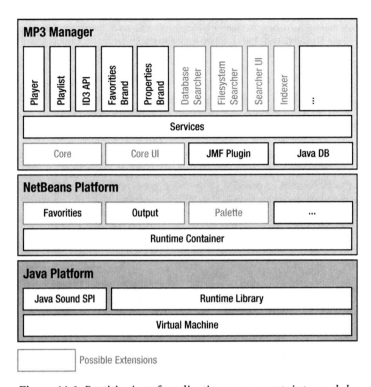

Figure 44-1. Partitioning of application components into modules

Creating a NetBeans Platform Application

The base of each NetBeans rich client application is a *NetBeans Platform Application project*. This project represents the application as a whole and contains the separate modules. Application branding (meaning naming of the application, splash screen, etc.) also occurs via the NetBeans Platform Application project. The NetBeans IDE provides a wizard for creating such a project. You can call this wizard via *File ➤ New Project*. Then, select the project type *NetBeans Platform Application* under *NetBeans Modules*. Press *Next* to get to the next page where you can enter a project name. You choose *MP3 Manager* this time. By clicking *Finish*, the Platform application is created. You can specifically adapt the appearance of your application to the product in the branding dialog which you can call via *Branding...* in the context menu of the Platform application. There, you can also adapt the title, different icons, and the splash screen, among other things.

So now that you have created the basis for your application, you can go on to the separate modules, meaning the application's components.

Support for MP3

To support playing MP3 files in your player module, use *Java Media Frameworks* (JMF) and an MP3 plugin. The *MP3 Plugin* is an implementation of the Java Sound API (which is part of the Java Platform) for MP3 files. Basically, this plugin would be sufficient for playing MP3s, but with the assistance of the

JMF implementation it is much easier. You create a *library wrapper module* for the two components, the JMF and the MP3 plugin, in order to integrate those two libraries into your application.

Creating the JMF Module

Download the JMF as a cross-platform edition as well as the MP3 plugin from `http://www.oracle.com/technetwork/java/javase/tech`. (You will also find both components in the Source Code/Download area for this book on the Apress web site at `www.apress.com`.) Copy both the JAR archive *lib/jmf.jar* from the JMF distribution, and *lib/ext/mp3plugin.jar* from the MP3 plugin distribution, into a directory. You can add both to a module afterwards. Call *File ➤ New Project... ➤ NetBeans Modules ➤ Library Wrapper Module*. Add both JAR archives which you copied in a directory (hold the *Ctrl* key, to select both archives) with *Browse*. Enter *JMF Plugin* as project name on the next page of the wizard and choose the NetBeans Platform application that had been created. Determine the *Code Name Base* of the modules via `javax.media` on the following page. Finally, press *Finish*, so the wrapper module is created and added to the MP3 manager.

Registering the MP3 Plugin

Bear in mind that the MP3 plugin is not immediately provided to the JMF; you must register this plugin at the `PlugInManager` of the JMF so it can be used. Pass the task to a *Module Installer* (you can find more about this in Chapter 3) in order to ensure that the plugin is always registered. The module installer is executed when loading the JMF plugin. Create the module installer via *File ➤ New File ➤ Module Development ➤ Installer / Activator*. Press *Finish* in the dialog that appears to create the installer. You implement the necessary registration for the `PlugInManager` in the `restored()` method. You must indicate the plugin's class, the input and output formats, and the plugin's type. Of course, in this case it is a codec plugin. Next, insert the following lines as shown in Listing 44-1.

Listing 44-1. Registering the MP3 Plugin at the JMF Plugin Manager During Startup

```
package javax.media;
import javax.media.format.AudioFormat;
import org.openide.modules.ModuleInstall;

public class Installer extends ModuleInstall {
    public void restored() {
        Format input1 = new AudioFormat(AudioFormat.MPEGLAYER3);
        Format input2 = new AudioFormat(AudioFormat.MPEG);
        Format output = new AudioFormat(AudioFormat.LINEAR);
        PlugInManager.addPlugIn(
                "com.sun.media.codec.audio.mp3.JavaDecoder",
                new Format[]{input1, input2},
                new Format[]{output},
                PlugInManager.CODEC);
    }
}
```

MP3 File Type

Another important base for easy-to-use and professional management of MP3 files within your application is a so-called MP3 file type. A *file type* is a concept of the NetBeans Platform which is used to manage files of a particular type. It consists of three main parts. First, there is a FileObject, which basically represents a wrapper for a File. Thus, it represents the concrete physical MP3 file. Based on this, there is a DataObject, which extends the FileObject by properties and functionalities in a flexible manner. The third component is a Node object, which is used to graphically represent a DataObject at the user interface that includes the ability to accept actions. More information related to this can be found in the Chapters 7 and 12.

Normally, the MP3 file type belongs to the core functionality of your MP3 manager, which means you could manage the MP3 file type in the Core module. For more flexibility and to avoid cyclic dependencies, however, you should create a separate module for the MP3 file type. To do this, call *File ➤ New Project... ➤ NetBeans Modules ➤ Module*. Assign *File Type* as name and com.hboeck.mp3manager.filetype as code name base. You can leave the remaining values. Clicking the *Finish* button closes the wizard and creates the module.

The components of a file type are created completely by the file type wizard which in turn is provided by the IDE. Call this wizard via *File ➤ New File ➤ Module Development ➤ File Type*. You use audio/mpeg as MIME type for MP3s, and of course, assign mp3 for the extension. On the next page, you enter Mp3 as the prefix for the class to create, and you can select an icon for this file type. Now all the required information is collected, and the MP3 file type can be created by clicking *Finish*.

The wizard registers a data object factory for the MP3 MIME type which is responsible for loading an Mp3DataObject. (See Listing 44-2.)

Listing 44-2. Each Data Object Factory Is Responsible for a Certain File Type and Is Served by the NetBeans Platform. This Is Why It Must Be Registered.

```
<folder name="Loaders">
  <folder name="audio">
    <folder name="mpeg">
      <folder name="Factories">
        <file name="Mp3DataLoader.instance">
          <attr name="SystemFileSystem.icon"
                urlvalue="nbresloc:/com/hboeck/mp3manager/filetype/mp3.png"/>
          <attr name="dataObjectClass"
                stringvalue="com.hboeck.mp3manager.filetype.Mp3DataObject"/>
          <attr name="instanceCreate"
                methodvalue="org.openide.loaders.DataLoaderPool.factory"/>
          <attr name="mimeType" stringvalue="audio/mpeg"/>
        </file>
      </folder>
    </folder>
  </folder>
</folder>
```

This factory creates an Mp3DataObject for each MP3 FileObject, which consists of the basic structure shown in Listing 44-3.

Listing 44-3. Implement the Logic of an MP3 File via the Mp3DataObject Class.

```java
import java.io.IOException;
import org.openide.filesystems.FileObject;
import org.openide.loaders.DataNode;
import org.openide.loaders.DataObjectExistsException;
import org.openide.loaders.MultiDataObject;
import org.openide.loaders.MultiFileLoader;
import org.openide.nodes.Node;
import org.openide.nodes.Children;
import org.openide.util.Lookup;

public class Mp3DataObject extends MultiDataObject {
    public Mp3DataObject(FileObject pf, MultiFileLoader loader)
        throws DataObjectExistsException, IOException {
        super(pf, loader);
    }

    @Override
    protected Node createNodeDelegate() {
        return new DataNode(this, Children.LEAF, getLookup());
    }

    @Override
    public Lookup getLookup() {
        return getCookieSet().getLookup();
    }
}
```

This class's task is to assign a common `FileObject` with logic. Furthermore, the `Mp3DataObject` delivers a node to you. By this node, the MP3 file can be simply and comfortably displayed in different views, such as the Favorites module or, for example, in a playlist. You implement such a playlist later in this chapter. By default, just the `DataNode` class is used. In the following section you want to equip the node with special feature and then create a special node class that derives from `DataNode`.

■ **Note** When implementing the first module, which uses the MP3 file type and therefore must define a dependency on the file type, you will see that this is not possible. The reason for this is that all packages of a module are not public, by default. This means, you must explicitly define which packages can be accessed from outside. You define this in the *Properties* of a module under *API Versioning*. The module is only shown in the list if at least one package is defined as public and contains modules that another module depends on.

ID3 Support

Inside an MP3 file, information about the file can be saved in an *ID3 tag*, in which you must distinguish between two different versions. The ID3v1 tag consists of a fixed number of fields (such as number, artist, and title), which each has a fixed size. The most important information, at least, can be stored in the file with that tag. The ID3v2 tag introduces a much more flexible concept. A much greater number of standardized fields are defined and furthermore, multiple customized fields can be added (a field is referred to as frame, as well). Nonetheless, the tag can also be read by applications that do not know about or interpret this field. The frames of an ID3v2 tag may vary in length. Also, a frame will only exist in a file if it is required, which means there are no empty frames.

ID3 API

Of course, you will reuse the information stored in this manner in your application. Therefore, you need an API that adequately supports retrieval and storage of ID3 data, according to the specification. On the Internet you will find a series of such ID3 APIs for free. Most of them are reasonably useful. For easy handling and simple integration, I started implementing my own ID3 APIs, though. Doing so, I consciously avoided the assistance of NetBeans APIs, in order to being able to use it in other applications, too. Although this library is still under development (only the editing of ID3v1 tags is possible at the moment), it is sufficient for this example, which merely demonstrates advantages and strengths of the NetBeans Platform. Of course, you are free to use another library. If you do, however, you must adapt resulting source locations to the selected API. As with the JMF libraries, you integrate the ID3 library using a library wrapper module. You can create such a module by clicking *File ➤ New Project...* and *NetBeans Modules ➤ Library Wrapper Module*. On the wizard's first page, select the library named com-hboeck-mp3manager-id3.jar (which can also be downloaded from the Source Code/Download area for this book on the Apress web site). Name the module *ID3 API* and add it to the MP3 manager. All other fields can be left with their default values.

You must define a dependency to the ID3 module in order to provide the ID3 API to the file type module. You can do this in the *Properties* of the file type module in the category *Libraries* (see Figure 44-2). Press the *Add Dependency...* button and just select the *ID3 API* module there.

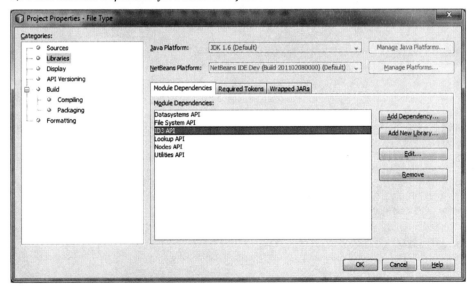

Figure 44-2. *Defining dependencies to the ID3 API*

As already mentioned, the class Mp3DataObject is responsible for the information and methods specific to MP3. As a result, you extend this class which facilitates accessing both the ID3v1 tag and the ID3v2 tag (see Listing 44-4). It is very important that you create the tags only when accessing the file itself, and here is why. If you open, for example, a folder containing a lot of MP3 files in the Favorites window, an Mp3DataObject is created for each file. If you read the ID3 tags of every file, you would eventually encounter a significant delay—a behavior to be avoided.

Listing 44-4. Extending the MP3 DataObject Class with Support for ID3

```
import com.hboeck.mp3manager.id3.v1.ID3v1Tag;
import com.hboeck.mp3manager.id3.v2.ID3v2Tag;
...
public class Mp3DataObject extends MultiDataObject {
    private ID3v1Tag id3v1 = null;
    private ID3v2Tag id3v2 = null;
    public Mp3DataObject(FileObject pf, MultiFileLoader loader)
            throws DataObjectExistsException, IOException {
        super(pf, loader);
    }
    ...

    public ID3v1Tag getID3v1Tag() {
        if(id3v1 == null) {
            id3v1 = new ID3v1Tag(FileUtil.toFile(getPrimaryFile()));
        }
        return id3v1;
    }

    public ID3v2Tag getID3v2Tag() {
        if(id3v2 == null) {
            id3v2 = new ID3v2Tag(FileUtil.toFile(getPrimaryFile()));
        }
        return id3v2;
    }
}
```

Using the DataObject method getPrimaryFile() you receive the FileObject of the MP3 file, which is managed by the Mp3DataObject instance (this is the object that is passed to the constructor by the data loader). You must pass a FileObject to the ID3 tag constructor. This file is obtained by using the method FileUtil.toFile(), which determines the file encapsulated by the FileObject.

Another way to obtain instances of the ID3v1Tag and ID3v2Tag classes could be to provide them using the Lookup of the Mp3DataObject. This enables you to retrieve these instances from a simple Node or DataObject instance, without special type safety:

```
Node n = ...
ID3v1Tag id3v1 = n.getLookup().lookup(ID3v1Tag.class);
```

ID3 Editor

Now you just need a way to display and edit the ID3 data. You can do this with the *Properties* module of the NetBeans Platform connected to your MP3 file type. It is the nodes' job to provide properties to be displayed in the user interface. Therefore, you now create the Mp3DataNode class. Connected to this class, you must change the createNodeDelegate() method of the Mp3DataObject class. An Mp3DataNode instance is created then.

In the newly created Mp3DataNode class, you overwrite the createSheet() method. This method provides the properties of the nodes using a Sheet instance; features can occur that can only be read or written. In this example, the ID3v1 data will be read as well as written, while the ID3v2 data is only read.

First, you invoke the createSheet() method of the DataNode superclass, which already creates a Sheet and adds some basic properties to it, such as file name, size, or the date of modification. If you do not want this data displayed, you can also directly create your own sheet using Sheet.createDefault(). Inside a Sheet object, properties are grouped using Set objects. These groups may be purposefully hidden or shown in the Properties window. A Set is created using the static createPropertiesSet() method.

You create two of them, in order to manage the ID3v1 and ID3v2 data separately. It is important that each Set is given a unique name, using the method setName(); otherwise, the sets will be overridden inside the sheets. (See Listing 44-5).

Listing 44-5. Providing ID3 Information in a Properties Sheet for Display and Editing Purposes

```java
import org.openide.nodes.PropertySupport;
import org.openide.nodes.Sheet;

public class Mp3DataNode extends DataNode {
    ...
    @Override
    protected Sheet createSheet() {
        Sheet sheet = super.createSheet();
        Sheet.Set set1 = Sheet.createPropertiesSet();
        Sheet.Set set2 = Sheet.createPropertiesSet();
        set1.setName("id3v1");
        set1.setDisplayName("ID3 V1");
        set2.setName("id3v2");
        set2.setDisplayName("ID3 V2");

        Mp3DataObject m = getLookup().lookup(Mp3DataObject.class);
        ID3v1Tag id3v1 = m.getID3v1Tag();
        ID3v2Tag id3v2 = m.getID3v2Tag();
        try {
            /* ID3v1 Properties */
            Property title1 =
                new PropertySupport.Reflection<String>(id3v1, String.class, "title");
            ...
            title1.setName("Title");
            set1.put(title1);
            /* ID3v2 Properties */
            Property album2 =
                new PropertySupport.Reflection<String>(id3v2, String.class, "getAlbum", null);
            ...
            album2.setName("Album");
            set2.put(album2);
        } catch (Exception e) { }
```

```
        sheet.put(set1);
        sheet.put(set2);
        return sheet;
    }
}
```

The Lookup of the Node provides an instance of the Mp3DataObject represented by that node. Using the previously created methods getID3v1Tag() and getID3v2Tag() you gain access to the ID3 information of the MP3 file. Then, you create an instance of the class PropertySupport.Reflection<T> for every property. Specify the type of the property (in this example, it is String) using a template. For the read and write properties you assign the name of the method (with which the properties can be read and written) without the prefixes get and set. Passing title to the constructor sets the title (for example, using the methods getTitle() and setTitle()). Properties that are read-only are passed to a special version of the constructor taking the names of the get and set methods separately. Passing null as set method will prevent modification of the property. Each property created is named using the method setName(). This name is displayed in the *Properties* window. Finally, add each instance to the Sheet object using the put() method, and return that sheet.

When starting the application and opening the favorites and the properties window via the *Window* menu, you get the window shown in Figure 44-3, if you select an MP3 file in the properties window.

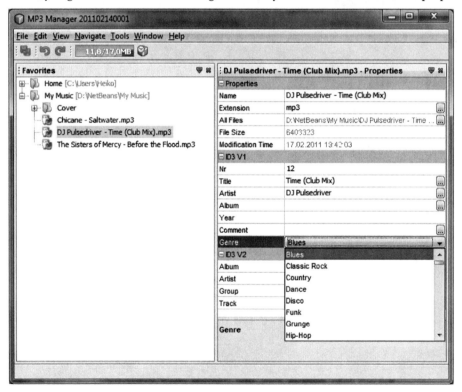

Figure 44-3. Using the Properties window as ID3 editor

In Chapter 19, you will learn how to provide a special editor (such as a combo box to select the values) for properties, such as the genre which can have a series of predefined values.

Media Library

In the previous section, you made use of the Favorites module provided by the NetBeans Platform. This module is also very good for the usage within your application, as a *Media Library*. The reason for this is that the user can add each file separately or the whole directory in a very simple manner to the Favorites module. That feature is not restricted to MP3 files only, but can be used to manage any file type. Thus, by adding the Image module from the idle cluster, for example, you can also manage and display covers of tracks in JPG format. Since you can bind actions to a particular MIME type via the layer file, you are able to work with MP3 files directly in the *Favorites* window. That means, for example, you can directly play files by merely double-clicking, or using the drag-and-drop feature to drag files to a separate window (e.g., a playlist). Bear in mind that the Favorites module or window is activated (meaning available) in your NetBeans Platform, in order to be able to use it. Open the *Properties* of the MP3 manager via the context menu and ensure that the *Favorites* module is activated in the *Libraries* category under the *platform* cluster.

Now you can also change the name and the menus of the Favorites module using a branding module. The branding module is automatically created by the NetBeans IDE. You just have to adapt the desired text in the branding dialog, which you can open via *Branding…* in the context menu of the Platform application. You can search for the texts to be substituted in the *Resource Bundles* register. You want to adapt the name of the window and the different menu entries as shown in Figure 44-4.

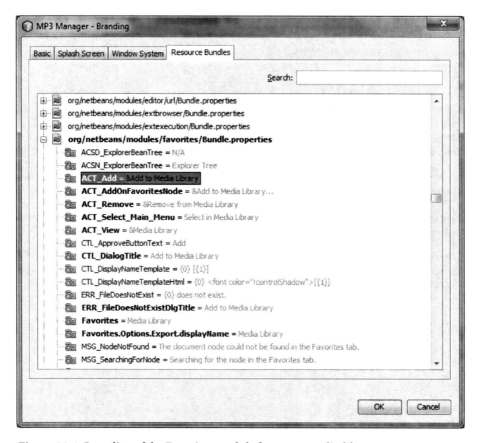

Figure 44-4. Branding of the Favorites module for use as media library

Services

Next, you will implement the main functionality of the application. It is divided into two sections: the *Service Interface* and the *Service Provider*. In conjunction with the registry mechanism of the service provider and the Lookup, you can implement the functionality that is absolutely decoupled and independent of specific modules. Therefore, you create a new module to bundle the service interfaces for a central provision (see Figure 44-1). From this point of view, the module can be seen as a link between different application modules. Use *File ➤ New Project...* to create a new module, as usual. For convenience, name it *Services* and set the code name base to `com.hboeck.mp3manager.services`. Even for this module, you must remember to enable public access for the packages, which you will do under *Properties ➤ API Versioning*, because only then can you define a dependency to the Services module and be able to use its classes.

MP3 Player

In the previous section, you created the base for your player design by dividing the services module into two parts: a service interface and a service provider. Now you consider the interfaces and the functionality the player should provide to other components of your application. You then describe these interfaces in an abstract class. You should therefore choose an abstract class, and not an interface, since the player will be a central global service. In other words, the requesting modules are usually only interested in a single player instance. As you will notice in the following sections, this behavior can be ensured much more easily using an abstract class.

Service Interface

Inside the services module, you create a new package named player with an abstract class named Mp3Player. Of course, a player must be able to play back, pause, and stop MP3 files. Additionally, a user should be able to mute the playback, control the volume, and see the current playback position and total duration. It should also be possible to influence the current playback position of the file. You specify all these desired functionalities which the player will provide via the abstract method in this class. (See Listing 44-6).

Listing 44-6. Defining the Player's Interfaces and Providing an Implementation Using the getDefault()
Method

```
package com.hboeck.mp3manager.services.player;
import com.hboeck.mp3manager.filetype.Mp3DataObject;
import java.util.ListIterator;
import org.openide.util.Lookup;
...
public abstract class Mp3Player {

    public static Mp3Player getDefault() {
        Mp3Player p = Lookup.getDefault().lookup(Mp3Player.class);
        if (p == null) {
            p = new DefaultMp3Player();
        }
        return p;
    }

    public abstract void play(Mp3DataObject mp3);
    public abstract void play(ListIterator<Mp3DataObject> mp3s);
    public abstract void pause();
    public abstract void stop();
    public abstract void previous();
    public abstract void next();
    public abstract void setMute(boolean mute);
    public abstract void setVolume(int volume);
    public abstract int getDuration();
    public abstract int getMediaTime();
    public abstract void setMediaTime(int seconds);
}
```

The most important part for the service requesters—meaning the modules that want to use the player—is the getDefault() method. This method actually searches for a registered Mp3Player implementation via the Lookup. If an implementation is found, the Lookup returns an instance of it. If no implementation is found, you nonetheless want to ensure that a requester never obtains a null reference, but always an instance of the Mp3Player class. Therefore, you provide a default implementation inside the abstract Mp3Player class, which is named DefaultMp3Player and will do—in the simplest case—nothing except tell the user it will do nothing. Another easy and smart solution would be to forward the MP3 file to an external application. (See Listing 44-7).

Listing 44-7. Providing a Default Implementation Inside the Abstract Class

```
public abstract class Mp3Player {
    ...
    private static class DefaultMp3Player extends Mp3Player {
        public void play(Mp3DataObject mp3) {
            Logger.getLogger(Mp3Player.class.getName()).info("not supported");
        }
        public void stop() { }
        ...
    }
}
```

If we imagine a module using the player, we will quickly notice that a module needs to be notified about the events that may occur in the player in order to react. Thus, a user interface, for example, needs to be informed about the end of the playback of an MP3 file. For this purpose, we specify a listener interface named Mp3PlayerEventListener interface, which might look like this in a simple version:

```
package com.hboeck.mp3manager.services.player;
import com.hboeck.mp3manager.filetype.Mp3DataObject;
import java.util.EventListener;

public interface Mp3PlayerEventListener extends EventListener{
    public void playing(Mp3DataObject mp3);
    public void stopped();
}
```

The functionality to add and remove Mp3PlayerEventListener to the player is implemented directly in the abstract class; the concrete implementation does not need to worry about this anymore. Additionally, you provide two fire methods equivalent to the listener interface with which the concrete classes are able to notify listeners about events, as shown in Listing 44-8.

Listing 44-8. Methods to Manage Listeners Interested in Events

```
import com.hboeck.mp3manager.filetype.Mp3DataObject;
import java.util.ListIterator;
import javax.swing.event.EventListenerList;
import org.openide.util.Lookup;

public abstract class Mp3Player {
    ...
    private final EventListenerList listeners = new EventListenerList();
```

```
    public void addEventListener(Mp3PlayerEventListener l) {
        listeners.add(Mp3PlayerEventListener.class, l);
    }

    public void removeEventListener(Mp3PlayerEventListener l) {
        listeners.remove(Mp3PlayerEventListener.class, l);
    }

    protected final void firePlayEvent(Mp3DataObject mp3) {
        for(Mp3PlayerEventListener listener :
            listeners.getListeners(Mp3PlayerEventListener.class)) {
            listener.playing(mp3);
        }
    }

    protected final void fireStopEvent() {
        for(Mp3PlayerEventListener listener :
            listeners.getListeners(Mp3PlayerEventListener.class)) {
            listener.stopped();
        }
    }
}
```

Service Provider

Your first service has been defined, so now you can start implementing the service provider. This means you use the JMF module and its functionality for the playback of MP3 files. Already this brings you back to the usage of your MP3 file type. As indicated previously in Figure 44-1, the MP3 player is implemented into a separate module. So, you create a new module again which you call Player and to which you will pass the code name base com.hboeck.mp3manager.player. Using *Properties* ➤ *Libraries*, you define the corresponding dependencies so this module can access the file type, the JMF plugin, and the service interface.

First, you create an Mp3PlayerImpl class, which inherits from the previously created service interface Mp3Player. You implement the abstract methods of the service interface MP3Player here via the Java Media Framework. Start with the play() method, which an MP3 file is passed to as Mp3DataObject. The central class of JMF is the Manager class. It is used to obtain system-dependent resources. This manager creates a Player instance for the MP3 file passed as a URL. Before starting that Player using the start() method, you register a ControllerListener for it, so that you will be informed of the different states of the Player. (See Listing 44-9.)

Listing 44-9. Implementation of the Service Provider Using the JMF

```
package com.hboeck.mp3manager.player;
import com.hboeck.mp3manager.filetype.Mp3DataObject;
import com.hboeck.mp3manager.services.player.Mp3Player;
import javax.media.ControllerEvent;
import javax.media.ControllerListener;
import javax.media.EndOfMediaEvent;
import javax.media.GainControl;
import javax.media.Manager;
import javax.media.Player;
```

```java
import javax.media.RealizeCompleteEvent;
import javax.media.Time;
...
public class Mp3PlayerImpl extends Mp3Player implements ControllerListener {

    private static final Logger LOG = Logger.getLogger(Mp3PlayerImpl.class.getName());
    private Player      player      = null;
    private GainControl volumeControl = null;
    private int      volume = 20;
    private boolean mute    = false;
    private Mp3DataObject                mp3  = null;
    private ListIterator<Mp3DataObject> list = null;

    public Mp3PlayerImpl() {
    }

    @Override
    public void play(Mp3DataObject mp3) {
        try {
            this.mp3 = mp3;
            if(player != null) {
                player.stop();
                player.close();
            }
            player = Manager.createPlayer(mp3.getPrimaryFile().getURL());
            player.addControllerListener(this);
            player.start();
        } catch(Exception e) {
            LOG.log(Level.SEVERE, e.getMessage(), e);
        }
    }

    @Override
    public void play(ListIterator<Mp3DataObject> mp3s) {
        list = mp3s;
        if(list.hasNext()) {
            play(list.next());
        }
    }

    @Override
    public void pause() {
        if(player != null) {
            player.stop();
        }
    }

    @Override
    public void stop() {
        if(player != null) {
            fireStopEvent();
```

```
        player.stop();
        player.setMediaTime(new Time(0));
        player.close();
    }
}

@Override
public void previous() {
    if (list != null && list.hasPrevious()) {
        play(list.previous());
    }
}

@Override
public void next() {
    if (list != null && list.hasNext()) {
        play(list.next());
    }
}
```

The ControllerListener interface defines the controllerUpdate() method, which is used to get the current state of the Player. We are particularly interested in two states: first, only if the Player is realized do you get access to the volume control; at the same time, you notify the listeners that the playback of the MP3 file already started (you do so via the firePlayEvent() method). The second event of interest is EndOfMediaEvent, which allows you to stop the Player, and then reset the current playback position to the beginning. If a list of MP3 files was passed to the play() method, you start playback with the next file in the list. (See Listing 44-10).

Listing 44-10. Reacting on the Events of the JMF Player

```
@Override
public void controllerUpdate(ControllerEvent evt) {
    if (evt instanceof RealizeCompleteEvent) {
        LOG.info("Realized");
        firePlayEvent(mp3);
        volumeControl = player.getGainControl();
        setVolume(volume);
        setMute(mute);
    } else if (evt instanceof EndOfMediaEvent) {
        LOG.info("End of Media");
        stop();
        if(list != null && list.hasNext()) {
            play(list.next());
        } else {
            list = null;
        }
    }
}
```

Finally, you also implement the missing control and information methods in your service provider class. (See Listing 44-11).

Listing 44-11. Methods to Control Volume and Playback Position

```
@Override
public void setVolume(int volume) {
    this.volume = volume;
    if(volumeControl != null) {
        volumeControl.setLevel((float)(volume/100.0));
    }
}

@Override
public void setMute(boolean mute) {
    this.mute = mute;
    if(volumeControl != null) {
        volumeControl.setMute(mute);
    }
}

@Override
public int getDuration() {
    return (int)player.getDuration().getSeconds();
}

@Override
public int getMediaTime() {
    return (int)player.getMediaTime().getSeconds();
}

@Override
public void setMediaTime(int seconds) {
    player.setMediaTime(new Time((double)seconds));
}
}
```

Accessing this implementation of the MP3 player should be done via the `Mp3Player.getDefault()` method. You must register the `Mp3PlayerImpl` class to enable this method to find the implementation using the Lookup. This is done by a `ServiceProvider` annotation. (See Listing 44-12).

Listing 44-12. Registering the Mp3Player Service Provider

```
import org.openide.util.lookup.ServiceProvider;
...
@ServiceProvider(service=Mp3Player.class)
public class Mp3PlayerImpl extends Mp3Player implements ControllerListener {
    ...
}
```

Playback of MP3 Files

Now that you have implemented the MP3 player service provider, you can register an action for your MP3 file type. Thus, it is possible to play an MP3 file via the context menu or just by double-clicking in the Favorites window, for example. Such an action can easily be created and registered using the NetBeans Action wizard. Call *File* ➤ *New File...* and select *Module Development* ➤ *Action*. Choose *Conditionally Enabled* as action type and Mp3DataObject as context interface. On the next page, you can associate this action with a predefined category or create a new one. You continue assigning the action to a menu. You activate the option *File Type Context Menu Item* so the action appears in the context menu of an MP3 file. Select audio/mpeg as content type, which you already defined when you created the MP3 file type. Finally, you define the class name, a label, and an icon on the last page of the wizard. You complete the wizard with *Finish*. Doing so, it becomes clear once more which relief the NetBeans IDE and the NetBeans Platform bring. You just have to insert one more line in the actionPerformed() method (see Listing 44-13).

Listing 44-13. Context-Sensitive Action to Play MP3 Files

```java
import com.hboeck.mp3manager.filetype.Mp3DataObject;
import com.hboeck.mp3manager.services.player.Mp3Player;
import java.awt.event.ActionListener;
import java.awt.event.ActionEvent;
import org.openide.awt.ActionRegistration;
import org.openide.awt.ActionReference;
import org.openide.awt.ActionReferences;
import org.openide.awt.ActionID;

@ActionID(
        category = "File",
        id = "com.hboeck.mp3manager.player.PlayAction")
@ActionRegistration(
        displayName = "#CTL_PlayAction",
        iconBase= "com/hboeck/mp3manager/player/gui/icons/play16.png")
@ActionReferences({
    @ActionReference(path = "Menu/File", position = 0),
    @ActionReference(path = "Loaders/audio/mpeg/Actions", position = 0)
})
public final class PlayAction implements ActionListener {
    private final Mp3DataObject context;

    public PlayAction(Mp3DataObject context) {
        this.context = context;
    }

    @Override
    public void actionPerformed(ActionEvent ev) {
        Mp3Player.getDefault().play(context);
    }
}
```

With this action, you can immediately test the MP3 player. Start the application and open the Favorites window. Add an MP3 file or a folder with MP3 files to the Favorites Window. Now you can start the playback by double-clicking or using the context menu.

User Interface

Having only an action is not really satisfying, so in this section you will create a complete user interface for an MP3 player. This user interface uses the functionality provided by the MP3 player service. You create a new package in the player module named com.hboeck.mp3manager.player.gui. With the help of the *Window* wizard, you create a TopComponent class. You can invoke this wizard like the previous ones via *File ➤ New File... ➤ Module Development.* For the window position, you can use explorer, for example, and for the class name prefix you can use Mp3Player. Then, you build a TopComponent using the Form Designer as shown in Figure 44-5.

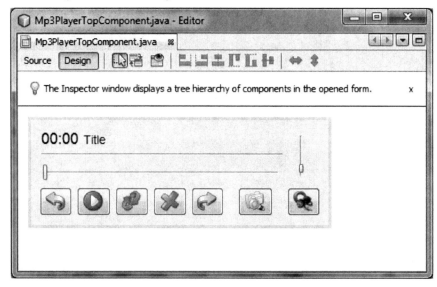

Figure 44-5. MP3 player user interface

Of course, it is not looking all that beautiful, but it is functional and offers all the relevant MP3 player functionalities. Most of the work required for designing the top component is done by the Form Designer. You simply have to implement the actions (see Listing 44-14). But first, give yourself access to an Mp3Player instance delivered by the getDefault() method in the constructor. For this instance, register an Mp3PlayerEventListener, for which you defined an interface in the "Service Interface" section, to be notified about the start and stop event of the MP3 file. These events are required to update information displayed on the user interface.

Listing 44-14. Most of the Methods Are Really Simple and Only Delegate the Relevant Values to the MP3 Player

```java
import com.hboeck.mp3manager.filetype.Mp3DataObject;
import javax.swing.JFileChooser;
import javax.swing.Timer;
import javax.swing.filechooser.FileNameExtensionFilter;
import org.openide.awt.ActionID;
import org.openide.awt.ActionReference;
...
@TopComponent.Description( preferredID = "Mp3PlayerTopComponent",
    iconBase="com/hboeck/mp3manager/player/gui/player.png",
    persistenceType = TopComponent.PERSISTENCE_ALWAYS)
@TopComponent.Registration( mode = "explorer",
    openAtStartup = true)
@ActionID( category = "Window",
    id = "com.hboeck.mp3manager.player.gui.Mp3PlayerTopComponent")
@ActionReference(path = "Menu/Window" /*, position = 333 */)
@TopComponent.OpenActionRegistration(
    displayName = "#CTL_Mp3PlayerAction",
    preferredID = "Mp3PlayerTopComponent")
public final class Mp3PlayerTopComponent extends TopComponent
    implements Mp3PlayerEventListener {
    private static final SimpleDateFormat SDF = new SimpleDateFormat("mm:ss");
    private JSlider       duration;
    private JSlider       volume;
    private JToggleButton mute;
    private JButton       next;
    private JButton       open;
    private JButton       pause;
    private JButton       play;
    private JButton       previous;
    private JButton       stop;
    private JLabel        time;
    private JLabel        title;
    private Timer       t      = null;
    private Mp3Player player = null;

    public Mp3PlayerTopComponent() {
        initComponents();
        ...
        player = Mp3Player.getDefault();
        player.addEventListener(this);
    }

    private void pauseActionPerformed(ActionEvent evt) {
        player.pause();
    }
```

```
private void stopActionPerformed(ActionEvent evt) {
    player.stop();
}

private void nextActionPerformed(ActionEvent evt) {
    player.next();
}

private void previousActionPerformed(ActionEvent evt) {
    player.previous();
}

private void muteActionPerformed(ActionEvent evt) {
    player.setMute(mute.isSelected());
}

private void volumeStateChanged(ChangeEvent evt) {
    player.setVolume(volume.getValue());
}

private void durationMouseReleased(MouseEvent evt) {
    player.setMediaTime(duration.getValue());
}
```

Clicking the *Play* button invokes the playActionPerformed() method, in which you can use the TopComponent.Registry (see Listing 44-15). This will provide the currently activated nodes independently of the TopComponent they belong to, that is, if an Mp3DataObject (or rather an Mp3DataNode) is selected in any top component (regardless of whether that is the Media Library window or, for example, the playlist) and the *Play* button is clicked, this file will be played back.

Listing 44-15. Using TopComponent.Registry, the Currently Selected MP3 File Can Be Played.

```
private void playActionPerformed(ActionEvent evt) {
    Node n[] = getRegistry().getActivatedNodes();
    if(n != null) {
        Mp3DataObject mp3 = n[0].getLookup().lookup(Mp3DataObject.class);
        if(mp3 != null) {
            player.play(mp3);
        }
    }
}

private void openActionPerformed(ActionEvent evt) {
    JFileChooser c = new JFileChooser();
    c.setFileFilter(new FileNameExtensionFilter("MP3 Files", "mp3"));

    if(c.showOpenDialog(this) == JFileChooser.APPROVE_OPTION) {
        try {
            player.play(Mp3DataObject.find(c.getSelectedFile()));
        } catch(Exception e) {
            Exceptions.printStackTrace(e);
        }
    }
```

```
    }
}
```

Within the playing() method, called by Mp3Player, you can display title and time information in the user interface. Thus, you are not restricted to the file name; you can also access the ID3 tag and display information out of the tag (see Listing 44-16). The timer is used to update playback time. In the stopped() method (indicating that the playback of the MP3 file was stopped), you reset all displayed information and stop the timer.

Listing 44-16. Updating the Displayed Information of the Current MP3 File

```java
public void playing(Mp3DataObject mp3) {
    resetInfos();
    title.setText(mp3.getName());
    duration.setMaximum(player.getDuration());
    ID3v1Tag id3v1 = mp3.getID3v1Tag();
    title.setText(id3v1.getArtist()+" - "+id3v1.getTitle());
    ActionListener updateInfo = new ActionListener() {
        public void actionPerformed(ActionEvent evt) {
            duration.setValue(player.getMediaTime());
            time.setText(SDF.format(new Date(player.getMediaTime() * 1000)));
        }
    };

    if (t != null) {
        t.stop();
    }
    t = new Timer(1000, updateInfo);
    t.start();
}

public void stopped() {
    resetInfos();
    if(t != null) {
        t.stop();
    }
}

private void resetInfos() {
    duration.setValue(0);
    time.setText("00:00");
    title.setText("Title");
}
}
```

Playlist

The objective of this section is to create a playlist. The user should be able to manage multiple playlists in parallel. And of course you want the user to be able to add MP3 files from the Media Library to the playlist by using drag-and-drop. All this functionality is provided in a separate module. So, you create a new module via *File* ➤ *New Project...* ➤ *NetBeans Modules* ➤ *Module*, name it *Playlist*, and set the code name base to `com.hboeck.mp3manager.playlist`. Add a dependency to the *File Type* and *Services* module.

For the playlist, another top component is used, containing a `TreeTableView` taken from the Explorer API. Using such a view eases the management of MP3 files with the help of the `Mp3DataNode` class.

Node View

Let us start with the view for the nodes. You use a `TreeTableView` and create the subclass `PlaylistView`. This class is used to hide the configuration and to have a handier class. The only thing you need to configure is the default action processor because, by default, a double-click in this view executes the default action of a node (that is, an `Mp3DataNode`), which is the `PlayAction` you created in the "Playback of MP3 files" section. But this action plays only a single file, while the desired behavior of a playlist is to play the complete list automatically. Therefore, you implement the `setDefaultActionProcessor()` method (see Listing 44-17), which takes an instance of an `ActionListener`. The `actionPerformed()` method of this listener is executed (instead of the node's default action) when the node is double-clicked or the *Enter* key is pressed.

Listing 44-17. This View Is Used to Represent MP3 Files in a List View.

```
package com.hboeck.mp3manager.playlist;
import org.openide.explorer.view.TreeTableView;

public class PlaylistView extends TreeTableView {

    public PlaylistView() {
        setRootVisible(false);
    }

    public void setDefaultActionProcessor(final ActionListener action) {
        setDefaultActionAllowed(false);
        tree.addMouseListener(new MouseAdapter() {
            @Override
            public void mouseClicked(MouseEvent me) {
                if (me.getClickCount() == 2) {
                    action.actionPerformed(null);
                }
            }
        });
        treeTable.registerKeyboardAction(action,
                KeyStroke.getKeyStroke(KeyEvent.VK_ENTER, 0, false),
                JComponent.WHEN_FOCUSED);
    }
}
```

Node Container

All nodes represented in the `PlaylistView` are managed by a container. A container is based on the class `Children`. There are different variants of this class, which should be chosen depending on the purpose. You will use the class `Index.ArrayChildren` as superclass for your node container (see Listing 44-18). The nodes to be added to a playlist are stored in an object of the type `ArrayList`. You provide this list with the method initCollection(). The list will initially be empty, because the nodes are inserted via drag-and-drop from the Media Library. Using the getRemaining() method, you return a list of remaining MP3 files, which can be directly passed to the player to play back the playlist.

Listing 44-18. Container Class to Manage MP3 files Contained in a Playlist

```
package com.hboeck.mp3manager.playlist;
import com.hboeck.mp3manager.filetype.Mp3DataObject;
import org.openide.nodes.Index;
import org.openide.nodes.Node;

public final class NodeContainer extends Index.ArrayChildren {
    private List<Node> list = new ArrayList<Node>();

    @Override
    protected List<Node> initCollection() {
        return list;
    }

    public ListIterator<Mp3DataObject> getRemaining(Node n) {
        List<Mp3DataObject> v = new ArrayList<Mp3DataObject>();
        for (Node n : list.subList(indexOf(n), list.size())) {
            v.add(n.getLookup().lookup(Mp3DataObject.class));
        }
        return v.listIterator();
    }

    public void add(Node n) {
        add(new Node[]{n});
    }
}
```

Top Component

Now you can begin creating the playlist. To do so, you need a top component again. You will create the top component using the Window wizard via *File ➤ New File... ➤ Module Development ➤ Window*. You assign the top component to the *editor* mode and assign the prefix Playlist. Thus, you have already created the basic structure of the playlist. A top component created this way is designed as a singleton instance by default. This means that only one window of that type can be opened. Since you want to manage multiple playlists at the same time, though, you must change this. To do so, you just have to delete the preferredID attribute of the TopComponent.OpenActionRegistration annotation. So, a new PlaylistTopComponent instance is created by the corresponding action with each invocation. (See Figure 44-6).

```
package com.hboeck.mp3manager.playlist;
import com.hboeck.mp3manager.filetype.Mp3DataObject;
import com.hboeck.mp3manager.services.player.Mp3Player;
import org.openide.explorer.ExplorerManager;
import org.openide.explorer.ExplorerUtils;
import org.openide.nodes.AbstractNode;
```

```java
@TopComponent.Description( preferredID = "PlaylistTopComponent",
   iconBase = "com/hboeck/mp3manager/playlist/playlist.png",
   persistenceType = TopComponent.PERSISTENCE_ALWAYS)
@TopComponent.Registration( mode = "editor",
   openAtStartup = false)
@ActionID( category = "Window",
   id = "com.hboeck.mp3manager.playlist.PlaylistTopComponent")
@ActionReference(path = "Menu/Window" /*, position = 333 */)
@TopComponent.OpenActionRegistration(
   displayName = "#CTL_PlaylistAction")
public final class PlaylistTopComponent extends TopComponent
   implements ExplorerManager.Provider {

   private static final String PREF_CURRENTDIR = "currentdir";
   private Preferences PREF = NbPreferences.forModule(PlaylistTopComponent.class)
   private ExplorerManager manager    = new ExplorerManager();
   private NodeContainer   container = new NodeContainer();
   private PlaylistView    playlist  = new PlaylistView();

   public PlaylistTopComponent() {
      initComponents();
      setName(NbBundle.getMessage(PlaylistTopComponent.class, "CTL_Playlist"));
      setToolTipText(NbBundle.getMessage(PlaylistTopComponent.class, "CTL_Playlist"));
      manager.setRootContext(new AbstractNode(container));
      playlist.setDefaultActionProcessor(new Play());
      associateLookup(ExplorerUtils.createLookup(manager, getActionMap()));
   }

   private final class Play implements ActionListener {
      @Override
      public void actionPerformed(ActionEvent e) {
         Mp3Player.getDefault().play(
            container.getRemaining(manager.getSelectedNodes()[0]));
      }
   }

   public ExplorerManager getExplorerManager() {
      return manager;
   }
   ...
}
```

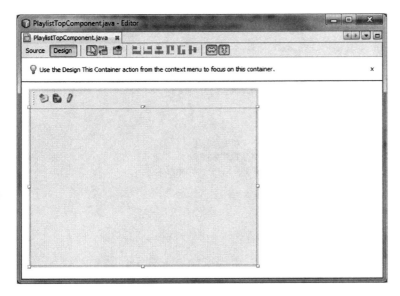

Figure 44-6. Playlist top component

You enhance the top component by adding a toolbar with three buttons, using the Form Designer.These buttons are used to add and remove files, and to name the playlist. Finally, you just add a panel that uses the BorderLayout and occupies the whole area of the top component. This panel is used as the container for the node view.

Managing the nodes in your PlaylistView is done by an explorer manager. You implement the ExplorerManager.Provider interface, create a private instance of the ExplorerManager, and return this manager in the getExplorerManager() method. Additionally, you create a NodeContainer instance. Every manager has a root context, which is a node that is used as root for all the other nodes. This context is set by the method setRootContext(). You will use an AbstractNode as the root context (because you do not want to display it anyway) and pass it to the container carrying the MP3 files of the playlist.

Finally, you create a PlaylistView instance to which you pass the action to be performed when double-clicking an MP3 file in the playlist. To pass the action, use the setDefaultActionProcessor() method. Your default behavior is to play back the complete list starting at the selected file. Therefore, the method getRemaining() delivers all files still remaining in the list. Finally, the view just needs to be added to the panel you already created in a previous step using the Form Designer. To do so, call *Customize Code* from the context menu of the panel and insert the following lines after the layout initialization (pre-population):

```
panel.add(playlist, BorderLayout.CENTER);
```

Of course, in the end, you should not forget the buttons in the toolbar of the playlist, since they are used to add and remove MP3 files by invoking a file chooser dialog, as well as to rename the playlist itself. It should be possible to add files in a way that multiple files and directories can be selected via the addActionPerformed() method. Therefore, you add the method addAllFiles(), which recursively parses the selection and adds all files to the node container. Removing files (done by the removeActionPerformed() method) is very easy, because the ExplorerManager returns all selected entries, and the remove() method of the container removes an array of nodes in one step. Renaming the playlist (invoked by the method renameActionPerformed()) is easy as well, using the Dialogs API. (See Listing 44-19).

Listing 44-19. Actions to Edit the Playlist

```
public final class PlaylistTopComponent extends TopComponent
    implements ExplorerManager.Provider {
    ...
    private void addActionPerformed(ActionEvent evt) {
        JFileChooser fc = new JFileChooser(PREF.get(PREF_CURRENTDIR, ""));
        fc.setFileSelectionMode(JFileChooser.FILES_AND_DIRECTORIES);
        fc.setFileFilter(new FileNameExtensionFilter("MP3 Files", "mp3"));
        fc.setMultiSelectionEnabled(true);
        if(fc.showOpenDialog(this) ==JFileChooser.APPROVE_OPTION) {
            addAllFiles(fc.getSelectedFiles());
            PREF.put(PREF_CURRENTDIR,
                fc.getCurrentDirectory().getAbsolutePath());
        }
    }

    private void addAllFiles(File[] files) {
        for(File f : files) {
            if(f.isFile()) {
                try {
                    container.add(Mp3DataObject.find(f).getNodeDelegate());
                } catch(Exception e) {}
            } else if(f.isDirectory()) {
                addAllFiles(f.listFiles());
            }
        }
    }

    private void removeActionPerformed(ActionEvent evt) {
        container.remove(manager.getSelectedNodes());
    }

    private void renameActionPerformed(ActionEvent evt) {
        NotifyDescriptor.InputLine nf = new NotifyDescriptor.InputLine(
            "New Playlist Name", "Rename");
        nf.setInputText(getName());
        if(DialogDisplayer.getDefault().notify(nf) == NotifyDescriptor.OK_OPTION) {
            setName(nf.getInputText());
        }
    }
}
```

Now you can start the application, open one or multiple playlists, and add MP3 files via the toolbar (see Figure 44-7).

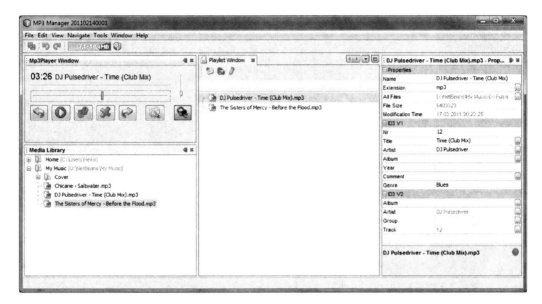

Figure 44-7. *Using the toolbar playlist, files can be added to the playlist.*

If you try to drag files from the Media Library window to the playlist you will quickly recognize that this is not possible. This is not possible, yet, because your Mp3DataNode class (containing the objects you want to transfer between windows) and the PlaylistView class are not yet prepared for dragging actions. We will cover this aspect of simple and intuitive usage in the next section.

Drag and Drop

First, you extend the Mp3DataNode class. The super class, AbstractNode, already implements the drag() method, which is invoked if a drag event occurs. For example, a drag event will be fired when you drag files from the Media Library to the playlist. This method must deliver a Transferable instance. So you will implement the Transferable interface and its methods in the Mp3DataNode class. You overwrite the drag() method and thus, a reference is returned to its own reference. To access the data, and for identification purposes, during a drag-and-drop operation you create a DataFlavor object that can be accessed from outside. (See Listing 44-20.)

Listing 44-20. *Extension to the Mp3DataNode Class to Enable Drag and Drop*

```
package com.hboeck.mp3manager.filetype;
import java.awt.datatransfer.DataFlavor;
import java.awt.datatransfer.Transferable;
import java.awt.datatransfer.UnsupportedFlavorException;
...
public class Mp3DataNode extends DataNode implements Transferable {
    public static final DataFlavor DATA_FLAVOR =
        new DataFlavor(Mp3DataNode.class, "Mp3DataNode");
    ...
```

```java
    @Override
    public Transferable drag() {
        return this;
    }

    @Override
    public DataFlavor[] getTransferDataFlavors() {
        return new DataFlavor[]{DATA_FLAVOR};
    }

    @Override
    public boolean isDataFlavorSupported(DataFlavor flavor) {
        return flavor == DATA_FLAVOR;
    }

    @Override
    public Object getTransferData(DataFlavor flavor) throws UnsupportedFlavorException {
        if(flavor == DATA_FLAVOR) {
            return this;
        } else {
            throw new UnsupportedFlavorException(flavor);
        }
    }
}
}
```

However an Mp3DataNode can now be transferred, your playlist is still not able to accept it. Now, you must add a DropTarget to the PlaylistView. You create a DropTarget object and pass a DropTargetAdapter to it. Via this DropTargetAdapter you are then notified regarding both drag-and-drop events. You only implement the methods dragEnter() and drop(). The dragEnter() method is called as soon as a file is dragged to your playlist. As you only want to allow drops of MP3 files, check the type of data using the data flavor. In case it is not an Mp3DataNode, you call the rejectDrag() method to prevent a drop. The drop() method is invoked during the real drop event. So, you extract the Mp3DataNode from the parameter and add the node to the ExplorerManager, or rather the container responsible for the view. (See Listing 44-21.)

Listing 44-21. To Enable the Addition of MP3 Files via Drag and Drop, a DropTarget Is Required for the PlaylistView.

```java
package com.hboeck.mp3manager.playlist;
import java.awt.dnd.DropTarget;
import java.awt.dnd.DropTargetAdapter;
import java.awt.dnd.DropTargetDragEvent;
import java.awt.dnd.DropTargetDropEvent;
...
public class PlaylistView extends TreeTableView {
    public PlaylistView() {
        setRootVisible(false);
        setDropTarget();
    }

    private void setDropTarget() {
```

```
DropTarget dt = new DropTarget(this, new DropTargetAdapter() {
    @Override
    public void dragEnter(DropTargetDragEvent dtde) {
        if(!dtde.isDataFlavorSupported(Mp3DataNode.DATA_FLAVOR)) {
            dtde.rejectDrag();
        }
    }

    @Override
    public void drop(DropTargetDropEvent dtde) {
        try {
            Mp3DataNode n = (Mp3DataNode)dtde.getTransferable().
                getTransferData(Mp3DataNode.DATA_FLAVOR);
            ExplorerManager.find(getParent()).
                getRootContext().getChildren().add(new Node[]{n});
        } catch(Exception e) {
            Exceptions.printStackTrace(e);
            dtde.rejectDrop();
        }
    }
});
setDropTarget(dt);
    }
}
```

Thus, you are now able to drag MP3 files from the Media Library or other sources directly into a playlist.

Saving the Playlist

You may have already noticed that the content of the playlist is lost when restarting the application. This is because the window system stores the playlist itself, but is unable to store the contained data. In other words, you have to extend the load and store functions for your application. A good approach is to store the lists in an embedded database (Java DB, for example, works very well for this). This client-side database system was already used in the "Java DB" section in Chapter 26. You integrate it into your application using a module, and thus you can use the database (in addition to the use for playlists) for other purposes.

The module is a library wrapper module, and is created like any other module—via *File ➤ New Project... ➤ NetBeans Modules ➤ Library Wrapper Module.* You add the files *lib/derby.jar* and *lib/derbyLocale_de_DE.jar* to it from the Java DB distribution. (Further information on how to integrate and use Java DB, as well as where to obtain a distribution, can be found in Chapter 26.) Name the module *Java DB* and use org.apache.derby for the code name base. After creating the module, add a module installer, which is used to initialize centralized access. Such an installer can be created via *File ➤ New File... ➤ Module Development ➤ Installer / Activator.* Afterward, rename it with *Refactor ➤ Rename...* to *Database.*

In the restored() method, called while starting the module, you set the system directory of Java DB and execute the initTables() method. This method will first check whether the table playlist exists by performing a SELECT query. If the table does not exist yet, a SQLException will be thrown, which you will catch in order to then create the table. Using the getConnection() method, you obtain a connection to the database. The close() method allows the database system to be correctly shut down after the application is finished. (See Listing 44-22.)

Listing 44-22. The Database Class Initializes the Database and Provides a Central Connection.

```
package org.apache.derby;
import java.sql.Connection;
import java.sql.DriverManager;
import java.sql.SQLException;
import java.sql.Statement;
import org.openide.modules.ModuleInstall;
import org.openide.util.Exceptions;

public class Database extends ModuleInstall {
    private static Connection conn = null;

    public void restored() {
        System.setProperty("derby.system.home",
            System.getProperty("netbeans.user",
            System.getProperty("user.home")) + "/databases");
        initTables();
    }

    private void initTables() {
        try {
            Statement stmt = getConnection().createStatement();
            stmt.executeQuery("SELECT id FROM playlist");
            stmt.close();
        } catch(SQLException e) {
            try {
                Statement stmt = getConnection().createStatement();
                stmt.execute("CREATE TABLE playlist (" +
                    "id VARCHAR(12)," +
                    "filename VARCHAR(100))");
                stmt.close();
            } catch(SQLException ex) {
                Exceptions.printStackTrace(ex);
            }
        }
    }

    public static Connection getConnection() throws SQLException{
        if(conn == null || conn.isClosed()) {
            conn = DriverManager.getConnection(
                "jdbc:derby:Mp3Manager;create=true",
                "user", "password");
        }
        return conn;
    }
```

```java
    public void close() {
        try {
            conn.close();
            DriverManager.getConnection("jdbc:derby:;shutdown=true");
        } catch (SQLException ex) {}
    }
}
```

Do not forget to make the org.apache.derby package containing the Database class public. To enable the *Playlist* module to access the database, specify a dependency to the Java DB module. As you already know, the nodes for a view have to be provided by the class NodeContainer. Knowing this, it would be best to just extend this class so it reads the content of the playlist from the database for itself and can store it when the application closes. To do so, add the methods load() and update() to the NodeContainer class. The load() method will perform a query to read all entries for a particular playlist. When the getNodeDelegate() method is used, each entry will result in an Mp3DataObject that delivers its corresponding node. (See Listing 44-23.)

Listing 44-23. The load() Method Reads All Entries from the Database and Adds Them to the Container.

```java
package com.hboeck.mp3manager.playlist;
import java.sql.PreparedStatement;
import java.sql.ResultSet;
import java.sql.SQLException;
import org.apache.derby.Database;
...
public final class NodeContainer extends Index.ArrayChildren {
    ...
    public void load(String id) {
        try {
            String sql="SELECT filename FROM playlist WHERE id = ?";
            PreparedStatement stmt = Database.getConnection().prepareStatement(sql);
            stmt.setString(1, id);
            ResultSet rs = stmt.executeQuery();
            while (rs.next()) {
                try {
                    add(Mp3DataObject.find(rs.getString(1)).getNodeDelegate());
                } catch(Exception e) {}
            }
            rs.close();
            stmt.close();
        } catch(SQLException e) {
            LOG.severe(e.toString());
        }
    }
```

To store the playlist, use the update() method. First, remove all entries of this specific playlist to avoid lost entries. Then use the getNodes() method to obtain all nodes of this container and store the path of the related MP3 file for each node. (See Listing 44-24.)

Listing 44-24. The update() Method Stores the Container's Entries in the Database.

```java
    public void update(String id) {
```

```
    try {
        String sql = "DELETE FROM playlist WHERE id = ?";
        PreparedStatement stmt = Database.getConnection().prepareStatement(sql);
        stmt.setString(1, id);
        stmt.execute();
        stmt.close();
        sql="INSERT INTO playlist (id, filename) VALUES (?, ?)";
        stmt = Database.getConnection().prepareStatement(sql);
        for(Node n : getNodes()) {
            stmt.setString(1, id);
            stmt.setString(2, n.getLookup().lookup(Mp3DataObject.class).
                getPrimaryFile().getPath());
            stmt.execute();
        }
        stmt.close();
    } catch(Exception e) {
        LOG.severe(e.toString());
    }
    }
}
}
```

You might ask who is calling these methods. The answer can be found if you open the Playlist class, since the base class, TopComponent, defines the componentOpened() method, called while opening the window. Here, you determine the unique ID of the top component, at first, while in a subsequent step you call the container's load() method with this ID. The writeExternal() method of the superclass is used to store data while the application is closing. Consequently, you will override this method and invoke the update() method with the ID you stored as a private variable. (See Listing 44-25.)

Listing 44-25. The Playlist Class Is Responsible for Loading and Storing the Container's Content.

```
public class PlaylistTopComponent extends TopComponent
    implements ExplorerManager.Provider {
    private String id = "";
    ...
    @Override
    public void componentOpened() {
        id = WindowManager.getDefault().findTopComponentID(this);
        LOG.log(Level.INFO, "Load playlist with ID: {0}", id);
        container.load(id);
    }

    void writeProperties(Properties p) {
        p.setProperty("version", "1.0");
        LOG.log(Level.INFO, "Save playlist with ID: {0}", id);
        container.update(id);
    }
}
```

Summary

In this chapter, we created a bigger example which enabled you to apply a lot of the concepts you learned about in previous chapters. First, you defined a modular application structure based on NetBeans modules. You created a module, enabling your example application to play MP3 files. The module contains the JMF classes, as well as the MP3 plugin.

To handle MP3 files within the NetBeans Platform, you created an MP3 file type, as explained in Chapter 7. Next, you included an ID3 library in your NetBeans Platform Application, implementing an MP3 player service module. In this module, you also implemented a small GUI for the player.

Next, you created playlist functionality. To that end, you created your own node view and node container. To implement drag-and-drop functionality from the Media Library window, you extended your Node class.

Finally, this chapter demonstrated how easy it is to incrementally build a modular NetBeans Platform application and highlighted the extensibility of such an application.

Appendix

This Appendix includes a list of important extension points in the NetBeans Platform followed by a list of Document Type Definitions (DTDs) for some important configuration files such as mode, toolbar, or top component group configurations.

Important NetBeans Platform Extension Points

Table A-1 lists the most important NetBeans Platform extension points. These are folders in the layer file, where you register your extensions. The chapters in which you can find more information about each extension point's usage are included.

Table A-1. Important Extension Points of the NetBeans Platform

Extension Point	Usage
Actions	Registers all actions used throughout the application. In other words, this extension point creates the central action pool, the content of which can be referenced from other classes. See Chapter 6.
Loaders	Data object factories for special MIME types are registered with this extension point. See Chapter 7.
Menu	Registers all the entries in the application menus. An application menu is built from the folders and files in this extension point. See Chapter 9.
Navigator/Panels	Registers all the available Navigator panels by MIME type. See Chapter 18.
OptionsDialog	Option panels with their own category are determined here (see Chapter 20).

Extension Point	Usage
OptionsDialog/Advanced	The option panels (registered with this extension point) are added to the standard category. See Chapter 20.
Services	Registers service providers that are available via the default Lookup. See Chapter 5.
Services/AutoupdateType	Registers update center configurations. See Chapter 36.
Services/JavaHelp	Registers JavaHelp helpsets, which are then combined with all helpsets from the other modules, resulting in a single JavaHelp system for the end user. See Chapter 16.
Services/MIMEResolver	Registers specific data types to a data loader, which in turn is a factory for its DataObject. See Chapter 7.
Shortcuts	Registers keyboard shortcuts for an action. Provides a central overview of all existing shortcuts. See Chapter 9.
TaskList/Groups	Registers task groups that are shown in the NetBeans Platform's task list. See Chapter 23.
TaskList/Scanners	Registers custom scanner implementations that provide tasks for the NetBeans Platform's task list. See Chapter 23.
TaskList/Scopes	Registers custom scopes for task list searches.
Toolbars	Registers new toolbars and their actions. You can also add actions to pre-existing toolbars with this extension point. See Chapter 9.
WarmUp	Registers instances of the Runnable class, which are executed automatically and asynchronously as applications start. See Chapter 8.
Windows2/Components	Registers module top components. See Chapter 10.
Windows2/Groups	Registers groups of related top components that should behave in concert with each other. See Chapter 10.
Windows2/Modes	Registers custom modes, i.e., areas within the application where top components can be displayed. See Chapter 10.

Important Configuration DTDs

Filesystem

```
<!-- -//NetBeans//DTD Filesystem 1.2//EN -->
<!-- XML representation of a fixed filesystem -->
<!-- as for example a module layer. -->
<!-- See: org.openide.filesystems.XMLFileSystem -->
<!ELEMENT filesystem    (file|folder|attr)* >
<!ELEMENT folder        (folder|file|attr)* >
<!ELEMENT file          (#PCDATA|attr)* >
<!ELEMENT attr             EMPTY >
<!ATTLIST filesystem >
<!ATTLIST folder
          name          CDATA #REQUIRED >
<!ATTLIST file
          name          CDATA #REQUIRED
          url           CDATA #IMPLIED >
<!ATTLIST attr
          name          CDATA #REQUIRED
          bytevalue     CDATA #IMPLIED
          shortvalue    CDATA #IMPLIED
          intvalue      CDATA #IMPLIED
          longvalue     CDATA #IMPLIED
          floatvalue    CDATA #IMPLIED
          doublevalue   CDATA #IMPLIED
          boolvalue     CDATA #IMPLIED
          charvalue     CDATA #IMPLIED
          stringvalue   CDATA #IMPLIED
          urlvalue      CDATA #IMPLIED
          methodvalue   CDATA #IMPLIED
          newvalue      CDATA #IMPLIED
          serialvalue   CDATA #IMPLIED
          bundlevalue   CDATA #IMPLIED >
```

Mode Definitions

```
<!-- //NetBeans//DTD Mode Properties 2.2//EN -->
<!ELEMENT mode (
   module?,
   name,
   kind,
   state,
   constraints?,
   (bounds | relative-bounds)?,
   frame?,
   active-tc?,
   empty-behavior?,
```

```
    slidingSide?,
    slideInSize*) >
<!ATTLIST mode
   version CDATA #REQUIRED >

<!ELEMENT module EMPTY >
<!ATTLIST module
   name CDATA #REQUIRED
   spec CDATA #IMPLIED >

<!ELEMENT name EMPTY >
<!ATTLIST name
   unique CDATA #REQUIRED >

<!ELEMENT kind EMPTY >
<!ATTLIST kind
   type (editor | view | sliding) #REQUIRED >

<!ELEMENT slidingSide EMPTY >
<!ATTLIST slidingSide
   side (left | right | bottom) #REQUIRED >

<!ELEMENT slideInSize EMPTY >
<!ATTLIST slideInSize
   tc-id CDATA #REQUIRED
   size  CDATA #REQUIRED >

<!ELEMENT state EMPTY >
<!ATTLIST state
   type (joined | separated) #REQUIRED >

<!-- This entry is used when a window is moved out of the applcation via the "Undock" function
-->
<!ELEMENT bounds EMPTY >
<!ATTLIST bounds
   x       CDATA #REQUIRED
   y       CDATA #REQUIRED
   width   CDATA #REQUIRED
   height CDATA #REQUIRED >
<!ELEMENT relative-bounds EMPTY >
<!ATTLIST relative-bounds
   x       CDATA #REQUIRED
   y       CDATA #REQUIRED
   width   CDATA #REQUIRED
   height CDATA #REQUIRED >

<!-- The current status of the windows. The value is represented by an integer. Settable
values can be found in the java.awt.Frame class. Default: Frame.NORMAL (0) -->
<!ELEMENT frame EMPTY >
<!ATTLIST frame
   state CDATA #IMPLIED >
```

```
<!ELEMENT constraints (path*) >
<!ATTLIST constraints >

<!ELEMENT path EMPTY >
<!ATTLIST path
   orientation (horizontal | vertical) #REQUIRED
   number      CDATA                    #REQUIRED
   weight      CDATA                    #IMPLIED >

<!ELEMENT active-tc EMPTY >
<!ATTLIST active-tc
   id CDATA #IMPLIED > // ID of the active top component

<!-If set to true permanently, the mode will continue to exist even when no top component is
docked within it -->
<!ELEMENT empty-behavior EMPTY >
<!ATTLIST empty-behavior
   permanent (true | false) #IMPLIED >
```

Configuration of Top Component in Mode

```
<!-- //NetBeans//DTD Top Component in Mode Properties 2.2//EN -->
<!ELEMENT tc-ref (
   module?,
   tc-id,
   state,
   previousMode,
   docking-status?,
   slide-in-status?) >
<!ATTLIST tc-ref
   version CDATA #REQUIRED>

<!-- This optional element is used to remove the top component reference when the specified
module is deactivated -->
<!ELEMENT module EMPTY >
<!ATTLIST module
   name CDATA #REQUIRED  // Code name base of the module
   spec CDATA #IMPLIED > // Specification version of the module

<!ELEMENT tc-id EMPTY >
<!ATTLIST tc-id
   id CDATA #REQUIRED >  // Unique ID of the top component

<!ELEMENT state EMPTY >
<!ATTLIST state
   opened (true | false) #REQUIRED >

<!-- This attribute is used by the sliding views to restore the top component in the previous
mode. -->
<!ELEMENT previousMode EMPTY >
```

```
<!ATTLIST previousMode
    name  CDATA
    index CDATA #IMPLIED>
<!ELEMENT docking-status EMPTY >
<!ATTLIST docking-status
    maximized-mode (docked | slided) #IMPLIED
    default-mode   (docked | slided) #IMPLIED >

<!ELEMENT slide-in-status EMPTY >
<!ATTLIST slide-in-status
    maximized (true | false) #IMPLIED >
```

Top Component Group Definition

```
<!-- //NetBeans//DTD Group Properties 2.0//EN -->
<!ELEMENT group (
    module?,
    name,
    state) >
<!ATTLIST group
    version CDATA #REQUIRED >

<!ELEMENT module EMPTY >
<!ATTLIST module
    name CDATA #REQUIRED
    spec CDATA #IMPLIED >

<!ELEMENT name EMPTY >
<!ATTLIST name
    unique CDATA #REQUIRED >

<!ELEMENT state EMPTY >
<!ATTLIST state
    opened (true | false) #REQUIRED >
```

Configuration of Top Component in Group

```
<!--//NetBeans//DTD Top Component in Group Properties 2.0//EN -->
<!ELEMENT tc-group (
    module?,
    tc-id,
    open-close-behavior) >
<!ATTLIST tc-group
    version CDATA #REQUIRED >

<!ELEMENT module EMPTY >
<!ATTLIST module
    name CDATA #REQUIRED
    spec CDATA #IMPLIED >
```

```
<!ELEMENT tc-id EMPTY >
<!ATTLIST tc-id
   id CDATA #REQUIRED > // Unique ID of the top component

<!ELEMENT open-close-behavior EMPTY >
<!ATTLIST open-close-behavior
   open       (true | false)  #REQUIRED
   close      (true | false)  #REQUIRED
   was-opened (true | false)  #IMPLIED >
```

Toolbar Definition and Configuration

```
<!-- //NetBeans//DTD Toolbar Configuration 1.1//EN -->
<!ELEMENT Configuration (Row+) >
<!ELEMENT Row (Toolbar*) >
<!ELEMENT Toolbar EMPTY >
<!ATTLIST Toolbar
   name       CDATA           #REQUIRED
   visible    (true | false)  #IMPLIED
   align      (left | right)  #IMPLIED
   draggable  (true | false)  #IMPLIED >
```

Palette Item Definition

```
<!-- //NetBeans//DTD Editor Palette Item 1.1//EN -->
<!ELEMENT editor_palette_item (
   (class|body),
   icon16,
   icon32,
   (description|inline-description)) >
<!ATTLIST editor_palette_item
   version CDATA #REQUIRED >

<!-- Name of the class that implements the
 org.openide.text.ActiveEditorDrop interface -->
<!ELEMENT class EMPTY>
<!ATTLIST class
   name CDATA #REQUIRED >

<!-- Textual description, which can also contain HTML tags. -->
<!ELEMENT body (#PCDATA)>

<!ELEMENT icon16 EMPTY>
<!ATTLIST icon16
   urlvalue CDATA #REQUIRED >
<!ELEMENT icon32 EMPTY>
<!ATTLIST icon32
   urlvalue CDATA #REQUIRED >
```

```
<!ELEMENT description EMPTY>
<!ATTLIST description
    localizing-bundle CDATA #REQUIRED
    display-name-key  CDATA #REQUIRED
    tooltip-key       CDATA #REQUIRED >

<!ELEMENT inline-description (display-name, tooltip)>
<!ELEMENT display-name (#PCDATA)>
<!ELEMENT tooltip (#PCDATA)>
```

Index

▓ T

■ X, Y

■ Z

CPSIA information can be obtained at www.ICGtesting.com
Printed in the USA
LVOW130229231211

260829LV00007B/1/P

9 781430 241010